TRANSPARENCY IN INTERNATIONAL INVESTMENT ARBITRATION

The topic of transparency in international investment arbitration is gaining increasing attention. This in-depth commentary analyses the UNCITRAL Rules on Transparency in Treaty-Based Investor-State Arbitration, one of the most recent and innovative developments in international law. Focusing on the application of these rules, contributors analyse the issue of transparency in investment law more broadly and provide in-depth guidance on how to apply the UNCITRAL Transparency Rules. Chapters encompass all treaty-based disputes between investors and States, examining the perspectives of disputing parties, third parties, non-disputing State parties and arbitral tribunals. The contributors each have a strong background in investment arbitration, in both professional practice and academia. This commentary will be of interest to all actors involved in investment arbitrations, especially practitioners, counsels, NGOs, and scholars in the fields of international law, commercial arbitration and investor-State arbitration.

DIMITRIJ EULER is a PhD candidate in the Faculty of Law at the University of Basel, Switzerland.

MARKUS GEHRING is a university lecturer in the Faculty of Law at the University of Cambridge.

MAXI SCHERER is a senior lecturer in International Arbitration and Energy at Queen Mary, University of London and a Special Counsel at Wilmer Cutler Pickering Hale and Dorr LLP, London.

TRANSPARENCY IN INTERNATIONAL INVESTMENT ARBITRATION

A Guide to the UNCITRAL Rules on Transparency in Treaty-Based Investor-State Arbitration

Edited by

DIMITRIJ EULER, MARKUS GEHRING AND MAXI SCHERER

Assistant editors

MEAGAN WONG AND REBECCA HADGETT

CAMBRIDGE
UNIVERSITY PRESS

CAMBRIDGE
UNIVERSITY PRESS

University Printing House, Cambridge CB2 8BS, United Kingdom

Cambridge University Press is part of the University of Cambridge.

It furthers the University's mission by disseminating knowledge in the pursuit of education, learning and research at the highest international levels of excellence.

www.cambridge.org
Information on this title: www.cambridge.org/9781107077935

First published 2015

Printed in the United Kingdom by Clays, St Ives plc

A catalogue record for this publication is available from the British Library

Library of Congress Cataloging-in-Publication Data
Transparency in international investment arbitration : a guide to the UNCITRAL Rules on Transparency in Treaty-Based Investor-State Arbitration / edited by Dimitrij Euler, Markus Gehring and Maxi Scherer ; Assistant Editors Meagan Wong and Rebecca Hadgett.
pages cm
Includes index.
ISBN 978-1-107-07793-5 (Hardback)
1. United Nations Commission on International Trade Law. UNCITRAL Rules on Transparency in Treaty-based Investor-State Arbitration (2014) 2. International commercial arbitration. 3. Transparency in government–Law and legislation. I. Euler, Dimitrij, editor. II. Gehring, Markus W., editor. III. Scherer, Maxi, editor. IV. Wong, Meagan, editor. V. Hadgett, Rebecca, editor.
K2400.T729 2015
346′.092–dc23 2014044868

ISBN 978-1-107-07793-5 Hardback

CONTENTS

CONTENTS

CONTRIBUTORS

DIMITRIJ EULER is a PhD student at the University of Basel. He was Visiting Scholar at the Lauterpacht Centre for International Law at the University of Cambridge in 2012/2013 and was Visiting Scholar at the British Institute for International and Comparative Law in January and February 2014. He holds a Masters in Transnational Law and a Bachelor of Law from the University of Basel. His field of research is transparency and confidentiality in international arbitration.

DR MARKUS GEHRING, MA (CANTAB), LLM (YALE), PHD (HAMBURG), is Deputy Director of the Centre for European Legal Studies (CELS) Faculty of Law, University of Cambridge, Fellow and Director of Studies in Law at Hughes and a Fellow of the Lauterpacht Centre for International Law. Previously he served for seven years as Fellow in Law at Robinson College. He holds a Jean Monnet Research Chair *ad personam* in Sustainable Development Law at the University of Ottawa Law Faculty in Canada and has been a Visiting Professor in several law faculties around the world. In his former department at Cambridge, Politics and International Studies (POLIS), he served as affiliated Lecturer in European and International Law and Senior Research Associate in the Centre for Rising Powers. He is also an affiliated Lecturer in the Department of Land Economy and an Associate of the Centre for Climate Mitigation Research. A member of the Frankfurt Bar, he practised European and international trade law with Cleary Gottlieb Steen & Hamilton LLP in their Brussels office. He also serves as Lead Counsel for Sustainable Trade, Investment and Finance Law with the Centre of International Sustainable Development Law (CISDL), based at McGill University.

DR MAXI SCHERER, MA (SORBONNE), LLM (COLOGNE), PHD (SORBONNE), is a tenured full-time faculty member of the Centre for Commercial Law Studies (CCLS) and the School of International Arbitration at Queen Mary, University of London. She is also the Director of the Queen Mary

Paris LLM. Other academic appointments include Global Professor at NYU Law School, Visiting Professor at Sciences Po Law School, Adjunct Professor at the Georgetown Centre of Transnational Legal Studies, as well as previous visiting positions at the University of Melbourne, Freie Universität Berlin, Sorbonne Law School, Université de Versailles, Université de Fribourg, University of Würzburg, Pepperdine Law School, University of Basel and Université de Paris X Nanterre. Maxi is admitted to the Paris Bar and as a solicitor (England and Wales) and has extensive experience in international arbitration and counsel, having practised in leading law firms for over fifteen years. She publishes extensively in the field of international arbitration and litigation.

MEAGAN WONG is currently a PhD candidate at Leiden University, the Netherlands. She spent the second year of her doctoral research as a Visiting Doctoral Student at the University of Oxford, and the third year as a Visiting Scholar at the Lauterpacht Centre for International Law, University of Cambridge. She has an LLM in public international law from University College London, and has also been called to the Bar of England and Wales (Middle Temple Inn). She is currently an Assistant Editor for the Chinese Journal of International Law (OUP).

REBECCA HADGETT is currently a student on the Bar Professional Training Course (BPTC) at City Law School, London. She holds a degree in law from Trinity College, University of Cambridge and a Masters in Law from Harvard Law School. While at Harvard, she was a Student Attorney at Harvard Defenders and Harvard's International Human Rights Clinic. She has previously worked as a Research Assistant in areas including EU constitutional law and gender equality issues in the jurisprudence of the European Court of Human Rights. After completion of the BPTC, she will become a Pupil Barrister and she intends to develop a broad practice in criminal, regulatory, public, extradition and international law.

PROFESSOR KRISTA NADAKAVUKAREN SCHEFER holds a Swiss National Research Foundation Professorship at the University of Basel Law School, where she teaches International Law and International Economic Law. She is also a fellow at the World Trade Institute, University of Bern. Having received her Juris Doctor from Georgetown University Law Center and after her bar admission, she moved to Switzerland where she completed a dissertation and habilitation while working for the

University of Bern and the World Trade Institute. A member of the executive board of the Society of International Economic Law, Krista's areas of research include both trade and investment law and the interactions of these regimes with general international law.

GIUSEPPE BIANCO is currently a Research Fellow at the University of Oslo and at Université Paris 1 Panthéon-Sorbonne. He holds a degree in law from the University of Pisa and a Masters from Université Paris 1 Panthéon-Sorbonne. He was a Visiting Fellow at the Lauterpacht Research Centre for International Law of the University of Cambridge, and a Postgraduate Research Scholar at the École Normale Supérieure of Paris, and at the Sant'Anna School of Advanced Studies of Pisa. He was also a scholar at the Centre for Studies and Research of the Hague Academy for International Law, and an Erasmus Scholar at the University of Granada, Spain. He worked at the Sherpa Office of the Organisation for Economic Co-operation and Development. His current research focuses on sovereign debt restructuring, investment arbitration and collective action clauses.

DR CHRISTOPHER KEE is Head of the Graduate School for the College of Arts and Social Sciences at the University of Aberdeen. Prior to joining Aberdeen in the middle of 2011, he was a co-author and senior researcher on the Global Sales Law Project at the University of Basel, Switzerland. He holds an appointment as an Honorary Fellow of Deakin Law School, Australia, and has been an Adjunct Professor at the City University of Hong Kong. He is a Barrister and Solicitor of the High Court of Australia and the Supreme Courts of Victoria and New South Wales, and specialises in international arbitration and international commercial law. His doctoral thesis involved a comparative analysis of validity in contract.

DR MARIEL DIMSEY is an Australian Barrister and Solicitor specialising in international arbitration, international commercial law and international investment law. She has an LLM from the University of Cologne and a PhD *summa cum laude* from the University of Basel, both in investment treaty arbitration. She has published extensively in her her areas of specialisation. She currently works in the Dispute Resolution practice of Cleary Gottlieb Steen & Hamilton LLP in Cologne/Frankfurt, and previously practised at law firms in Düsseldort and Frankfurt and the ICC International Court of Arbitration. In addition to private practice, she lectures on International

Commercial and Investment Arbitration at the Universities of Bonn and Frankfurt.

DR MARTINS PAPARINSKIS, DPHIL (OXON), is Lecturer at the Faculty of Laws, University College London. He is a general international lawyer with a particular interest in international dispute settlement and international investment law. Martins' publications include articles in the *British Yearbook of International Law* and the *European Journal of International Law*, a compilation of *Basic Documents on International Investment Protection* (Hart 2012), and a monograph, *The International Minimum Standard and Fair and Equitable Treatment* (OUP 2013, in paperback with a new introduction 2014). Martin is a Book Review Editor of the *Journal of World Investment and Trade*, a member of the Academic Review Board of the *Cambridge Journal of International and Comparative Law*, a member of the International Law Association's Study Group on the Use of Domestic Law Principles for the Development of International Law, a member of the International Law Association's Committee on Non-State Actors, and a member of the Panel of Arbitrators of the International Centre for Settlement of Investment Disputes.

JESSICA HOWLEY is a DPhil candidate at Magdalen College, University of Oxford. She completed a BA and LLB at the University of Queensland, Australia, and a BCL and MPhil at the University of Oxford. Her research relates to State responsibility in public international law.

PROFESSOR KLINT ALEXANDER is Dean and Professor of Law at the University of Wyoming College of Law. As an attorney and UK solicitor he has counseled at Baker Donelson and is a member of the firm's Global Business Law group. He concentrates his practice in the areas of international trade and investment law, government regulation and dispute resolution, with an emphasis on UK and EU regulatory matters. Dr Alexander has represented and counselled governments and multinational corporations on international and domestic law matters throughout the world. During the 1990s, Dr Alexander served as a trade negotiator in the Office of GATT/ WTO Affairs, Office of the US Trade Representative (USTR) in the Clinton Administration. Dr Alexander is an expert on international trade law and agreements, and teaches international trade and investment law at Vanderbilt University Law School in Nashville and the University of London's Institute of Advanced Legal Studies. He has written and published extensively on international trade law matters and counsels clients on export and import trade compliance matters, economic sanctions, anti-dumping and countervailing duties, anti-boycott measures, WTO and NAFTA rules and procedures and dispute resolution.

THIERRY P. AUGSBURGER is a bilingual (French/German) Swiss advocate and an international arbitration and litigation specialist. He regularly represents parties from the commodities trading and transport, trade finance, construction/infrastructure, renewable energy, defence, and licencing/distribution sectors in international arbitration proceedings, arbitration-related court proceedings or commercial litigation, and advises them, *inter alia*, on investment-related matters. He holds both a lic.iur. degree from the University of Zurich and an LLM degree with a Specialisation in International Law from the University of Cambridge. He was also a Max-Planck Scholar at the Max Planck Institute for Comparative Public Law and International Law, Heidelberg. He currently practises with Bratschi Wiederkehr & Buob Ltd. in Switzerland as a Junior Partner.

KATHLEEN CLAUSSEN is a Visiting Assistant Professor at the Indiana University Maurer School of Law. She came to the Law School from the Permanent Court of Arbitration in The Hague, where she served as Legal Counsel. Her teaching and research focus on US and international commercial arbitration, international investment law, public international law and federalism. Before joining the Permanent Court of Arbitration in 2011, Claussen clerked for the Honorable David F. Hamilton of the US Court of Appeals for the Seventh Circuit. She was also a Brandon Research Fellow at the University of Cambridge's Lauterpacht Centre for International Law.

DR JOHANNES KOEPP is a partner in Baker Botts' International Arbitration & Dispute Resolution Group. His practice focuses on international arbitration, both commercial and public international law disputes. He has represented clients before most major arbitral institutions, as well as in ad hoc proceedings. He is experienced in multijurisdictional disputes arising out of energy, joint ventures, mergers and acquisitions, telecommunications and financial services. Dr Koepp worked as a research fellow at the University of Geneva for two years. During this time, he completed his doctoral thesis, which analysed and compared various third-party procedures in the field of international dispute settlement. He has taught law at universities in Switzerland, Germany and Spain.

CAMERON SIM is an associate in Baker Botts' International Arbitration & Dispute Resolution Group. His practice focuses on international arbitration, including both commercial and public international law disputes. He is dual qualified in the jurisdictions of England and Wales and Australia. He spent one year working as judicial assistant to Lord Neuberger of Abbotsbury, President of the Supreme Court of the United Kingdom. He has also worked as a research assistant at the Centre for Corporate Law and Securities Regulation at the University of Melbourne and at the Institute of European and Comparative Law at the University of Oxford.

FOREWORD

Investment disputes often engage matters of the public interest. One of the most significant challenges facing international investment law today is the need to balance the interests of investors in the protection of their investment with the regulatory interests of host States. At times, ad hoc tribunals deciding investment treaty claims have produced decisions with seemingly little regard for the latter interests. This contributes to a concern on the part of States that international investment law is becoming one-sided, favouring claimant investors over host States.

The UNCITRAL Rules on Transparency in Treaty-based Investor-State Arbitration underline the public interest function of those tribunals and should help to render these disputes more visible. The UNCITRAL Rules, analysed in this book, could facilitate third parties' access to proceedings and thereby increase the transparency of these disputes in the public interest.

The editors, Dimitrij Euler, Maxi Scherer and Markus Gehring, all have strong research and professional links to investment law. Dimitrij Euler, a PhD researcher at the University of Basel and a former Visiting Scholar at the Lauterpacht Centre for International Law in Cambridge, focuses his research on transparency and arbitration. Dr Maxi Scherer, a Senior Lecturer at Queen Mary, University of London (School of International Arbitration) and Special Counsel at Wilmer Cutler Pickering Hale and Dorr LLP, is a distinguished scholar and has acted as arbitrator in investment arbitration. Dr Markus W. Gehring, MA (Cantab), LLM (Yale), Dr jur (Hamburg), is Deputy Director of the Centre for European Legal Studies (CELS) at the Faculty of Law, University of Cambridge and a Fellow at Hughes Hall and at the Lauterpacht Centre. He has worked extensively on sustainable development in investment and trade law.

Their edited commentary reflects the search for increased transparency in investment law and provides a useful insight into the history and interpretation of the UNCITRAL Rules. They have gathered together contributions from authors with diverse backgrounds in academia, private and public legal practice and international organisations. These different perspectives add to our understanding of this new set of international standards. Their analysis of the history and of relevant international cases and awards provides a useful resource for academics and practitioners in the field of investment law. Transparency in investment arbitration has to seek viable compromises between the interests of the parties and the interest of the public. This volume contributes usefully to this discussion.

James Crawford
Lauterpacht Centre for International Law
University of Cambridge

ACKNOWLEDGEMENTS

The editors owe their gratitude to the institutions and all the people who made this book possible: the University of Basel; the University of Cambridge, in particular the Lauterpacht Centre for International Law in Cambridge; the Centre for European Legal Studies and Trinity Hall; the School of Law at Queen Mary, University of London; the British Institute of International and Comparative Law; and the Centre for International Sustainable Development Law.

We especially thank the Freiwillige Akademische Gesellschaft Basel, Portland Stiftung and Max Geldner Stiftung Basel, which greatly supported this project and our workshops and research meetings to prepare this commentary. We thank all reviewers and commentators as well as the active participants in our book workshop and their institutions.

We express our thanks to our authors Krista Nadakavukaren Schefer, Giuseppe Bianco, Christopher Kee, Mariel Dimsey, Martins Paparinskis and Jessica Howley, Klint Alexander, Thierry P. Augsburger, Kathleen Claussen, Johannes Koepp and Cameron Sim and their institutions. We also add our thanks to Meagan Wong and Rebecca Hadgett, who greatly assisted in the various iterations of the editing process. We would also like to thank those lawyers who have guided this project through their work, such as Natalie Bernasconi (IISD), Daniel Costelloe (WilmerHale), Dennis Schwaninger (University of Basel), and Henriette Sigmund (House of Finance, Goethe-University Frankfurt).

No book would be possible without the wonderful support from our publisher, Cambridge University Press, especially Kim Hughes, Elizabeth Davey, Deborah Hey, Richard Woodham and Finola O'Sullivan and their respective teams.

The book has incorporated all material up to 1 March 2014. We were able to include selected references and some major developments between March and July 2014. All websites were accurate as of 1 July 2014.

Editors

TREATIES, GUIDELINES AND RULES

UNCITRAL Arbitration Rules (2010)

Arbitration Rules (2010, as adopted 2013)	Chapter	Article	Paragraph
(Generally)	**1**	**I**[1]	7
	2	**P**[2]	14–43
	3	**1**	5, 10–43, 45
	4	**2**	13, 48
	5	**3**	2, 4, 60
	6	**4**	36
	8	**6**	16, 18
	10	**8**	19
	11	**A**[3]	31
Article 1	**3**	**1**	32
Article 1(1)	**3**	**1**	62
	11	**A**	32
Article 1(3)	**3**	**1**	32
	5	**3**	2
	9	**7**	172
Article 1(4)	**11**	**A**	31
Article 2(1)	**4**	**2**	13
Article 3(2)	**4**	**2**	2, 3
Article 3(3)	**4**	**2**	13, 17, 23
Article 3(4)	**4**	**2**	13, 17
Article 3(5)	**4**	**2**	13
Article 4(1)	**4**	**2**	13, 15
Article 17(1)	**3**	**1**	66
	5	**3**	17, 60, 61
	6	**4**	36
	9	**7**	88, 141, 175
	11	**A**	37, 38, 39
Article 17(3)	**8**	**6**	13
Article 17(5)	**6**	**4**	24

(*cont.*)

Arbitration Rules (2010, as adopted 2013)	Chapter	Article	Paragraph
Article 27(3)	**9**	**7**	5
Article 28(3)	**4**	**2**	48
	8	**6**	14, 18
	9	**7**	16
	11	**A**	35
Article 29(1)	**5**	**3**	64
Article 34(5)	**4**	**2**	48
	5	**3**	5
	9	**7**	16
	11	**A**	34
Article 37	**5**	**3**	93
Article 38	**5**	**3**	93
Article 39	**5**	**3**	93
Article 42(1)	**9**	**7**	182
Article 42(2)	**9**	**7**	182

[1]Chapter: Introduction.
[2]Chapter: The Public Interest in Investment Arbitration.
[3]Chapter: The Application of Transparency.

UNCITRAL Arbitration Rules (1976)

Arbitration Rules (1976)	Chapter	Article	Paragraph
(Generally)	**1**	**I**	7
	2	**P**	14–16, 43
	3	**1**	10–30, 45
	4	**2**	48
	5	**3**	19, 22, 24
	6	**4**	42, 166
	8	**6**	2, 9, 31
	9	**7**	20, 26
	11	**A**	31
Article 1	**3**	**1**	31
	11	**A**	32
Article 15	**1**	**I**	7
	3	**1**	11, 12
	5	**3**	17
	6	**4**	35, 41, 44, 59, 79

(*cont.*)

Arbitration Rules (1976)	Chapter	Article	Paragraph
	8	**6**	9
	9	**7**	88
	11	**A**	37, 38
Article 25(4)	**4**	**2**	48
	11	**A**	35
Article 32(5)	**3**	**1**	17
	4	**2**	48
	5	**3**	5
	11	**A**	34

CASES

Case name	Court or Tribunal	Reference	Ch.	Art.	Para.
Abaclat and Others (formerly known as *Giovanna A Beccara and Others)* v. *Argentina*	ICSID	ICSID Case No. ARB/07/5	**9**	**7**	71
Achmea B.V. (formerly known as *Eureko B.V.*) v. *The Slovak Republic*	PCA	PCA Case No. 2008-13	**6**	**4**	65–8, 90, 106, 115, 167
			7	**5**	6
			8	**6**	19
ADC and ADC & ADMC Management Limited v. *Hungary*	ICSID	ICISD Case No. ARB/03/16	**9**	**7**	140
ADF Group Inc. v. *United States of America*	ICSID	ICSID Case No. ARB(AF)/00/1	**7**	**5**	4, 26
			8	**6**	17
AES Summit Generation Limited and AES-Tisza Erömü Kft v. *Hungary*	ICSID	ICSID Case No. ARB/07/22	**6**	**4**	65, 141, 167
			7	**5**	6

(*cont.*)

Case name	Court or Tribunal	Reference	Ch.	Art.	Para.
Aguas del Tunari SA v. *Bolivia*	ICSID	ICSID Case No. ARB/02/3	**5**	**3**	21
			6	**4**	46, 47, 105, 110, 170
			7	**5**	6
			12	**C**[4]	8
Mr A. J. O. v. *Slovak Republic*	Ad-hoc Geneva	BIT Case	**8**	**6**	19
Alabama Claims (United Kingdom v. *United States of America*	Ad-hoc Geneva		**12**	**C**	9
Ali Shipping Corporation v. *'Shipyard Trogir'*	English Court of Appeal	[1998] 1 Lloyd's Rep 643	**11**	**A**	84
AMCO Asia Corporation and others v. *Indonesia,*	ICSID	ICSID Case No. ARB/81/1	**9**	**7**	140
Apotex Holdings et al. v. *United States of America; Apotex v United States of America*	ICSID; Ad-hoc New York	ARB(AF)/12/1; NAFTA Case	**6**	**4**	80–7, 96 112, 149, 164–6, 174
			7	**5**	4
			9	7	6, 98, 174, 181, 192
Archer Daniels Midland Company et al. v. *Mexico,*	ICSID	ICSID Case No. ARB(AF)/04/05	**7**	**5**	5, 6
Azurix Corp. v. *Argentina*	ICSID	ICSID Case No. ARB/03/30	**8**	**6**	37
Bernard von Pezold and Others v. *Zimbabwe*	ICSID	ICSID Case No. ARB/10/15	**6**	**4**	69–73, 122 136, 143, 161, 163, 178, 187, 205

(*cont.*)

Case name	Court or Tribunal	Reference	Ch.	Art.	Para.
Border Timbers Limited, Border Timbers International (Private) Limited, and Hangani Development Co. (Private) Limited v. *Zimbabwe*	ICSID	ICSID Case No. ARB/10/25	**6**	**4**	69–73
Biwater Gauff Limited v. *Tanzania)*	ICSID	ICSID Case No. ARB/05/22, IIC 31 (2006)	**1**	**I**	8
			2	**P**	11
			3	**1**	70
			5	**3**	17, 29
			6	**4**	19, 22, 52, 54, 89, 105, 109, 114, 116, 126, 132, 142, 175, 187, 190, 208
			8	**6**	7
			9	7	37, 59, 124, 140, 144, 147, 151
			11	**A**	50
Bulgarian Foreign Trade Bank Ltd v. *A.I. Trade Finance Inc ('Bulbank')*	Supreme Court of Sweden	T 1881-99, 27 October 2000 (NJA 2000 s. 538)	**4**	**2**	75
Caratube International Oil Company LLP v. *Kazakhstan*	ICSID	ICSID Case No. Arb/08/12	**12**	**C**	8
Chemtura Corporation v. *Canada*	PCA	NAFTA Case	**7**	**5**	4
			8	**6**	17

(*cont.*)

Case name	Court or Tribunal	Reference	Ch.	Art.	Para.
Chevron Corporation and Texaco Petroleum Corporation v. *Ecuador*	PCA	PCA Case No. 2009-23	**6** **12**	**4** **C**	79, 92 8
Claude Reyes and others v. *Chile*	IACHR	IACHR Series C No. 151	**2**	**P**	17
Continental Casualty Company v. *Argentina*	ICSID	ICSID Case No. ARB/03/9	**8** **9**	**6** **7**	37 133
CMS Gas Transmission Company (formerly known as *Blue Ridge Investment)* v. *Argentina*	ICSID	ICSID Case No. ARB/01/8	**8** **9**	**6** **7**	37 131
Detroit International Bridge Company v. *Canada*	PCA	PCA Case No. 2012-25	**3** **5** **7** **8** **9**	**1** **3** **5** **6** 7	71 13 4, 5, 14 17, 18, 22 106, 192
Dolling-Baker v. *Merrett*	*English Court of Appeals*	*(1991) 2 All ER 890*	**11**	**A**	84
Eastern Sugar B.V. v Czech Republic	SCC	SCC No. 088/2004	**8**	**6**	19
EDF (Services) Limited v. *Romania*	ICSID	ICSID Case No. ARB/05/13	**9**	**7**	140, 144
Electrabel S.A. v. *Hungary*	ICSID	ICSID Case No. ARB/07/19	**6** **7** **10**	**4** **5** **6**	65, 167, 172 6 19

(cont.)

Case name	Court or Tribunal	Reference	Ch.	Art.	Para.
Esso Australia Resources Ltd v. *The Honourable Sidney James Plowman (Esso/BHP* v. *Plowman*	Australian High Court	(1995) 183 CLR 10	**2**	**P**	14, 16
			5	**3**	4
			11	**A**	84
Ethyl Corporation v. *Canada*	Ad-hoc Toronto	NAFTA Case	**7**	**5**	4
Fireman's Fund Insurance Company v. *Mexico*	ICSID	ICSID Case No. ARB(AF)/02/1	**7**	**5**	4, 6
			10	**6**	19
GAMI v. *Mexico*	Ad-hoc Vancouver	NAFTA Case	**7**	**5**	4
			8	**6**	17
Giacobazzi Crandi Vini SpA v. *Renfield Corp*	US District Court, Southern District of New York	No 85 Civ, 6434, US Dist Ct, SDNY (10 March 1987), (1987) US Dist LEXIS 1783	**11**	**A**	84
Glamis Gold Ltd. v. *United States of America*	ICSID	NAFTA Case	**6**	**4**	22, 55–7, 105, 108, 194, 208
			8	**6**	28, 31
			9	**7**	71, 91, 103
Grand River Enterprises Six Nations, Ltd et al. v. *United States of America*	ICSID	NAFTA Case	**6**	**4**	58, 125
			7	**5**	4
Hassneh Insurance Co of Israel v. *Mew*	English High Court	[1993) 2 Lloyd's Rep 243	**11**	**A**	84
Industrotech Constructors Inc v. *Duke University*	Court of Appeals of North Carolina	(1984) 67 NC App 741	**11**	**A**	84

(*cont.*)

Case name	Court or Tribunal	Reference	Ch.	Art.	Para.
*International Thunderbird Gaming Corp.*v. *Mexico*	ICSID	NAFTA Case	**7**	**5**	4
John Forster Ennott v. *Michael Wilson & Partners Limited*	English Court of Appeals	[2008] EWCA Civ 184	**11**	**A**	84
Libananco Holdings v. *Turkey*	ICSID	ICSID Case No. ARB/06/8	**9**	**7**	158
Loewen Group, Inc and Raymond Loewen v. *United States of America*	ICSID	ICSID Case No. ARB(AF)/98/3	**3**	**1**	69
			5	**3**	26
			7	**5**	4
			9	**7**	86
Mercer International Inc. v. *Canada*	ICSID	ICSID Case No. ARB(AF)/12/3	**5**	**3**	13, 17
			9	**7**	49
Merrill & Ring Forestry L.P. v. *Canada*	ICSID	NAFTA Case	**5**	**3**	15
			6	**4**	59
			7	**5**	4
Metalclad Corporation v. *Mexico*	ICSID	Case No. Arb (AF)/97/1	**3**	**1**	69
			5	**3**	23
			7	**5**	4, 5
			9	**7**	140, 170
Methanex Corporation v. *United States of America*	ICSID	NAFTA Case	**1**	**I**	7
			2	**P**	15
			3	**1**	69, 70
			5	**3**	22, 23
			6	**4**	7, 27, 29, 39–41, 114, 116, 159, 160, 187, 193, 195, 197
			7	**5**	4, 30
			8	**6**	10
			11	**A**	39, 40

(cont.)

Case name	Court or Tribunal	Reference	Ch.	Art.	Para.
Mobil v. *Canada*	ICSID	Case No. ARB (AF)07/4	7	5	4
National Grid plc v. *Argentina*	ICSID	UNCITRAL	7	5	6
			8	**6**	37
Pac Rim Cayman LLC v. *El Salvador*	ICSID	ICSID Case No. ARB/09/12	**6**	**4**	74–8
			7	5	4
			8	**6**	11
Philip Morris Asia Limited v. *Australia*	PCA	PCA Case No. 2012-12	**8**	**6**	22
			9	7	50, 84, 90, 98, 124, 192
Piero Foresti and others v. *South Africa*	ICSID	ICSID Case No ARB(AF)/07/1	**6**	**4**	60–4, 102, 116, 176, 180, 187, 189, 194, 206
Pope & Talbot Inc. v. *Canada*	Ad-hoc Montreal	NAFTA Case	**2**	**P**	33
			5	3	24, 25
			7	5	4, 26
			8	**6**	17
			9	7	59, 108, 167, 184
Quiborax S.A., Non Metallic Minerals S.A. and Allan Fosk Kaplún v. *Bolivia*	ICSID	ICSID Case No. ARB/06/2	**9**	7	144
Railroad Development Corporation v. *Guatemala*	ICSID	ICSID Case No. ARB/07/23	5	3	66
			7	5	4
Renco Group Inc. v. *Peru*	ICSID	ICSID Case No. UNCT/13/1	7	5	4, 5
			9	7	188
*San Sebastián Gold Mines, Inc.*v. *El Salvador*	ICSID	ICSID Case No. ARB/09/17	7	5	4

(*cont.*)

Case name	Court or Tribunal	Reference	Ch.	Art.	Para.
Saipem S.p.A. v. *Bangladesh*	ICSID	ICSID Case No. ARB/05/07	**9**	**7**	17
			10	**8**	34
SD Myers v. *Canada*	Ad-hoc Toronto	NAFTA Case	**7**	**5**	4
			8	**6**	17
SGS Société Générale de Surveillance S. A. v. *Pakistan*	ICSID	Case No. ARB/ 01/12	**7**	**5**	4, 6, 13
SGS Société Générale de Surveillance S.A. v. *Philippines,*	ICSID	ICSID Case No. ARB/02/6	**10**	**8**	33
Siemens A.G. v. *Argentina*	ICSID	ICSID Case No. ARB/02/08	**7**	**5**	6, 13
Suez, Sociedad General de Aguas de Barcelona S.A., and InterAguas Servicios Integrales del Agua S.A. v. *Argentina*	ICSID	ICSID Case No. ARB/03/17	**1**	**I**	17
			6	**4**	3, 22, 51, 110, 113, 114, 118, 122, 137, 139
			8	**6**	37
Suez, Sociedad General de Aguas de Barcelona S.A. and Vivendi Universal S.A. v. *Argentina*	ICSID	ICSID Case No. ARB/03/19	**1**	**I**	8
			5	**3**	27, 28, 30
			6	**4**	18, 22, 31, 48–51, 104, 108, 114, 116, 120, 162, 187, 195, 208
			8	**6**	37
Társaság A Szabads ágjogokért v. *Hungary*	ECtHR	Application No. 37374/05	**2**	**P**	28

(*cont.*)

Case name	Court or Tribunal	Reference	Ch.	Art.	Para.
TECO Guatemala Holdings Inc. v. *Guatemala*	ICSID	ICSID Case No. ARB/10/23	**7**	**5**	4
United States – Continued Suspension of Obligations in the EC – Hormones Dispute and *Canada – Continued Suspension of Obligations in the EC – Hormones Dispute*	World Trade Organisation (Appellate Body)	WT/DS320/AB/R, WT/DS321/AB/R	**8**	**6**	6
United States of America v. *Panhandle Eastern Corp*	Federal District Court of Delaware	(D Del 1988) 118 FRD 346	**11**	**A**	84
United Parcel Service of America Inc. ('UPS') v. *Canada*	ICSID	NAFTA Case	**5**	**3**	19, 20
			6	**4**	7, 27, 29, 42–5, 102, 105, 108, 116, 126, 130, 136, 138, 163, 172, 173, 195
			8	**6**	9, 18
			11	**A**	39, 40
Vattenfall AB, Vattenfall Europe AG, Vattenfall Europe Generation AG & CO KG v. *Germany*	ICSID	ICSID Case No. ARB/09/06	**2**	**P**	8

(*cont.*)

Case name	Court or Tribunal	Reference	Ch.	Art.	Para.
Veteran Petroleum Limited (Cyprus) v. *Russia*	PCA	PCA Case No. AA 228	**12**	**C**	8
Vito G. Gallo v. *Canada*	PCA	PCA Case No. 55798	**9**	**7**	71
William Ralph Clayton, William Richard Clayton, Douglas Clayton, Daniel Clayton and Bilcon of Delaware Inc. v. *Canada*	PCA	PCA Case No. 2009-04	**7**	**5**	4
			9	**7**	49, 71, 98, 174, 181, 192
World Duty Free v. *Kenya*	ICSID	ICSID Case No. ARB/00/7	**6**	**4**	188
			9	**7**	1400

[4]Chapter: Conclusion.

ABBREVIATIONS

AAA	American Arbitration Association
ADR	Alternative Dispute Resolution
Arbitration Rules	United Nations Commission on International Trade Law Arbitration Rules
Arbitration Rules (1976)	United Nations Commission on International Trade Law Arbitration Rules (1976)
Arbitration Rules (2010)	United Nations Commission on International Trade Law Arbitration Rules (as revised in 2010)
ATIA	Access to Information Act
BIT	Bilateral Investment Treaty
CAFTA-DR	Dominican Republic–Central America Free Trade Agreement
CETA	Comprehensive Economic and Trade Agreement (Canada-EU)
CIEL	Center for International Environmental Law
COMESA	Common Market for Eastern and Southern Africa
Convention	United Nations Convention on Transparency in Treaty-based Investor-state Arbitration
ECCHR	European Center for Constitutional and Human Rights
EFTA	European Free Trade Association
EU	European Union
FDI	Foreign Direct Investment
FOI	Freedom of Information
FIPA	Foreign Investment Promotion and Protection Agreement
FTA	Free Trade Agreement
FTC	Free Trade Commission
HGA	Host Government Agreement
IBA	International Bar Association
IBA Rules	IBA Rules on the Taking of Evidence in International Arbitration
ICC	International Chamber of Commerce
ICC Rules	International Chamber of Commerce Rules of Arbitration
ICJ	International Court of Justice
IIA	International Investment Agreement

ILA	International Law Association
ILC	International Law Commission
ICSID	International Centre for Settlement of Investment Disputes
ICSID AFR	ICSID Additional Facility Arbitration Rules
ICSID Rules	Collective term for the International Centre for Settlement of Investment Disputes Convention, Regulations, Institution Rules, Rules of Procedure for Arbitration and Additional Facility Arbitration Rules
IISD	International Institute for Sustainable Development
JAMS	Judicial Arbitration and Mediation Services
LCIA	London Court of International Arbitration
NAFTA	North American Free Trade Agreement
NGO	Non-Governmental Organisation
NULC	Nyahode Union Learning Centre
OECD	Organisation for Economic Co-operation and Development
PCA	Permanent Court of Arbitration
PCIA	Paris Court of International Arbitration
QIN	Quechan Indian Nation
Rules	United Nations Commission on International Trade Law Rules on Transparency in Treaty-based Investor-State Arbitration
SCC Institute	Arbitration Institute of the Stockholm Chamber of Commerce
SCC Rules	Rules of the Arbitration Institute of the Stockholm Chamber of Commerce
TNC	Trans-National Corporations
UNCITRAL	United Nations Commission on International Trade Law
UNCTAD	United Nations Conference on Trade and Development
USTR	Office of the United States Trade Representative
VCLT	Vienna Convention on the Law of Treaties
VCC	Vale Columbia Center on Sustainable Development
WG	United Nations Commission on International Trade Law Rules Working Group II (Arbitration and Conciliation)
WIPO	World Intellectual Property Organization
WTO	World Trade Organization

1

Introduction

MAXI SCHERER,* MARKUS GEHRING**
AND DIMITRI EULER***

1.1 Transparency and the hybrid nature of investment arbitration

1. The topic of transparency in international investment arbitration has gained, and continues to gain, increased attention.[1] The heightened public awareness is justified: investment disputes between foreign investors and host States before international tribunals typically involve high-stakes – usually financial, but often also political. Host State governments have much at stake in the political equations arising out of these often sensitive disputes. Sometimes, it may be a population within the host State that most directly bears the effects of a foreign investment project, rather than the host State's government.[2]

* Dr Maxi Scherer, MA (Sorbonne), LLM (Cologne), PhD (Sorbonne), is Senior Lecturer at Queen Mary, University of London (School of International Arbitration) and Special Counsel at Wilmer Cutler Pickering Hale and Dorr LLP.

** Dr Markus Gehring, MA (Cantab), LLM (Yale), PhD (Hamburg), is Deputy Director of the Centre for European Legal Studies (CELS) Faculty of Law, University of Cambridge, Fellow and Director of Studies in Law at Hughes and a Fellow of the Lauterpacht Centre for International Law.

*** Dimitrij Euler is a PhD student at the University of Basel.

1 See e.g. Nathalie Bernasconi-Osterwalder, 'Transparency and Amicus Curiae in ICSID Arbitrations', in Marie-Claire Cordonier Segger, Markus W. Gehring and Andrew Newcombe (eds.), *Sustainable Development in World Investment Law* (Kluwer Law International, 2011); Julie Maupin, 'Transparency in International Investment Law: The Good, the Bad, and the Murky', in Andrea Bianchi and Anne Peters (eds.), *Transparency in International Law* (Oxford University Press, 2013); Stefan W. Schill, 'Editorial: Five Times Transparency' (2014) 15 *International Investment Law Journal of World Investment & Trade* 363–74. On public interest generally, see Andreas Kulick, *Global Public Interest in International Investment Law* (Cambridge University Press, 2012).

2 See Jose Daniel Amado, 'From Investors' Arbitration to Investment Arbitration: A Mechanism for Allowing the Participation of Host State Populations in the Settlement of Investment Conflicts', http://papers.ssrn.com/sol3/papers.cfm?abstract_id=2385776.

2. It is in these circumstances that the concept of transparency in investor-State arbitration has gained increased visibility as a topic of concern. Because of the involvement of a State, investment arbitration has the potential to affect 'public interest' issues, i.e. issues that concern a broader public than just the parties to the dispute. Commentators and civil society groups have thus called for increased public involvement in investment arbitration proceedings, in order to incorporate broader policy considerations into the dispute resolution process. The perception of 'secrecy' in investor-State proceedings has been a contributing factor in the growing dissatisfaction with this type of dispute resolution mechanism as a whole, which has, in some cases, culminated in States' denunciation of bilateral investment treaties.[3]

3. This 'legitimacy crisis' of investment arbitration, of which the transparency debate forms an important part, can be explained, in part, by the hybrid nature of investment arbitration at the crossing of the public and private spheres.[4] On the one hand, investment arbitration is a creature of public international law. The dispute involves a State, and the parties' substantive rights, as well as the agreement to arbitrate (in treaty-based investment arbitration), arise out of an instrument of public international law, i.e. the treaty. On the other hand, arbitration is a private form of dispute resolution, away from State courts, and proceeds under procedural rules shaped and chosen by the parties.

4. This hybrid nature of investment arbitration affects the debate as to whether and, if so, how much transparency is needed. From one point of view, investment disputes or, more precisely, their outcomes, may have fairly immediate effects for large numbers of individuals and for the host State's economy. These disputes involve matters of legitimate public concern, including, for example, the environment or public health, or even human rights or corruption. Therefore, under this view, it is difficult to see why such proceedings ought to enjoy the protections of confidentiality in the manner that commercial arbitrations typically do. Moreover, being based on a treaty, confidentiality protections that exist under purely contractual disputes do not enjoy the same level of justification.

[3] For example, Indonesia in 2014 announced its intention to review or terminate numerous bilateral investment treaties. Further, Venezuela in 2012 submitted a notice to ICSID denouncing the ICSID Convention. Bolivia and Ecuador had done likewise in 2007 and 2009, respectively.

[4] See e.g. Zachary Douglas, 'The Hybrid Foundations of Investment Arbitration' (2003) 74 *British Yearbook of International Law* 151.

5. From a different perspective, investment arbitration remains a private dispute resolution mechanism. As such, irrespective of the parties' identities or the source of the arbitration agreement, these proceedings should remain confidential, precisely because they do not occur before State courts. Where the parties have decided to refer a dispute to arbitration, rather than to litigate it in court, their right to confidentiality should be respected.

6. The various chapters of this book will show that the UNCITRAL Rules on Transparency in Treaty-based Investor-State Arbitration (the Rules) attempt to strike a balance between the different interests at stake. Also, as discussed in more detail in the conclusion of this book, they arguably successfully level the playing field between investors and host States, and contribute to increasing the legitimacy of investment arbitration as a system.[5]

1.2 The development of the transparency rules

7. The drafters of the Rules were not the first to consider the thorny issue of transparency. Even before the adoption of the Rules, certain tribunals constituted under the UNCITRAL Arbitration Rules had shown themselves amenable to transparency-based arguments, at least as far as third-party written submissions were concerned. Notable among these instances was the decision of the tribunal in *Methanex* v. *United States of America* that certain third parties or *amici* – the International Institute for Sustainable Development, Communities for a Better Environment and the Earth Island Institute specifically – were permitted to make written submissions to the tribunal.[6] It was the first investment tribunal to hold that Article 15(1) of the UNCITRAL Arbitration Rules gave it the power to accept *amicus* briefs, even against the wishes of one of the disputing parties, thereby signalling a recognition of public concerns associated with the transparency of proceedings. The *Methanex* tribunal offered a powerful statement in this order on third party submissions and transparency: [7]

[5] See Dimitrij Euler and Maxi Scherer, 'Conclusion', [7]–[11].

[6] *Methanex Corporation* v. *United States of America*, Decision of the Tribunal on Petitions from Third Persons to Intervene as 'Amici Curiae', 15 January 2001. Third party refers to both third person and non-disputing party.

[7] *Ibid.* at [49].

> There is an undoubtedly public interest in this arbitration. The substantive issues extend far beyond those raised by the usual transnational arbitration between commercial parties. This is not merely because one of the Disputing Parties is a State: there are of course disputes involving States which are of no greater general public importance than a dispute between private persons. The public interest in this arbitration arises from its subject-matter, as powerfully suggested in the Petitions. There is also a broader argument, as suggested by the Respondent and Canada: the Chapter 11 arbitral process could benefit from being perceived as more open or transparent; or conversely be harmed if seen as unduly secretive. In this regard, the Tribunal's willingness to receive amicus submissions might support the process in general and this arbitration in particular; whereas a blanket refusal could do positive harm.

8. By way of comparison, similar developments occurred in arbitrations under the ICSID Rules. Notably, the tribunal in *Aguas Argentinas* v. *Argentina* decided to allow a third-party written submissions despite the opposition of the investor.[8] More recently, the tribunal in *Biwater Gauff* v. *Tanzania* allowed an *amicus* submission under the revised ICSID Rules.[9] These cases, and others, are discussed in more detail in the relevant chapters of this book.[10]

9. It is against this background of developing case law and awareness of transparency issues that the UNCITRAL's Working Group II (Arbitration and Conciliation) (WG) began to develop the Rules. The transparency debate commenced in earnest during the WG's forty-eighth session in 2008. Certain non-governmental organisations (NGOs) and States pushed the topic of transparency onto the agenda at that session, and the Commission created a mandate for the WG with respect to the topic of transparency.[11] The Rules were finally adopted during its forty-sixth session in 2013.[12] The Rules are thus the product of over four years of work by the WG and the Commission itself. However, the WG's efforts did not stop here, since the UN General Assembly adopted the

[8] *Aguas Argentinas, S.A., Suez, Sociedad General de Aguas de Barcelona, S.A. and Vivendi Universal, S.A.* v. *Argentina* (Order in Response to a Petition for Transparency and Participation as *Amicus Curiae*), 19 May 2005 and 12 February 2007.

[9] *Biwater Gauff* v. *Tanzania* (Procedural Order No. 5), 29 September 2006, [46]–[61].

[10] See e.g. Christopher Kee, 'Article 3' [18]–[23]; Mariel Dimsey, 'Article 4', [37]–[87]; Martins Paparinskis and Jessica Howley, 'Article 5', [3]–[5]; Klint Alexander, 'Article 6', [7]–[12]; Thierry P. Augsburger, 'Article 7', [37]; Johannes Koepp and Cameron Sim, 'Application of Transparency', [50].

[11] See Markus Gehring and Dimitrij Euler, 'Public interest in investment arbitration', [14]–[44].

[12] *Ibid.* [44].

WG's elaborated Convention on Transparency in Treaty-Based Investor-State Arbitration on 10 December 2014 open for signature since 17 March 2015, which aims at broadening the scope of application of the Rules, as discussed in Chapter 11 and the conclusion of this book.[13]

1.3 What is transparency?

10. The first difficulty when looking at the Rules stems from the very word 'transparency'. It is not a straightforward term or concept in the present context. First, the term could be defined negatively and refer to a (full or partial) absence of confidentiality. For instance, this would allow the arbitrators and the parties to report about the disputes in public, as they deem fit. Second, transparency could also be understood as referring to certain mechanisms which aim to safeguard public interest and involve the public as a whole. These might include, for instance, opening the hearing to the public or inviting third party submissions.

11. In the context of the Rules (and thus in this book), the term 'transparency' operates broadly. It can be described as an umbrella term that includes a number of components, notably but not exclusively the publication of information about the arbitral proceedings, access to various documents from the arbitration file and to the hearings, as well as involvement of third parties in the conduct of proceedings. Collectively, all of these elements fall under the heading of 'transparency' as that term is typically used in connection with international investment arbitration.

12. Based on this broad use of the term 'transparency', the Rules thus have a symbolic significance in that they facilitate public access to investment arbitration proceedings, and provide certain tools for doing so. Whether they will, in application, render these objectives concrete remains to be seen and will be considered in this book.

13. The chapters of this book discuss the notion of 'public interest' in investment arbitration more broadly (Chapter 2); the scope of application of the Rules (Chapter 3); the publication of information at the commencement of the arbitral proceedings (Chapter 4); the publication of, and access to, documents filed in the arbitration (Chapter 5); the possibilities for third parties to make submissions, i.e. submissions by a third person (Chapter 6) or by a non-disputing party to the underlying

[13] See Johannes Koepp and Cameron Sim, 'The Application of Transparency', [8]; Dimitrij Euler and Maxi Scherer, 'Conclusion', [10]–[15].

treaty (Chapter 7); the use of public hearings (Chapter 8); the exceptions to transparency allowed under the Rules (Chapter 9); the organisation and use of a repository to collect published information (Chapter 10); and, finally, how the Rules will apply in practice in combination with other instruments (Chapter 11).

2

Public interest in investment arbitration

MARKUS GEHRING* AND DIMITRIJ EULER**

2.1 Absence of public interest in investment disputes

1. Investment agreements, either in the form of contracts or treaties, are problematic because the State agrees to exclude a dispute from its jurisdiction and instead offers investment arbitration. States accept this limitation because they believe arbitration to be one significant factor for foreign investors to assess where they intend to invest. Thus, the arbitration clause, in addition to other protections, shall attract investments and promote growth in the long run. In contracts, the dispute is defined under the arbitration clause. Treaties, however, are more problematic than contracts because States need to determine the term 'investment' related to unknown disputes in their investment treaty. The term is not defined under customary international law. Assuming that protection of all kinds of investment creates growth, States prefer to include a very broad definition of investment in their respective investment treaties.

2. Investment treaties are highly problematic for a host State if they omit a clear definition of investment whilst still containing an offer to arbitrate with the investor. Host States risk violating investors' rights with any measure domestically enacted, irrespective of whether it is in the national or international public interest. The lack of definition, in combination with the offer to arbitrate, allows the investor to file for arbitration against the State more easily. Once arbitration is undertaken and an award is made, it is generally enforceable under the New York

* Dr Markus Gehring, MA (Cantab), LLM (Yale), PhD (Hamburg), is Deputy Director of the Centre for European Legal Studies (CELS) Faculty of Law, University of Cambridge, Fellow and Director of Studies in Law at Hughes and a Fellow of the Lauterpacht Centre for International Law. He holds an ad personam Jean Monnet Chair at the University of Ottowa. This chapter shares thoughts with his previous collaborative work, in particular with Dr Marie-Claire Cordonier Segger, Dr Avidan Kent and Dr Jarrod Hepburn.

** Dimitrij Euler is a PhD student at the University of Basel.

Convention on Recognition and Enforcement of Foreign Arbitral Awards (NY Convention) or directly under the International Centre for Settlement of Investment Disputes (ICSID) Convention if it was an ICSID tribunal. States have no right to appeal.

3. An additional problem arises with regard to the legitimacy of these treaties. The investment treaties discussed here sometimes fail to have the requisite degree of democratic legitimacy, especially when compared to national laws. States at times negotiate these treaties in the absence of any political debate and the public misses the opportunity to comment on or contribute to their content. The departments of foreign affairs usually negotiate such treaties in a sphere beyond the reach of the public.[1]

4. Once States conclude investment treaties, the arbitration clause in the treaties excludes disputes concerning State interference with a foreign investor's right protected under these treaties from the scope of their courts. These courts are generally expected to act in the public interest with independence and impartiality. However, the arbitral tribunal also acts in the interest of the disputing parties in a fair and efficient manner, and endeavours to resolve the dispute under its jurisdiction concerning a question based on the disputing parties' submissions. Outside the disputing parties' submission and the arbitral tribunal's jurisdiction, an arbitral tribunal cannot address any third person submission. Thus, investment disputes concern the public interest but are beyond the reach of the public.

2.2 Transparency as an answer to the public interest

5. The system of investor-State arbitration borrows its main elements from the system of commercial arbitration. One of the most cited advantages of commercial arbitration as opposed to court proceedings is the level of confidentiality without public disclosure that the parties enjoy.[2] The existence of the dispute remains private; hearings are treated confidentially and the publication of awards often depends on the decision of the parties. In commercial disputes, confidentiality aims to expedite

[1] Philip Allot, *The Health of Nations, Society and Law beyond the State* (Cambridge University Press, 2002) (Kindle), Loc 3240.

[2] See Julian D. M. Lew, Loukas A. Mistelis and Stefan Michael Kröll, 'Arbitration as a Dispute Settlement Mechanism' in *Comparative International Commercial Arbitration* (Kluwer Law International, 2003) 1, 3.

arbitrations, whilst also serving to protect the confidentiality of information and reputation. However, investor-State disputes often raise public interest issues that are usually absent from international commercial arbitration. The involvement of a State in the investment context can lead to arbitral decisions that affect a significantly broader range of actors than the two parties to the dispute. Commentators and civil society groups have thus called for increased public involvement in investment arbitration proceedings in order to incorporate broader policy considerations into the dispute resolution process and add a measure of transparency.

6. There are sometimes fundamental questions raised with regard to investor-State arbitrations as such, largely because those disputes typically involve public interests. As one NGO publication suggests, the allegation is that these disputes create public problems while enhancing private rights.[3] Certainly it is a legitimate question to ask whether confidentiality should be granted to investors when their dispute concerns important public interest values such as human rights or sustainable development more broadly. More concretely, it is questionable whether environmental priorities and socio-economic development imperatives should be solely represented by the State party in dispute. When the public is concerned, and arguably in sustainable development disputes that is often the case, the State might not be able to represent all public interests at issue.

7. The promise of sustainable development, as an objective, is to achieve transparency in an integrated manner. 'Sustainable development' has been recognised by countries of the world in a progressive series of international policy debates and declarations over the past three decades.[4] The concept draws attention to the long-term sustainability of development progress, especially whether this progress can respect

[3] IISD-WWF, *Private Rights, Public Problems* (IISD, 2001) www.iisd.org/pdf/trade_citizens guide.pdf.

[4] See *inter alia* 'The Rio Declaration on Environment and Development' (1992) UN Doc. A/CONF.151/26 www.un.org/documents/ga/conf151/aconf15126-1annex1.htm (*Rio Declaration on Environment and Development*); 'Johannesburg Declaration on Sustainable Development' (2002) UN Doc. A/CONF/199/20; 'Doha Ministerial Declaration (Ministerial Conference, Fourth Session, 14 November 2001)' (2001) WTO Doc. WT/MIN(01)/DEC/W/1. For a more detailed review, see Marie-Claire Cordonier Segger and Ashfaq Khalfan, *Sustainable Development Law: Principles, Practices, and Prospects* (Oxford University Press, 2004) 3–4.

social, economic and environmental priorities in a balanced and coherent manner.[5] The prospect of a 'global green economy' in the context of poverty eradication and sustainable development addresses precisely these issues, supporting the trade, investment and development efforts that spur more ecologically and socially beneficial outcomes.[6] It is usually assumed that investment law includes several features that protect an investment, such as protection for the transfer of funds, long-term activity, as well as protection of the investor's participation in the management of the project.[7] The promotion of foreign direct investment (FDI) is regulated mainly by international investment agreements (IIAs). These treaties are designed to provide security and certainty for foreign investors, in order to promote FDI, with the object of achieving the ultimate goal of development.

8. The relationship between FDI and sustainable development can be described as 'dual-natured'.[8] On the one hand, the activity of transnational corporations (TNCs) and other foreign investors can, and often does, promote certain aspects of sustainable development. This is evident from experiences such as foreign investment in renewable energy technologies and infrastructure that can help to mitigate climate change, investment in watershed restoration that improves water supplies for people, investment in new agricultural techniques that support organic farming, or investment in information and communications technologies that improves quality of life and opens new educational opportunities in developing countries. On the other hand, the activities of investors may also frustrate sustainable development, promoting economic development projects that externalise social and environmental costs as significant negative impacts on the environment and on communities. Similarly, some FDI also adversely affects the global environment, such as investments that seek to establish new coal-based

[5] Cordonier Segger and Khalfan (n. 4) 3–4.

[6] See e.g. Céline Kauffmann and Cristina Tébar Less, *Transition to a Low-Carbon Economy: Public Goals and Corporate Practices* (OECD, 2010), paras 105–9 www.oecd.org/dataoecd/40/52/45513642.pdf.

[7] Rudolf Dolzer and Christoph Schreuer, *Principles of International Investment Law* (Oxford University Press, 2008) 60.

[8] This term was recently used to describe the more specific relationship between FDI and climate change, see United Nations Conference on Trade and Development, *World Investment Report 2010, Investing in a Low Carbon Economy* (United Nations Publications, 2010) 136.

power plants in a carbon-constrained world.[9] The prospect of the 'green economy' in the context of poverty eradication and sustainable development addresses precisely these issues, supporting the trade, investment and development efforts that spur more ecologically and socially beneficial outcomes.[10] Moreover, ignoring sustainable development issues can be bad for business. These economic impacts should be prevented, not ignored.

9. For example, the principle of public participation, as phrased by the International Law Association's New Delhi Declaration of Principles of International Law Relating to Sustainable Development,[11] can be integrated through the inclusion of the public's right to submit *amicus curiae* briefs in investment disputes, or by allowing free access to documents as now mandated through the Rules to which this book is dedicated.[12] While much of the impact of dispute settlement will depend on the underlying substantive rules, the complete absence of all forms of investor-State arbitration could also hamper sustainable development. What if an EU investor faces challenges for a renewable energy project in one of the US states and US state and federal courts (many judges directly elected) are proving to be disinclined to help a 'foreign' company, but the Commission and our investor's EU Member State are unwilling to intervene? Surely the complete absence of all forms of investor-State arbitration cannot support sustainable development in these circumstances.

10. From a sustainable development perspective, the main challenge faced by treaty negotiators is to balance the conflicting interests present in the essence of foreign investments. In this sense, enhanced transparency is only one of many changes that could be made to international investment law. Treaty negotiators, for example, should design tools that will promote sustainable investments by providing them a secure and stable business environment. On the other hand, they also need to secure ample regulatory flexibility so that States will be able to reform and adapt

[9] See e.g. the factual background of the *Vattenfall* case, *Vattenfall AB, Vattenfall Europe AG, Vattenfall Europe Generation AG & Co. KG (Sweden and Europe)* v. *The Federal Republic of Germany* (Award) [2011] ICSID Case No. ARB/09/6 (ECT).

[10] See e.g. Kauffmann and Tébar Less (n. 6), [105]–[109].

[11] International Law Association, 'New Delhi Declaration of Principles of International Law Relating to Sustainable Development' (2002) 49(2) *Netherlands International Law Review* 299.

[12] UNCITRAL, *UNCITRAL Rules on Transparency in Treaty-based Investor-State Arbitration* (2014) www.uncitral.org/pdf/english/texts/arbitration/rules-on-transparency/Rules-on-Transparency-E.pdf.

their policies. One approach adopted by States is the inclusion of references to sustainable development objectives in preambles to IIAs as already discussed for FTAs. The importance of preambular language can be understood from Article 31(2) of the 1969 Vienna Convention on the Law of Treaties (VCLT), according to which the context and the purpose of a treaty is to be derived *inter alia* from the treaty's preamble.[13] In light of the different interpretations given to legal terms such as 'expropriation', 'legitimate expectations' and 'like-circumstances', and the effects these can have on sustainable development objectives,[14] the role preambular language can fulfil is significant.[15] A second type of preambular language, while not referring to sustainable development as a treaty objective *per se*, imposes upon parties the duty to behave consistently with this objective. This type of language can be found in US IIAs. The preamble to the US–Rwanda IIA, for example, defines as treaty objectives *inter alia* the promotion of economic cooperation, the stimulation of private investment, and the creation of a stable business environment. It continues, however, by stating that the parties are: '*Desiring* to achieve these objectives in a manner consistent with the protection of health, safety, and the environment, and the promotion of internationally recognised labor rights'.[16] A third example of preambular language can be defined as 'non-derogation' language. This language can be found in many of the IIAs signed by States such as Finland, the Netherlands, Japan and the US.[17] According to these references, the treaty's objectives (often economic in nature) are to be achieved without relaxing regulatory standards in fields such as the environment, health or safety. Lastly, on very rare occasions, references to sustainable development treaties can be found in the preamble to IIAs.

[13] See Vienna Convention on the Law of Treaties, Article 31(2).

[14] For a review of these terms and their relation to sustainable development, see Marie-Claire Cordonier Segger and Andrew Newcombe, 'An Integrated Agenda for Sustainable Development in International Investment Law' in Marie-Claire Cordonier Segger, Markus W. Gehring and Andrew Newcombe (eds.), *Sustainable Development in World Investment Law* (Kluwer Law International, 2011).

[15] Marie-Claire Cordonier Segger and Andrew Newcombe, 'An Integrated Agenda for Sustainable Development in International Investment Law' in Cordonier Segger, Gehring and Newcombe (n. 14) 101, 126.

[16] See similar language in the US 2004 Model BIT, and the *US–Uruguay BIT* (2006).

[17] See e.g. *Finland–Ethiopia BIT* (2006); *Finland–Armenia BIT* (2004); *Netherlands–Suriname BIT* (2005); *Netherlands–Burundi BIT* (2007); *US–Mozambique BIT* (1998); *US–Jordan BIT* (2003); *US–Bahrain BIT* (2001); *Japan–Korea BIT* (2002); *Japan–Vietnam BIT* (2003).

Examples of this can be found in the preamble to the Singapore–European Free Trade Association free trade agreement (EFTA FTA) (which includes investment protection), in which the parties reaffirm 'their commitment to the principles set out in the United Nations Charter and the Universal Declaration of Human Rights',[18] and in the Energy Charter Treaty, in which the parties are '[r]ecalling the United Nations Framework Convention on Climate Change, the Convention on Long-Range Transboundary Air Pollution and its protocols, and other international environmental agreements with energy-related aspects'.[19]

11. Sustainable development is no longer optional. In many ways the social licence of investment protection rules depends on its ability to balance economic and environmental priorities. That means primarily three consequences. Current uses of existing IIAs have to be re-thought and transparency is an important part of it. They should be less a second chance for a foreign investor to have another attempt at difficult governmental negotiations or even mean exceedingly preferential treatment of the foreign investor in comparison to domestic companies. Rather, investment law should serve the development, writ nowadays sustainable development, of the host country. It is not inconceivable that investors in future will have to demonstrate that they have done precisely that. The standards are also becoming increasingly clear. A wealth of international sustainable development treaties[20] provide international standards that must influence how we interpret 50-year-old treaty instruments. The norm users of investment law, particularly arbitrators on tribunals, are under a special obligation to engage in the kind of balancing of economic and environmental priorities as discussed above. Dispute settlement is becoming increasingly transparent and the Rules could influence how the majority of arbitral tribunals will regard the matter. But this kind of procedural innovation should also be coupled with a contemporary interpretation of investment obligations. Some arbitrators have tried to make amends in the award stage, such as in the *Biwater* decision,[21] but further

[18] The EFTA States Iceland, Liechtenstein, Norway and Switzerland signed a free trade agreement with Singapore in Egilsstaðir, Iceland, on 26 June 2002, entry into force 1 January 2003.

[19] Energy Charter Treaty, opened for signature 17 December 1994, 34 ILM 360, 385 (ECT).

[20] UN Treaty Secretariat, *Multilateral Treaty Framework an Invitation to Universal Participation: 2010 Treaty Event: Towards Universal Participation and Implementation* (United Nations, 2010).

[21] *Biwater Gauff (Tanzania) Limited* v. *United Republic of Tanzania*, ICSID Case No. ARB/05/22, Procedural Order No. 3 (29 September 2006).

development, for example with regard to the burden of proof, is recommended. The precautionary principle allows for reversal or lessoning of the burden of proof, as has long been the case in the world trading system.[22]

12. With the arrival of the EU as a new actor,[23] many IIAs will need to be re-written or re-concluded. This window of opportunity should allow for better balancing provisions and procedural innovations to be enshrined.

13. The Rules attempt to include the public interest in investment disputes. In response to the need for greater representation of the public interest, the Rules apply to treaty-based investor-State arbitration but not investment arbitration in general.[24] Disclosure at the very outset of proceedings of some information allows the public to be aware of these proceedings.[25] The public may request some detailed information.[26] The Rules establish rights of third persons and non-disputing States to submit their views.[27] The hearings are generally held in public.[28] However, these rights are limited by exceptions.[29] Insofar as the Rules function properly, the repository acts as an information custodian.[30] The Rules aim to have an impact in the arena of investment arbitration beyond tribunals' established the Arbitration Rules.[31]

2.3 Implementing transparency in investment arbitration

14. In 2006, at its forty-fourth session, UNCITRAL, in its Working Group II (Arbitration and Conciliation) (WG), discussed possibilities for future improvements. Previous issues were addressed concerning the revision of the Arbitration Rules.[32] In its January session, the WG referred to documents of 2000 that discussed the confidentiality of information in arbitral

[22] Marie-Claire Cordonier Segger and Markus Gehring, 'Precaution, Health and the WTO: Moving Towards Sustainable Development' (2003) 29 *Queens Law Journal* 133.

[23] See A. Dimopoulos, *EU Foreign Investment Law* (Oxford University Press, 2011).

[24] See Krista Nadakavukaren Schefer, 'Article 1'.

[25] See Giuseppe Bianco, 'Article 2'.

[26] See Christopher Kee, 'Article 3'.

[27] See Mariel Dimsey, 'Article 4' and Martins Paparinskis and Jessica Howley, 'Article 5'.

[28] See Klint Alexander, 'Article 6'.

[29] See Thierry P. Augsburger, 'Article 7'.

[30] See Kathleen Claussen, 'Article 8'.

[31] See Johannes Koepp and Cameron Sim, 'The application of transparency'.

[32] See UNCITRAL, 'Report of the Working Group on Arbitration and Conciliation on the work of its forty-fourth session (New York, 23–27 January 2006)' (2006) UN Doc. A/CN.9/592 [89]–[95].

proceedings as an area open for improvements,[33] largely in response to the decision of *Australian High Court Esso* v. *Plowman* in 1994,[34] where the court had decided in favour of transparency.[35] Despite this decision, the WG in 2000 regarded issues of confidentiality as not being of high priority and saw a greater need for discussion of other issues.[36]

15. In 2006, the WG started to revise the UNCITRAL Arbitration Rules. It was agreed, during the 2006 sessions, that there was no need for a general provision requiring confidentiality in the Arbitration Rules. Various views were expressed with regard to an explicit confidentiality requirement, but there was no general support towards more confidentiality.[37] However, referring to the discretion of the tribunal to conduct proceedings and recalling the *Methanex* decision to accept *amicus* submission,[38] the WG 'agreed that third party intervention in arbitral proceedings was a matter closely connected to the confidentiality of proceedings'.[39]

16. At the same sessions in 2006, Paulsson and Petrochilos issued a report suggesting which provisions in the Arbitration Rules (1976) needed revision. This report only addressed transparency in passing and provided no momentum for improvement to the situation with regard to third party submissions and access to the proceedings.[40] This report was then distributed to the WG delegates and observers. The NGO CIEL, being an observer, criticised the fact that this:

> report commissioned by UNCITRAL . . . was written by two distinguished members of the arbitration bar with apparently no input from civil society; and it does not adequately reflect transparency and public

[33] See UNCITRAL, 'Report of the Working Group on Arbitration on the work of its thirty-second session (Vienna, 20–31 March 2000)' (2000) UN Doc. A/CN.9/468 [107].

[34] See 'The Decision of the High Court of Australia in *Esso/BHP* v. *Plowman*' 11 *Arbitration International* 109.

[35] See UNCITRAL, 'International Commercial Arbitration: Possible future work in the area of international commercial arbitration, Note by the Secretariat' (1999) UN Doc. A/CN.9/460 [62].

[36] See UNCITRAL, 'Report of the United Nations Commission on International Trade Law on the work of its thirty-second session (17 May–4 June 1999)' (1999) UN Doc. A/54/17 [358]–[359].

[37] See UNCITRAL, 'Report of the Working Group on Arbitration and Conciliation on the work of its forty-fifth session (Vienna, 11–15 September 2006)' (2006) UN Doc. A/CN.9/614 [81]–[86].

[38] *Ibid.* [81]. [39] *Ibid.* [83].

[40] See Jan Paulsson and Georgios Petrochilos, *Revision of the UNCITRAL Arbitration Rules* (Freshfields Bruckhaus Deringer, 2006).

> participation concerns as they apply to State arbitrations. In addition, UNCITRAL has not reached out to civil society or other institutions (e.g., United Nations Environment Programme and the World Trade Organization) with interests and expertise in this area.[41]

17. The work of UNCITRAL was influenced by the decisions of other courts and various commission decisions. In the same year, the Intra-American Human Rights Commission decided that the Chilean Government had violated the right to information by declining a request for information in investor-State proceedings.[42] Thereby, this decision established the active right to receive information.

18. Since proceedings under the North American Free Trade Agreement (NAFTA) had already changed towards more transparency, and the revised ICSID Convention had clarified the position of third person submissions, to express a view against transparency was difficult to argue in the WG. The forty-fifth session, in 2006, moved slightly towards transparency. The WG recognised a need for explicit provisions on third party submissions in proceedings established under the Arbitration Rules. The WG acknowledged that whatever rules were created should be applied to disputes between private commercial parties, ad hoc tribunals, investor-State disputes, and State-to-State disputes. Broad support was expressed towards arbitration rules that would apply in all contexts.[43] Thus, these rules were to apply to those proceedings that were comparable, or even similar, to investor-State arbitration under NAFTA or in accordance with the ICSID Convention.

19. In this regard, the application of the Arbitration Rules reflected very general legal relationships between disputing parties. In 2007, the WG decided that a dispute merely required a defined legal relationship, whether contractual or not.[44] Strong support existed to integrate a mechanism that would automatically apply the most recent rules.[45] The

[41] CIEL, 'UNCITRAL Arbitrations Involving State as a Party – Transparency, Public Participation and Accountability' (16 September 2008) http://ciel.org/Publications/UNCITRAL_Statement_18Sep06.pdf.

[42] See *Claude Reyes and others* v. *Chile*, Merits, reparations and costs (19 September 2006) IACHR Series C No. 151 (IACHR, 2006) IHRL 1535.

[43] See UNCITRAL (n. 37) [17]–[19].

[44] See UNCITRAL, 'Report of the Working Group on Arbitration and Conciliation on the work of its forty-sixth session (New York, 5–9 February 2007)' (2007) UN Doc. A/CN.9/619 [22]–[24].

[45] *Ibid.* [35].

defined relationship should, in future disputes, refer to the Arbitration Rules. This would lead to the application of the most recent arbitration rules and not earlier ones. The WG called this principle 'the generic approach'.[46] Additionally, some countries pushed for explicit provisions providing public access to documents, proceedings and *amicus* briefs, as well as ensuring publication of the awards.[47] In response, some delegates attempted to introduce confidentiality provisions.[48] Thus, the WG agreed on a broad scope of application, but disagreed on the substance of those provisions concerning transparency.

20. The question of confidentiality was then settled in the following session, the forty-seventh, when it was understood that parties could agree to confidentiality against mandatory law to disclose an award in pursuit of legal rights or during legal proceedings. Meanwhile, the WG asked the Secretariat to further consider awards being made public.[49] Other issues of transparency were not explicitly mentioned. The WG also agreed to discuss the application of the Arbitration Rules in the context of investor-State disputes.[50]

21. The NGOs CIEL and IISD all pushed towards increased transparency. Both NGOs proposed a working paper on this subject,[51] and this was then discussed in a side meeting.[52] In response to the WG's report, both NGOs proposed a revised version of their paper in December 2007.[53] Both versions stressed the need for enhancing transparency in treaty-based investor-State arbitration, and proposed applying transparency in 'arbitrations brought by a foreign investor against a State under the terms of a treaty ("investor-State arbitrations")'.[54] Although both NGOs honoured the definition of investment in Article 25 ICSID Convention, as this definition sufficed to distinguish investor-State arbitration from genuine commercial arbitration, they nevertheless rejected the

[46] *Ibid.* [62]. [47] *Ibid.* [61].

[48] See UNCITRAL (n. 44) [61]–[69]; CIEL and IISD, 'Revising the UNCITRAL Arbitration Rules to Address Investor-State Arbitrations: Revised Version December 2007' (2007) [11] www.iisd.org/pdf/2008/investment_revising_uncitral_arbitration_dec.pdf.

[49] See UNCITRAL, 'Report of the Working Group on Arbitration and Conciliation on the work of its forty-seventh session (Vienna, 10–14 September 2007)' (2007) UN Doc. A/CN.9/641 [97]–[98].

[50] *Ibid.* [113].

[51] CIEL and IISD, Revising the UNCITRAL Arbitration Rules to Address State Arbitrations (February 2007) www.iisd.org/pdf/2007/investment_revising_uncitral_arbitration.pdf.

[52] See CIEL and IISD, 'Proposed Revisions to the UNCITRAL Arbitration Rules for Investor-State Arbitrations' (12 September 2007).

[53] See CIEL and IISD (n. 48). [54] *Ibid.* at 3.

same wording under the scope of a future transparency standard, as that scope should address 'treaty-based' arbitration as the relevant criteria.[55] It is interesting to note that both NGOs did accept that transparency should apply in treaty-based arbitration and therefore did not affect international commercial arbitration in general, despite agreeing that public interest might also be relevant in these disputes.[56] Thus, the NGOs only accepted a future transparency standard in treaty-based investor-State arbitration, but not in contract-based investor-State arbitration.

22. The CIEL and IISD again stated that enhancing transparency would not eliminate other investor-State arbitration flaws. In 2007, the IISD recalled its wish to have an international court to deal with investor-State issues and called for the appeal tribunal to improve the coherency of investor-State awards. They also repeated that other institutions of commercial arbitration other than ICSID were inappropriate for resolving disputes because such proceedings, and their ensuing awards, had to remain confidential.[57] However, both NGOs maintained their request that the 'UNCITRAL rules ought to be adapted so that they require the public disclosure of any investment treaty arbitrations launched pursuant to those rules, as well as public access to the arbitral hearings and documents'.[58] Thus, the NGOs concentrated on one aim only – transparency – with both NGOs repeating their previous standpoints in the NAFTA and ICSID tribunals. For example, they submitted that transparency was key because citizens of disputing States needed to know about the conduct of their own governments and that transparency was vital because it strengthened good governance, influenced public policy, was a valuable tool against corruption and because compensation to investors would be paid with tax-payers' money.[59]

23. The CIEL's position remained unaltered, although the CIEL used slightly different categories of international arbitration than the WG had previously done. The CIEL distinguished disputes involving public interest and at least one disputing State party from international commercial arbitration, from disputes not involving public interest and between private parties of different States.[60] Thus, the call for transparency was

[55] *Ibid.* at 7. [56] See UNCITRAL (n. 49) [7].

[57] See Luke Eric Peterson, 'Investment Treaty News: 2006 Year in Review' (2007) 15 www.iisd.org/pdf/2007/itn_year_review_2006.pdf.

[58] *Ibid.* at 17. [59] See CIEL and IISD (n. 51) 1f; Ciel and IISD (n. 48) 1f. [60] *Ibid.*

broader than the future transparency standard in treaty-based investor-State arbitration.

24. The WG began its debate concerning the transparency standard in 2008, during its forty-eighth session, when it actively discussed the subject. The broad scope of the Arbitration Rules, contract-based and treaty-based arbitration, dominated the discussion on how to deal with public interest in treaty-based investor-State arbitration.[61] The Special Representative of the Secretary-General on human rights and transnational corporations and other business enterprises pointed out that the arbitral tribunal's decision would have significant effects on the governance of States, governance of corporations and human rights in general.[62] The Representative to the Secretary-General, John Ruggie, stated that 'adequate transparency where human rights and other state responsibilities are concerned is essential if publics are to be aware of proceedings that may affect the public interest' and further noted that 'such transparency lies at the very foundation of what the United Nations and other authoritative entities have been promulgating as the precepts of good governance'.[63] He supported both NGOs and urged governments to support the issue in the WG.[64] Thus, the position of the parties in favour of transparency became stronger.

25. However, not everyone was enthusiastic. The Club of Milan favoured confidentiality, and attempted to shift the debate back in that direction.[65] They used traditional arguments, such as the fact that the general nature of arbitration, being based on party autonomy, required confidentiality. As the side in favour of confidentiality decreased in force, some of the delegates that had previously favoured a broad scope of the arbitration rules expressed their concerns that it was a mistake to

[61] See UNCITRAL, 'Report of the Working Group on Arbitration and Conciliation on the work of its forty-eighth session (New York 4–8 February 2008)' (2008) UN Doc. A/CN.9/646 [54]–[69] Statement made on behalf of the Special Representative of the Secretary-General on Human Rights and Transnational Corporations and Other Business Enterprises.

[62] *Ibid.* [57] and Annex I (n. 61) [61]–[65], Annex I and Annex III Statement by the Center for International Institute for Sustainable Development (IISD); ibid.

[63] UNCHR, 'Statement of the UN Secretary-General's Special Representative on Business and Human Rights, Professor John Ruggie to the UNCITRAL Working Group II (Arbitration and Conciliation), 48th session, New York, USA February 4–8, 2008', cited in CIEL and IISD, 'CIEL and IISD call for an end to an era of secrecy in investor-State arbitration: UN body must support transparency in new arbitration rules' (June 2008) 2.

[64] See UNCITRAL (n. 61) [61]–[65], Annex I and Annex III Statement by the Center for International Institute for Sustainable Development (IISD); ibid.

[65] See UNCITRAL (n. 61) [60] and Annex II Statement by the Milan Club of Arbitrators.

understand commercial arbitration as also encompassing investor-State arbitration.[66] An alternative was to establish the term 'generic' or 'ordinary' commercial arbitration as opposed to 'treaty-based'.[67]

26. This session was a success for all those in favour of transparency, and in particular for the observer NGOs, CIEL and IISD. The WG accepted that, firstly, treaty-based investor-State arbitration raised, to some extent, issues that differed from ordinary commercial arbitration. Secondly, in response to these issues, additional provisions addressing treaty-based investor-State arbitration were regarded as desirable. Lastly, it was recognised that the issue of transparency needed further consideration.[68] Hence, the CIEL and the IISD, together with Argentina, other South American countries, Canada, South Africa, Switzerland and Norway, successfully pushed transparency onto the official WG agenda, despite very strong opposition from other States and the Club of Milan. In early July 2008, the Commission gave the WG the mandate to address transparency.[69] The WG was to still continue its revision of the Arbitration Rules (1976), but transparency was also to be addressed, at a later stage.

27. In a follow-up to this session, in 2008, a senior counsel of the IISD, Howard Mann, reflected upon Ruggie's intervention in the WG in the light of the tribunal's need to address human rights in investor-State disputes, stating that he understood human rights in the broader sense including political, civil, economic, social and cultural rights.[70] Confidentiality of treaty-based investor-State arbitration collided with human rights, and prevented civil society from scrutinising their democratically elected government, or from reacting in the form of democratic debates on the issues raised in the arbitral procedures.[71]

28. Both NGOs referred to the human right to obtain information and expressed concern that arbitral tribunals might violate this right by protecting confidentiality. Under slightly different circumstances, the

[66] UNCITRAL, Model Law on International Commercial Arbitration (1985), with amendments as adopted in 2006 art 1 Footnote ('The definition of commercial arbitration is in most cases implied by the Model Law on International Commercial Arbitration').

[67] UNCITRAL (n. 61) [67]. [68] *Ibid.* [69].

[69] See CIEL and Nathalie Bernasconi-Osterwalder, 'Shedding Light Onto Investment Arbitration', 13th International Anti-Corruption Conference Athens, Greece, 30 October–2 November 2008, 4.

[70] See Howard Mann, 'International Investment Agreements, Business and Human Rights: Key Issues and Opportunities (February 2008)' (2008) 8 www.iisd.org/pdf/2008/iia_business_human_rights.pdf.

[71] *Ibid* 29.

European Court of Human Rights in the *Hungarian Civil Liberties Union* case *Társaság a Szabadságjogokért* v. *Hungary*, Judgment of 14 April 2009,[72] decided that an NGO has a right to access information of public interest in accordance with the right to information protected under Article 10 the European Human Rights Charter. In this case, the respondent did not contest that an active right to information existed under the right to information under Article 10, but stated that its data protection act had precedence over the right to information.[73] The Court repeated at the outset that 'Article 10 does not . . . confer on the individual a right of access to a register containing information on his personal position, nor does it embody an obligation on the Government to impart such information to the individual'.[74] However, the court considered that 'the State had an obligation not to impede the flow of information sought by the applicant'.[75] Hindering an NGO from gathering information that would otherwise be available would adversely affect the role of the NGO in its position as a public watchdog. Individuals who are linked to a public matter may not, therefore, rely on their privacy rights.[76] Even though the court decided that generally available information may not be barred for whatever reason, the judgment lacked the express wording that an active right to information existed that would otherwise remain confidential. It thus depended on domestic law and, in particular, the relevant freedom of information act, or data protection act, as to whether the information might be considered generally available or confidential.

29. On 27 June 2008, in New York, the WG had to agree on a schedule for discussing the issue of transparency in treaty-based investor-State arbitration. Despite their mandate, the group had, until that time, difficulties in reaching a consensus. The United Kingdom, the United States and Canada, as well as some developing countries, particularly Uganda among them, supported the CIEL and IISD position in establishing transparency.[77] Some delegates, however, predominantly commercial

[72] See *Társaság A Szabadságjogokért* v. *Hungary*, Application No. 37374/05, Judgment Strasbourg (14 April 2009; Final 14 July 2009).

[73] *Ibid.* [21]: 'Within the framework of the Data Act 1992, the right of access to data of public interest was restricted by the right to the protection of personal data. The Government maintained that this restriction met the requirements laid down in the Convention, in that it was prescribed by law, it was applied in order to protect the rights of others and it was necessary in a democratic society'.

[74] *Ibid.* [35]. [75] *Ibid.* [36]. [76] *Ibid.* [37].

[77] CIEL and IISD, 'UN body supports transparency in new arbitration rules' (3 July 2008) http://ciel.org/Trade_Sustainable_Dev/UNCITRAL_Transparency_3Jul08.html.

arbitrators, 'rebuffed calls by many States and civil society to introduce transparency requirements into investment arbitrations'.[78] In response, the countries concerned and their civil societies were dissatisfied with their own delegates and several delegates were replaced before the start of the transparency debate scheduled for 2010.[79]

30. In the 2008 sessions, the WG had agreed on a schedule. Its first task was to complete the rules revision and then propose a transparency standard 'as a matter of priority'.[80] It then confirmed its earlier approach that the general applicability was regarded as being of great importance also with regard to future discussions.[81] In the first session of 2010, the WG finished its revision and began with its new task.[82]

31. In 2010, UNCITRAL entrusted this WG with the mandate of preparing a legal standard on transparency in treaty-based investor-State arbitration.[83] Work began in the fifty-third session in Vienna in response to the forty-first UNCITRAL session held a decade earlier.[84] Despite the mandate to increase transparency, some delegates remained sceptical, but had no new arguments. The discussion immediately focused on the question of the scope of application. Some delegates who were previously in favour of a broad application of the Arbitration Rules pointed out the differences between commercial arbitration and investor-State arbitration. Now the roles were reversed; those delegations in favour of transparency argued for a broad application of the rules, whereas those opposed argued for a narrow application. The need for an opt-in or opt-out mechanism was also raised.[85] At this stage, the standard should address publication of the commencement of the arbitral proceedings,

[78] *Ibid.* at 1. [79] *Ibid.*

[80] See UNCITRAL, 'Report of Working Group II (Arbitration and Conciliation) on the work of its fiftieth session (New York, 9–13 February 2009)' (2009) UN Doc. A/CN.9/669 [121].

[81] *Ibid.*

[82] See UNCITRAL, 'Report of Working Group II (Arbitration and Conciliation) on the work of its fifty-second session (New York, 1–5 February 2010)' (2010) UN Doc. A/CN.9/688.

[83] See UNCITRAL, 'Report of the United Nations Commission on International Trade Law Forty-third session (21 June–9 July 2010)' (2010) UN Doc. A/65/17 (General Assembly Official Records Sixty-fifth session Supplement No. 17 2010) [190].

[84] See UNCITRAL, 'Report of the United Nations Commission on International Trade Law Forty-first session (16 June–3 July 2008)' (2008) UN Doc. A/63/17 (Official records of the General Assembly, Sixty-third session, Supplement No. 17, 2008) [314].

[85] See UNCITRAL, 'Report of Working Group II (Arbitration and Conciliation) on the work of its fifty-third session (Vienna, 4–8 October 2010)' (2010) UN Doc. A/CN.9/712 [16]–[21].

access to documents, public hearings, criteria for *amicus* briefs, publication of the awards and any exceptions in the case of confidential business information or essential security interest of a State, and perhaps even exceptions to an exception. Not all topics were clear; for example, the WG made no reference to non-disputing State-party submissions, but only addressed *amicus* briefs submissions.[86]

32. In the eyes of the CIEL and IISD, a transparent international dispute resolution procedure is far from being perfect, as transparency is not the only issue in investor-State disputes; the senior counsel of IISD, Fiona Marshall, outlined three ongoing issues, namely transparency, arbitrators' independence and impartiality, and, finally, consistency of the decisions.[87] Today, however, of these three, only transparency is now discussed. Even though both NGOs remained concerned about the investor-State arbitration system, the UNCITRAL mandate of preparing a legal standard on transparency in treaty-based investor-State arbitration may be seen as a major achievement. It is indeed an example of what NGOs may achieve on the international level.

33. In October 2010, the WG discussed methods to implement transparency. Both NGOs favoured implementing transparency in the form of an appendix to the Arbitration Rules (2010) and submitted a set of principles that ensured the greatest extent of transparency.[88] It is particularly noteworthy that both of the NGOs and Canada supported the same position, as they had once not always seen eye to eye, recalling how Canada dealt with the claimant's request for information in the *Pope & Talbot* v. *Canada* tribunal.[89] From October 2010, Canada, the CIEL and IISD gave the impression that they were working together as a team.

34. The scope of application remained an unresolved issue, and the delegates held fast to their positions. In the fifty-fourth session, 7–11 February 2011, the WG dealt with the controversial issue of the applicability of the standard to existing treaties. Here, there were two clashing positions: opt in or opt out. One side took the position that the

[86] *Ibid.* [30]–[31].

[87] See Fiona Marshall, *Defining New Institutional Options for Investor-State Dispute Settlement* (IISD, 2009) www.iisd.org/pdf/2009/defining_new_institutional_options.pdf.

[88] IISD and CIEL, 'Ensuring Transparency in Investor-State Dispute Resolution under the UNCITRAL Arbitration Rules, UNCITRAL Working Group II, Vienna, October 4–8, 2010' (2010) 2.

[89] See Letter from the Arbitral Tribunal, NAFTA UNCITRAL Investor-State Claim Pope & Talbot Inc and the Government of Canada, 21 March 2001, available at www.international.gc.ca.

standard on transparency would apply unless the State parties to the investment treaty opted out, which meant that a State party in favour of confidentiality had to renegotiate the treaty in question. It also meant that if the standard went below an existing transparency standard in a treaty, for example the transparency standards under NAFTA or the ICSID Convention, in this case, the State party in favour of transparency would have to renegotiate the treaty. The other side took the opposite position, arguing that arbitrations had to be confidential by default; therefore, State parties to an investment treaty had to opt in if they intended to apply transparency standards in disputes initiated under existing treaties. If the State parties had agreed, in an already existing treaty, to a broader transparency standard, such as under NAFTA or the ICSID Convention, the State party in favour of the narrow, new UNCITRAL standard would need to start the negotiation. The NGOs stated that, at a minimum, the standard needed to mirror the European Court of Human Rights and the Intra-American Commission for Human Rights decisions.[90]

35. Another issue was the submissions of non-disputing State parties. The WG addressed what had already been established under NAFTA proceeding, i.e. that the home State of an investor, or a non-involved third State, could address legal interpretations in ongoing arbitral disputes.[91] However, not all members of the group agreed as to what non-disputing State parties' rights could be.

36. The scope of application remained unresolved, the debate continuing in the fifty-fifth session, when major arbitration institutions were invited to express their views.[92] Would an extensive application of the scope violate institutional rules, for example the rules of the Stockholm Chamber of Commerce or the International Chamber of Commerce in Paris?

37. Another issue was examined concerning the differentiation between non-disputing State parties' submissions or third persons'

[90] See UNCITRAL, Report of Working Group II (Arbitration and Conciliation) on the work of its fifty-fourth session (New York, 7–11 February 2011), UN Doc. A/CN.9/717 [14]–[32].

[91] UNCITRAL, 'Report of the United Nations Commission on International Trade Law Forty-fourth session (27 June–8 July 2011), UN Doc. A/66/17 (General Assembly Official Records Sixty-sixth session Supplement No. 17) [124].

[92] UNCITRAL, Report of Working Group II (Arbitration and Conciliation) on the work of its fifty-fifth session (Vienna, 3–7 October 2011), UN Doc. A/CN.9/736 [28].

submission, for example NGOs'.[93] The question was whether non-disputing State parties or third persons had the same rights, and could address questions of law, fact and legal or factual issues within or beyond the disputing parties' submissions.

38. Finally, the WG listed various instruments to implement transparency, such as rules, model clauses, guidelines, catalogues of principles or conventions.[94] The choice of instruments to be used would depend on the transparency standard's scope. The CIEL and IISD proposed using rules with a broad scope that encompassed future disputes initiated under existing treaties, as well as future treaties. Both NGOs believed that if the scope of the guidelines were to be limited to future treaties, it would be an unnecessary limitation that would hinder establishing transparency. The question to exclude existing treaties from the scope was one of interpretation of the arbitration clause in the treaty, and therefore outside the mandate of the WG.[95] Those delegates who were for transparency had already clearly made it known that they would support a convention if the WG agreed to a narrow scope.

39. In February 2011, the IISD issued a best-practice report that supported the integration of the Rules into treaties. The reasoning behind this was that as most treaties offer several for a to resolve an investor-State dispute, and as the host State has limited influence upon the choice of the legal seat once a dispute has arisen, it was the investor party that could determine the degree of transparency in the investor-State dispute. This choice would be eliminated if State parties to the treaty incorporated the Rules into the treaty.[96] However, such a pathway could be risky in that the standard valid among the State parties could be lowered.[97]

40. The scope of application remained controversial. In the fifty-sixth session, in 2012, the WG continued its discussion on the subject. One delegation suggested a compromise, which was to have an opt-in for

[93] *Ibid.* [78]–[98].

[94] See Nathalie Bernasconi-Osterwalder, 'Ensuring Transparency in Investor-State Dispute Resolution under the UNCITRAL Arbitration Rules' (CIEL and IISD, 2011) 1 www.iisd.org/publications/pub.aspx?id=1428 accessed 23 September 2013.

[95] *Ibid.* 4.

[96] See Lise Johnson and Nathalie Bernasconi-Osterwalder, 'Transparency in the Dispute Settlement Process: Country Best Practices' (IISD, 2011) 2 www.iisd.org/pdf/2011/transparency_dispute_settlement_processes.pdf.

[97] See CIEL and IISD, 'Comments on the Scope of Application of UNCITRAL's Draft Rules on Transparency in Investor-State Arbitration, Working Group II, February 6–10, 2012' (2012) 1 www.iisd.org/pdf/2012/ciel_iisd_uncitral_feb_2012.pdf.

existing treaties and an opt-out for future treaties.[98] Not all were satisfied with this solution, and some suggested using a dynamic approach to the application of the Rules. They believed that the scope of the rules should be interpreted in accordance with the VCLT.[99] Canada and the US favoured the dynamic interpretation; the Swiss delegation, however, attempted to find a consensus among the different delegations.

41. Despite these diverging viewpoints, the WG did make progress, attributable to the outstanding capabilities of its president. In October 2012, the IISD announced that the WG might achieve consensus upon the transparency issue, but other issues were still to be resolved.[100] In particular, it was the scope of application that still needed to be clarified. The opt-out and dynamic approach was further discussed in the fifty-seventh session.[101] Argentina, Australia, Canada, Mexico, Norway, the US and others disagreed with the proposed compromise of opt-in for existing treaties and opt-out for future treaties, and filed a common understanding of the scope of application.[102]

42. For the NGOs, the compromise was not a satisfactory solution; CIEL and IISD opined that some proposed options in the transparency debate were below the then current transparency standards under the ICSID Convention, and treaties such as NAFTA or CAFTA-DR.[103] In the eyes of these NGOs, some delegates were using the discussions for their own purposes by attempting to lower the current standards of transparency in treaty-based investor-State arbitration.[104] It was not clear at that point in time whether some delegations were attempting to

[98] See UNCITRAL, 'Report of Working Group II (Arbitration and Conciliation) on the work of its fifty-sixth session (New York, 6–10 February 2012)' (2012) UN Doc. A/CN.9/741 [13]–[59].

[99] *Ibid.* [55].

[100] See Lise Johnson, 'Inching Towards Consensus: An Update on the UNCITRAL Transparency Negotiations' (IISD, 30 October 2012) 1.

[101] UNCITRAL, 'Report of Working Group II (Arbitration and Conciliation) on the work of its fifty-seventh session (Vienna, 1–5 October 2012)' (2012) UN Doc. A/CN.9/760 [131].

[102] UNCITRAL, 'Settlement of Commercial Disputes: Preparation of a legal standard on transparency in treaty-based investor-State arbitration. Proposal by Governments of Argentina, Australia, Canada, Mexico, Norway, South Africa, and the United States of America' (2012) UN Doc. A/CN.9/WG.II/WP.174.

[103] CIEL and IISD, 'Comments on Draft Rules on Transparency in Investor-State Arbitration' (2011) 3.

[104] See Lise Johnson, 'Countries Continue to Pursue Efforts to Increase Transparency in Investor-State Dispute Settlement' (IISD, 2012) 1 www.iisd.org/pdf/2012/com_increase_transparency.pdf.

jeopardise the work of the group.[105] Thus, the consensus seemed to be as close to reachable as in the previous session, but it was doubtful whether the WG could come to an agreement.

43. The IISD, CIEL and VCC urged the participants to accept that the scope of transparency encompasses existing treaties, and that transparency required, besides the proposed documents, procedural orders and the decisions of various authorities supporting the arbitral procedure, whether those decisions were dissenting or supporting opinions.[106]

44. The question of scope was finally resolved in the fifty-eighth session, when the WG proposed to apply the standard to disputes also arising out of future treaties. The WG decided to address the question of the application of the standard to disputes initiated under existing treaties in future sessions. The delegates agreed in the draft document that the convention would allow a State to apply the Rules by signature and that no pressure should be put on States to ratify the convention.[107] In 2013, the standard on transparency in investor-State arbitration was finally adopted; a convention was agreed upon in 2014 and will serve as a tool to increase transparency.[108]

[105] See Nathalie Bernasconi-Osterwalder, 'A Critical Opportunity for Transparency in Investor-State Disputes as Government Delegations and Arbitration Experts Meet in New York, February 2012' (IISD, 2012) 1 www.iisd.org/publications/pub.aspx?id=1547.

[106] IISD, CIEL and VCC, Submission to Working Group II on International Arbitration, Vienna October 1–5, 2012, Comments on Draft Articles 1, 3, 7 and 8 (2012) 1.

[107] UNCITRAL, 'Report of Working Group II (Arbitration and Conciliation) on the work of its fifty-eighth session (New York, 4–8 February 2013)' (2013) UN Doc. A/CN.9/765 [16]–[40].

[108] See UNCITRAL, 'Report of the United Nations Commission on International Trade Law Forty-sixth session (8–26 July 2013)' (2013) UN Doc. A/68/17 (General Assembly Official Records Sixty-eighth session Supplement No. 17) [14].

3

Article 1. Scope of application

KRISTA NADAKAVUKAREN SCHEFER*

Applicability of the Rules

1. The UNCITRAL Rules on Transparency in Treaty-based Investor-State Arbitration ("Rules on Transparency") shall apply to investor-State arbitration initiated under the UNCITRAL Arbitration Rules pursuant to a treaty providing for the protection of investments or investors ("treaty")* concluded on or after 1st April 2014 unless the Parties to the treaty** have agreed otherwise.
2. In investor-State arbitrations initiated under the UNCITRAL Arbitration Rules pursuant to a treaty concluded before 1 April 2014, these Rules shall apply only when:
   (a) the parties to an arbitration (the "disputing parties") agree to their application in respect of that arbitration; or
   (b) the Parties to the treaty or, in the case of a multilateral treaty, the State of the claimant and the respondent State, have agreed after 1 April 2014 to their application.

Application of the Rules

3. In any arbitration in which the Rules on Transparency apply pursuant to a treaty or to an agreement by the Parties to that treaty:
   (a) the disputing parties may not derogate from these Rules, by agreement or otherwise, unless permitted to do so by the treaty;
   (b) the arbitral tribunal shall have the power, beside its discretionary authority under certain provisions of these Rules, to adapt the requirements of any specific provision of these Rules to the particular circumstances of the case, after consultation with the disputing parties, if such adaptation is necessary to conduct the arbitration in a practical manner and is consistent with the transparency objective of these Rules.

* Prof Krista Nadakavukaren Schefer holds a Swiss National Research Foundation Professorship at the University of Basel Law School, where she teaches international economic law. She also teaches at the World Trade Institute, University of Bern.

(cont.)

Discretion and authority of the arbitral tribunal

4. Where the Rules on Transparency provide for the arbitral tribunal to exercise discretion, the arbitral tribunal in exercising such discretion shall take into account:
   (a) the public interest in transparency in treaty-based investor-State arbitration and in the particular arbitral proceedings; and
   (b) the disputing parties' interest in a fair and efficient resolution of their dispute.
5. These Rules shall not affect any authority that the arbitral tribunal may otherwise have under the UNCITRAL Arbitration Rules to conduct the arbitration in such a manner as to promote transparency, for example by accepting submissions from third persons.
6. In the presence of any conduct, measure or other action having the effect of wholly undermining the transparency objectives of these Rules, the arbitral tribunal shall ensure that those objectives prevail.

Applicable instrument in case of conflict

7. Where the Rules on Transparency apply, they shall supplement any applicable arbitration rules. Where there is a conflict between the Rules on Transparency and the applicable arbitration rules, the Rules on Transparency shall prevail. Notwithstanding any provision in these Rules, where there is a conflict between the Rules on Transparency and the treaty, the provisions of the treaty shall prevail.
8. Where any of these Rules is in conflict with a provision of the law applicable to the arbitration from which the disputing parties cannot derogate, that provision shall prevail.

Application in non-UNCITRAL arbitrations

9. These Rules are available for use in investor-State arbitrations initiated under rules other than the UNCITRAL Arbitration Rules or in ad hoc proceedings.

* For the purposes of the Rules on Transparency, a "treaty" shall be understood broadly as encompassing any bilateral or multilateral treaty that contains provisions on the protection of investments or investors and a right for investors to resort to arbitration against Parties to the treaty, including any treaty commonly referred to as a free trade agreement, economic integration agreement, trade and investment framework or cooperation agreement, or bilateral investment treaty.

** For the purposes of the Rules on Transparency, any reference to a "Party to the treaty" or a "State" includes, for example, a regional economic integration organization where it is a Party to the treaty.

3.1 Introduction

1. Transparency in international arbitration has been a topic of attention since the 1980s, but the intensity of discussions increased with the growth of investor-State dispute settlements beginning at the start of the twenty-first century. It was the North American region that began the move towards greater public access to information about and participation in arbitrations involving claims against governments. In 2001, the Free Trade Commission (FTC) of the North American Free Trade Agreement (NAFTA) issued a statement that '[n]othing in the NAFTA imposes a general duty of confidentiality on the disputing parties' to an investor-State arbitration brought on the basis of the treaty.[1] Moreover, the Commission revealed, the three NAFTA parties agreed 'to make available to the public in a timely manner all documents submitted to, or issued by, Chapter Eleven tribunals'.[2] Thus, while confidential or privileged information must be redacted, the dispute settlement documentation will be published.[3] The FTC further opened NAFTA proceedings to the public over the next five years. In 2003, the acceptance of *amicus* submissions was clarified to be within tribunal discretion rather than subject to party will,[4] and the following year Mexico supported the US and Canada's offer to allow for public hearings within the context of Chapter 11 arbitrations.[5]

2. As the US and Canada continued to pursue the transparency agenda in their bilateral and regional investment relationships, other investment fora took up the issue. By 2006, the main international forum for investor-State dispute settlement had adopted revisions of its rules to permit greater public access. The International Centre for Settlement of Investment Disputes (ICSID) revised its Arbitration Rules (ICSID Rules) by adding several provisions to increase non-parties' access to information and to the proceedings. Characterised as 'modest, incremental and conservative',[6] the additions nevertheless do suggest a preference for more openness of the proceedings by making open hearings the

[1] NAFTA Free Trade Commission, Notes of Interpretation of Certain Chapter 11 Provisions (31 July 2001) A.1, A.2(a) www.state.gov/documents/organization/38790.pdf.

[2] *Ibid.* A.2(b). [3] *Ibid.*

[4] NAFTA Free Trade Commission, Statement of the Free Trade Commission on Non-Disputing Party Participation (7 October 2003).

[5] NAFTA Free Trade Commission, Joint Statement on the Decade of Achievement (San Antonio, 16 July, 2004).

[6] Jarrod Wong and Jason Yackee, 'The 2006 Procedural and Transparency-Related Amendments to the ICSID Arbitration Rules: Model Intentions, Moderate Proposals, and Modest Returns' in Karl P. Sauvant (ed.), *Yearbook on International Investment Law and Policy* (Oxford University Press, 2010).

default rule.[7] They also give tribunals a clear mandate to determine whether non-party submissions will be accepted[8] and mandate that at least 'excerpts of the legal reasoning of the Tribunal' be published once the Award has been issued.[9]

3. It is not surprising, then, that the United Nations Commission on International Trade Law (UNCITRAL) – the source of the second most frequently used rules of investment arbitration[10] – also faced the question of how to enhance public access to investor-State arbitrations conducted under its rules. Though its Working Group II (Arbitration and Conciliation) (WG) declined to take up the questions surrounding openness within their discussion of the general revision of the Arbitration Rules,[11] by 2010 one of the delegates to the WG stated with confidence, 'the issue is not whether to include an additional section governing transparency third-party participation in State arbitrations . . . but rather to determine the scope and level of this transparency and access to information'.[12]

4. He was right and, soon afterward the WG took up the negotiation of a separate set of principles: the UNCITRAL Rules on Transparency in Treaty-Based Investor-State Arbitration, adopted at the Commission's forty-sixth session, and effective as of 1 April 2014 (the Rules).

5. The Rules are the most recent and most detailed result of efforts to strengthen the legitimacy of international arbitration between States and private investors through increasing the visibility of these processes and the awareness of their results. While the precise content of the individual rules will determine the intensity of light to be shed on the process, the scope provided for in Article 1 determines the extent of this light. Clearly covering treaty-based arbitrations conducted under UNCITRAL's own Arbitration Rules, the Rules are potentially much

[7] ICSID, Arbitration Rules, Rule 32(2). [8] *Ibid.* Rule 37(2). [9] *Ibid.* Rule 48(4).

[10] Jonathan Sutcliffe and Aníbal Sabater, 'UNCITRAL Arbitration: New Rules on Transparency?' (May 2008) 23(5) *Mealey's International Arbitration Report* 1 https://www.mealeysonline.com/mealey/ppv/addToCart.do?itemType=MLART&itemID=4SMD-R1W0-0141-R1FP&itemName=UNCITRAL+Arbitration%3A+New+Rules+On+Transparency%3F%2C23-5+Mealey%27s+Intl.+Arb.+Rep.+20+%282008%29%2C+May+2008.

[11] See e.g. UNCITRAL, 'Report of the Working Group on Arbitration and Conciliation on the work of its forty-eighth session (New York, 4–8 February 2008)' (2008) UN Doc. A/CN.9/646 [69].

[12] Ignacio Torterola, 'The Transparency Requirement in the New UNCITRAL Arbitration Rules: A Premonitory View' (23 September 2010) *Investment Treaty News* www.iisd.org/itn/2010/09/23/the-transparency-requirement-in-the-new-uncitral-arbitration-rules-a-premonitory-view/.

more broadly applicable and promise to significantly influence investment arbitration in multiple fora.

6. This chapter will set forth the underlying nature of the Rules together with their substantive and temporal application. It begins with an overview of the purpose of Article 1. A brief review of the negotiating history of Article 1 precedes the explanation and analysis of its individual provisions. The paragraphs are grouped as found in the original, with the significance of particular terms highlighted.

3.2 Purpose

7. Motivated by the same desire of enhancing public access to investor-State arbitrations, the UNCITRAL negotiations on the Rules differed in a key respect from the attempts to increase transparency in other arbitration fora – the WG not only had to agree on the applicable standard, it had to decide on the scope of that standard's application. The complexity of this question arises particularly for UNCITRAL because UNCITRAL itself provides neither a forum for dispute settlement nor a treaty basis to tie the procedural rules to any substantive ones that are at issue in a particular case. The UNCITRAL WG establishes only the procedural rules that parties can select to govern arbitration. These rules, moreover, were designed (and continue) to apply to commercial arbitration but they also can be (and are) called upon to apply to investor-State dispute resolution in any number of fora or before ad hoc tribunals.

8. As a result, any UNCITRAL rules that would enhance transparency could have an extremely wide field of application. Did the Members want to change what was, until 2010 at least, a fundamental belief about arbitration in general – that one of the attractions of this form of Alternative Dispute Resolution (ADR) was its commitment to confidentiality? Or should they restrict the push towards openness to particular arbitrations (such as 'public' rather than 'commercial' ones)? Or to particular parties (States rather than private actors)? And should the parties be allowed to choose how much transparency they wished, as is usually the case in arbitration, subject, perhaps, to some minimal openness? And, given that transparency can involve time-consuming (not to mention costly) efforts by the parties and the administering institution, should tribunals be granted discretion to adjust the Rules (as they often may for procedural issues) in order to ensure that the time and money-saving attributes of ADR remain intact? Moreover, should the Rules apply to arbitrations that are based on investment treaties that are currently in

force? Or only to proceedings that are based on a claim arising out of a treaty that comes into effect after the Rules do?

9. The answers to these questions needed to be discussed and, ultimately, set forth in the Rules. Thus, the provision on the scope of the Rules is lengthy and touches upon several legal issues not relevant to the transparency rules of other institutions.

3.3 Background

10. The history of the Rules begins with the negotiation of the revision of the Arbitration Rules (1976), for it was in the midst of these talks that the calls for more transparency in investor-State arbitration were taken up by the NAFTA tribunals and ICSID, and international attention to the issue was blooming. Greater transparency was recognised as offering several benefits to arbitration: systemic advantages, such as an increased awareness of prior decisions that could lead to a more unified and predictable body of law and a greater equality between parties, but also a higher level of legitimacy among the public of arbitration decisions; and the general advantages of better governance, which would follow from increased information to and from the public and from greater accountability on the part of government administrations.[13]

11. Aware of the discussions of transparency going on around it, the WG was beginning to consider the contents of the new Arbitration Rules when the idea of re-considering the appropriate level of confidentiality of arbitrations was brought up. The WG had, however, set forth for itself a programme of changing only that which was necessary, motivated in large part to protect parties' expectations in their existing agreements.[14] Thus, any wording that would only clarify a provision would generally be

[13] See generally OECD, 'Transparency and Third Party Participation in Investor-State Dispute Settlement Procedures: Statement by the OECD Investment Committee' (June 2005) [44]–[46] www.oecd.org/investment/internationalinvestmentagreements/34786913.pdf.

[14] See UNCITRAL, 'Report of the Working Group on Arbitration and Conciliation on the work of its forty-fifth session (Vienna, 11–15 September 2006)' (2006) UN Doc. A/CN.9/614 [15] ('the mandate . . . provided, inter alia, that revision of the UNCITRAL Arbitration Rules should not alter the structure of the text, its spirit and drafting style and that it should respect the flexibility of the text rather than make it more complex.'); UNCITRAL, 'Report of the Working Group on Arbitration and Conciliation on the work of its forty-sixth session (New York, 5–9 February 2007)' (2007) UN Doc. A/CN.9/619 [18] ('generally agreed principle that the Working Group should avoid making unnecessary changes to the Rules').

left as is, and any changes would be considered in light of how they would affect existing agreements that made reference to the earlier version of rules.

12. Most importantly, the WG viewed any significant departures from traditional ways of approaching arbitration with suspicion. When looking at Article 15 of the Arbitration Rules (1976), for example, it noted: [15]

> that matter [of confidentiality] was quite complex, that there were diverse views expressed on the importance of confidentiality, and that the practice and the law were still evolving. It was said that regulating that issue in too much detail would constitute a major departure from the UNCITRAL Arbitration Rules. It was observed that the scope of confidentiality needed could depend on the subject matter of the dispute and the applicable regulatory regimes.

13. The same concerns were expressed in regard to creating a separate provision on confidentiality of the proceedings.[16]

14. This caution extended to the use of words not traditionally associated with arbitration – words such as 'transparency'. The term 'transparency' itself was, in this early stage, only used in connection with the appointment of arbitrators in the context of multiple parties.[17] Openness was discussed as an aspect of 'confidentiality'.

15. It was in the February 2007 session that the WG first faced a call for 'transparency' in arbitration.[18] Here, a proposal was made to include a special regulation for notice to be given of investor-State arbitrations in the general Arbitration Rules.[19]

16. The WG's cautionary approach from its previous session continued, however. Thus, it balked at the suggestion to include a call for transparency in investor-State arbitrations in their draft revision of the Arbitration Rules.[20] There were two main reasons given for this. For one thing, the WG did not approve of different rules for different types of arbitration. The Arbitration Rules should be revised on a 'generic approach that sought to identify common denominators that applied to all types of arbitration irrespective of the subject matter of the dispute'.[21] Inserting a rule to foster transparency only in investor-State proceedings would go against this approach. Secondly, the WG continued to consider the idea of agreeing to rules on still-evolving legal topics as inappropriate:

[15] UNCITRAL (n. 14) UN Doc. A/CN.9/614 [85]. [16] *Ibid.* [85]. [17] *Ibid.* [63].
[18] UNCITRAL (n. 14) UN Doc. A/CN.9/619 [61]–[62]. [19] *Ibid.* [61]. [20] *Ibid.*
[21] *Ibid.*

'[i]t was recalled that, since practice in various areas, including in investor-State dispute settlement, was still developing, it would be undesirable to seek to design specific provisions at the current stage'.[22] Averse to leading the transparency-fostering movement, the WG decided to wait to take up the issue.

17. By the next 2007 session, however, transparency as an issue of particular significance for investor-State arbitrations had gained credibility.[23] Looking at the confidentiality of award decisions, the WG had to determine whether Article 32(5) of the Arbitration Rules (1976) would need adjustment to allow a single party to publicise the decision. Here, the WG agreed that it would need to consider whether awards of arbitrations involving States would need to be published, 'considering that States have to respond to public interest'.[24]

18. The idea of considering the interests of the public in the investor-State arbitration context was therefore brought into the open. This led to agreement on the advisability of taking up the considerations of transparency in a special instrument available for cases of state involvement in arbitration.

19. In its February 2008 session, although the WG continued to adhere to its commitment to formulating 'generic . . . common denominator'[25] rules in its Arbitration Rules revision process, the issue of investor-State disputes had gained enough traction to include a statement by John Ruggie, Special Representative of the Secretary-General on Human Rights and Transnational Corporations and Other Business Enterprises, on the topic of corporate investors' impacts on human rights in host countries.[26] It was at this meeting that the WG agreed to consider the specific needs of transparency in the context of investor disputes with public entities as a means of promoting good governance.[27]

20. Convinced that confidentiality was still an 'essential feature' of commercial arbitration, the delegates were willing to admit that under

[22] *Ibid.*

[23] UNCITRAL, 'Report of the Working Group on Arbitration and Conciliation on the work of its forty-seventh session (Vienna, 10–14 September 2007)' (2007) UN Doc. A/CN.9/641.

[24] *Ibid.* [99]. [25] UNCITRAL (n. 11) UN Doc. A/CN.9/646 [7].

[26] *Ibid.* [56]; see also UNCITRAL, UN Doc. A/CN.9/646, Annex I (attached text of Ruggie's statement, 'Statement made on behalf of the Special Representative of the Secretary-General on Human Rights and Transnational Corporations and Other Business Enterprises').

[27] *Ibid.* [56]–[69].

'the principles of good governance, governmental activities might be subject to the basic requirements of transparency and public participation'.[28] The WG was clearly looking at investor-State arbitration as exceptional, and at transparency as a tool to assist the public's understanding of – and consequently its acceptance of – arbitration as a way for their governments to resolve disputes with investors.[29] At the same time, some delegates held to the belief that UNCITRAL should offer an alternative to the ICSID-style of opening up: 'it was observed that . . . it was also desirable to provide parties to investor-States disputes with real alternative solutions'.[30]

21. Both of these viewpoints affected the WG's session results. By the end of the session, there was a basic agreement that the transparency of the proceedings and publication of the award were principles to foster, but also that the revision of the general Arbitration Rules should precede any substantial commitments to the development of specific transparency rules.[31]

22. By the fiftieth session, the WG had mainly completed its work on the general Arbitration Rules and was ready to consider the topic of transparency in 'treaty-based investor-State arbitration . . . as a matter of priority' as soon as the generic rules were complete.[32]

23. It was thus in the autumn 2010 session that the transparency work became an item of direct action for the WG.[33] Although the idea of

[28] *Ibid.* [57]. [29] *Ibid.*

[30] *Ibid.* [58]. Discussions about increased arbitral transparency in ICSID rules often bring up the argument that requiring too much transparency in one forum will simply cause complainants to select a highly confidential alternative, with an overall loss of public awareness. One author indicates a distinction between 'pre-' and 'post-award' transparency, suggesting that it is only the 'pre-award' transparency that might cause forum shopping. Katharina Diel-Gligor, 'Competing Regimes in International Investment Arbitration: Choice between the ICSID and Alternative Arbitral Systems'(2011) 22 *Am. Rev. Int'l Arb.* 677, 701 ('an overly high degree of transparency in the "pre-award" stage should be avoided in order to strengthen the ICSID regime's appeal to private investors, who are often the ones who have the final choice between the different applicable arbitral frameworks provided by numerous BITs. [*footnote omitted*] An over-the-top degree of transparency during the pendency of the process would most likely deter them from choosing ICSID arbitration. As a result, more and more investment disputes would be resolved in commercial arbitration systems – providing neither for "pre-award transparency", nor for sufficient "post-award transparency"').

[31] UNCITRAL (n. 11) UN Doc. A/CN.9/646 [69].

[32] UNCITRAL, 'Report of Working Group II (Arbitration and Conciliation) on the work of its fiftieth session (New York, 9–13 February 2009)' (2009) UN Doc. A/CN.9/669 [121].

[33] UNCITRAL, 'Report of Working Group II (Arbitration and Conciliation) on the work of its fifty-third session (Vienna, 4–8 October 2010)' (2010) UN Doc. A/CN.9/712.

drafting a set of transparency rules as a separate instrument was not immediately agreed upon,[34] several guiding principles were. Of those most relevant to this chapter's focus on scope were the delegates' assumptions about what they were doing. The nature of the Rules, from the viewpoint of the WG, was to lend investor-State arbitration legitimacy, not to reconceive of arbitration procedures more fundamentally. This is implicit from the report, which indicated:

(1) the WG's decision to limit the negotiation of the Rules to arbitrations in which the State is involved as a party;[35]
(2) its view of transparency as a tool to promote sustainable development, good governance and the legitimacy of international investment law;[36] and
(3) some of the delegates' commitment to avoid impinging on either arbitration's consensual nature or the efficiency of arbitral processes.[37]

As will be shown, each of these basic tenets informed the Rules' scope.

24. The WG's February 2011 session continued the discussions on specific provisions against a policy-oriented background.[38] While recognising that 'transparency must give full effect to the mandatory character of human rights' (such as the right of access to information), the WG was in 'general agreement' that States must consent to the application of any rules requiring more transparency.[39] The question that divided WG opinion was the manner in which States must do so – expressly ('opt-in') or by presumption, with the possibility of refusing such consent ('opt-out'). This item became a central point of contention and will be discussed further below.

25. Related to the opt-in/opt-out issue was that of the extent to which new transparency standards would apply to existing investment treaties that included a reference to the possibility of dispute resolution according to 'UNCITRAL Arbitration Rules'.[40] Questions as to whether interpretation of such provisions by means of 'dynamic reference' would violate international legal norms of non-retroactivity – and even

[34] UN, 'Official Records of the General Assembly, Sixty-fifth session' UN Doc. A/65/17 [191] (as cited by UNCITRAL (n. 33) UN Doc. A/CN.9/712 [3]).

[35] UNCITRAL (n. 33) UN Doc. A/CN.9/712 [19]. [36] *Ibid.* [17]. [37] *Ibid.* [21].

[38] UNCITRAL, 'Report of Working Group II (Arbitration and Conciliation) on the work of its fifty-fourth session (New York, 7–11 February 2011)' (2011) UN Doc. A/CN.9/717.

[39] *Ibid.* [19]. [40] *Ibid.* [36]–[41].

whether non-retroactivity is indeed a norm of international law – drove these WG discussions.[41]

26. One issue that was resolved even by this early stage was that of whether the investor could choose to avoid the Rules' applicability.[42] The WG agreed that investor-led derogation would not be allowed. Not only would a possibility of derogation give the investor a privilege over the State, but transparency itself was a norm to benefit society, not merely the parties.[43] Hence, they correctly reasoned, it would be antithetical to the purposes of the Rules to permit the investor to decide unilaterally to avoid them.

27. The next session took up the opt-in/opt-out discussions based on a draft text.[44] While the draft's offering of various opt-in/opt-out provisions led to fundamentally opposing views between delegates, the focus on proposed wordings for such provisions permitted comments to be more precise. It also led to an important recognition: that there are two related but separate aspects of scope – the material and the temporal. Coming to a decision on the material question (i.e., to what arbitrations the Rules will apply), the delegates realised, can be assisted by considering the temporal question (as of what date will the Rules apply) on its own.

28. The solution to these divisive issues was proposed in the first 2012 session.[45] There, the WG considered using a suggestion to take a binary approach – using the opt-out for future treaties and the opt-in for existing agreements. In the WG's 'spirit of finding a solution and ... willingness to further work towards a compromise solution',[46] this suggestion gathered significant support, as it addressed both the interests of broad application and the concerns about State consent to be bound to

[41] For a more detailed description of the various perspectives on the issue, see Proposal by Governments of Argentina, Australia, Canada, Mexico, Norway, South Africa, and the United States of America in UNCITRAL, 'Settlement of Commercial Disputes: Transparency in Treaty-Based Investor-State arbitration – Compilation of Comments by Governments' (2012) UN Doc. A/CN.9/WG.II/WP.174; CIEL; and IISD, 'Comments on the Scope of Application of UNCITRAL's Draft Rules on Transparency in Investor-State Arbitration', Working Group II, February 6–10, 2012.

[42] UNCITRAL (n. 39) UN Doc. A/CN.9/717 [53]. [43] *Ibid.* [50].

[44] UNCITRAL, 'Report of Working Group II (Arbitration and Conciliation) on the work of its fifty-fifth session (Vienna, 3–7 October 2011)' (2011) UN Doc. A/CN.9/736.

[45] UNCITRAL, 'Report of Working Group II (Arbitration and Conciliation) on the work of its fifty-sixth session (New York, 6–10 February 2012)' (2012) UN Doc. A/CN.9/741.

[46] *Ibid.* [54].

international rules. While not yet firmly accepted, the issue was substantially resolved.[47] Discussion could thus turn to other issues.

29. The provisions clarifying the extent of party and tribunal discretion to alter the Rules, the relationship between the Rules and any treaty provisions on transparency, and the possibility of applying the Rules to non-UNCITRAL arbitrations raised few difficulties. Progress in the negotiations, therefore, continued.

30. By the WG's February 2013 session, the draft provisions were substantially in place.[48] At the beginning of October 2013, the text of the Rules was released.[49] The following examines the individual terms and provisions.

3.4 Title

31. The title of Article 1 of the Rules is 'Scope of application'. The WG had already discussed the title of Article 1 of the Arbitration Rules (1976) during its revision of those provisions.[50] At that time, there had been some discussion as to whether that provision should be titled 'Applicability' rather than 'Scope of application'.[51] The former arguably better highlighted the fact that Article 1 regulates more than simply the breadth of subject matter.[52] Nevertheless, the majority decided to retain the 1976 language ('Scope of application') so as to not disturb the text without a compelling reason to do so.[53]

32. In the context of the Rules' drafting, Article 1 mirrors Article 1 of the Arbitration Rules (2010) by taking up the depth of application, the temporal dimension, and the position of the Rules in comparison to other norms, as well as the scope. Thus, once again, there was a good argument for naming the provision 'Applicability'. Nevertheless, the

[47] The WG II's September 2013 decision to commence discussions on a convention on transparency in treaty-based investor-State arbitration helped relieve the fears of the Rules' critics by foreseeing an opt-in approach for existing treaties within the Convention. See UNCITRAL, 'Report of Working Group II (Arbitration and Conciliation) on the work of its fifty-ninth session (Vienna, 16–20 September 2013)' (2013) UN Doc. A/CN.9/794 [17]–[22].

[48] See generally, UNCITRAL, 'Report of Working Group II (Arbitration and Conciliation) on the work of its fifty-eighth session (New York, 4–8 February 2013)' (2013) UN Doc. A/CN.9/765 [16]–[40].

[49] UNCITRAL, 'Rules on Transparency in Treaty-based Investor-State Arbitration, Pre-Release Draft' (2 October 2013). An earlier Pre-Release draft was available as of 30 July 2013.

[50] UNCITRAL (n. 14) UN Doc. A/CN.9/619 [18]. [51] *Ibid.* [52] *Ibid.* [53] *Ibid.*

parties' commitment to their earlier 'generally agreed principle that the Working Group should avoid making unnecessary changes' seems to have driven their decision to remain with the old label for the Article.[54] Thus, maintaining a close adherence to the language of the Arbitration Rules, the title of Article 1 is the same for both – 'Scope of application'.

3.5 Structure

33. The body of Article 1 is composed of nine paragraphs and two footnotes. The paragraphs are grouped into five headings: Applicability of the Rules; Application of the Rules; Discretion and authority of the Arbitral Tribunal; Applicable instrument in case of conflict; and Application in non-UNCITRAL arbitrations. The remainder of this chapter will follow the same structure.

3.6 Article 1(1) and 1(2): Applicability of the Rules

1. The UNCITRAL Rules on Transparency in Treaty-based Investor-State Arbitration ("Rules on Transparency") shall apply to investor-State arbitration initiated under the UNCITRAL Arbitration Rules pursuant to a treaty providing for the protection of investments or investors ("treaty")* concluded on or after 1 April 2014 unless the Parties to the treaty** have agreed otherwise.
2. In investor-State arbitrations initiated under the UNCITRAL Arbitration Rules pursuant to a treaty concluded before 1 April 2014, these Rules shall apply only when:
   (a) The parties to an arbitration (the "disputing parties") agree to their application in respect of that arbitration; or
   (b) The Parties to the treaty or, in the case of a multilateral treaty, the State of the claimant and the respondent State, have agreed after 1 April 2014 to their application.

* For the purposes of the Rules on Transparency, a "treaty" shall be understood broadly as encompassing any bilateral or multilateral treaty that contains provisions on the protection of investments or investors and a right for investors to resort to arbitration against Parties to the treaty, including any treaty commonly referred to as a free trade agreement, economic integration agreement, trade and investment framework or cooperation agreement, or bilateral investment treaty.

** For the purposes of the Rules on Transparency, any reference to a "Party to the treaty" or a "State" includes, for example, a regional economic integration organization where it is a Party to the treaty.

[54] *Ibid.*

34. Paragraphs 1 and 2 relate to when the Rules will apply – to their applicability. Their applicability is limited in two significant ways: materially and temporally. First, the type of arbitrations to which the Rules apply is materially restricted to investor-State processes brought under an investment protection treaty. Second, the application is temporally limited according to the date on which the underlying investment treaty was concluded. Structurally, however, these two aspects are not clearly set apart, with the first paragraph establishing the material scope of the Rules and then putting forth the first of the temporal scope elements and the second paragraph setting out the second set of temporal restrictions. These aspects will be addressed in turn.

3.7 Material applicability of the Rules

3.7.1 'Rules shall apply'

35. The language of paragraph 1 is clearly mandatory. Using the word 'shall', the sentence leaves no room for parties, disputing parties or tribunals to choose not to recognise the Rules' validity where applicable.[55] The obligatory nature of the Rules supports the background intention of the delegates to promote 'good governance, due process, and rights to access to information' in investor-State dispute settlement as well as to lend greater legitimacy to these arbitration processes.[56] These goals were deemed important enough to require them to secure the 'highest standards on transparency'[57] – a concept that the delegates felt necessitated not only precise rules, but also binding ones. While their preliminary discussions do not reflect debate on the Rules' use of 'shall', their consideration – and ultimate rejection – of drafting discursive 'guidelines' that would have set out options[58] rather than 'rules'

[55] Compare UNCITRAL (n. 14) UN Doc. A/CN.9/619 [58] (discussion in the context of the revision of the Arbitration Rules on whether to make Article 3(5) optional, and therefore whether to replace 'shall' with 'may'). Note that Article 1.3(b) does afford tribunals discretion to adjust the application of the rules to fit the circumstances of the case. This does not mean, however, that the tribunal may refuse to apply the Rules entirely. See also below at 3.9.

[56] UNCITRAL (n. 39) UN Doc. A/CN.9/717 [25]. [57] *Ibid.* [58].

[58] UNCITRAL, 'Settlement of Commercial Disputes: Transparency in Treaty-based Investor-State Arbitration: Proposals by Governments and International Organizations: Note by the Secretariat' (20 December 2010) UN Doc. A/CN.9/WG.II/WP.164; UNCITRAL, 'Settlement of Commercial Disputes: Preparation of a Legal Standard on Transparency in Treaty-based Investor-State Arbitration: Note by the Secretariat' (9 December

indicates that they determined that adopting hard obligations, voluntarily accepted, was the optimal approach to fostering the aims of good governance and legitimacy.[59]

3.7.2 'to investor-State arbitration'

36. The fundamental limitation of the Rules' applicability 'to investor-State arbitration' emerges within the first part of paragraph 1's sentence as well as in the title. The idea that the Rules would only apply to investor-State proceedings was present from the beginning of the negotiation of the Rules,[60] and the incorporation of the expression of the scope as limited to 'investor-State' proceedings has the advantage of avoiding determinations about whether an arbitration is to be considered an 'investment' arbitration or whether an investment arbitration in which a State is a disputant addresses a 'commercial' or 'public' matter.[61] Thus, according to Article 1(1), only the party – not the content of the dispute – determines the application of the Rules to an arbitration.

37. The reference to 'investor-State' is significant for more than its clarity. It distinctly reflects the WG's conception of why transparency is important: for good governance and for the legitimacy of the arbitration system in matters affecting State policymaking and finance.[62] Transparency, they indicate, is important for shedding light on State activities.

2010) UN Doc. A/CN.9/WG.II/WP.162 [15]. (See also Germany's statement supporting a guidelines approach on the basis of ensuring broader acceptance of the principles, as well as ensuring that national laws on access to information are not undercut. Note by Secretariat, 'Proposals by Governments and International Organizations: Proposal by the Government of Germany'.)

59 See UNCITRAL (n. 59) UN Doc. A/CN.9/WG.II/WP.162 [26] (delegates preferring guidelines agreed to proceed on the basis of a draft set of rules, subject to the availability of States to consent to their application).

60 The 'specific situation' of investor-State arbitration was recognised at the beginning of the revisions of the 1976 Arbitration Rules (5 October 2006). UNCITRAL (n. 14) UN Doc. A/CN.9/614 [19]. At that time, a generic approach was considered the most appropriate for the Arbitration Rules negotiations (UN Doc. A/CN.9/614 [19]). The topic of addressing investor-State arbitration in a separate instrument was determined by 2008, when the WG decided to keep the Arbitration Rules general, and to take up transparency in the context of investor-State disputes in some other type of instrument (UN Doc. A/CN.9/646 [69]).

61 See UNCITRAL (n. 11) UN Doc. A/CN.9/646 [67] (setting out the argument that under the UNCITRAL Arbitration Rules, the term 'commercial' explicitly includes 'investment').

62 The term 'good governance' stems from the concept of 'governance', which itself means essentially 'the manner in which power and authority are acquired, organized and exercised and the way that the relation existing between the authority and those subject

38. Many commentators agree that arbitrations involving the State should be subject to standards of transparency because good governance requires the opportunity for public participation in matters that affect policymaking and public finances, and that the public will only accept arbitration awards as legitimate if they can access information about the process through which the decisions are made.[63] The WG, too, subscribed to this idea of why transparency is important. This instrumental view of transparency eliminates any reason for the Rules to apply to non-State arbitration processes: openness is not necessary for the arbitration process itself (indeed it reiterated its commitment to maintaining confidentiality in private arbitrations[64]); it is necessary for the public.

39. Could this be too restrictive? Certainly, there are arguments that such a narrow view of the benefits of transparency is fundamentally problematic. One commentator noted that:

> the debate over the appropriate form and content of transparency norms within international investment law cannot be reduced to the parallel debate over amicus curiae participation in investor-State arbitration proceedings. Nor should it be conflated with the ongoing discussions as to how best to make investor-State dispute resolution more politically accountable to various key constituencies and how to increase the IIL regime's stability, predictability, and legitimacy overall. Transparency plays an instrumental role in all of these debates, but it also has an inherent value which transcends them. Focusing on transparency for its own sake can thus help to advance our understanding on multiple fronts simultaneously.[65]

to it (or affected by it) takes place'. Juanita Olaya, 'Good Governance and International Investment Law: The Challenges of Lack of Transparency and Corruption', SIEL Second Biennial Global Conference 8–10 July 2010 at www.ssrn.com/link/SIEL-2010-Barcelona-Conference.html. Transparency is just one of the constituent elements of good governance. Accountability, legitimacy and rule of law are also seen as necessary to ensuring that power and authority are well organised and exercised (Olaya).

[63] E.g. Joachim Delaney and Daniel Barstow Magraw, 'Procedural Transparency' in Peter Muchlinski et al. (eds.), *Oxford Handbook of International Investment Law* (Oxford University Press, 2008) 721–88, 761 ('transparency serves democratic values and the right to know, informing those who are affected by government activities about those activities'); Gus Van Harten, *Investment Treaty Arbitration and Public Law* (Oxford University Press, 2008) 159–64; Cindy Buys, 'The Tensions between Confidentiality and Transparency in International Arbitration' (2003) *Am. Rev. Int'l Arb.* 121, 134.

[64] UNCITRAL (n. 11) UN Doc. A/CN.9/646 [57].

[65] Julie A. Maupin, 'Transparency in International Investment Law: The Good, the Bad, and the Murky' in Andrea Bianchi and Anne Peters (eds.), *Transparency in International Law* (Cambridge University Press, 2013) 142–71, 148–50.

40. One need not expect the UNCITRAL WG to try to implement a general notion of transparency to apply to all areas of economic activities to question its restriction to investor-State arbitration.[66] It is easy to imagine commercial arbitrations between private actors that could also impact upon issues in which the public may have an interest or of which they should be informed. The financial crisis of 2007/2008 demonstrated the extent to which the multi-billion dollar transactions of private multinational corporations can impact on policymaking and public finances, as well as on individuals and communities. The State, too, may have an interest in private arbitrations, particularly when awards are brought to local courts for enforcement.[67] Yet, while there are some voices calling for more transparency in commercial arbitration as well as in investor-State arbitration,[68] the Rules clearly do not challenge the tradition of confidentiality in arbitration between private parties.

41. Finally, and even less understandably, the Rules' scope fails to create any transparency obligations in State-to-State investment arbitrations. A forerunner to investor-State arbitration, the possibility of State-to-State arbitration has long existed for the resolution of investment

[66] The WG itself recognised that increasing transparency in investor-State arbitration is only one aspect of supporting transparency in investment relations. UNCITRAL (n. 39) UN Doc. A/CN.9/717 [14] ('Beyond treaty-based investor-State arbitration, transparency was said to be essential (i) for the conduct of States' investment-related administrative procedures, (ii) for the design and implementation of domestic investment laws and regulations, (iii) for investment promotion and States' efforts to attract development enhancing investment, and (iv) for States' specific interactions with individual investors').

[67] See Anjanette H. Raymond, 'Confidentiality in a Forum of Last Resort: Is the Use of Confidential Arbitration a Good Idea for Business and Society?' (2005) 16 *Am. Rev. Int'l Arb.* 479, 486 ('despite institutional rules and party choice determining confidentiality of proceeding and awards, the State, in many instances, still has an interest in arbitral decisions. This interest may be at its highest when the State is asked to enforce, through its sovereign power, the arbitration award').

[68] Buys (n. 63) 135–8 ('setting out the benefits of arbitral transparency that are independent of whether there is a state party, including: increased consistency of awards, further development of the law, better avoidance of future disputes, greater opportunities to improve the system; and more efficiency in determining which arbitrator is most suitable to one's case'); Raymond (n. 67): Raymond gives a particularly interesting account of the benefits of eliminating confidentiality to avoid the large advantages enjoyed by 'repeat players' in arbitration (Raymond 498–501). Basing her analysis on Marc Galanter's theory of 'Haves' benefiting by frequent use of the legal system (the same results having been established in employment arbitration), Raymond urges businesses to reject confidentiality in arbitration in order to ensure that 'competitive information' circulates among all players, not just the ones who repeatedly engage in processes, the lessons of which are then kept confidential (Raymond 502).

disputes. The lack of scholarly attention given to these procedures stems mainly from their infrequent invocation relative to the investor-State dispute provisions. This infrequence, however, may be changing, bringing with it a new era of 'hybrid' investment arbitrations – one in which the system provides for host State challenges of investors' actions in addition to the possibility of investor challenges of acts of hosts.[69]

42. In many aspects, State-to-State arbitration is less disturbing to the international system than are investor-State disputes. For one thing, as claimants, host governments will presumably balance foreign policy interests with the likely benefits of initiating a claim, potentially lowering the total number of claims brought against a developing country host. Additionally, by bringing a single claim on behalf of a number of investors, a home State's claim would reduce the likelihood that a host will have to engage in multiple proceedings on the same issue. Further, States as claimants are perhaps more likely to strive for negotiated settlements than private entities would, thus shortening the time periods in which disputes are ongoing. Moreover – and quite significantly from the point of view of the public – any awards will be paid to the coffers of the home State (presumably benefiting the population as a whole) rather than being left to an investor's private benefit.

43. Despite these substantial differences in the frequency and possible financial results of State-to-State arbitrations and investor-State proceedings, when the issue is transparency, there is little to differentiate. The benefits of procedural openness in the case of one State's claims against another are the same as the benefits of openness in the case of an investor's claims against a host. Public interests are still at stake, public knowledge is still desirable, public acceptance of awards would still be higher, and public moneys are still at risk. The WG gave no indication of the reasons for its decision to avoid applying the Rules to State-to-State arbitrations. This is unfortunate, as – from the perspective of transparency as an instrument for good governance – the issues are indistinguishable.

3.7.3 'initiated under the UNCITRAL Arbitration Rules'

44. Paragraph 1 also sets out that the Rules will apply to an arbitration conducted under the Arbitration Rules.

[69] See Anthea Roberts, 'State-to-State Investment Treaty Arbitration: A Hybrid Theory of Interdependent Rights and Shared Interpretive Authority' (2014) 55(1) *Harv. Int'l L. J.* 1.

45. There was significant consideration of whether to include a reference to the UNCITRAL Arbitration Rules in the drafting phase and, if it were to be included, precisely how to word such a reference.[70] The discussions were made more complex by the fact that the Arbitration Rules (1976) were still in effect for some parties, while others would be bound by the Arbitration Rules (2010). Some delegations expressed concern over the possibility that some parties to UNCITRAL would not yet have made the Arbitration Rules (2010) applicable to their treaties, and proposed that this be reflected in the wording of the Rules. Others noted that international legal principles of treaty succession exist already and that tribunals could determine which set of Arbitration Rules would apply by using the customary norms of interpretation. In the end, the agreement to treat existing and future investment treaties differently eliminated these concerns, and the general reference to 'UNCITRAL Arbitration Rules' sufficed.

46. The more interesting aspect of this language is that it indicates self-restraint on the part of the WG drafters. General international treaty law prohibits treaty-making States from agreeing to provisions that would impose legal obligations on third parties.[71] As set forth in the UNCITRAL discussions, the idea (not referred to as such during the negotiations) of *pacta tertiis nec nocent nec prosunt* kept the WG delegates from using more expansive language. While the WG was convinced of the benefits of transparency for investor-State dispute settlement and hoped to create a widely acceptable framework for its promotion, they did not purport to legislate towards a generally applicable norm. Limiting, in Article 1, the applicability to arbitrations under 'UNCITRAL Arbitration

[70] E.g. UNCITRAL (n. 33) UN Doc. A/CN.9/712 [27], [87]–[89]; UNCITRAL (n. 39) UN Doc. A/CN.9/717 [37]–[39].

[71] Codified in the Vienna Convention on the Law of Treaties, Article 34, this general principle of international law is based on the principle of State consent, itself a reflection of sovereignty (Vienna Convention on the Law of Treaties, Article 34). Ian Sinclair, *The Vienna Convention on the Law of Treaties* (2nd edn., Manchester University Press, 1984) 99. See also Malgosia Fitzmaurice, 'Third Parties and the Law of Treaties' in J. A. Frohwein and R. Wolfrum (eds.), 6 *Max Planck YB United Nations Law* (2002) 37–137 (Kluwer Law Int'l, 2002); Theodor Schweisfurth, 'International Treaties and Third States' (1985) 45 ZaöRV 653. But see Ilias Bantekas, 'The Need to Amend Article 12 of the ICC Statute: Remedying the Effects of Multilateral Treaties upon Third Parties' (2009) 12 *New Crim. L. R.* 485, fn. 1 on p. 486 (explaining that Sinclair, as Special Rapporteur, conceded some instances in which third parties could be bound by obligations in a treaty 'but the underlying factor in all cases is that the third state has played some part in the formation of a rule in a particular treaty (e.g., it has signed it, it has accepted the binding nature of a relevant custom, the rule concerned relates to an accepted boundary, etc.)').

Rules' indicates that for all its enthusiasm, the WG did not presume to be creating broader international (soft) law. Rather, it is setting out standards to govern those States that have consciously consented to UNCITRAL's authority in the arbitration sphere. The language of paragraph 9, as will be shown below, permits the Rules to be invoked in further fora, but it does not – because UNCITRAL rules cannot – make this mandatory.

3.7.4 'pursuant to a treaty providing for the protection of investments or investors ("treaty")'

47. Not every UNCITRAL-governed investor claim against a State will come within the scope of the Rules. The arbitration must have been brought on the basis of a 'treaty' provision setting out the investor or investment protection. Defined as 'an international agreement concluded between states in written form and governed by international law' in the Vienna Convention on the Law of Treaties (VCLT),[72] UNCITRAL's term 'treaty' is given a special footnote in the Rules. Footnote 1 sets out that, for purposes of the Rules, the term '"treaty" shall be understood broadly', explicitly including both bilateral and multilateral investment agreements. Interestingly, despite opening the scope beyond pure investment protection treaties to trade or cooperation agreements, the provision requires that any such agreement include an investor-State arbitration clause: 'encompassing any ... treaty that contains provisions on the protection of investments or investors *and* a right for investors to resort to arbitration against Parties to the treaty'.[73] This juxtaposition deserves a few comments.

48. First, the Rules' explicit emphasis on the wish to 'broadly' define the term 'treaty' causes rather more confusion than less. The VCLT definition of the same term would clearly include at least those trade and economic integration area agreements, cooperation agreements, and bi- or multilateral investment agreements referred to in footnote 1.[74] The

[72] Vienna Convention on the Law of Treaties, Article 2.1(a). [73] Emphasis added.

[74] Vienna Convention on the Law of Treaties, Article 2.1(a) (defining a treaty for purposes of the Convention as 'an international agreement concluded between States in written form and governed by international law, whether embodied in a single instrument or in two or more related instruments and whatever its particular designation'). See Mark E. Villiger, 'Article 2: Use of Terms' in *ibid.*, *Commentary on the 1969 Vienna Convention of the Law of Treaties* (Brill, 2009) 65–97, 76–84 (commentary on the Convention's provision 2.1(a), emphasising that the State-to-State nature and an agreement's governance by

only real limitation that the VCLT imposes on recognising State-to-State agreements as treaties is that they must be (1) written; and (2) governed by international law. Each of the agreements mentioned in footnote 1 would clearly fulfil these requisites. The International Court of Justice, in fact, has interpreted 'treaty' to include any agreement between States that sets out rights and obligations. As Klabbers explains, this means that even political agreements will be seen as binding treaties:[75]

> If commitments, once consented to, by definition are of legal character, then the claim that some commitments can be merely politically binding is dismissed. Of course, apart from being legally binding, commitments may be political commitments as well ... but they can never exclusively be political commitments. The creation of commitments, according to the Court, by necessity implies the creation of legal rights and obligations.

49. As customary international law, the VCLT would be applicable in any UNCITRAL arbitration so mentioning the types of agreements that are included as 'treaties' by name adds nothing. In fact, by omitting the mention of several possible types of international agreements that the Vienna Convention would accept as treaties (memoranda of understanding, declarations, even minutes of an official meeting have been viewed as 'treaties' under general international law[76]), the WG's note is actually suggesting a more limited definition than its silence would have permitted.[77] By saying one thing (i.e. that it adopts a 'broad' definition of treaty) and doing another (i.e. accepting only a subset of possible treaties), the Rules create unnecessary confusion.

50. There are other limitations contained within the Rules' 'broadly understood' term of 'treaty' that are of greater practical significance for

international law are particularly important elements characterising a 'treaty' for purposes of the Vienna Convention).

[75] Jan Klabbers, 'Qatar v. Bahrain: The Concept of "Treaty" in International Law' (1995) 33 *Archiv des Völkerrechts* 361, 370.

[76] See *Maritime Delimitation and Territorial questions between Qatar and Bahrain*, Jurisdiction and Admissibility, Judgment ICJ Report No. 7, 1994, 112. The *Qatar/Bahrain* case before the ICJ demonstrates the extent of the notion of 'treaty', with the judges determining that the document recording the discussions of the foreign ministers' meeting was an 'international agreement' for purposes of Court jurisdiction (rather than simply minutes of the meeting). See also Klabbers (n. 75) 366 (noting that the Court arguably – and questionably – raised the Vienna Convention definition of 'treaty' to the level of customary international law); Shabtai Rosenne, 'The Qatar/Bahrain Case: What is a Treaty? A Framework Agreement and the Seising of the Court' (1995) 8(1) *Leiden J. Int'l L.* 161.

[77] The text of footnote 1 does use the term 'including', which indicates a non-exclusive list. Still, the list is superfluous.

the promotion of transparency in investor-State arbitration. Two restrictions are inherent in the language of footnote 1, both resting on the fact that investor-State arbitrations can be initiated on the basis of arbitration clauses found in numerous legal instruments.

51. One significant omission is the failure of the Rules to apply to contract-based arbitrations. The prevailing view of the drafters appeared to be that most investor-State arbitrations are arising – and will continue to arise – from treaty-based claims,[78] so extending the Rules' coverage to arbitrations based on violations of other instruments would not add much to transparency. This is an empirical issue the accuracy of which is difficult to ascertain on available evidence. As such, the limitation may be ill-advised, particularly given the lack of comprehensive knowledge about the existence of non-ICSID proceedings. Unaffected by the Rules, ad hoc arbitrations in particular (about which there is currently the least information available) will remain intransparent. This leaves the public's knowledge about these most confidential arbitrations lacking.[79]

52. Nor do the Rules apply to the settlement of investment disputes brought under national law. As States' putting foreign investment protection obligations into national investment codes becomes 'a growing trend in developing countries',[80] arbitration transparency efforts will need to target the broader international arbitration environment. Given the interest of non-disputing parties in having access to such proceedings, an extension of the rules to legislation-based processes would have been desirable for securing real openness.[81]

53. Finally, although the Rules apply to arbitration 'pursuant to a treaty', not all investment treaties are available as the basis for

[78] UNCITRAL (n. 46) UN Doc. A/CN.9/741 [19].

[79] See e.g. IA Reporter, 'After failure of claim under Kazakh statute, Canadian miner hopes that USSR–Canada investment treaty permits arbitration with Kazakhstan' (18 December 2013) www.iareporter.com/articles/20131218. (An early arbitration between WWM and Kazakhstan was brought on the basis of a Kazakh law rather than any bilateral treaty. While it is known that that claim failed due to the time bar, the award remains confidential. In such a case, the Transparency Rules would not apply, leaving the details unknown to the wider public.)

[80] Makane Moïse Mbengue, 'Consent to Arbitration through National Investment Legislation' (19 July 2012) *Investment Treaty News* www.iisd.org/itn/2012/07/19/consent-to-arbitration-through-national-investment-legislation/ (mentioning the laws of Mauritius, Mongolia, Myanmar and the Seychelles as having foreign investor protections in their national law).

[81] One must, of course, acknowledge that gaining agreement on such an extension would have been likely to have been extremely difficult. Good governance is easier to discuss for international processes than for domestic ones.

transparent proceedings. Footnote * also restricts the Rules' applicability to investor-State arbitrations arising out of treaties with investor-State arbitration clauses. Treaties without such clauses are therefore excluded from the scope. In the context of current renegotiation of investment treaties and a greater hesitancy on the offering of investor-State dispute settlement, this double-criteria approach could prove to limit the usefulness of the Rules.[82]

3.8 Temporal applicability of the Rules

54. Long debated among the delegates, clarifying the temporal scope was key to gaining acceptance of the Rules. The differing views on the temporal scope were based to a large extent on the differing views of the material scope. Were the provisions of the Rules to be applicable without explicit State consent? Were they to apply at all to existing treaties? These questions could only be resolved by taking seriously both the concerns of delegates who insisted on preserving the consensual nature of arbitration (and therefore valued explicit expressions of consent to the application of new rules) and those who were eager to see actual improvements in arbitral transparency (and therefore wanted the Rules to apply as soon and as widely as possible, and who feared that basing acceptance on explicit consent would undermine these goals). The result was a dual approach, with both opt-out and opt-in aspects to the material scope added to the temporal application of the Rules to prospective and existing treaties.

*3.8.1 Arbitrations pursuant to a treaty 'concluded on or after 1 April 2014 unless the Parties to the treaty** have agreed otherwise'*

55. The latter half of paragraph 1 stipulates that the Rules will apply to arbitrations brought on the basis of a treaty that comes into effect on or after 1 April 2014, unless the treaty's parties explicitly decide not to incorporate the Rules. This 'opt-out' provision ensures the broadest application without violating either the rules on retroactivity of laws or States' ability to avoid international obligations to which they have not consented.

[82] Australia and South Africa are among the most recent States to have determined not to offer further investor-State arbitration provisions in their bilateral investment treaties.

56. The assumption behind the acceptability of the opt-out mechanism is that by 1 April 2014, States will know of the Rules and decide whether to accept or reject them. If they do nothing, the Rules will apply 'as an extension of the UNCITRAL Arbitration Rules', and, thus, will be applicable.[83] By making their applicability the default, it is likely that the Rules will attract more adherents than if States had to undertake a positive step to accept them. Libertarian paternalism, or 'nudge theory', supports the validity of the WG's choice to support transparency in this way.[84] Still, the possibility of opting out maintains a State's ultimate control over its obligations.

57. Footnote 2 clarifies that the term 'Party' or 'State' includes multi-State entities that have concluded a treaty. The inclusion of such parties is important, given that there is a growing number of agreements providing for investment protection that bring together free trade agreements or other economic groupings as one of their parties.[85] The European Union, of course, is an obvious target of this language. The Commission's competence to conclude investment agreements between the EU and other States increases the potential practical importance of footnote 2.[86]

[83] UNCITRAL, 'Note by the Secretariat' (30 March 2011) UN Doc. A/CN.9/734 [20].

[84] Libertarian paternalism is a theory on how to best regulate, based on behavioural economics and psychology made popular in law by Cass Sunstein and Richard Thaler. Under this view, regulation is most effective if it sets options such that no action is required to accept the socially desired choice, while active rejection is required to avoid this and make a socially non-desirable choice. See Richard H. Thaler and Cass R. Sunstein, *Nudge: Improving Decisions about Health, Wealth and Happiness* (Penguin Books, 2009).

[85] ASEAN has a network of economic cooperation agreements with non-Member Asian countries (including Korea, India and China) that foresee the conclusion of investment agreements. Discussions between the US and ASEAN regarding a framework agreement have been reported. See American Chamber of Commerce Vietnam, US–ASEAN TIFA (Trade and Investment Framework Agreement) Under Consideration (11 July 2006) www.amchamvietnam.com/947/u-s-asean-tifa-trade-and-investment-framework-agreement-under-consideration/. Mercosur also has increased investment opportunities set out as a goal in their cooperation agreement with Canada. Trade and Investment Cooperation Arrangement and Action Plan Between Canada and Mercosur, Art. 2 (16 June 1998). While offering no binding protections currently, if harder obligations evolve, they could be included within the Rules.

[86] The EU is currently in negotiations with Canada over a free trade agreement, which is planned to include a chapter on investment protection. As such, the Comprehensive Economic Trade Agreement (CETA) would come within the scope of Article 1 of the Rules. Interestingly, information from the EU indicates that the CETA will incorporate the UNCITRAL Rules on Transparency in its investment chapter anyway. See European Commission, Investment Provisions in the EU–Canada free trade agreement (CETA), 3 December 2013 http://trade.ec.europa.eu/doclib/docs/2013/november/tradoc_151918.

The language, however, is open to any other preferential trade organisation that exercises similar powers.

3.8.2 Arbitrations 'pursuant to a treaty concluded before 1 April 2014'

58. Paragraph 2 deals with the opposite situation. For existing investment protection agreements concluded before 1 April 2014, the Rules will only apply if either the disputing parties (i.e. the parties to the arbitration) or the treaty parties (i.e. the parties to the investment treaty) agree to the application of the Rules following their coming into force. This 'opt-in' formula was chosen to assuage concerns about (i) applying new rules where they may not have been foreseen when the treaty was concluded;[87] and (ii) requiring tribunals to engage in 'dynamic interpretation'[88] to bring the Rules to effect in a particular arbitration.[89]

59. The WG discussions revolved around the recognition that, given the thousands of international investment agreements that already exist, the purely prospective application of the Rules would greatly reduce their value for the near future. This could be avoided by making the Rules an extension of the Arbitration Rules, and thus applicable to any arbitration for which the parties had selected the Arbitration Rules. Some delegates, however, disapproved of subjecting disputing parties to rules that they could not have expected when they agreed to them. Given the consensual nature of arbitration, the WG determined that some expression of acceptance of the Rules was a necessary forerunner to their application. Thus, for the purpose of existing treaties, the Rules are considered 'stand-alone' rules.[90]

pdf. But, see Howard Mann, 'CETA Text: Devil's Still in the Details' (2003) http://www.ipolitics.ca/2013/12/19/the-ceta-text-devils-still-in-the-details/) (criticising the lack of public information about the negotiating draft of the CETA).

87 See UNCITRAL (n. 46) UN Doc. A/CN.9/741 [43]–[46].

88 A 'dynamic interpretation' of the Rules would arise where arbitral tribunals decide upon the application of the Rules in dispute in accordance with the applicable rules of treaty interpretation. For the arguments of Argentina, Australia, Canada, Mexico, Norway, South Africa and the United States of America in support of using this approach for the Rules, see Paragraph 54 of UN Doc. A/CN.9/741.

89 *Ibid.* [54].

90 Contra UNCITRAL draft Convention on Transparency, Art. 3 (setting forth an opt-in rule for the Rules' application to treaties concluded on or after 1 April 2014). See UNCITRAL, 'Settlement of Commercial Disputes: Draft Convention on Transparency

3.9 Article 1(3): Application of the Rules

3. In any arbitration in which the Rules on Transparency apply pursuant to a treaty or to an agreement by the Parties to that treaty:
   (a) The disputing parties may not derogate from these Rules, by agreement or otherwise, unless permitted to do so by the treaty;
   (b) The arbitral tribunal shall have the power, besides its discretionary authority under certain provisions of these Rules, to adapt the requirements of any specific provision of these Rules to the particular circumstances of the case, after consultation with the disputing parties, if such adaptation is necessary to conduct the arbitration in a practical manner and is consistent with the transparency objective of these Rules.

60. Paragraph 3 of Article 1 aims to ensure that the Rules will be applied in any arbitration falling within its scope, limiting the discretion of both the disputing parties and the tribunal, far beyond the level that is customarily available in UNCITRAL proceedings. The provision first establishes that the consensual nature of arbitration cannot override the interests of transparency. It then ensures that the other practical benefits of arbitration may be preserved to the extent compatible with the basic goals of openness.

61. The WG's commitment to ensuring transparency in investor-State arbitrations is set forth strongly in subparagraph (a). This provision sets forth clearly that the parties to the arbitration 'may not derogate . . . by agreement or otherwise'. Thus, neither the investor nor the host State can unilaterally avoid the Rules, nor can they mutually agree to do so. This goes against much of arbitration's classic deference to parties' will when addressing procedure. 'Party autonomy', as one author states, 'is one of the hallmarks of arbitration and choices made by the parties ought to be respected by arbitrators, arbitral institutions, and courts'.[91] In treaty-based proceedings, however, there are also the interests of the governmental treaty parties to take into account.

62. In balancing these interests, the WG inserted provision 1(3)(a) to prevent disputing parties from changing a decision that States had taken to adhere to the Rules. The provision was necessary in light of the Rules' 'supplemental' nature in relation to the Arbitration Rules. Because both

in Treaty-based Investor-State Arbitration: Note by the Secretariat' (27 November 2013) UN Doc. A/CN.9/WGII/WP.181 [7], [18].

[91] Buys (n. 63) 138. The WG members also expressed their conviction that 'a central feature of arbitration' is the 'consensual nature' of the process. UNCITRAL (n. 33) UN Doc. A/CN.9/712 [19].

sets of rules are presumably applicable to any arbitration, the Rules would not automatically trump the disputing parties' choice of applicable arbitration rules. Since the Arbitration Rules generally provide parties with discretion to modify them,[92] if the Rules had not provided for a special status for transparency-enhancing norms, it would not have been obvious that the Rules could not be modified as well. To ensure that the Rules will be approached differently from other procedural rules, non-derogation is explicitly stated.[93]

63. The WG was also concerned that disputing parties' attempts to limit transparency would negatively impact the interests of non-parties. Because transparency is valuable for the general public as well as the parties, the WG recognised, the Rules should not offer the parties the possibility of restricting it.[94] International law of treaties recognises that even though treaty parties are free to extend benefits to third parties, they are not free to withdraw such benefits at will.[95] Applied to the Rules, this principle supports the non-derogation principle as set out in provision 1(3)(a).

64. Unlike the non-derogation principle of the Rules as applying to the disputants, however, the underlying treaty may offer the possibility of derogation from the Rules. Like the opt-out clause discussed above,[96] this possibility allows States to maintain their sovereign right to determine which laws they accept. Thus States engaged in the negotiation of a bilateral investment treaty may insert language to prevent the Rules from being applied even if they accept the Arbitration Rules. This option is protected despite the WG's belief in the governance benefits of

92 UNCITRAL Arbitration Rules (2010), Article 1(1).

93 UNCITRAL (n. 46) UN Doc. A/CN.9/741 [63].

94 UNCITRAL (n. 46) UN Doc. A/CN.9/741 [61]; UNCITRAL (n. 45) UN Doc. A/CN.9/736 [33].

95 Vienna Convention on the Law of Treaties, Article 37. See Pierre d'Argent, 'Article 37: Convention of 1969' in Olivier Corten and Pierre Klein (eds.), 1 *The Vienna Convention on the Law of Treaties: A Commentary* (Oxford University Press, 2011) 943–7. See also *Free Zones of Upper Savoy and District of Gex (France* v. *Switzerland)*, 1932 PCIJ (series A/B) No. 46 (7 June) (the Permanent Court finds that benefits extended to Switzerland through the Treaty of Versailles could not be withdrawn by France without Swiss consent); but see Arthur K. Kuhn, 'The Case of the Free Zones of Upper Savoy and District of Gex' (1932) 26 (4) *Am. J. Int'l L.* 801, 802 (noting that the PCIJ had actually found Switzerland had not needed to accede to the Treaty of Versailles, so that country's position as a third party was questionable and arguing that the Court's finding that consent of the third State is required was not an established principle of law at that time).

96 See above [24]–[30] and [54]–[57].

transparency in order to safeguard the traditionally high status placed on State sovereignty in international law.

65. Although the disputing parties cannot choose to avoid transparency obligations, subparagraph (b) offers parties a reassurance that the Rules are not meant to be applied in disregard of the circumstances of the dispute. Here, the text affords tribunals the competence to adapt to (not to deviate from[97]) individual requirements contained in the rules if that is necessary to ensure the efficiency of the proceeding.[98] It is important to note that the WG was clear that this competence to adapt the requirements was not to be seen as a power to declare exceptions to the Rules (which it limited to the Rules Article 7).[99] Enhancing efficiency under Article 1(3)(b), therefore, is not to lessen transparency.

66. Also interesting is that, unlike the typical discretion offered by the Arbitration Rules,[100] the competence to adapt the requirements is to be exercised only 'after consultation with the disputing parties'. This suggests two things: first, that both disputing parties' interests are to be taken into account, rather than the interests of just one of the parties; but, second, that the tribunal is not bound to garner their consent before it acts. The term 'after consultation' suggests a duty of conduct rather than a duty of result – so as long as discussions are held, the tribunal is permitted to decide to act against the disputants' views if it sees fit. While such decisions are certain to be rare, the possibility that a tribunal can act on its own belief in what is best opens the possibility of a new set of challenges for the traditional practice of party-led arbitration.

67. Constraining the discretion of the tribunal is the availability of the power to adapt the requirements only if 'necessary to conduct the arbitration in a practical manner'. The mention of conducting the arbitration in a 'practical manner' is vague, but should include considerations of time-, effort- and money-saving.[101] These interests, widely perceived

[97] UNCITRAL (n. 46) UN Doc. A/CN.9/741 [71]–[73].

[98] For example, while a tribunal could not refuse to accept third party submissions at all, it might limit their length or set a time limit on their submission to avoid overburdening the process.

[99] UNCITRAL, 'Report of Working Group II (Arbitration and Conciliation) on the work of its fifty-eighth session (New York, 4–8 February 2013)' (2013) UN Doc. A/CN.9/765 [35].

[100] UNCITRAL Arbitration Rules (2010), Article 17(1).

[101] UNCITRAL (n. 46) UN Doc. A/CN.9/741 [67] (mentioning the adjustment of time periods).

as the advantages of arbitration over court proceedings, are important to parties, and tribunals need to be able to ensure procedural efficiency if parties are not to turn away from UNCITRAL arbitration.[102] This 'necessity' limitation offers a reasonable curb on tribunals' over-zealous protection of such private interests at the cost of the public's interest in transparency. It is not to be expected that paragraph 3's terms will impose a strict 'necessity' test on tribunals in the sense of requiring an analysis that demonstrates that there are no less transparency-restricting means available to achieve such ends.[103] One could assume, however, that tribunals are not to engage in softening the Rules for mere convenience – either their own or the disputing parties'. Thus, minor cost savings should not justify the avoidance of requirements that would offer enhanced transparency.

68. Moreover, the tribunal is prohibited from exercising its Rules-adaptation power in a way that is inconsistent with the document's 'transparency objectives'. What this means is left somewhat open, as the Rules have no preamble setting out the objectives as is usual in international treaties. Still, the WG's views on this matter were repeated throughout their various sessions and can be taken as accepted. The goals as set forth in the documents include fostering good governance and supporting due process and the public's right to access information, and enhancing the legitimacy of and public interest in investor-State arbitration through greater public participation.[104] Thus, the tribunals may only take advantage of the discretion to adapt requirements if these aims are upheld. Future practice will undoubtedly reveal the difficulties in determining how to balance efficiency and effectiveness with openness and legitimacy.

[102] Indeed, one author explains the presumed benefits of ADR as being of an entirely different nature from courtroom dispute settlement: 'Thus, in most cases the best measure of effective ADR is not as a surrogate for public adjudication, but as an intervention strategy to promote what a trial was not designed to accomplish: getting quicker and less costly resolution, tailoring creative solutions, serving business goals, improving relationships, enhancing the quality of human interaction, and "opening up" the dispute resolution process to the broader community'. Thomas J. Stipanowich, 'ADR and the "Vanishing Trial": The Growth and Impact of "Alternative Dispute Resolution"' (2004) 1(3) *J. Empirical Leg. Stud.* 843, 848.

[103] UNCITRAL (n. 46) UN Doc. A/CN.9/741 [69] ('recording a suggestion' came to include a 'higher threshold than merely exercising discretion').

[104] E.g. UNCITRAL (n. 45) UN Doc. A/CN.9/736 [14]. There were also less-frequently mentioned aims of fairness and equity. UNCITRAL (n. 33) UN Doc. A/CN.9/712 [17].

3.10 Articles 1(4), 1(5) and 1(6): Discretion and authority of the arbitral tribunal

4. Where the Rules on Transparency provide for the arbitral tribunal to exercise discretion, the arbitral tribunal in exercising such discretion shall take into account:
   (a) The public interest in transparency in treaty-based investor-State arbitration and in the particular arbitral proceedings; and
   (b) The disputing parties' interest in a fair and efficient resolution of their dispute.
5. These Rules shall not affect any authority that the arbitral tribunal may otherwise have under the UNCITRAL Arbitration Rules to conduct the arbitration in such a manner as to promote transparency, for example by accepting submissions from third persons.
6. In the presence of any conduct, measure or other action having the effect of wholly undermining the transparency objectives of these Rules, the arbitral tribunal shall ensure that those objectives prevail.

69. Arbitral tribunals are generally left substantial discretion to run the arbitration as they see fit, within the bounds of the parties' agreement. Arbitrator competence to make procedural determinations has been implied by their obligation to issue a decision, but this authority can come under challenge when such determinations go against the interests of a party to the dispute. A number of arbitrations opened the particular question of the extent to which a tribunal may – independent of the parties' consent – invite or accept non-party requests for involvement in the proceedings.[105]

70. By the time of the Rules' drafting, the extent of a tribunal's discretion to increase the transparency of proceedings without the parties' consent had been addressed both by NAFTA's FTC and by the ICSID.[106]

[105] E.g. *Metalclad* v. *United Mexican States*, Decision on a Request by the Respondent for an Order Prohibiting the Claimant from Revealing Information Regarding ICSID Case ARB(AF)/97/1, para. 9 (27 October 1997); *Methanex Corporation* v. *United States of America* (UNCITRAL Rules), Decision of the Tribunal on Petitions from Third Persons to Intervene as 'Amici Curiae' (15 January 2001); *The Loewen Group, Inc. and Raymond L. Loewen* v. *United States of America*, ICSID Case No. ARB(AF)/98/3. See Jack J. Coe, Jr., 'Transparency in the Resolution of Investor-State Disputes – Adoption, Adaptation and NAFTA Leadership' (2006) 54 *Kansas L. Rev.* 1339, 1364–78 (for a discussion of the early cases and the FTC interpretation and the responses to them).

[106] E.g. *Methanex Corporation* v. *United States of America* (n. 105); *Biwater Gauff (Tanzania) Limited* v. *United Republic of Tanzania*, ICSID Case No. ARB/05/22, Procedural Order No. 5 on *amicus curiae* (2 February 2007); *Suez, Sociedad General de Aguas de Barcelona S.A. and Interagua Servicios Integrales de Agua S.A.* v. *Argentine Republic*,

As set out below, NAFTA and other US-Free Trade Agreements (FTAs) clearly provide authority to tribunals to accept amicus submissions.[107] As these agreements also call for open hearings and the governments have agreed to publish their submissions, the tribunals have no need of supplemental authority to promote these aspects of transparency. The ICSID tribunals, too, have the authority to accept non-party submissions, but their discretionary power to render the hearings public exists only if neither party objects.[108] Comments submitted by NAFTA parties reflected positively on the inclusion of transparency norms, and regarded fears about investor avoidance as unfounded.[109]

71. Paragraphs 4, 5 and 6 of Article 1 fail to take as unambiguous a position on the tribunal's competence to promote transparency beyond the parties' wishes. Paragraph 4, for example, states that the tribunal 'shall take into account' the good governance role of transparency and the parties' 'interest in a fair and efficient' settlement of their dispute. Yet, it precedes this by including the phrase 'in any matter where the tribunal has discretion to exercise', indicating that this paragraph does not give authority to determine the level of transparency to be fostered by the process. Instead, it merely prescribes that where such authority exists already, a compromise must be struck between the interest in fostering public knowledge of and participation in government and the interest in upholding the parties' expectations of a timely and fair proceeding.[110]

ICSID Case No. ARB/03/17, Order in response to a Petition for Participation as Amicus Curiae (17 March 2006).

[107] See also Johannes Koepp and Cameron Sim, 'The application of transparency'.

[108] UNCITRAL, 'Settlement of Commercial Disputes: Transparency in Treaty-based Investor-State Arbitration: Comments by the International Centre for Settlement of Investment Disputes (ICSID): Note by the Secretariat' (8 August 2011) UN Doc. A/CN.9/WG.II/WP.167. (The ICSID Secretariat set out its transparency rules and practice in a document submitted to the WG. See Note by the Secretariat, 'Comments by the International Centre for Settlement of Investment Disputes (ICSID)'). It is interesting that the CAFTA-DR FTA's Article 10.21 leaves no tribunal discretion in terms of opening the hearings. One author remarks that it 'truly embraces transparency'. James Harrison, 'Recent Developments to Promote Transparency and Public Participation in Investment Treaty Arbitration' (2010) *University of Edinburgh School of Law Working Paper* Series No. 2011/01, 14 (text available at http://ssrn.com/abstract=1739181).

[109] See UNCITRAL, 'Note by the Secretariat: Comments of the Governments of Canada and of the United States of America on transparency in treaty-based investor-State arbitration under Chapter Eleven of the North American Free Trade Agreement (NAFTA)' (7 December 2010) UN Doc. A/CN.9/WG.II/WP.163.

[110] It is interesting to consider whether Canada's request for its NAFTA partners to be able to attend the hearings in the *Detroit Bridge* dispute would have been different had the

72. Paragraph 5 offers a reassurance to transparency advocates that this balancing of interests should not undermine any existing authority to accept non-party submissions. The tribunal could not, then, say that such submissions cannot be accepted because it would take too long to consider them. Thus, a minimum level of transparency seems guaranteed – to the extent the Arbitration Rules permit tribunals to make decisions to enhance transparency, the discretion offered by the Rules shall not extend to reducing this. The proceeding's transparency will, at the very least, not be lower than it would be without the Rules.

73. Paragraph 6 is more striking. Characterisable as a sort of emergency provision, it not only grants the tribunal a right to promote transparency in the face of actions that would make arbitrations more confidential, it imposes an obligation on the tribunal to actively counter any such actions. The tribunal, it states, 'shall ensure that [transparency] objectives prevail'. The text does not indicate whether the objectionable conduct would be from the investor or the State, so both are presumably included, as would actions by any non-party.

3.11 Articles 1(7) and 1(8): Applicable instrument in case of conflict

> 7. Where the Rules on Transparency apply, they shall supplement any applicable arbitration rules. Where there is a conflict between the Rules on Transparency and the applicable arbitration rules, the Rules on Transparency shall prevail. Notwithstanding any provision in these Rules, where there is a conflict between the Rules on Transparency and the treaty, the provisions of the treaty shall prevail.
> 8. Where any of these Rules is in conflict with a provision of the law applicable to the arbitration from which the disputing parties cannot derogate, that provision shall prevail.

74. The Rules are not the only legal provisions on transparency in investor-State arbitration, and disputing parties may find themselves involved in a dispute based on a treaty that contains its own rules on

Rules been in applicable at the time. In the context of this arbitration, the claimant's argument that its parallel case against the United States could be jeopardised if the tribunal granted Canada's request influenced the tribunal members to uphold the disputing parties' confidentiality agreement. Given that the pending US case may have in fact heightened the public's interest in the company's case against Canada, it is possible that the interests would have weighed in favour of transparency. See NAFTA Arbitration, *Detroit International Bridge Company* v. *Canada*, Procedural Order No. 8 (12 May 2014).

non-party access or the publication of materials. Where newer treaties may prefer greater transparency than the WG agreed to, other treaty rules may well prioritise confidentiality over transparency, given arbitration's traditional emphasis on avoiding public attention. In such a situation, a conflict of rules may arise and tribunals will be faced with resolving which set of rules to apply.[111]

75. Some of the WG delegates were concerned with ensuring that the Rules would establish a minimum standard for transparency in UNCITRAL investor-State arbitrations. Their application should be ensured in contexts where confidentiality rules were stronger, but any higher treaty standards of transparency should be permitted to trump the Rules.[112] Others felt treaty standards should always override the Rules, independent of the strength of the standard contained.[113] Further, all delegates realised that there are some national legal provisions that protect confidentiality on grounds of national security, human rights or commercial interest. Such provisions, they agreed, should remain in effect.[114]

76. Article 1's paragraphs 7 and 8 set forth a guide for tribunals to determine which transparency rules will apply in the case of conflict between (i) the Rules and other arbitration rules; (ii) the Rules and the investment treaty; and (iii) the Rules and national laws. As will be explained below, only in the first will the Rules prevail.

[111] See also Johannes Koepp and Cameron Sim, 'The application of transparency'.

[112] UNCITRAL (n. 45) UN Doc. A/CN.9/736 [31].

[113] See, e.g., UNCITRAL Working Group II (Arbitration and Conciliation) Fifty-third session (Vienna 4–8 October 2010), Settlement of commercial disputes, Transparency in treaty-based investor-State arbitration, Compilation of comments by Governments, Note by the Secretariat, Addendum Comments of Bahrain, UN Doc. A/CN.9/WGII/WP.159 p. 8 (2010); UNCITRAL Working Group II (Arbitration and Conciliation) Fifty-third session (Vienna 4–8 October 2010), Settlement of commercial disputes, Transparency in treaty-based investor-State arbitration, Compilation of comments by Governments, Note by the Secretariat, Addendum Comments of Poland, UN Doc. A/CN.9/WGII/WP.159/Add.3 p. 2; UNCITRAL Working Group II (Arbitration and Conciliation) Fifty-third session (Vienna 4–8 October 2010), Settlement of commercial disputes, Transparency in treaty-based investor-State arbitration, Compilation of comments by Governments, Note by the Secretariat, Addendum Comments of Russia, UN Doc. A/CN.9/WGII/WP.159/Add.3, p. 3; UNCITRAL Working Group II (Arbitration and Conciliation) Fifty-third session (Vienna 4–8 October 2010), Settlement of commercial disputes, Transparency in treaty-based investor-State arbitration, Compilation of comments by Governments, Note by the Secretariat, Addendum Comments of Turkey, UN Doc. A/CN.9/WGII/WP.159/Add.3 p. 7.

[114] E.g., UNCITRAL (n. 33) UN Doc. A/CN.9/712 [70].

77. The first sentence of paragraph 7 characterises the Rules as 'supplemental' to other arbitration rules, indicating a preference for a finding of no conflict between the different sets of applicable rules. The second sentence, however, immediately establishes the priority of the Rules should the other applicable arbitration rules conflict. International courts define the term 'conflict' strictly to refer to a situation which arises (only) where two mutually exclusive legal obligations exist: for example, all awards must be published in order to be in compliance with the Rules and simultaneously, the applicable arbitration rules prohibit the publication of the award in question. In such a situation, the Rules would prevail and the award would be made public. As a result, the Rules ensure that the claimant cannot choose to bring a claim under arbitration rules that would demand less transparency than the Rules would require.

78. When it comes to the level of transparency determined by the law applicable to the arbitration, however, the Rules defer to governments' sovereignty. The third sentence ensures that if there is a conflict between the Rules and the treaty out of which the claim arises, the treaty's provisions 'shall prevail'. While this enhances transparency where the treaty demands openness, where the treaty calls for the strong protection of confidentiality, the level of transparency will be the lower one.

79. Similarly, paragraph 8 upholds the prioritisation of any other rules (such as national laws) applying to the arbitration where such rules are non-derogable. Again, where these rules include a citizen's legal right to access governmental information (such as Freedom of Information (FOI) legislation[115]), this may in fact result in more transparency than the Rules alone would. Yet, if the applicable law incorporates a broader concept of confidential information than is considered mandatory, the Rules will be left aside.

80. Do paragraphs 7 and 8 ensure the goals of the delegates to protect a minimum standard of transparency in UNCITRAL investor-State

[115] The United States' Freedom of Information Act, enacted in 1966, was the first major piece of legislation to give citizens a right to access governmental information. A large and growing number of States today have such laws in place. E.g., Australia's Freedom of Information Act 1982; Canada's Access to Information Act 1983; Germany's Gesetz zur Regelung des Zugangs zu Informationen des Bundes (Informationsfreiheitsgesetz) vom 5. September 2005; India's Right to Information Act of 2005; and Liberia's Freedom of Information Act 2010. Other States have constitutional protection of access to information (e.g. Belgium's Article 32; Brazil's Article 5.XXXIII; South Africa's section 32), sometimes with additional legislation. Yet others grant access rights through administrative law (e.g., Greece's Administrative Procedural Code, Article 5, Law 2690/1999).

arbitrations? Clearly not. Even accepting that openness would logically yield to confidentiality in situations where the public interest in transparency is low and the disputing parties' interest in confidentiality is high, the third sentence of paragraph 7 and paragraph 8 leave two large gaps in ensuring transparent investor-State arbitrations. Transparency cannot be ensured unless both existing international investment agreements and national arbitration laws are adapted to reflect current concerns with heightened public access to information and participation. Where confidentiality remains explicitly protected by States, the Rules will give way.

3.12 Article 1(9): Application in non-UNCITRAL arbitrations

> 9. These Rules are available for use in investor-State arbitrations initiated under rules other than the UNCITRAL Arbitration Rules or in ad hoc proceedings.

81. Proposed originally within the first paragraph, the ninth paragraph offers disputing parties an opportunity to extend the Rules' material scope. How, precisely, this last paragraph will become operable remains to be seen. Given the traditional concern with consent in arbitration, one can presume that both disputing parties would need to agree to the Rules' application in a non-UNCITRAL setting. Moreover, where applied as procedural rules, the degree to which a non-UNCITRAL tribunal could adapt the requirements within the Rules becomes an important question. Given the clear objective of transparency, however, a strong argument could be made for strictly and fully using the Rules in any non-UNCITRAL or ad hoc proceedings for which they are adopted.

82. Given the underlying goal of broadening transparency for good governance, this provision fits well with the preceding content of Article 1. It is also a welcome – even if partial – remedy to the potentially too limited material scope set out in paragraph 1.

3.13 Conclusion

83. The scope of the Rules is the delicately balanced result of the interests and concerns of the UNCITRAL WG members regarding opening the arbitration process to enhanced public scrutiny. Heavily influenced by the broader international law trend of promoting governmental accountability and legitimacy through transparent processes of rule-making and

rule-application, the Rules' negotiators succeeded in securing a legal foundation so that the majority of investors' legal disputes with host governments can be made public. UNCITRAL's new Transparency Convention continues to push States to explicitly consent to the Rules' application in the context of arbitrations brought on the basis of treaties concluded before the Rules came into effect, thus broadening the Rules' temporal scope.

84. While the Rules are a welcome step in increasing the public awareness and acceptance of investor-State arbitration mechanisms, substantial room for improved transparency remains. The Rules still permit, for instance, States to avoid improvements in transparency by allowing mandatory provisions in the law applicable to the arbitration to override the Rules. They also allow a tribunal to sacrifice some level of transparency in the interest of an efficient process. The lack of a minimum standard of transparency could thus slow the spread of transparency in those contexts in which it may be most beneficial.

85. More importantly, the material scope of the Rules is too limited to ensure that the goal of enhancing transparency in investment disputes can be secured. While that goal itself is admirable, it is too narrowly defined – as a value of importance to the public and the aims of good governance. Moreover, as discussed above, limiting the Rules' applicability to disputes of a private investor based on a treaty claim prevents a whole class of arbitrations from coming within their range. Clarifying the desired level of transparency for contract-based claims and State-to-State arbitrations may be the next step in the search for shedding light on the investment arbitration regime.

4

Article 2. Publication of information at the commencement of arbitral proceedings

GIUSEPPE BIANCO*

Once the notice of arbitration has been received by the respondent, each of the disputing parties shall promptly communicate a copy of the notice of arbitration to the repository referred to under article 8. Upon receipt of the notice of arbitration from the respondent, or upon receipt of the notice of arbitration and a record of its transmission to the respondent, the repository shall promptly make available to the public information regarding the name of the disputing parties, the economic sector involved and the treaty under which the claim is being made.

4.1 Introduction

1. Article 2 regulates the publication of information at the commencement of arbitral proceedings. It does so in a rather concise manner, as it only consists of one paragraph. From a systematic point of view, Article 2 is the first provision of the UNCITRAL Rules on Transparency in Treaty-based Investor-State Arbitration (the Rules) to deal substantively with the issue of transparency, after the meticulous definition of the scope of application of the Rules provided by Article 1. Articles 2 to 6 establish the transparency obligations introduced by the Rules. Article 2 makes an express reference to Article 8, which is concerned with the repository of published information.[1]

2. Article 2 imposes the first transparency obligation also from a chronological perspective. The temporal reference point for Article 2 is the commencement of the arbitration, i.e., the moment when the Respondent received the notice of arbitration. Article 3(2) of the Arbitration Rules

* Giuseppe Bianco is PhD Fellow at University of Oslo and at Université Paris 1 Panthéon-Sorbonne. The author wishes to thank Anna de Luca for her helpful comments on a previous draft. Any errors and omissions are the sole responsibility of the author.

[1] See Kathleen Claussen, 'Article 8'.

(2010)[2] stipulates: 'Arbitral proceedings shall be deemed to commence on the date on which the notice of arbitration is received by the respondent'. Consequently, as soon as the arbitration commences, the transparency mechanism of Article 2 is triggered.

3. Article 2 imposes two obligations. The first one is the obligation for the parties to communicate a copy of the notice of arbitration to the repository. The second obligation requires the repository to make available to the public information regarding the name of the disputing parties, the economic sector involved and the treaty under which the claim is being made.

4.2 Background and purpose

4. The publication of information at the commencement of the arbitral proceedings concerns the first or 'simplest form' of transparency, requiring 'that information is available about the arbitration process'.[3] This is of paramount importance for transparency and legitimacy purposes. It allows stakeholders and other interested parties to become aware of the existence of the dispute and to intervene as *amici curiae*.

5. Together with Article 8 ('Repository of published information'), Article 2 allows for information on investor-State disputes to be published and available at a single registry. This will not only improve transparency and public awareness, but might also – in the long term – increase consistency among arbitral decisions and awards.

6. Scepticism towards transparency requirements in investor-State arbitration generally stems from the fear that investors may have to disclose confidential business information, strategies, trade secrets and other information that could impinge on their future economic perspectives. Governments, on the other hand, might be unwilling to gain an exaggerated reputation as a 'poor host for foreign investment'.[4]

7. Nevertheless, such concerns are gradually waning in the face of the growing awareness by governments and economic actors alike that the

[2] It must be recalled that the UNCITRAL Transparency Rules can be used also for investor-State arbitrations initiated under rules other than the UNCITRAL Arbitration Rules or in ad hoc proceedings, as stipulated by Article 1(9). Nevertheless, examples in this chapter will be made mostly to the UNCITRAL Arbitration Rules for ease of reference.

[3] James Harrison, 'Recent Developments to Promote Transparency and Public Participation in Investment Treaty Arbitration' (2011) University of Edinburgh School of Law Working Paper, No. 2011/01, 2.

[4] Christopher F. Dugan, Don Wallace Jr., Noah Rubins and Borzu Sabahi, *Investor-State Arbitration* (Oxford University Press, 2008) 707.

viability of investor-State arbitration necessitates higher legitimacy in the eye of the public. In order to achieve it, the promotion of greater transparency and publicity is essential. Indeed, part of the legal scholarship had long suggested a move towards higher levels of transparency, starting with the publication of information at the commencement of the arbitral proceedings: 'A new generation treaty (or rule changes) could provide for express publicity of all new claims, along the lines of the information provided by the International Centre for the Settlement of Investment Disputes (ICSID) on its website'.[5]

8. Most debates and analyses about transparency focus on the public nature of hearings and on the publication of the outcomes of judicial deliberations, such as awards and courts' decisions.[6] The Rules are innovative in that they specifically spell out obligations related to the publication of information at the commencement of arbitral proceedings.

9. In ICSID arbitration, the 2006 revision of the ICSID Rules (mainly aimed at increasing the transparency of arbitral proceedings) did not explicitly address this question.[7] However, as will be further discussed below, pursuant to Regulation 22(1) of the ICSID Administrative and Financial Regulations, the Centre indicates on its website[8] the date of registration of the request for arbitration, the name of the parties and the subject matter of the dispute (whereas the Rules require the disclosure of the economic sector, and of the treaty under which the claim is made).

10. In the debate over the UNCITRAL negotiations on the Rules, several non-governmental organisations (NGOs) focused on the issue of the publication of information at the commencement of arbitral tribunals. In particular, they expressed their dissatisfaction with the fact that 'there [wa]s no requirement that even the existence of an arbitration proceeding . . . be made public'.[9]

[5] Nigel Blackaby, 'Public Interest and Investment Treaty Arbitration' in Albert Jan van den Berg (ed.), *International Commercial Arbitration: Important Contemporary Questions* (Kluwer Law International, 2003) 363.

[6] Thore Neumann and Bruno Simma, 'Transparency in International Adjudication' in Andrea Bianchi and Anne Peters (eds.), *Transparency in International Law* (Cambridge University Press, 2013) 436–76.

[7] ICSID, 'Suggested Changes to the ICSID Rules and Regulations', Working Paper of the ICSID Secretariat, 12 May 2005 https://icsid.worldbank.org/apps/ICSIDWEB/resources/Documents/Suggested%20Changes%20to%20the%20ICSID%20Rules%20and%20Regulations.pdf.

[8] https://icsid.worldbank.org/ICSID/Index.jsp.

[9] Center for International Environmental Law (CIEL) and International Institute for Sustainable Development (IISD), 'CIEL and IISD call for an end to an era of secrecy in

11. Two of the most active NGOs, the Center for International Environmental Law (CIEL) and the International Institute for Sustainable Development (IISD), advocated the publication of the whole notice of arbitration. The draft rule they put forward was as follows:

Public notice of arbitration

> Promptly upon communicating a notice of arbitration to the respondent, the claimant shall forward a copy of the notice of arbitration to the UNCITRAL secretariat (or other designated institution), which shall post the notice of arbitration on its website without delay. Promptly upon communicating a response to the notice of arbitration, the respondent shall forward a copy of the response to the UNCITRAL Secretariat (or other designated institution), which shall post the response on its website without delay.[10]

12. NGOs emphasised the importance of the automatic, prompt disclosure of the existence of an arbitral dispute. In light of the length of time that the establishment of the tribunal can require, it was suggested that the publication be done by disclosing the notice of arbitration (if necessary, after redacting confidential information), as this would have ensured 'an optimal level of transparency without involving a sacrifice of current rights and protections'.[11]

4.3 Parties' obligation

4.3.1 *'Once the notice of arbitration has been received by the respondent'*

13. The provision indicates that the obligation arises '[o]nce the notice of arbitration has been received by the respondent'. The Arbitration Rules (2010) leave the parties free to choose the means of communication, as Article 2(1) stipulates that: 'A notice, including a notification, communication or proposal, may be transmitted by any means of communication

investor-State arbitration: UN body must support transparency in new arbitration rules', June 2008 www.iisd.org/pdf/2010/pr_uncitral_2010.pdf.

10 'Proposed Legal Annex for UNCITRAL Rules' in CIEL and IISD, 'Ensuring Transparency in Investor-State Dispute Resolution under the UNCITRAL Arbitration Rules', UNCITRAL Working Group II, Vienna, 4–8 October 2010 www.iisd.org/pdf/2010/unicitral_ensuring_transparency.pdf.

11 Nathalie Bernasconi-Osterwalder and Lise Johnson, 'Comments on Draft Rules on Transparency in Investor-State Arbitration' (CIEL and IISD, 2011) 8 www.iisd.org/pdf/2011/uncitral_comments_draft_rules.pdf.

that provides or allows for a record of its transmission'. The reception of the notice of arbitration by the respondent can take place when the notice has been delivered to the address designated by the party specifically for this purpose or authorised by the arbitral tribunal.[12] If the notice of arbitration is transmitted by electronic means, it is deemed to have been received on the day when it reaches the addressee's electronic address.[13] In the absence of a designation by the respondent or an authorisation by the tribunal, the notice is received when it is physically delivered to the respondent, or is deemed to have been received when it is delivered at the place of business, habitual residence or mailing address of the respondent.[14] If, after reasonable efforts, neither method is available, the notice is deemed to have been received when it is sent to the respondent's last-known place of business, habitual residence or mailing address by registered letter or any other means that provides a record of delivery or of attempted delivery.[15]

4.3.2 'each of the disputing parties shall'

14. The first sentence of Article 2 addresses the disputing parties' obligation to provide the notice of arbitration to the repository. This obligation concerns both the claimant and the respondent. The report of UNCITRAL Working Group II (Arbitration and Conciliation) (WG) noted that 'any party, and not only the respondent, should be entitled to communicate the notice of arbitration to the registry'.[16] In case of a plurality of claimants or a plurality of respondents, this should be understood as having each of them as an addressee.

4.3.3 'promptly'

15. When the notice of arbitration has been received by the respondent, by whatever means, each disputing party will then have an obligation to

[12] United Nations Commission on International Trade Law, UNCITRAL Arbitration Rules (with new Article 1, paragraph 4, as adopted in 2013), United Nations, New York, 2014 www.uncitral.org/pdf/english/texts/arbitration/arb-rules-2013/UNCITRAL-Arbitration-Rules-2013-e.pdf, Article 3(2).

[13] UNCITRAL Arbitration Rules, Article 3(5).

[14] UNCITRAL Arbitration Rules, Article 3(3).

[15] UNCITRAL Arbitration Rules, Article 3(4).

[16] UNCITRAL, 'Report of Working Group II (Arbitration and Conciliation) on the Work of its Fifty-Fifth Session (Vienna, 3–7 October 2011)' (2012) UN Doc. A/CN.9/736 [44].

communicate a copy of it 'promptly'. The indication of the time at which the copy of the notice of arbitration should be sent to the repository is thus not well specified. Nevertheless, since the obligation consists merely in the communication of a copy of the notice of arbitration, and since both disputing parties are to act in good faith, the interval between the receipt by the respondent and the communication to the repository should be short. This is different, for instance, from the timeframe within which the respondent has to communicate to the claimant a response to the notice of arbitration. Pursuant to Article 4(1) of the Arbitration Rules (2010), the respondent has thirty days from the receipt of the notice of arbitration to do so, because the response needs careful preparation. Since the copy of the notice of arbitration does not require such preparation, the meaning of 'promptly' must be taken to mean significantly less than thirty days.

4.3.4 'communicate . . . the notice of arbitration'

16. The content of the obligation consists of the communication of a copy of the notice of arbitration to the repository. The obligation established by this sentence allows the repository to obtain the information, which it will then make available to the public, pursuant to the second obligation enshrined in Article 2.

17. According to Articles 3(3) and 3(4) of the Arbitration Rules (2010), if they apply, the notice of arbitration has a mandatory content consisting of:

(a) A demand that the dispute be referred to arbitration;
(b) The names and contact details of the parties;
(c) Identification of the arbitration agreement that is invoked;
(d) Identification of any contract or other legal instrument out of or in relation to which the dispute arises or, in the absence of such contract or instrument, a brief description of the relevant relationship;
(e) A brief description of the claim and an indication of the amount involved, if any;
(f) The relief or remedy sought;
(g) A proposal as to the number of arbitrators, language and place of arbitration, if the parties have not previously agreed thereon.

And an optional content including:

(a) A proposal for the designation of an appointing authority referred to in article 6, paragraph 1;

(b) A proposal for the appointment of a sole arbitrator referred to in article 8, paragraph 1;
(c) Notification of the appointment of an arbitrator referred to in article 9 or 10.

18. The Transparency Registry (the UNCITRAL Secretariat) has published Guidelines on 'How to Submit Documents'.[17] Article A(1) specifies that '[t]he notice of arbitration shall be accompanied with information on the name of the disputing parties, the economic sector of the dispute and the treaty under which the claim arises'. This is further made clear in a template prepared for disputing parties.[18] This increases the content of the documents to be sent by the parties, and is meant to facilitate the work of the Registry itself, as will be seen below.

19. As regards the technical method for sending documents to the Registry, the Guidelines stipulate that the submission may be made 'by email, through upload to http:// or by courier, on USB stick, CD-ROM or DVD' (Article D(1)). Furthermore, the communication with the Registry shall be 'to the extent possible . . . in one of the working languages of the UN Secretariat, i.e. English or French' (Article D(3)). Although such articles refer to the arbitral tribunal, they should also be applicable to parties' submissions. Finally, Article E is dedicated to the format of the documents.[19]

4.3.5 *'to the repository'*

20. The recipient of the copy of the notice of arbitration is the repository of published information. Article 8 of the Rules designates to this end the Secretary-General of the United Nations or an institution named by

[17] Available at www.uncitral.org/transparency-registry/en/guidelines.html#_ftn1.
[18] www.uncitral.org/documents/transparency-registry/Template_for_disputing_parties.doc
[19] Article E reads:

(1) The documents shall be sent electronically, in searchable pdf format, 300 dpi. The document size shall not exceed 5 MB. If the document is larger, it should be divided into smaller documents of 5 MB or less each.
(2) As all submitted documents may be published, confidential or protected information shall be edited by the arbitral tribunal in accordance with the Transparency Rules. Documents shall be redacted by striking out the confidential or protected information. The blackened (or redacted) sections shall be neither searchable nor recoverable.
(3) No hard copy shall be sent to the Registry.
(4) The Registry will publish information in the form and language in which it receives it.

UNCITRAL.[20] Pursuant to the deliberations of UNCITRAL and General Assembly Resolution 68/106 of 16 December 2013,[21] the function of the Transparency Registry is undertaken by the Secretary-General of the United Nations, through the UNCITRAL secretariat.[22]

4.4 Repository's obligation

4.4.1 *'Upon receipt of the notice of arbitration, the repository'*

21. The second sentence of Article 2 contains the second obligation of this provision. The publication of essential information concerning the arbitral dispute is the responsibility of the repository, since the arbitral tribunal has not yet been established at this point.

22. This obligation takes its inception when the parties' obligation mandated by the first sentence of Article 2 is fulfilled. It occurs when either (i) the repository receives the notice of arbitration from the respondent; or (ii) the claimant communicates to the repository both the notice of arbitration and a record of its transmission to the respondent. In both cases, the purpose of the provision is to ensure that, when the repository acts, the respondent has already received the notice of arbitration. Otherwise, the information concerning the arbitral proceedings might be in the public domain before the respondent has had cognizance of it, and this would violate procedural fairness.

4.4.2 *'shall make available ... the name of the disputing parties, the economic sector involved and the treaty under which the claim is being made'*

23. The obligee, i.e. the repository, has to make available to the public some information related to the arbitral proceedings. It consists of the name of the disputing parties, the economic sector involved and the treaty under which the claim is being made. These pieces of information can be taken directly from the notice of arbitration, as the WG noted: 'the registry [will] extract therefrom the relevant information ... for publication'.[23]

[20] See Kathleen Claussen, 'Article 8', [19]–[27].

[21] UN Resolution adopted by the General Assembly on 16 December 2013; Report of the United Nations Commission on International Trade Law on the work of its forty-sixth session, A/RES/68/106.

[22] Website: www.uncitral.org/transparency-registry/registry/index.jspx.

[23] UNCITRAL (n. 11) UN Doc. A/CN.9/736 [44].

This is true for the name of the disputing parties (Article 3(3)(b) of the Arbitration Rules (2010): 'The names and contact details of the parties') and the treaty (Article 3(3)(c) of the Arbitration Rules (2010): 'Identification of the arbitration agreement that is invoked'). As to the economic sector, it can be inferred from the notice of arbitration, from the contractual or other relationship between the parties (Article 3(3)(d) of the Arbitration Rules (2010): 'Identification of any contract or other legal instrument out of or in relation to which the dispute arises or, in the absence of such contract or instrument, a brief description of the relevant relationship') and from the claim itself (Article 3(3)(e) of the Arbitration Rules (2010): 'A brief description of the claim and an indication of the amount involved'). However, it must be noticed that the WG discussed the proposal 'to refer to "a brief description of the subject matter of the claim" instead of the "economic sector involved" in order to convey more precise information to the public'.[24] Since the final wording retained was 'the economic sector involved', this indication should be understood as being essential and concise, and less detailed than a description of the subject matter (required for instance by the ICSID Rules) would have been. A list of possible economic sectors has been included in the Guidelines published by the Transparency Registry.[25] As will be seen

[24] UNCITRAL, 'Report of Working Group II (Arbitration and Conciliation) on the work of its fifty-fourth session (New York, 7–11 February 2011)' (2011) UN Doc. A/CN.9/717 [68].

[25] 'Possible economic sectors:

- Agriculture, forestry and fishing
- Mining and quarrying
- Manufacturing
- Energy supply
- Water supply; sewerage, waste management and remediation activities
- Construction
- Wholesale and retail trade
- Transportation and storage
- Accommodation and food service activities
- Information and communication
- Financial and insurance activities
- Real estate activities
- Professional, scientific and technical activities
- Administrative and support service activities
- Public administration
- Education
- Human health and social work activities
- Arts, entertainment and recreation
- Other service activities
- Other (please specify).'

more in depth later, the WG decided not to require the publication of the full notice of arbitration, because of the confidential information it may contain.

4.4.3 *'promptly'*

24. The repository has to fulfil its obligation 'promptly'. Just as the parties' obligation examined above, the time limit is not further specified. Therefore, it is to be understood as requiring the repository to make the information publicly available in a timely manner, taking into account its administrative and logistic capacities.

25. The issue of timing was clearly present to the members of the WG. Opinions were divided as to whether to publish information at the very beginning or to wait for the constitution of the arbitral tribunal. The former view was supported by those who highlighted the importance of raising public awareness on the procedural steps of the arbitration. Others suggested that such early publication was not appropriate, since the arbitral proceedings eventually might not take place, and because only a tribunal could ensure the reliability of the information published.[26]

26. Indeed, the WG discussed at length what information should be published at the commencement of the arbitral proceedings. The first option was to publish the notice of arbitration, but this raised several concerns. Its publication might provide imbalanced information on the case. Furthermore, it could give rise to 'various issues such as protection of confidential or sensitive information and risks of frivolous claims'.[27] The second option was to publish only essential information:

> It was suggested that providing only preliminary information regarding the parties involved, their nationality, and the economic sector concerned might be sufficient. The example of publication by the ICSID Secretariat was given. It was highlighted that for arbitration under the ICSID Convention, the Secretariat did not make the notice of arbitration public and posted on its website, after registration, the name and subject matter of the case as well as the date of registration of the case in accordance with the ICSID Convention.[28]

27. The views were not unanimous, and the possibility of also publishing the notice of arbitration at the beginning of the proceedings remained on

[26] UNCITRAL, 'Report of Working Group II (Arbitration and Conciliation) on the work of its fifty-third session (Vienna, 4–8 October 2010)' (2010) UN Doc. A/CN.9/712 [34].
[27] *Ibid.* [33]. [28] *Ibid.*

the table. At the following meeting of the WG, the Secretariat put forward a proposal that contained both options:

> Information regarding the name of the parties, their nationalities and the economic sector involved shall be made publicly available once [the notice of arbitration has been received by the respondent] [and the arbitral tribunal has been constituted].[29]

28. The compromise found was to defer the publication of the notice of arbitration to a later stage, when the arbitral tribunal had been constituted. However, 'there should also be disclosure of information on the existence of the proceedings . . . promptly upon the receipt of the notice of arbitration'.[30] It was agreed that the first bracket (when 'the notice of arbitration has been received by the respondent') would be retained, and the second one (when 'the arbitral tribunal has been constituted') deleted. In particular, the analogy with the procedure followed by the ICSID was considered important, as many States were already familiar with it.[31]

4.5 Possible exceptions to the publication?

4.5.1 The lack of an express reference to Article 7

29. Article 3, on the publication of documents,[32] includes an express reference to Article 7 of the Rules,[33] which contains exceptions to transparency. The latter can concern either confidential or protected information (paragraphs 1–5), or the integrity of the arbitral process (paragraphs 6–7).

30. In contrast, Article 2 does not contain any such reference to Article 7. Even in the absence of an express reference in Article 2, it is necessary to reflect on how to coordinate the publication of information at the commencement of the arbitral proceedings with the exceptions to transparency. This is because Article 7 refers to Article 2, both in its paragraph 1 and in its paragraph 6:

[29] UNCITRAL, 'Settlement of commercial disputes: Preparation of a legal standard on transparency in treaty-based investor-State arbitration, Note by the Secretariat' (2011) UN Doc. A/CN.9/WG.II/WP.162/Add.1 [45].

[30] UNCITRAL (n. 17) UN Doc. A/CN.9/717 [66]. [31] *Ibid.* [68].

[32] Cf. Christopher Kee, 'Article 3'.

[33] This is discussed further in Thierry Augsburger, 'Article 7'.

1. Confidential or protected information, as defined in paragraph 2 and as identified pursuant to the arrangements referred to in paragraphs 3 and 4, shall not be made available to the public pursuant to articles 2 to 6;

...

6. Information shall not be made available to the public pursuant to articles 2 to 6 where the information, if made available to the public, would jeopardize the integrity of the arbitral process as determined pursuant to paragraph 7.

31. In most cases, it would be hard to imagine that the publication of the name of the disputing parties, the economic sector involved and the treaty under which the claim is made can pose an issue. This information could hardly represent confidential or protected information, which, according to Article 7(2), consists of:

(a) Confidential business information;
(b) Information that is protected against being made available to the public under the treaty;
(c) Information that is protected against being made available to the public, in the case of the information of the respondent State, under the law of the respondent State, and in the case of other information, under any law or rules determined by the arbitral tribunal to be applicable to the disclosure of such information; or
(d) Information the disclosure of which would impede law enforcement.

32. It would be equally difficult to hypothesise that the publication of the information mandated by Article 2 would 'jeopardize the integrity of the arbitral process because it could hamper the collection or production of evidence, lead to the intimidation of witnesses, lawyers acting for disputing parties or members of the arbitral tribunal' (Article 7(7)), or that the respondent State would consider the disclosure of such information 'to be contrary to its essential security interests' (Article 7(5)).

4.5.2 Article 7 exceptions to publication

33. Three possible interpretations could be given to harmonise Article 2 and Article 7.

34. The first interpretation is that the burden of ensuring the application of Article 7 would be borne by the repository. Upon receipt of the notice of arbitration from either disputing party, the repository should check whether the information (name of the parties, treaty and economic sector involved) would constitute confidential or protected information

and whether its publication would jeopardise the integrity of the arbitral process for the purposes of Article 2. It should then publish only those pieces of information that have withstood this scrutiny, or refrain from making anything public. However, such activity does not feature among those functions assigned to the repository, which emerges as a neutral registry merely tasked with the publication of information and not with the evaluation of the nature of the information. This can be easily inferred from the *travaux préparatoires*. The WG considered, for instance, that the 'screening of the notice of arbitration would go beyond the role of a registry'.[34] Furthermore, such scrutiny is not contemplated among the tasks mentioned in the questionnaire circulated by the Secretariat among arbitral institutions potentially interested in serving as repositories.[35]

35. The second possible interpretation of Article 7's reference to Article 2 is that the arbitral tribunal would be charged with the preliminary examination of the information to be published at the commencement of the proceedings. This solution would echo the one chosen for the publication of documents, as enshrined in Article 3(4):

> The documents to be made available to the public pursuant to paragraphs 1 and 2 shall be communicated by the arbitral tribunal to the repository referred to under article 8 as soon as possible, subject to any relevant arrangements or time limits for the protection of confidential or protected information prescribed under article 7. The documents to be made available pursuant to paragraph 3 may be communicated by the arbitral tribunal to the repository referred to under article 8 as they become available and, if applicable, in a redacted form in accordance with article 7.

36. According to this interpretation, the repository, in case of doubt, would leave the decision concerning the publication to the arbitral tribunal. The difference between Article 3 and Article 2 is, however, that the arbitral tribunal is certainly constituted when the former applies, but would normally not yet be in place when Article 2 is to operate. Therefore, in order to put this interpretation into practice, the

[34] UNCITRAL (n. 11) UN Doc. A/CN.9/736 [50].

[35] UNCITRAL, 'Settlement of commercial disputes, Transparency in treaty-based investor-State arbitration, Comments by arbitral institutions regarding the establishment of a repository of published information ('registry'), Note by the Secretariat' (2012) UN Doc. A/CN.9/WG.II/WP.170.

timing of Article 2 would need to be diluted, and the 'prompt' publication would not really be such.

37. The third approach would be that the publication of the name of the disputing parties, the treaty under which the claim is made and the economic sector would be made without any preliminary check by entities other than the parties. The presence of confidential or protected information, or the publication of information capable of jeopardising this integrity of the arbitral process, could not be prevented.

38. The history of the elaboration of the Rules can shed some light on this conundrum.

39. As discussed under section 4.4.3, the *travaux préparatoires* demonstrate that the interpretation to be retained is that the information under Article 2 is to be made available to the public before the arbitral tribunal is constituted. Therefore, the exceptions of Article 7 cannot be applicable. This is further corroborated by the will of the WG to include only essential, non-contentious information. Consequently, it was agreed that it would include 'a reference to the investment treaty under which the claim was brought, as it was seen as a factual matter unlikely to create debate'.[36] On the other hand, any piece that might be problematic was to be excluded from the information to be published at the commencement of the proceedings. For instance, 'the nationalities of the parties, as well as a brief description of the claim, contained in [a previous proposal], should not be part of the information communicated to the public at the early stage of the proceedings, as that information could be contentious'.[37]

40. Where the information to be published could give rise to issues of confidentiality or at any rate be the subject of divergent views between the parties, it was considered necessary that the arbitral tribunal should be in place to settle the question. For example, the publication of the notice of arbitration was removed from the information publishable at the commencement of the proceedings pursuant to Article 2, and was inserted into Article 3. The view of the WG was that 'the arbitral tribunal would be best placed to oversee matters of confidential and sensitive information that might be contained in the notice of arbitration, and that screening of the notice of arbitration would go beyond the role of a registry'.[38]

41. Such a conclusion is further supported by the practice followed by the ICSID. As we shall see later, under Regulation 22(1) of the ICSID

[36] UNCITRAL (n. 11) UN Doc. A/CN.9/736 [43]. [37] *Ibid.* [43]. [38] *Ibid.* [50].

Administrative and Financial Regulations, the Secretary-General publishes information about the beginning of the proceedings. Consequently, 'the existence of disputes will be publicized by the Centre and it is not possible for the parties to keep the dispute a secret'.[39]

42. A question that remains to be examined is why Article 7 contains a reference to Article 2, even though it is not applicable to it, as we have seen. The answer might lie in the drafting history of Article 7. When the first version of Article 7 was drafted, in the form 'Exceptions to transparency' and with an explicit mention of Article 2 ('1. The rules set out in articles 2 to 6 are subject to the following express exceptions'),[40] the second option for the draft Article 2 (entitled 'Initiation of arbitral proceedings'), read as follows:

> Once the notice of arbitration has been received by the respondent, the respondent shall promptly [communicate to the repository referred to under article 8][make available to the public] (i) information regarding the name of the disputing parties, their nationalities [and][the economic sector involved][and][a brief description of the subject matter of the claim]; and (ii) the notice of arbitration,
>
> Variant 1: except with respect to any portion of the notice to which either the claimant (at the time it submits the notice) or the respondent objects on the ground that it contains confidential and sensitive information as defined under article 7, paragraph 2.
>
> Variant 2: [unless any disputing party objects to its publication.][provided all disputing parties agree to its publication.][41]

43. Thus, the option of publishing the notice of arbitration at the very beginning of the arbitral proceedings was still being considered. Since the notice could contain confidential or protected information, or information whose disclosure might undermine the integrity of the arbitral process, the exceptions of Article 7 were to be applicable also to Article 2. It does not seem too far-fetched to hypothesise that the subsequent discussion leading to the elimination of the publication of the notice of arbitration under Article 2 was not reflected in the wording of Article 7. Therefore, the reference to Article 2 in Article 7 is merely a testimony to these two articles' drafting histories, and should not be given too much weight.

[39] Harrison (n. 3) 4.

[40] UNCITRAL, 'Settlement of commercial disputes: preparation of a legal standard on transparency in treaty-based investor-State arbitration, Addendum, Note by the Secretariat' (2011) UN Doc. A/CN.9/WG.II/WP.166/Add.1, 2.

[41] *Ibid.* [24].

44. The only outstanding issue would concern situations where the mere knowledge of the existence of a dispute between such investor and such State would be problematic, because it would be against the State's security interests (Article 7(5)) or because of a special, exceptional circumstance (which is the open clause allowed by Article 7(7)). The intervention of the arbitral tribunal under Article 7(3) or Article 7(7) to order the withdrawal of some of the information published would take place some time (potentially, several months) after the publication at the commencement of the proceedings. Therefore, such withdrawal would probably not be sufficient to eliminate any damage that had already occurred.

4.6 Breach of the parties' obligation

45. Lack of compliance on the part of the disputing parties with their obligation to send a copy of the notice of arbitration to the repository is not provided with a specific sanction under Article 2. The issue was raised before the WG, but it was considered that 'the question of sanctions was a difficult matter to address in an instrument of the nature of the rules'.[42] It was thus left unanswered. Since the publicity of the commencement of the arbitral proceedings is of great importance, the arbitral tribunal might react pursuant to Article 1(6) if no party sends a copy of the notice of arbitration to the repository. Article 1(6) provides:

> In the presence of any conduct, measure or other action having the effect of wholly undermining the transparency objectives of these Rules, the arbitral tribunal shall ensure that those objectives prevail.

46. Consequently, immediately after its constitution, the tribunal might proceed to communicate a copy of the notice of arbitration directly to the repository, and order it to publish the name of the disputing parties, the treaty under which the claim is made, and the economic sector involved. This is confirmed by the Guidelines published by the Transparency Registry, whose Article D(2) stipulates that '[t]he arbitral tribunal shall also submit the notice of arbitration to the Registry, if the disputing parties have failed to do so'. Thus, the objective of making such information available to the public at large would be achieved, albeit later than foreseen by Article 2.

[42] UNCITRAL (n. 16) UN Doc. A/CN.9/736 [45].

4.7 Comparative overview

47. This section will compare Article 2 with other provisions and practices on the publication of information at the commencement of the arbitral proceedings. As a preliminary remark, it is worth noting that '*il n'existe pas un concept unique de la confidentialité dans l'arbitrage*'.[43] This diversity in the general treatment of confidentiality and transparency is reflected in the debate on whether and what information should be made available to the public at the commencement of an arbitral dispute.

4.7.1 *Publication of information under the Arbitration Rules*

48. The UNCITRAL Arbitration Rules do not regulate the question of public access to procedural documents, neither in the 1976 version, nor in the revised version of 2010. Whereas Article 28(3) (revising Article 25(4)) and Article 34(5) (revising Article 32(5)) of the Arbitration Rules (2010) contain provisions on the confidentiality of hearings and awards, respectively, they do not cover the confidentiality of the proceedings, as such, or of the materials (including pleadings) before the arbitral tribunal.[44] Consequently, confidentiality currently needs to be agreed upon by the parties; without such agreement, it has to be determined by the arbitral tribunal.

49. The WG often took inspiration from ICSID practice. Regulation 22 (1) of the ICSID Administrative and Financial Regulations provides that:

> 1. The Secretary-General shall appropriately publish information about the operation of the Centre, including the registration of all requests for conciliation or arbitration and in due course an indication of the date and method of the termination of each proceeding.
> 2. If both parties to a proceeding consent to the publication of:
>   (a) reports of Conciliation Commissions;
>   (b) arbitral awards; or
>   (c) the minutes and other records of proceedings, the Secretary-General shall arrange for the publication thereof, in an appropriate form with a view to furthering the development of international law in relation to investments.

[43] 'There is not a unified concept of confidentiality in arbitration', Jean-François Poudret and Sébastien Besson, *Droit comparé de l'arbitrage international* (Schulthess, Zurich, 2002) 334.

[44] Corinne Montineri, 'UNCITRAL Rules and their use in ad hoc arbitration' in Giuditta Cordero-Moss (ed.), *International Commercial Arbitration. Different Forms and Their Features* (Cambridge University Press, 2013) 104.

50. Thus, upon registration of a request for conciliation, arbitration, an application for post-award remedies under the ICSID Convention or upon granting access to the Additional Facility Rules, the Centre indicates on its website the date of registration of the request or application, the name of the parties and the subject matter of the dispute.[45]

51. The Arbitration Rules of the International Chamber of Commerce (ICC) do not explicitly address the issue of the publication of information at the commencement of arbitral proceedings. On the other hand, there is no rule requiring the parties to maintain as confidential the information concerning the proceedings. Article 30.1 provides for non-disclosure of procedural documents and awards:

> 1. Unless the parties expressly agree in writing to the contrary, the parties undertake as a general principle to keep confidential all awards in their arbitration, together with all materials in the proceedings created for the purpose of the arbitration and all other documents produced by another party in the proceedings not otherwise in the public domain – save and to the extent that disclosure may be required of a party by legal duty, to protect or pursue a legal right or to enforce or challenge an award in bona fide legal proceedings before a state court or other judicial authority.

52. Since this provision does not mention non-disclosure of the existence of the dispute, it might be inferred *a contrario* that parties are free to make available to the public information such as that mentioned by Article 2 of the Rules.

53. The Arbitration Rules of the Arbitration Institute of the Stockholm Chamber of Commerce (SCC) contain a general principle of confidentiality at Article 46: 'Unless otherwise agreed by the parties, the SCC Institute and the Arbitral Tribunal shall maintain the confidentiality of the arbitration and the award'. Consequently, the publication of essential information about the existence of the arbitral proceedings would necessitate the agreement of the disputing parties.

54. As for the International Arbitration Rules of the International Centre for Dispute Resolution,[46] two important provisions are Article 30(3) and Article 37(1). Article 30(3) stipulates that:

> An award may be made public only with the consent of all parties or as required by law, except that the Administrator may publish or otherwise

[45] https://icsid.worldbank.org/ICSID/Index.jsp.

[46] International Centre for Dispute Resolution, International Arbitration Rules, Rules Amended and Effective 1 June 2014, available at www.icdr.org.

> make publicly available selected awards, orders, decisions, and rulings that have become public in the course of enforcement or otherwise and, unless otherwise agreed by the parties, may publish selected awards, orders, decisions, and rulings that have been edited to conceal the names of the parties and other identifying details.

Article 37(1) provides that:

> Except as provided in Article 30, unless otherwise agreed by the parties or required by applicable law, the members of the arbitral tribunal and the Administrator shall keep confidential all matters relating to the arbitration or the award.

The principle enshrined in these Rules, therefore, is that confidentiality about the arbitral proceedings (also about its very existence) is the standard rule. By way of exception, only when the disputing parties agree, or the applicable law mandates it, will information concerning the dispute be made available to the public.

55. The *Optional Rules for Arbitrating a Dispute between Two Parties, Of Which Only One is a State* (1993) of the Permanent Court of Arbitration follow similar principles. Article 32(5) stipulates that an award may only be made public with the consent of the parties. However, since this provision only concerns the award, it might be inferred that the parties are free to disclose to the public the existence of the dispute, the name of the other disputing party, the economic sector involved and the treaty under which the claim is made.

56. The Arbitration Rules of London Court of International Arbitration (LCIA)[47] are particularly attached to the principle of confidentiality, enshrined in Article 30 after the 2014 revision. Even before, it was generally held that the obligation of confidentiality covered all documents created for or submitted to the proceedings, as well as the very existence of the arbitration.[48] This is now confirmed by Articles 30(1) and 30(3):

> 30.1 The parties undertake as a general principle to keep confidential all awards in the arbitration, together with all materials in the arbitration created for the purpose of the arbitration and all other documents produced by another party in the proceedings not otherwise in the public domain, save and to the extent that disclosure may be required of a party by legal duty, to protect or pursue a legal right, or

[47] LCIA Arbitration Rules, effective 1 October 2014, available at www.lcia.org/Dispute_Resolution_Services/lcia-arbitration-rules-2014.aspx.

[48] Johannes Koepp, Dorine Farah and Peter Webster, 'Arbitration in London' in Cordero-Moss (n. 44) 263.

to enforce or challenge an award in legal proceedings before a state court or other legal authority.

. . .

30.3 The LCIA does not publish any award or any part of an award without the prior written consent of all parties and the Arbitral Tribunal.

4.7.2 Publication of information under bilateral and multilateral investment treaties

57. The practice under the North American Free Trade Agreement (NAFTA) was brought before the WG for consideration. Chapter Eleven of NAFTA allows for treaty-based investor-State arbitration, and contains transparency provisions, such as NAFTA Article 1137 and Annex 1137.4 (on the publication of the award). Moreover, the *Notes of Interpretation of Certain* Chapter 11 *Provisions* published by the NAFTA Free Trade Commission (FTC) on 31 July 2001[49] clarify the question of access to documents as follows:

> Nothing in the NAFTA imposes a general duty of confidentiality on the disputing parties to a Chapter Eleven arbitration and, subject to the application of Article 1137 (4), nothing in the NAFTA precludes the Parties from providing public access to documents submitted to, or issued by, a Chapter Eleven tribunal.

58. Therefore, the United States,[50] for instance, promptly makes available to the public, subject to the redaction of protected information, documents regarding the initiation of arbitral proceedings and notices of arbitration that it receives, by posting them on its website.[51]

59. Canada also complies with NAFTA transparency obligations by making information about claims brought against it available to the public. It does so 'by posting the initiating documents submitted by potential claimants on the website of the Department of Foreign Affairs

[49] NAFTA Free Trade Commission, North American Free Trade Agreement: Notes of Interpretation of Certain Chapter 11 Provisions, 31 July 2001, http://www.sice.oas.org/tpd/nafta/Commission/CH11understanding_e.asp.

[50] UNCITRAL, 'Settlement of commercial disputes, Transparency in treaty-based investor-State arbitration, Comments of the Governments of Canada and of the United States of America on transparency in treaty-based investor-State arbitration under Chapter Eleven of the North American Free Trade Agreement (NAFTA), Note by the Secretariat' (2011) UN Doc. A/CN.9/WG.II/WP.163, Annex 2(1).

[51] See NAFTA Investor-State Arbitrations, US Department of State www.state.gov/s/l/c3439.htm.

and International Trade[52] as soon as possible, and in all cases, prior to the appointment of the arbitral tribunal', and it publishes 'promptly upon receipt from an alleged investor, the Notice of Intent to Submit a Claim to Arbitration'.[53] The notice of intent does not mark the beginning of arbitral proceedings, as the claimant needs to wait for 90 days after filing it before submitting a claim to arbitration.[54]

60. The Investment Agreement for the Common Investment Area of the Common Market for Eastern and Southern Africa (COMESA) contains a very broad obligation on the transparency of arbitral proceedings. Article 28 on 'Investor-State Disputes' provides that: '5. All documents relating to a notice of intention to arbitrate, the settlement of any dispute pursuant to Article 28, the initiation of an arbitral tribunal, or the pleadings, evidence and decisions in them, shall be available to the public'. This is tempered only by the exception in paragraph 7, protecting confidential business information.

61. The level of transparency required by bilateral investment treaties (BITs) and free trade agreements (FTAs) greatly varies. Many of them contain provisions requiring transparency of arbitral proceedings. The United States declared that they pursue the following objectives in the negotiation of free trade agreements:

> [E]nsur[e] the fullest measure of transparency in the dispute settlement mechanism, to the extent consistent with the need to protect information that is classified or business confidential, by –
> (i) ensuring that all requests for dispute settlement are promptly made public;
> (ii) ensuring that –
> (I) all proceedings, submissions, findings, and decisions are promptly made public; and
> (II) all hearings are open to the public.[55]

62. Consequently, the 2004 US Model BIT requires a high level of publicity pursuant to its Article 29(1) of Section B:

> (1) Subject to paragraphs 2 and 4, the respondent shall, after receiving the following documents, promptly transmit them to the non-disputing Party and make them available to the public:
> (a) the notice of intent;
> (b) the notice of arbitration;

[52] See www.state.gov/documents/organization/38790.pdf.
[53] UNCITRAL (n. 50) UN Doc. A/CN.9/WG.II/WP.163, Annex 1(I). [54] *Ibid.* n. 2.
[55] Trade Act 2002, s 102(b)(3)(H), quoted in Harrison (n. 3) 1.

(c) pleadings, memorials, and briefs submitted to the tribunal by a disputing party and any written submissions submitted pursuant to Article 28 (2) [Non-Disputing Party submissions] and (3) [Amicus Submissions] and Article 33 [Consolidation];
(d) minutes or transcripts of hearings of the tribunal, where available; and
(e) orders, awards, and decisions of the tribunal.

63. BITs based on this model include, for example: US–Uruguay BIT, Article 29; US–Rwanda BIT, Article 29; US–Central America and the Dominican Republic (CAFTA-DR), Article 10.21; US–Chile FTA, Article 10.20; US–Colombia Trade Promotion Agreement, Article 10.21; US–Peru Trade Promotion Agreement, Article 10.21; US–Korea FTA, Article 11.21; US–Morocco FTA, Article 10.20; US–Oman FTA, Article 10.20; US–Panama Trade Promotion Agreement, Article 10.21; and US–Singapore FTA, Article 15.20.[56]

64. Canadian investment agreements have also followed the path of increasing transparency requirements. In 2003 and 2004, Canada revised its Model Foreign Investment Promotion and Protection Agreement (FIPA) to align it with its experience in arbitration and to promote transparency.[57] In particular, Article 38 stipulates:

(3) All documents submitted to, or issued by, the Tribunal shall be publicly available, unless the disputing parties otherwise agree, subject to the deletion of confidential information.
(4) Notwithstanding paragraph 3, any Tribunal award under this Section shall be publicly available, subject to the deletion of confidential information.

65. In contrast, bilateral or multilateral treaties entered into by China do not feature any provision on transparency or publicity regarding treaty-based investment arbitration.[58] The same applies to agreements stipulated by the Russian Federation,[59] France[60] and Germany.[61] Many of these investment protection agreements, however, refer to the ICSID dispute settlement procedure, which in turn contains transparency and publicity requirements.

[56] UNCITRAL (n. 50) UN Doc. A/CN.9/WG.II/WP.163, Annex 2(1).
[57] UNCITRAL, 'Settlement of commercial disputes, Transparency in treaty-based investor-State arbitration, Compilation of comments by Governments, Note by the Secretariat, Addendum' (2010) UN Doc. A/CN.9/WG.II/WP.159/Add.1 [17]–[18].
[58] UNCITRAL (n. 57) UN Doc. A/CN.9/WG.II/WP.159/Add.1, 12.
[59] UNCITRAL (n. 57) UN Doc. A/CN.9/WG.II/WP.159/Add.3, 3.
[60] UNCITRAL (n. 57) UN Doc. A/CN.9/WG.II/WP.159/Add.2, 4.
[61] *Ibid.* [6].

66. The 1994 Energy Charter Treaty does not include a specific provision on the publication of information at the commencement of arbitral proceedings. However, the Model Host Government Agreement (HGA) for agreements between an individual State and the project investors for cross-border pipelines presented to the Energy Charter Conference in 2007 stipulates in its Article 19(11) that '[a] copy of the award shall be deposited with the Energy Charter Secretariat, which shall make it generally available'.

4.7.3 Publication of information under State practice

67. Furthermore, individual States have adopted practices that promote transparency in investor-State arbitration and specifically cover the publication of information at the commencement of arbitral proceedings. For instance Canada, since the beginning of 2000:

> has provided public notice of the existence of all of the above matters [(a) that the public is given notice of the existence of the arbitration; (b) that documents submitted to the tribunal or issued by it are publicly available; (c) that hearings are open to the public; and (d) that confidential or privileged information is adequately protected] via the website of the Department of Foreign Affairs and International Trade.[62]

68. Other States do not promote transparency in investment-related arbitration proceedings. For instance, before the WG, Russia asserted that the 'investment dispute arbitration practices in the Russian Federation show that the principle of confidentiality is observed'.[63]

4.7.4 Publication of information in international commercial arbitration

69. It is not easy to compare international investment and international commercial arbitration on the issue of transparency. International commercial arbitration proceedings are 'supposed to have little impact beyond the disputing parties and their immediate affiliates',[64] whereas international investment arbitrations might bring about a change in the

[62] UNCITRAL (n. 57) UN Doc. A/CN.9/WG.II/WP.159/Add.1 [5].
[63] UNCITRAL (2010) UN Doc. A/CN.9/WG.II/WP.159/Add.3, 3.
[64] Julie A Maupin, 'Transparency in International Investment Law: The Good, the Bad and the Murky' in Andrea Bianchi and Anne Peters (n. 6) 148.

legislation or the practice of the State, and result in payment obligations incurred by the State that will eventually be borne by its taxpayers.[65] Furthermore, international commercial arbitration usually takes place on the basis of arbitral clauses included in contracts concluded by private parties: consent is thus mutual and specific. In contrast, international investment arbitration generally stems from the encounter between the offer to arbitrate by the State expressed in a treaty and the subsequent acceptance by the investor, and therefore the State's consent is somehow broader and can be relied upon for a variety of disputes. Thus, public information about investment arbitration is more needed than information about commercial arbitration.

70. The basic principle in international commercial arbitration is confidentiality, which is 'perceived as encouraging efficient, dispassionate dispute resolution, rather than emotive "trial by press release" or efforts to gain extraneous leverage; reducing the risks of damaging disclosure of commercially-sensitive information to competitors, customers and others; and facilitating settlement by minimizing the role of public posturing'.[66]

71. Consequently, confidentiality is seen as 'good practice for the tribunal and the parties to treat as confidential the existence of the arbitral proceedings, any materials disclosed and pleadings exchanged during the proceedings, and the arbitral award itself', unless the parties agree otherwise, or unless there is a conflicting obligation stemming from domestic or international law or from judicial proceedings.[67]

72. Nevertheless, there is not a unanimous view on the role and scope of confidentiality in international commercial proceedings.[68] Statutes and case law usually do not deal with the issues of confidentiality and privacy; even when they do, the decisions they reach are considerably different from one jurisdiction to another.[69]

73. Party autonomy is taken as the reference point, meaning that the disputing parties are left free to decide whether and what information and documentation should be made known to third parties or to the public. Furthermore, the disclosure of the existence of arbitral

[65] Cindy Galway Buys, 'The Tensions between Confidentiality and Transparency in International Arbitration' (2003) 14(121) *American Review of International Arbitration* 134.

[66] Gary B. Born, *International Commercial Arbitration* (Wolters Kluwer, 2009) 2250–1.

[67] Georgios Petrochilos, *Procedural Law in International Arbitration* (Oxford University Press, 2004) 223.

[68] Born (n. 66) 2252. [69] *Ibid.* 2253.

proceedings or of other information is generally justified when it is required by securities regulatory requirements or governmental disclosure obligations.[70]

74. In Germany, the legislation follows the UNCITRAL Model Law on International Commercial Arbitration. It does not explicitly deal with the question of confidentiality. It is thus considered that disputing parties do not have an obligation of confidentiality. Consequently, they are free to disclose to the public the existence of a dispute or details related to it.[71]

75. A similar approach is followed by Swedish law. As the famous *Bulbank*[72] case has made clear, there is no presumption of confidentiality in the arbitration agreement. Therefore, if parties wish to maintain the dispute as confidential, they have to include an explicit clause in their agreement.[73]

76. Under English law, in the absence of a statutory provision, the courts have held that the principle of confidentiality applies to the documents prepared for and used in the proceedings, or disclosed or produced in the course of the arbitration, transcripts and notes of the evidence in the arbitration, and the award. However, it is not clear whether the issue of the existence of the arbitral proceedings is itself covered by the obligation of confidentiality.[74]

77. French law is also gradually moving towards greater transparency. On the one hand, it is true that Article 1464(4) of the Code of Civil Procedure, on domestic arbitration, stipulates that the arbitral proceedings are under the principle of confidentiality, unless the law or the parties decide otherwise. This is understood as covering the existence of the arbitration, its procedure and its outcome.[75] Indeed, French scholarship highlights that the mere knowledge of the existence of the proceedings might weaken a party in its economic environment or in its private sphere. Furthermore, the disclosure of the content of the dispute might have significant consequences, especially from a competition law perspective.[76]

[70] *Ibid.* 2285. [71] Jens Bredow, 'Arbitration in Germany' in Cordero-Moss (n. 44) 178.

[72] *Bulgarian Foreign Trade Bank Ltd* v. *A.I. Trade Finance Inc.*, T 1881–99, 27 October 2000 (NJA 2000, s. 538).

[73] Henrik Fieber and Eva Storskrubb, 'Arbitration in Sweden' in Cordero-Moss (n. 44) 341.

[74] Remy Gerbay, 'Confidentiality vs. Transparency in International Arbitration: The English Perspective' (University of Warsaw Conference on Confidentiality and Arbitration, Warsaw, Poland, 9 February 2011) 3.

[75] Henri-Jacques Nougein and Romain Dupeyré, *Règles et pratiques du droit français de l'arbitrage* (Lextenso, Gazette du Palais, 2012) 23–4.

[76] *Ibid.*

On the other hand, however, this provision is not applicable to international arbitration: if parties want their proceedings to be confidential, they need to agree on it in their arbitration clause or in another express agreement.[77]

4.8 Conclusion

78. Article 2 sets the tone for the entire body of the Rules. It is the first to spell out transparency obligations. It deals with the very information about the commencement of arbitral proceedings even before the arbitral tribunal is established. The explicit requirement by the Rules for the publication of information at this early stage of the investor-State arbitral proceedings is a novelty.

79. Article 2's requirement is essential in guaranteeing effectiveness to the rest of the Rules. The publication of information related to the proceedings allows the population of the defendant State, other States, NGOs and the wider public to become aware of the existence of the dispute. This is the necessary prerequisite for them to exercise the rights that the Rules bestow upon them, such as filing submissions or attending public hearings. Furthermore, this early publication will put the proceedings under the spotlight, so that individuals and organisations outside of the dispute can be watchful as to the compliance with the Rules.

80. The content of the information to be made available was the result of a compromise between conflicting views and objectives. During the negotiations, several NGOs had advocated the publication of the entire notice of arbitration. They saw this as ensuring the optimal level of transparency, as well as a prompt, straightforward rule.

81. On the other hand, businesses and several governments were concerned with the protection of confidential business information, which might be included in the notice of arbitration. The redaction of such information could have given rise to disagreements, for which the arbitral tribunal would have been needed. This would have delayed the publication.

82. Consequently, the publication of the information related to the dispute was confined to the disputing parties, the economic sector involved and the treaty. This outcome is to be welcomed, since it allows for public awareness of the essential details of the dispute.

[77] Emmanuel Gaillard and Pierre de Lapasse, 'Le nouveau droit français de l'arbitrage interne et international' (2011) 175 *Recueil Dalloz* [28].

83. Whilst in international commercial arbitration, confidentiality of the existence of the dispute remains the rule, transparency is gaining ground in investor-State arbitration. The practice under ICSID (which publicises on its website the name of the parties and the subject matter of the dispute) is a prime example. The provisions of several multilateral and bilateral investment protection treaties, as well as the voluntary unilateral practice of several States, further corroborate this view.

84. The Rules bring this trend one step further. They explicitly require that information be made available at the very commencement of arbitral proceedings. Moreover, they establish for the first time a repository that will be the central registry for information on arbitral proceedings. These two requirements work together to ensure a high level of transparency in treaty-based investor-State arbitration.

5

Article 3. Publication of documents

CHRISTOPHER KEE*

1. Subject to Article 7, the following documents shall be made available to the public: the notice of arbitration, the response to the notice of arbitration, the statement of claim, the statement of defence and any further written statements or written submissions by any disputing party; a table listing all exhibits to the aforesaid documents and to expert reports and witness statements, if such table has been prepared for the proceedings, but not the exhibits themselves; any written submissions by the non-disputing Party(ies) to the treaty and by third persons, transcripts of hearings, where available; and orders, decisions and awards of the arbitral tribunal.
2. Subject to Article 7, expert reports and witness statements, exclusive of the exhibits thereto, shall be made available to the public, upon request by any person to the arbitral tribunal.
3. Subject to Article 7, the arbitral tribunal may decide, on its own initiative or upon request from any person, and after consultation with the disputing parties, whether and how to make available exhibits and any other documents provided to, or issued by, the arbitral tribunal not falling within paragraphs 1 or 2 above. This may include, for example, making such documents available at a specified site.
4. The documents to be made available to the public pursuant to paragraphs 1 and 2 shall be communicated by the arbitral tribunal to the repository referred to under Article 8 as soon as possible, subject to any relevant arrangements or time limits for the protection of confidential or protected information prescribed under Article 7. The documents to be made available pursuant to paragraph 3 may be communicated by the arbitral tribunal to the repository referred to under Article 8 as they become available and, if applicable, in a redacted form in accordance with Article 7. The repository shall make all documents available in a timely manner, in the form and in the language in which it receives them.

* Dr Christopher Kee is Senior Lecturer in Law and the Head of the Graduate School for the College of Arts and Social Sciences at the University of Aberdeen. He is an Australian Lawyer (non-practising).

5. A person granted access to documents under paragraph 3 shall bear any administrative costs of making those documents available to that person, such as the costs of photocopying or shipping documents to that person, but not the costs of making those documents available to the public through the repository.

5.1 Introduction

1. Article 3 addresses the publication of documents. It comprises five paragraphs that largely deal with issues of process. Paragraph 1, for instance, sets out a list of documents that are to be automatically made available. Paragraph 2 identifies documents that are to be made available upon request by any person. Paragraph 3 gives the arbitral tribunal the discretion to make available documents not encompassed in paragraphs 1 or 2. This discretion can be exercised in response to a request from any person, or an act of the tribunal's own volition. Documents made available pursuant to paragraph 3 are not necessarily done so through the repository. Paragraph 4 addresses the relationship between the tribunal and the repository again from a process perspective. Paragraph 5 addresses the costs issues associated with any paragraph 3 documents.

2. Article 3 is not, then, itself an article that gives or grants a right of access to information. This article is drafted in a manner that, in the first instance, assumes such a right already exists in relation to certain documents (see here paragraphs 1 and 2 of Article 3), and may exist with respect to other documents. The right of access is established by the application of the Rules as a whole, which, with reference to the Arbitration Rules (2010), would be Article 1(4), as adopted in 2013. The reference in paragraph 5 to granting access should therefore be understood as 'gaining' access.

5.2 Background and purpose

3. Article 3, like the Rules themselves, embodies, on the one hand, the culmination of steps towards transparency, but almost equally signifies a significant departure from what existed before. To reconcile these two seemingly opposite observations, a brief consideration of the background and context of document publication in arbitration, and particularly investment arbitration, is useful.

4. [1]The general Arbitration Rules were principally and originally drafted with private commercial arbitration in mind.[2] Yet despite this, they 'are the second most used rules for resolving investor-States disputes' (after the Arbitration Rules of the International Centre for Settlement of Investment Disputes (ICSID)).[3] Given their original, and indeed continuing, purpose, the Arbitration Rules themselves do not promote transparency. Indeed, to the contrary, both versions clearly demonstrate a preference for privacy.[4] Furthermore, it can be said of the Arbitration Rules (2010) in particular, that those rules do not even actively promote confidentiality. During the preparation of the 2010 revisions, the WG considered whether to specifically include a confidentiality provision. The decision was to not do so, but rather to leave the matter to the arbitral tribunal to deal with on a case-by-case basis.[5] Confidentiality in commercial arbitration is a complex subject.[6] Different positions are adopted by jurisdictions with regard to whether arbitrations are simply by their nature confidential, or if some further agreement of the parties is required. This is different to privacy. Privacy, if described and defined by reference to such things as the right to have hearings held in camera, is something that virtually all, if not all, arbitral rules recognise.[7] The difference may therefore be said to be one of a right to prevent someone being present, as opposed to a right to prevent publication. Julian Lew has very succinctly explained the difference between privacy and confidentiality in the following manner:

[1] See Krista Nadakavukaren Schefer, 'Article 1', [7]–[32].

[2] Clyde Croft, Christopher Kee and Jeffrey Waincymer, *A Guide to the UNCITRAL Arbitration Rules* (Cambridge University Press, 2013) 6.

[3] UNCITRAL, 'Report of the Working Group on Arbitration and Conciliation on the work of its forty-eighth session' (2008) UN Doc. A/CN.9/646 [58].

[4] See 2010 UNCITRAL Rules, Article 28(3), and 1976 UNCITRAL Rules, Article 25(4).

[5] UNCITRAL, 'Report of the Working Group on Arbitration and Conciliation on the work of its forty-fifth session' (2006) UN Doc. A/CN.9/614 [86]. Cindy G. Buys, 'The Tensions Between Confidentiality and Transparency in International Arbitration' (2003) 14 *American Review of International Arbitration* 121, 133–4.

[6] See generally Ileana M. Smeureanu, *Confidentiality in International Commercial Arbitration* (Kluwer Law International, 2011); see also the discussion of this topic in Croft, Kee and Waincymer (n. 2), [17.30]ff. A further indicator of the complexity is the amount of academic commentary the topic has generated. Albeit a crude measure, the fact that the search term (confidentiality AND 'commercial arbitration') returns 150 pages of results on kluwerarbitration is indicative.

[7] See e.g. ICC Rules, Article 26(3); ICDR Rules, Article 23(6); LCIA Rules, Article 19(4); SCC Rules, Article 27(3); DIAC Rules, Article 28(3); SIAC Rules, Article 21(4); HKIAC Rules, Article 22(7); CIETAC Rules, Article 36(1).

> Privacy is concerned with the right of persons other than the arbitrators, parties and their necessary representatives and witnesses, to attend the arbitration hearing and to know about the arbitration. Confidentiality, by contrast, is concerned with the obligation on the arbitrators and the parties not to divulge or give out information relating to the content of the proceedings, evidence and documents, addresses, transcripts of the hearings or the award.[8]

5. Given that the Arbitration Rules do not contain provisions on confidentiality, they are therefore largely silent on the publication of documents. Both versions do, however, have provisions relating to the publication of the award. The Arbitration Rules (1976) state that awards may be made public only with the consent of both parties.[9] In the Arbitration Rules (2010), this position was supplemented by a right to publish the award to the extent that such was necessary pursuant to a legal duty to do so, to protect or pursue a legal right, and in relation to legal proceedings before a court or other competent authority.[10] The 2012 PCA Arbitration Rules adopt the same stance.[11]

6. As noted below, the most commonly used rules for investment arbitration cases are the ICSID Arbitration Rules.[12] The ICSID Arbitration Rules do not address the issue of publication of documents directly. It would be wrong, however, to leave an impression that the ICSID Arbitration Rules did not at least implicitly favour transparency. ICSID maintains a publicly available register of the cases filed under its auspices and much of this register is available online. Furthermore, amendments to the ICSID Arbitration Rules in 2006 have led to greater transparency – though not at the level that will be seen under the Rules. ICSID Rule 48 still subjects publication of the award to the consent of the parties, but it mandates that excerpts of the legal conclusions of the tribunal must be published.[13]

7. In light of the above discussion it can be seen that the purpose of Article 3 of the Rules, or perhaps more appropriately its function, is to clarify the position on the publication of documents in those arbitrations to which it applies, because the underlying arbitration rules may not.[14]

[8] Expert Report of Julian Law in *Esso* v. *Plowman* (1995) 183 CLR 10 (High Court of Australia) (reprinted in 1995) 11 *Arbitration International* 283, 285, para 16.

[9] 1976 UNCITRAL Arbitration Rules, Article 32(5).

[10] 2010 UNCITRAL Arbitration Rules, Article 34(5). See also Croft, Kee and Waincymer (n. 2), paras 34.29ff for discussion of this amendment.

[11] PCA Arbitration Rules, Article 34(5).

[12] Klint Alexander, 'Article 6', [8]f.

[13] Christina Knahr and August Reinisch, 'Transparency versus Confidentiality in International Investment Arbitration – The *Biwater Gauff* Compromise' (2007) 6 *The Law and Practice of International Courts and Tribunals* 97, 100.

[14] See Article 1(7) of the Rules, and the commentary of Krista Nadakavukaren Schefer thereon earlier in this book, 'Article 1', [71]–[76].

Notably, this will, in some instances, mean that it effectively reverses the confidentiality presumption that is often, but not always, found in commercial arbitration.[15]

8. Separately from the applicable arbitration rules, provisions on publication of documents may be found in the relevant treaty, through applicable domestic statutory laws or, in common law jurisdictions, case precedent.

9. At the treaty level, a prominent example for consideration is the North American Free Trade Agreement (NAFTA). Many of the cases that demonstrate the issues associated with document publication have been NAFTA cases.[16] The circumstances of these cases have been such that the NAFTA Free Trade Commission (FTC), which has the power to issue binding interpretative statements, has pronounced on this issue. In its 'Notes of Interpretation of Certain Chapter Eleven Provisions (Free Trade Commission, July 31, 2001)', the FTC made clear that there was no separate stand-alone confidentiality obligation to be found in the NAFTA agreement that would, of itself, prevent the parties to the arbitration from publishing documents.[17] The Note also indicated the ability of the NAFTA parties to share arbitration documents (i.e. publish them) to subnational government officials.[18]

10. Article 1(7) of the Rules confirms that 'where there is a conflict between the Rules on Transparency and the treaty, the provisions of the treaty shall prevail'. It will be important to review how this provision is subsequently interpreted in practice, as there are two conceivable approaches. The question will be whether Article 1(7) is intended to apply to a conflict of principle or a conflict of standard. If the rule applies

[15] See e.g. ICC Rules, Article 34(5); ICDR Rules, Article 37; LCIA Rules, Article 30; SCC Rules, Article 46; DIS Rules, Section 43(1); DIAC Rules, Article 41(1); SIAC Rules, Article 35; HKIAC Rules, Article 42; CIETAC Rules, Article 36(2).

[16] See below 5.3 'Case law concerning confidentiality' for some examples. For commentary on NAFTA and confidentiality, see also Fulvio Fracassi, 'Confidentiality and NAFTA Chapter 11 Arbitrations' (2001) 2 *Chicago Journal of International Law* 213; Adrián Vázquez, 'Protection of Confidential Information in the Mexican Trade Remedy System' (2014) 9(7/8) *Global Trade and Customs Journal* 298–306; Sergio Puig, 'The Role of Procedure in the Development of Investment Law: The Case of Section B of Chapter Eleven of NAFTA' in Chester Brown and Kate Miles (eds.), *Evolution in Investment Treaty Law and Arbitration* (Cambridge University Press, 2012).

[17] NAFTA Free Trade Commission, North American Free Trade Agreement, Notes of Interpretation of Certain Chapter 11 Provisions, NAFTA Free Trade Commission (31 July 2001) www.state.gov/documents/organization/38790.pdf. See above, paras [3]–[10].

[18] *Ibid.*

to principles rather than standards, then there would, in theory, be no conflict with a treaty that endorses transparency, notwithstanding that the transparency rule in the treaty is of a higher or lower standard. The effective result of that interpretation would be that the approach and standard set by the Rules was applicable and could displace any procedures or standards set out in the treaty. In an international commercial arbitration this would be analogous to the circumstances dealing with challenges to arbitrators – rules that prohibited challenges would be contradictory and the *lex arbitri* would prevail, but rules that simply set out different procedures and tests for arbitrator challenges are not a conflict.

11. From the perspective of applicable domestic statutory laws, there are two types that are of particular relevance. The first is the statutory arbitration law of the seat of the arbitration.[19] Increasingly these statutes contain provisions on confidentiality. Very few, if any, of these provisions would be considered mandatory, and so in the usual fashion that arbitral rules, as a manifestation of the parties' agreement, prevail over non-mandatory law, Article 3 would prevail and be applicable. The impact of a consideration of Article 3 against these laws may therefore be of limited relevance.

12. However the second type of domestic statutory laws to be considered are those relating to freedom of information requests (FOI regimes). According to one source, ninety-five countries have FOI regimes.[20]

13. Numerous tribunals have now considered and/or addressed the impact of the freedom of information laws.[21] A recent example can be found in the *Mercer International Inc* v. *Canada* case.[22] There, the tribunal's confidentiality order included a provision that states:

> Notwithstanding any other provision in this Confidentiality Order, any request for documents, or for the production of documents under the

[19] It would not be uncommon to refer to the *lex arbitri* in this context. The statutory arbitration law is a very significant part of the *lex arbitri* but it is not the entirety of it. The *lex arbitri* is comprised of any law at the seat of the arbitration which is applicable to the arbitration by virtue of the fact that the arbitration is seated in that jurisdiction.

[20] freedominfo.org, 'Guyana Law Made Effective July 10; 95th in World' (19 September 2013) www.freedominfo.org/regions/global/foi-regimes/.

[21] See e.g. *Detroit International Bridge Company* v. *Canada*, UNCITRAL, PCA Case No. 2012–25, Confidentiality Order (27 March 2013) (although in this order the reference is not explicit but refers generally to a disclosure pursuant to a legal process, paragraph 6(f)).

[22] See *Mercer International Inc* v. *Canada*, Confidentiality Order (24 January 2013).

> *Access to Information Act*, R.S., 1985, c. A-1, the *Canada Evidence Act*, R.S., 1985, c. C-5, the *Privacy Act*, R.S. 1985, c. P-21, and the B.C. *Freedom of Information and Protection of Privacy Act*, RSBC 1996, Chapter 165, or any other applicable federal, provincial, or territorial legislation, including documents produced to Canada in these proceedings, shall be wholly governed by the relevant legislation.[23]

14. The practice of some States, particularly countries such as Canada and the United States, in actively and consistently asserting the potential impact of FOI regimes[24] has, it might be argued, forced tribunals to address any applicable FOI regime almost as a matter of course in confidentiality orders. In the example provided above, it appears that the tribunal is deferring the situation completely. The Canadian legislation is said to wholly govern the production should a request be made under the legislation. This would mean that the head of the relevant government institution would decide whether any of the exclusions to access applied – not the tribunal. If information is not disclosed then it is the Canadian Federal Court that hears the third person's appeal.

15. The inclusion of these provisions has not been without controversy. The investor in *Merrill & Ring Forestry L.P.* v. *Canada* argued strongly against the application of the Canadian FOI legislation to document (and information more generally) publication.[25] This argument was ultimately unsuccessful.

16. It would seem likely that the provisions of an FOI regime will almost always prevail over Article 3 of the Rules, based on the plain wording of the Rules themselves. However, a reasoned policy argument could be made that this should not necessarily be the case,[26] and, as such, a determination would be needed on a case-by-case basis. In the first instance the application of the FOI regime may be determined an

[23] *Ibid.* [15].

[24] See Joachim Delany and Daniel Barstow Magraw, 'Procedural Transparency' in Peter Muchlinski, Federico Ortino and Christoph Schreuer (eds.), *The Oxford Handbook of International Investment Law* (Oxford University Press, 2008) 744.

[25] See 'The Investors Submissions on Confidentiality' (9 November 2007) www.international.gc.ca/trade-agreements-accords-commerciaux/assets/pdfs/disp-diff/merrill-po-03.pdf; Canada's procedural submission (9 November 2007) www.international.gc.ca/trade-agreements-accords-commerciaux/assets/pdfs/disp-diff/merrill-po-05.pdf; and the Confidentiality Order of the Tribunal (21 January 2008) www.international.gc.ca/trade-agreements-accords-commerciaux/assets/pdfs/disp-diff/merrill-po-10.pdf.

[26] See Krista Nadakavukaren Schefer, 'Article 1', [70]–[80] and Thierry P. Augsburger, 'Article 7', [67], [78], [168]–[174].

applicable treaty.[27] Second, it is very unlikely that the FOI regime would not be considered a mandatory aspect of the *lex arbitri* and on that basis, pursuant to Article 1 paragraph 8 of the Rules, the FOI regime would also prevail. There does not appear to be the same issue regarding a conflict of principle versus a conflict of standard in Article 1 paragraph 8. This paragraph is worded differently, clearly opposing provision against provision. A provision such as Article 3 paragraph 3, which gives discretion to the tribunal, is clearly in conflict with a provision that gives a functionally similar decision to a state bureaucrat or judicial officer.

17. The argument that Article 3 should prevail over an FOI regime might, in brief, be as follows. Article 1(8) refers to applicable domestic laws. The question is then one of whether the FOI regime is in and of itself applicable. On its face, the FOI legislation will purport to be applicable because it will involve government organs. However, the applicability is a question of law to be determined by the tribunal.[28] Assuming that in the first instance the applicable law is international law, then the tribunal would need to determine whether the Rules reflected international law on this point. If they were found to so reflect the law, then they should prevail over the FOI regime. The prospect of the Rules reflecting the international law on this point seems quite likely, particularly given the United Nations Convention on Transparency in Treaty-based Investor-State Arbitration is open for signature, though not get in force.[29] In addition to a seemingly plausible legal basis for the non-application of the FOI regime, there are additionally sound policy

[27] See e.g. Article 38(8) of the Canadian Model Foreign Investment Promotion and Protection Agreement.

[28] UNCITRAL, 'Report of Working Group II (Arbitration and Conciliation) on the work of its fifty-fourth session' (2011) UN Doc. A/CN.9/717 [79]: 'In response to a general question whether there should be an analysis of the applicable law under which the arbitral tribunal would exercise any power conferred to it under the provision on publication of documents, it was said that the approach would be very similar to that adopted under article 15 of the 1976 UNCITRAL Arbitration Rules, or article 17 of the 2010 UNCITRAL Arbitration Rules, and that the question of applicable law was not intended to be dealt with under the rules on transparency. A view was expressed that investment treaties usually contained provisions on applicable law that would be relevant to that determination.'

[29] See www.uncitral.org/uncitral/en/uncitral_texts/arbitration/2014Transparency_Convention_status.html.

reasons.[30] As the *Mercer International Inc* v. *Canada* example above alluded to, the application of the FOI regime would take the decision away from the tribunal. The mere application of the Rules would be a manifestation of the parties' objective intent that it should be the tribunal that handles these matters. Furthermore, investment arbitration tribunals have a duty 'to conduct the proceedings so as to avoid unnecessary delay and expense and to provide a fair and efficient process for resolving the parties' dispute'.[31] It may be argued that where a tribunal does not have control over the documents that may or may not be published pursuant to a discretion exercised by an external body, that tribunal cannot then be certain of its ability to ensure performance of its duty.

5.3 Case law concerning access

18. It is useful to see how some of the arbitral tribunals that have been specifically called upon to consider the publication of documents have done so. In many cases, the request for document publication is, in effect, a subsidiary application to one seeking *amici curiae* status. The Rules address third person participation in Article 4 and, as such, many of the cases also involving confidentiality are identified and discussed in more detail in the next chapter.[32] However, several key cases are considered below. The cases that follow have been grouped into those that demonstrate the need for a rule like that found in Article 3, and those that may have some relevance to the operation of Article 3.

5.3.1 Demonstrating the need for an Article 3-like provision

5.3.1.1 *UPS* v. *Canada*

19. In the *United Parcel Service of America Inc. (UPS)* v. *Canada* case,[33] the tribunal was asked by the Canadian Union of Postal Workers and the Council of Canadians (who were both seeking to be admitted as either parties or *amicus*) for 'disclosure of the statement of claim

[30] See Krista Nadakavukaren Schefer, 'Article 1', [75] and Thierry P. Augsburger, 'Article 7', [168]–[174].

[31] See e.g. Revised UNCITRAL Arbitration Rules, Rule 17(1). See, for a similar statement describing the obligation, *Biwater Gauff (Tanzania) Limited* v. *Tanzania*, ICSID Case No. ARB/05/22, Procedural Order No. 3 (29 September 2006) [155].

[32] Mariel Dimsey, 'Article 4'.

[33] *United Parcel Service of America Inc* v. *Canada*, UNCITRAL. See also Mariel Dimsey, 'Article 4', [42]–[45].

and defence, memorials, counter-memorials, pre-hearing memoranda, witness statements and expert reports, including appendices and exhibits to such submissions, and any applications or motions to the tribunal'.[34] This was a NAFTA case conducted pursuant to the Arbitration Rules (1976).

20. Distinguishing between privacy and confidentiality, the tribunal noted that '[u]nder Chapter 11 and the UNCITRAL Rules provision is made for the communication of pleadings, documents and evidence to the other disputing party, the other NAFTA parties, the tribunal and the Secretariat – and to no one else'.[35] It further noted that principles of transparency argued in favour of a general order and dismissed this aspect of the application.

5.3.1.2 *Aguas del Tunari SA* v. *Republic of Bolivia*

21. *Aguas del Tunari SA* v. *Bolivia*[36] was an ICSID arbitration with reference to the Bolivia–Netherlands BIT. The arbitral tribunal received a joint petition from several NGOs and individuals to join the arbitration as parties, or alternatively as *amicus*. The petitioners additionally sought 'public disclosure of the statements of claim and defense; memorials and counter-memorials; pre-hearing memoranda; supplemental submissions; witness statements and expert reports; transcripts of hearings; appendices and exhibits to any submissions made to the tribunal; and any other submissions made to the tribunal'.[37] The tribunal in a letter denying the request noted its unanimous opinion that it did not have the power to accede to the petitioners' core requests, which included the publication of documents.[38] The tribunal noted that this situation could be altered with the parties' consent, but that the parties, had not so consented.

[34] Decision of the Tribunal on Petitions for Intervention and Participation as Amici Curiae [1(iii)] www.state.gov/documents/organization/6033.pdf.

[35] *Ibid.* [68].

[36] *Aguas del Tunari SA* v. *Bolivia*, ICSID Case No. ARB/02/3. Mariel Dimsey, 'Article 4', [46]–[47].

[37] Petition of La Coordinadora Para La Defensa Del Agua y Vida, La Federación Departamental Cochabambina de Organizaciones Regantes, Semapa Sur, Friends of the Earth-Netherlands, Oscar Olivera, Omar Fernandez, Father Luis Sánchez, and Congressman Jorge Alvarado to the Arbitral Tribunal (29 August 2002), [63(iii)] www.italaw.com/sites/default/files/case-documents/ita0018.pdf.

[38] *Aguas del Tunari* v. *Bolivia*, Letter from President of Tribunal Responding to Petition (29 January 2003) 1 www.italaw.com/sites/default/files/case-documents/ita0019_0.pdf.

5.3.1.3 *Methanex* v. *USA*

22. The *Methanex* v. *United States of America* case was brought under NAFTA and pursuant to the Arbitration Rules (1976). In this case the tribunal was called upon to consider the acceptance of *amici curiae* briefs. The tribunal found that it had the power to accept such briefs but that without the parties' consent this was limited to written submissions. A logical corollary of the third party requests had been to obtain access to the arbitration documents. This case, like most of the other cases discussed in this section, had had a confidentiality order issued by the tribunal. The tribunal considered the question of confidentiality under the Arbitration Rules (1976) and noted the conflicting decisions and general complexity of the area. However, the tribunal took the view that the confidentiality order already issued was controlling. In its order, the tribunal provided that the major pleadings could be disclosed by a party, subject to the protection of trade secret information. The tribunal observed that this, then, was a decision for the parties rather than itself.[39]

23. During the course of reaching its decision, the *Methanex* tribunal considered jurisprudence from the *Metalclad* case.[40] The tribunal in *Metalclad* had reached the conclusion that there was no general principle of confidentiality in any of the NAFTA, the ICSID (Additional Facility Arbitration Rules (AFR), the Arbitration Rules (1976) or the ILC's Draft Articles on Arbitration. The *Methanex* tribunal echoed those conclusions.

5.3.2 *Potential operational assistance*

5.3.2.1 *Pope & Talbot* v. *Canada*

24. The *Pope & Talbot* v. *Canada* case was also brought under NAFTA and was conducted pursuant to the Arbitration Rules (1976). It too concerned the Canadian C Trade mechanism, however in this instance the tribunal found that Canada should be permitted to provide documents to the state and territory officials. While the eventual outcome was reasonably straightforward, the sequence of events leading to it were not so. The tribunal had initially issued a procedural order

[39] *Methanex* v. *United States of America*, Decision of the Tribunal on Petitions from Third Persons to Intervene as 'Amici Curiae' (15 January 2001).

[40] *Metalclad Corporation* v. *Mexico*, ICSID Case No. Arb (AF)/97/1 (30 August 2000).

regarding confidentiality.[41] Disclosure by Canada through the C Trade mechanism would have been contrary to the terms of this order. However, the tribunal was persuaded by Canada that the order should be amended so as to allow the publication.[42] This procedural order was subsequently amended again on 17 September 2002 by mutual agreement of the parties.[43] This amendment was significant for two reasons in particular: it contemplates Canada's disclosure (i.e. publication) of documents from the arbitration pursuant to the Access to Information Act[44] (ATIA) but does not subject the publication of documents to that act; and it expressly prohibits the publication of the so-called 'rolling text' without the combined consent of Canada, the United States and Mexico. The rolling text had been the subject of considerable dispute. Pope & Talbot had sought discovery of the *travaux préparatoires* of the NAFTA. Canada had denied any such documents existed. It was not until a very late stage that documents said to be rolling text (as opposed to *travaux préparatoires*) were produced.

25. For the purposes of Article 3, this case may have relevance to the question of the applicability of FOI regimes. Perhaps ironically, given the present subject, the amendment was made by consent and the correspondence between the parties leading to that agreement does not appear to have been published. However, it is conceivable that someone with standing under ATIA[45] may request access to that correspondence.

5.3.2.2 *Loewen Group, Inc and Raymond Loewen* v. *USA*

26. The *Loewen* case was the first NAFTA-based claim brought against the United States. It was conducted pursuant to the ICSID AFR. For the purposes of this chapter, the interesting consideration that came before the tribunal in this case was the impact of the US FOI laws, and the public access rights that accrued to interested non-parties as a result. Initially the parties appeared to have quite different understandings of the confidentiality obligations imposed on them by a decision on confidentiality that had been rendered early on by the tribunal. The USA, in

[41] *Pope & Talbot* v. *Canada*, Procedural Order No. 5 (17 December 1999).

[42] *Pope & Talbot* v. *Canada*, Letter from the Tribunal to the Parties (2 April 2000) http://italaw.com/documents/AmendmentProceduralOrder5_Myers.pdf.

[43] *Pope & Talbot* v. *Canada*, Amended Procedural Order on Confidentiality No. 5 (17 September 2002) www.italaw.com/sites/default/files/case-documents/ita0687.pdf.

[44] Access to Information Act (RSC, 1985, c. A-1).

[45] See Access to Information Act (RSC, 1985, c. A-1), s. 4.

the apparent belief that the decision was intended to restrict only the tribunal and ICSID Secretariat, released the minutes and audio recording of a hearing. The USA's understanding is perhaps not as extraordinary as it may at first seem, as the tribunal's earlier decision had considered Article 44(1) of the ICSID AFR, which noted that transcripts could not be published without the parties' consent. This rule, the tribunal had noted, was principally directed at the tribunal. Loewen's position was that the decision prevented all publication without each party's consent. The tribunal confirmed Loewen's understanding, but noted that the decision was not intended to impact any statutory disclosure obligation that fell on any party. The USA then continued to make public documents, as it was called upon to do by the domestic FOI laws.[46]

5.3.2.3 *Suez/Vivendi* v. *Argentina*

27. The *Suez, Sociedad General de Aguas de Barcelona, S.A. and Vivendi Universal, S.A.* v. *Argentina* case[47] involved a joint request by five NGOs to participate as *amicus*. In their initial submission the NGOs sought 'timely, sufficient, and unrestricted access to all of the documents in the case'.[48] The tribunal acknowledged in principle its ability to permit *amici*; however, it found that their assistance was not needed at that point in the hearings. The tribunal deferred any decision on access to documents until such time as it had actually decided to admit the *amici*. Subsequently, on 1 December 2006, the five NGOs again approached the tribunal, and on this occasion were permitted to make an *amici* submission. The tribunal now also needed to address the NGOs' request for access to the record. Noting that '[a]s a general proposition, an amicus curiae must have sufficient information on the subject matter of the

[46] See generally *The Loewen Group, Inc. and Raymond L. Loewen* v. *United States of America*, ICSID Case No. ARB(AF)/98/3, Decision on hearing of Respondent's objection to competence and jurisdiction www.state.gov/documents/organization/3921.pdf. For confirmation that the '[d]ecision was intended to affect or qualify, or could affect or qualify, any statute-imposed obligation of disclosure by which any party to the arbitration might be bound', see [28].

[47] *Suez, Sociedad General de Aguas de Barcelona, S.A. and Vivendi Universal, S.A.* v. *Argentina*, ICSID Case No. ARB/03/19 (formerly *Aguas Argentinas, S.A., Suez, Sociedad General de Aguas de Barcelona, S.A. and Vivendi Universal, S.A.* v. *Argentina*). See also Mariel Dimsey, 'Article 4', [52]–[54].

[48] *Suez/Vivendi* (*ibid.*) Order in Response to a Petition for Transparency and Participation as Amicus Curiae (19 May 2005) [1(c)] www.italaw.com/sites/default/files/case-documents/ita0815.pdf.

dispute to provide "perspectives, expertise and arguments" which are pertinent and thus likely to be of assistance to the tribunal. Otherwise the entire exercise serves no purpose'.[49] The tribunal nevertheless went on to deny the request in this case. The tribunal found that the NGOs had already demonstrated that they had gained considerable information from other sources, such that further access was not needed.

28. This decision is an interesting and might also be considered a pragmatic one. As noted elsewhere,[50] the arbitration was an ICSID arbitration pursuant to the pre-revised ICSID Arbitration Rules, and as such the tribunal was relying on its 'residual power'.[51] The decision to allow the *amici* was therefore on already potentially contentious legal grounds, particularly as it appears the claimant had consistently objected. Furthermore, and somewhat intriguingly, the NGOs' request only sought disclosure of the record to the NGOs themselves, and not publication to the public at large. This meant that the tribunal did not need to consider transparency as a whole, but could instead focus very specifically on the NGOs. Once satisfied that the NGOs were sufficiently informed to assist, the decision to avoid further controversy would have been a fairly straightforward one.

5.3.2.4 *Biwater Gauff* v. *Tanzania*

29. In the *Biwater Gauff (Tanzania) Ltd.* v. *Tanzania* case[52] the tribunal was asked to permit several NGOs access to 'the initial notice of arbitration and statement of defense, if any was prepared; the decisions, orders and directions of the tribunal not already in the public domain, if any; the pleadings and written memorials of the arbitrating parties, and relevant witness statements and transcripts of any witness examinations'.[53] This case was the first to use the revised ICSID Arbitration Rules, and as such the petitioners commented:

[49] *Suez/Vivendi* (n. 47) Order in Response to a Petition by Five Non-Governmental Organizations for Permission to make an amicus curiae Submission (12 February 2007) [24] www.italaw.com/sites/default/files/case-documents/ita0823.pdf.

[50] See also Mariel Dimsey, 'Article 4', [48]–[51].

[51] *Suez/Vivendi* (n. 47) Order in Response to a Petition for Transparency and Participation as Amicus Curiae (19 May 2005) [10] www.italaw.com/sites/default/files/case-documents/ita0815.pdf.

[52] *Biwater Gauff (Tanzania) Ltd.* v. *Tanzania*, ICSID Case No. ARB/05/22.

[53] *Biwater Gauff* (*ibid.*) Petition for Amicus Curiae Status (27 November 2006) 15 www.italaw.com/sites/default/files/case-documents/ita0090.pdf.

> it [fell] to this tribunal to sort out, as necessary, the kinds of difficulties or lacunae that the initial uses of the new Rules might highlight in practice. In this case, the question arises of how to square the issuance of a broad confidentiality order with the exercise of the right of non-parties to apply for status as an amicus curiae in a manner that complies with the letter and spirit of the new Rules that apply to this arbitration.[54]

Although the tribunal allowed the NGOs to submit one joint written submission, access to the documents was denied.[55] The tribunal took the view that the issues that the NGOs were addressing had been widely publicised. If the NGOs were invited to make further submissions, then the access issue was to be revisited. That did not prove necessary.[56]

30. This decision, and that of *Suez/Vivendi* v. *Argentina*,[57] may be of relevance to the exercise of discretion in Article 3 paragraph 3, particularly when associated with a submission by a third person pursuant to Article 4, though not limited to that. The necessity of the publication of the documents relative to the purposes of the person requesting that publication will be a factor for consideration.

5.4 WG's deliberations

31. The simplicity of the principle that lies behind this Article, and indeed these Rules in general, belies the drafting complexity. That complexity exists at two distinct, but inextricably combined, levels. The first is the structure of the Rules themselves. Should this rule be a simple one-line expression of the principle, leaving the task of detail and exceptions to be left to other articles? Or should this article already attempt to deal at some level with those issues? The second is the natural corollary to a decision that the article should deal with detail and exceptions – what are those details and exceptions? The various draft versions of what would become Article 3 reflects the manner in which the WG addressed these questions, and provides insights into how the final version of Article 3 should be understood.

32. The drafting proposals first put by the UNCITRAL Secretariat to the WG (in Vienna at the fifty-fifth session, 3–7 October 2011) bear out

[54] *Ibid.*, 12.

[55] *Biwater Gauff* (n. 52) Procedural Order No. 5 (2 February 2007) [65] www.italaw.com/sites/default/files/case-documents/ita0091_0.pdf.

[56] For a detailed discussion of this case on the issue of publication of documents, see Knahr and Reinisch (n. 13).

[57] See section 1.3.2.3 above.

the two levels of complexity noted above.[58] These proposals had been informed by the earlier 'brainstorming' sessions of the WG.[59] It is also worth noting that at this time it was not certain whether, ultimately, the document would take the form of rules or guidelines.[60]

33. *Option 1, variant 1* was a simple statement of principle and would have left all detail to further articles.[61] *Option 1, variant 2* took a more prescriptive approach by listing the documents that must be made public.[62] The wording 'shall' is an imperative, suggesting that this rule itself contained no exceptions (other than being subject to section 6 – limitations on transparency) or discretion, though that may of course have been introduced by another rule. *Option 2* places complete discretion in the hands of the arbitral tribunal, and, on its face, appears very similar to the position that one would already find in international arbitration rules.[63]

34. In its consideration of these drafting options, the WG made a number of observations. Of *Option 1, variant 1,* it was observed that it

[58] UNCITRAL, 'Settlement of commercial disputes: preparation of a legal standard on transparency in treaty-based investor-State arbitration' (2011) UN Doc. A/CN.9/WG.II/WP.166 [32]–[40]: 'Publication of documents'.

[59] See e.g. UNCITRAL, 'Report of Working Group II (Arbitration and Conciliation) on the work of its fifty-third session' (2010) UN Doc. A/CN.9/712 [40]–[45].

[60] UNCITRAL, 'Settlement of commercial disputes: Preparation of a legal standard on transparency in treaty-based investor-State arbitration: Addendum' (2010) UN Doc. A/CN.9/WG.II/WP.162/Add.1 [43].

[61] *Ibid.* [46]:'Option 1, Variant 1: *"All documents submitted to, or issued by, the arbitral tribunal shall be made publicly available [unless all parties agree otherwise,] subject to section 6 below".*' UN Doc. A/CN.9/717 [77]: 'It was clarified that "section 6" mentioned in the proposals under consideration referred to the possible limitations to transparency to be further defined in the legal standard on transparency. It was also clarified that the bracketed text referring to the right of parties to agree otherwise would be further considered in the light of the decision to be made on whether the disputing parties were free to agree to depart from the legal standard on transparency after the dispute had arisen (see above, paras. 54 and 55) and would therefore not be extensively discussed in the context of each proposal. It was further clarified that the publication of the arbitral award would be dealt with separately (see below, paras. 93 to 100).'

[62] UNCITRAL (n. 60) UN Doc. A/CN.9/WG.II/WP.162/Add.1 [46]: 'Variant 2: *"The following documents shall be made publicly available: the notice of arbitration; pleadings, submissions to the tribunal by a disputing party and any written submissions by the non-disputing party and amicus curiae; minutes or transcripts of hearings of the tribunal, where available; and orders, awards, and decisions of the tribunal [unless the disputing parties otherwise agree,] subject to section 6 below".*'

[63] UNCITRAL (n. 60) UN Doc. A/CN.9/WG.II/WP.162/Add.1 [47]: 'Option 2: *"The arbitral tribunal shall decide, in consultation with the parties, which documents to make publicly available".*'

certainly promoted the idea of full transparency, but against it was a question of the cost and burden that might follow from such an approach, for both the arbitral tribunal and the parties, given the potentially extensive evidentiary record produced in such an arbitral proceeding.[64] *Option 1, variant 2* was felt to be a good approach to the manner in which the rule should be drafted, but it is evident from the record of the discussions that questions of what documents should be included in the list, unsurprisingly, arose. It was noted that the drafting did not contain reference to 'documentary evidence, witness statements, [or] expert witness reports'.[65] The observation was also made that sometimes the most interesting information is not contained in any of the documents that had been listed in the draft and, as such, a mechanism that allowed access to other specific documents might be required in addition to the list of specified documents. Of *Option 2,* it was said that it would allow a case-by-case approach; however, against the option, it was noted that it gave complete discretion to the arbitral tribunal without any guidance.[66]

35. The WG concluded that its discussions of these proposals had given rise to four 'new' approaches,[67] which it then tasked the Secretariat with reflecting in future drafts. These new approaches were: (1) the arbitral tribunal should determine the documents for publication subject to objection by a party; (2) all documents should be published subject to practical limitations, the effect of which could then be overcome by potentially allowing access to specific documents on request; (3) a (limited) list of documents that would always be published should be identified, with the ability of the arbitral tribunal to order publication of other documents; or (4) a list of documents that could be made publicly available for the arbitral tribunal to use on a case-by-case basis should be provided.[68]

36. Although *Option 1, variant 2* specifically includes reference to awards, there had been some feeling within the WG that a simple statement requiring the specific publication of awards was warranted. It was noted that the exception in the proposed statement, which referred to 'unless all parties agreed', meant that all parties would need to agree not to publish, rather than allowing a party to have a right of veto.[69]

37. The WG had determined that the work on transparency should take the form of rules during its February 2011, New York, meeting[70]

[64] UNCITRAL (n. 28) UN Doc. A/CN.9/717 [80]–[82]. [65] *Ibid.* [84]. [66] *Ibid.* [86]. [67] *Ibid.* [87]. [68] *Ibid.* [88]–[91]. [69] *Ibid.* [97]. [70] *Ibid.* [26], [58].

and, as such, the drafting proposals presented by the Secretariat took that format in the subsequent Vienna meeting. The decision of form is a significant one from a drafting perspective. Guidelines would have allowed more scope for a discursive approach and a freedom to elaborate ideas and intentions more clearly. However, what guidelines gain in this respect they lose in weight and likely impact. Reading between the lines of the WG Report it appears that this was quite a contentious issue.[71]

38. The drafting proposals presented to the WG[72] largely correspond to those that had been articulated at the end of the previous meeting – though not necessarily in the same order. *Option 1* was the broad principle, limited only by confidentiality and practical issues. *Option 2* gave discretion to the arbitral tribunal with significant party input. *Option 3* attempted to articulate a position of compromise by including both a list of documents to be automatically published with discretionary provisions regarding other documents. The WG was also asked to consider some practical questions regarding publication – the most central being who should be responsible for the publication, but additionally when publication should occur. The drafting options presented on this issue placed the responsibility with the arbitral tribunal or the respondent respectively. It may be useful to recall that the respondent will always be a State.

39. The WG Report on its work during this session reveals *Options 1* and *2* both appear to have been disposed of fairly quickly.[73] In the process it was observed that *Option 2* was in fact stricter than the Arbitration Rules, in that it gave a party a right of veto, and as such probably would not enhance transparency.

40. Of *Option 3*, it was said that there was strong support.[74] However, it is also evident from the WG Report that that support was quite varied. Some delegations favoured altering paragraph 1 to a general 'publish all' position and eliminating paragraphs 2 and 3. This, it would seem, would have fundamentally changed the nature of the provision back to a position that had previously been dismissed – so one may wonder whether this could really be described as support for *Option 3*.

[71] Note the language in UNCITRAL (n. 28) UN Doc. A/CN.9/717, [26] in particular.
[72] UNCITRAL (n. 58) UN Doc. A/CN.9/WG.II/WP.166.
[73] UNCITRAL, 'Report of Working Group II (Arbitration and Conciliation) on the work of its fifty-fifth session' (2011) UN Doc. A/CN.9/736 [55]–[56].
[74] *Ibid.* [58].

41. What was to become the final version of Article 3 can clearly be seen to be taking shape at the fifty-sixth session (though there were some further changes yet to be made). Consequently this analysis will now also follow the structure of the article.

5.5 Article 3(1): Access to listed documents

42. The draft of Article 3(1) that was put to the WG at the fifty-sixth session now clearly included the principle of automatic production of a significant number of types of documents. This was maintained and can be seen in the final wording of the paragraph:

> Subject to Article 7, the following documents shall be made available to the public: the notice of arbitration, the response to the notice of arbitration, the statement of claim, the statement of defence and any further written statements or written submissions by any disputing party; a table listing all exhibits to the aforesaid documents and to expert reports and witness statements, if such table has been prepared for the proceedings, but not the exhibits themselves; any written submissions by the non-disputing Party(ies) to the treaty and by third persons, transcripts of hearings, where available; and orders, decisions and awards of the arbitral tribunal.

43. This paragraph is expressly stated to be subject to Article 7, which sets out the exceptions to transparency, and is discussed in detail elsewhere in this book.[75]

44. The documents to which this paragraph applies are presented in the order in which they would typically appear in arbitration proceedings. This is a logical and seemingly obvious approach, but it has the consequence of hiding the controversial documents in the middle of the list.

45. It can be inferred from the WG Report that the automatic production of the pleadings and written statements or submissions by the parties was relatively uncontroversial.[76] Similarly relatively uncontroversial were orders, decisions and awards of the arbitral tribunal. From a drafting perspective the inclusion of awards within the remit of Article 3 meant that the then Article 4 was no longer required and so could be removed.[77]

[75] See Thierry P. Augsburger, 'Article 7', [18]–[31].

[76] See UNCITRAL, 'Report of Working Group II (Arbitration and Conciliation) on the work of its fifty-seventh session' (2012) UN Doc. A/CN.9/760 generally.

[77] *Ibid.* [38].

46. There does appear to have been a reasonable level of debate about the exhibits or a list thereof, along with expert reports and witness statements. The concerns about these were motivated by differing reasons. It had been suggested that publication of exhibits may be unduly burdensome, though there seems to have been no concern with the principle that exhibits should be one of the categories of documents to be made available. It was agreed, therefore, that reference to exhibits would be moved from automatic production and instead included in a paragraph that contained a provision for tribunal discretion.[78] This, however, raises a practical difficulty – how would an interested person know of the existence of the exhibit in order to ask for it? To overcome that difficulty, the drafting proposal had suggested that a list of exhibits be automatically published. Some delegations expressed concern about the level of work that would be involved in the production of a list of this kind as well. Others noted that in many instances it is ordinarily produced at the request of the tribunal in any case. The compromise position reached was that if the list existed it should be automatically published, but that there was no obligation on the parties to create the list if none existed.[79]

47. The decision to include transcripts within paragraph 1 had been of some contention in early stages, but it was confirmed and the position clarified to ensure that there was no obligation to have transcripts made in the first instance.[80]

48. In an October 2012 submission to the WG, a number of NGOs presented proposed amendments to paragraph 1.[81] These amendments sought to specifically include the orders and decisions of appointing authorities, as well as separate statements and dissenting opinions. As the final text of the paragraph demonstrates, these proposals were not adopted. Consideration can therefore be given as to whether these documents already fall within this paragraph, another paragraph or are outside the boundaries of Article 3 altogether.

49. It is generally recognised that dissenting opinions or personal statements are permitted in international investment arbitration.[82]

[78] *Ibid.* [15]. [79] *Ibid.* [16]. [80] *Ibid.* [24].

[81] IISD, CIEL and CCSI, 'Submission to Working Group II on International Arbitration, Vienna October 1–5, 2012, Comments on Draft Articles 1, 3, 7 and 8' (2012) www.iisd.org/sites/default/files/pdf/2012/uncitral_submission_working_group_ii_2012.pdf.

[82] Albert Jan van den Berg, 'Dissenting Opinions by Party-Appointed Arbitrators in Investment Arbitration' in Mahnoush Arsanjani et al. (eds.), *Looking to the Future: Essays on International Law in Honor of W. Michael Reisman* (Martinus Nijhoff, 2011) 821.

The vast majority of arbitral institutional rules do not make reference to dissenting or separate statements.[83] The *travaux préparatoires* of the Arbitration Rules indicate that the permissibility of a dissenting opinion is deliberately left to the law applicable at the seat of the arbitration.[84] Assuming a dissent or separate statement is allowed, these would still not technically be part of the award, and thus do not expressly fall under paragraph 1. For example, Article 48(4) of the ICSID Convention states '[a]ny member of the Tribunal may attach his individual opinion to the award, whether he dissents from the majority or not, or a statement of his dissent'.[85] The act of attaching a statement to the award indicates that the statement cannot itself form part of the award in the first instance.

50. In the ordinary course of events, one would nevertheless expect the arbitral tribunal to publish a dissenting opinion or separate statement, where these exist, alongside the award. However, there may be reasons for not doing so, such as where the dissenting opinion discloses confidential aspects of the deliberative process of the award. This would then be a matter for Article 3(3). The question of whether documents detailing or used in the deliberative process are encompassed within this Article are addressed below in the discussion of paragraph 3.[86]

5.6 Article 3(2): Access to expert opinions and witness statements

> Subject to Article 7, expert reports and witness statements, exclusive of the exhibits thereto, shall be made available to the public, upon request by any person to the arbitral tribunal.

51. Like paragraph 1, paragraph 2 is expressly subject to Article 7.

52. It is clear from the WG Report[87] that automatic production of experts' reports and witness statements were considerably difficult issues,

[83] S. Greenberg, C. Kee and J. R. Weeramantry, 'International Commercial Arbitration – An Asia-Pacific Perspective' (Cambridge University Press, 2011) [8.75].

[84] UNCITRAL, Yearbook of the United Nations Commission on International Trade Law (Volume VII, 1976) 178 (Article 27(4) commentary [10]). UNCITRAL, 'Draft convention on the carriage of goods by sea: draft provisions concerning implementation reservations and other final clauses' (1976) UN Doc. A/CN.9/115/Add.1. See also David D. Caron and Lee M. Caplan, *The UNCITRAL Arbitration Rules: A Commentary* (Oxford University Press, 2013) 753.

[85] ICSID Convention, Regulations and Rules (2006) Article 48(4) https://icsid.worldbank.org/ICSID/StaticFiles/basicdoc/CRR_English-final.pdf.

[86] See below [71]–[76].

[87] UNCITRAL (n. 76) UN Doc. A/CN.9/760.

as it is noted that there were delegations who did not favour it, and who specifically requested that their objection be noted in the report.[88]

53. The WG reports do not set out in any detail the motivation of those delegations who wished to have it excluded. The fifty-sixth session report only suggests that the point was made that these documents could have been accessed by the parties or other interested persons pursuant to the other paragraphs and therefore there was no disadvantage in removing them from the ambit of automatic production.[89] Some hints as to the motivation of those delegations who wished to have it excluded may be found in later discussion regarding the protection of witnesses generally and the intellectual property of experts.[90] Those that disagreed with this approach argued that putting these within the discretionary provisions would place an unreasonable burden and workload on the tribunal. The compromise position, which was eventually agreed, still provides for automatic production but only upon request. The drafting presented to the fifty-sixth session did not accommodate that possibility and as such a new paragraph was required. That 'new' paragraph is now paragraph 2 as extracted above.

54. The Rules do not set out what the request described in paragraph 2 should look like, nor give any indication of where it should be sent, other than it must be made to the arbitration tribunal. As a practical matter, the contact details of the arbitrators are usually contained in a document such as the first procedural order, and so any person wanting to make an Article 3(2) request should, in the first instance, look for the appropriate contact details in the documents that will have been automatically published pursuant to paragraph 1. Where an arbitral institution is involved in the administration of the arbitration, correspondence to the arbitral tribunal should be able to be sent care of that institution. At the very least, the institution would be able to advise the correct correspondence address details. Care should be taken, though, not to confuse an appointing authority with an arbitral institution involved in the administration. Frequently, a single institution may be performing both roles, but where an institution or individual is simply and only acting as an appointing authority, that institution would not be an appropriate contact address for the arbitral tribunal.

55. In the absence of any specific requirements, it may be assumed that the request will take the form of a letter to the tribunal. While on the

[88] *Ibid.* [18]. [89] *Ibid.* [25]. [90] *Ibid.* [21].

plain words of Article 3, the mere action of requesting the expert reports and witness statements should trigger the publication, it would seem prudent to set out the *bona fides* of the request in the correspondence. The arbitral tribunal does not have the power to evaluate the merits of the request, but it must necessarily have the power to determine whether something actually amounts to a request in the first instance. If this were not the case, the purpose of making the publication subject to a request would be rendered effectively useless. In this regard it would therefore also seem prudent to make the request with as much specificity as is possible. The more the generic the purported request is, the less credible it will appear.

5.7 Article 3(3): Access to any other document

> Subject to Article 7, the arbitral tribunal may decide, on its own initiative or upon request from any person, and after consultation with the disputing parties, whether and how to make available exhibits and any other documents provided to, or issued by, the arbitral tribunal not falling within paragraphs 1 or 2 above. This may include, for example, making such documents available at a specified site.

56. Paragraph 3, like the two before it, is subject to Article 7; however, unlike paragraphs 1 and 2, it grants a discretion to the arbitral tribunal. The drafting history of paragraph 3 is interesting, as the perspective of the paragraph was changed quite significantly at a reasonably late stage. It can be of particular importance to bear this in mind when considering other contemporaneous publications and submissions. For example, the 'Submission to Working Group II on International Arbitration, Vienna October 1–5, 2012, Comments on Draft Articles 1, 3, 7 and 8 by CIEL, IISD, Vale' considers an older structure of Article 3.[91]

57. At its fifty-sixth session, the WG identified what might be called an inconsistency in approach with regard to the manner in which the then draft paragraphs 2 and 3 had been drafted.[92] Both referred to 'any other

[91] That proposal suggested deleting paragraph 3 and combining it with paragraph 2. The two paragraphs the proposal is addressing are reproduced in the next footnote. The merging in fact happened; however, this combined paragraph ultimately ended up being numbered paragraph 3, as a new paragraph 2 was created.

[92] UNCITRAL, 'Settlement of commercial disputes: preparation of a legal standard on transparency in treaty-based investor-State arbitration' (2011) UN Doc. A/CN.9/WG.II/WP.169 [29]:

document' and instead distinguished between the parties or persons requesting a document. In other words, the point of differentiation was who was making the request rather than the type of document. The WG looked back to its own original motivation for this drafting, and observed that it was motivated by reasons of the practicalities of publication rather than a desire to distinguish between persons. The view was that some documents did not lend themselves easily to publication, but rather to access,[93] and that this had been the original intent. The drafting as it had been presented to the WG did not clearly reveal this intention, and the WG noted that it would seem difficult to conceive of a situation where a tribunal would refuse access to one person but grant it to another.[94]

58. The proposed way around this was to combine draft paragraphs 2 and 3. The proposal included giving the arbitral tribunal the right to act on its own initiative or in response to a request. There appears to have been some disquiet about allowing the tribunal to act on its own initiative but it was eventually agreed.[95]

5.7.1 The arbitral tribunal may decide

59. As noted above, this paragraph grants the tribunal the discretion, after consulting with the parties, whether and how to make available the documents in question. The question of what is a document is addressed below.[96] The exercise of the tribunal's discretion is in the first instance informed by Article 1 paragraph 4 of the Rules, which states:

Discretion and authority of the arbitral tribunal

> 4. Where the Rules on Transparency provide for the arbitral tribunal to exercise discretion, the arbitral tribunal in exercising such discretion shall take into account:
> (a) the public interest in transparency in treaty-based investor-State arbitration and in the particular arbitral proceedings; and
> (b) the disputing parties' interest in a fair and efficient resolution of their dispute.

60. However, in circumstances where the Arbitration Rules (2010) apply, Article 17(1) of those rules is also applicable.

[93] UNCITRAL (n. 76) UN Doc. A/CN.9/760 [27]. [94] *Ibid.* [26]. [95] *Ibid.* [29]–[30].
[96] See below [65]–[70].

Article 17

1. Subject to these Rules, the arbitral tribunal may conduct the arbitration in such manner as it considers appropriate, provided that the parties are treated with equality and that at an appropriate stage of the proceedings each party is given a reasonable opportunity of presenting its case. The arbitral tribunal, in exercising its discretion, shall conduct the proceedings so as to avoid unnecessary delay and expense and to provide a fair and efficient process for resolving the parties' dispute.

61. The wording of the two articles in the two sets of rules is similar, but not identical. Article 1(7) explains that the Rules are intended to supplement the Arbitration Rules, except where there is conflict, in which case the Rules prevail. Although different, Article 17(1) of the Arbitration Rules (2010) does not conflict with Article 1(4) of the Rules. Therefore the additional obligations found in Article 17(1) upon arbitrators to conduct the proceedings so as to avoid unnecessary delay and expense for the parties remains applicable to the arbitral tribunal. There is nevertheless a potential tension between this obligation and the transparency principles. Cost-effective procedures may, for example, involve strictly controlling document production requests, limiting the length of witness statements, and/or 'hot tubbing' expert witnesses.[97] This might be seen to restrict transparency. If used properly none of these procedures will in fact impact on transparency. The purpose behind many of the processes employed by a tribunal is to ensure that the dispute is focused, and does not become a fishing exercise.[98] The Rules should similarly not be allowed to be abused.

62. Requiring exhibits and any other documents provided to, or issued by, the arbitral tribunal not falling within paragraph 1 or 2 above to be made available will involve cost. Article 3 paragraph 5 addresses the issue of cost.

5.7.2 Upon request from any person

63. No form requirement has been stipulated for the request required to activate the discretion. Similar to the observations made in connection

[97] Croft, Kee and Waincymer (n. 2) [17.9].

[98] Addressing this issue under the notion of 'procedural integrity', see Knahr and Reinisch (n. 13) 100–6.

with paragraph 2, the request should demonstrate the *bona fides* of the person making the request. However, differently to paragraph 2, consideration should be given to the requirement upon the tribunal to consult with the disputing parties. This requirement will almost certainly mean that the parties are given the opportunity to comment on the request, and it would therefore be prudent to bear this in mind when the request was being drafted. A further difference that should be considered is that there may be cost implications to the production and it would therefore be similarly prudent to address this issue in the request.[99]

5.7.3 After consultation with the disputing parties

64. The arbitral tribunal is required by the wording of paragraph 3 to exercise its discretion only after consultation with the disputing parties. The expression 'consultation with the disputing parties' is used in a number of instances throughout the Rules.[100] It is similarly found in Article 29(1) of the Arbitration Rules (2010). What amounts to consultation is not clearly expressed in either set of rules.[101] It can, however, clearly be inferred that while the tribunal should take the views of the parties, it is under no obligation to defer to any of those views.[102] To be in a position to consult with the arbitral tribunal, it can be expected that the parties would be given the request that had been sent to the tribunal.

5.7.4 What is a document?

65. Paragraph 3, like the Article as a whole, refers specifically to 'documents'. The documents in paragraphs 1 and 2 are clearly defined. The question that may then arise is: what is a document in the context of paragraph 3?

66. The definition of documents proposed by the claimant in *Railroad Development Corporation* v. *Guatemala* was quite broad:

[99] See below [82]–[85].

[100] See e.g. Article 4(1) of the Rules. Mariel Dimsey, 'Article 4', [86]–[89].

[101] See Caron and Caplan (n. 84) 49, for a discussion of the consultation requirement in Article 17(2) of the 2010 UNCITRAL Arbitration Rules.

[102] Jeff Waincymer, *Procedure and Evidence in International Arbitration* (Kluwer Law International, 2012) 385 (discussing the phrase in the context of ICC Rules Article 18 (2)).

> 'Documents' means each and every form of communication and each and every written, recorded or graphic matter of any kind, type, nature, or description that is or has been in the Republic of Guatemala's possession, custody, or control, including, but not limited to, all printed and electronic copies of emails, notes, correspondence, memoranda, work papers, calendars, registries of entrance to public or private offices/buildings, tapes, stenographic or handwritten notes, written forms of any kind, charts, blueprints, drawings, sketches, graphs, plans, articles, specifications, diaries, letters, telegrams, photographs, minutes, contracts, agreements, reports, surveys, computer printouts, data compilations of any kind, teletypes, telexes, facsimiles, invoices, order forms, checks, drafts, statements, credit memos, reports, summaries, books, ledgers, notebooks, schedules, transparencies, recordings, catalogs, advertisements, promotional materials, films, video tapes, audio tapes, brochures, pamphlets, spreadsheets, or any written or recorded materials of any other kind, however stored (whether in tangible or electronic form), recorded, produced, or reproduced, and also including, but not limited to, drafts or copies of any of the foregoing that contain any notes, comments, or markings of any kind not found on the original documents or that are otherwise not identical to the original documents.[103]

67. The request to which this definition is related was one in which the claimant was seeking an interim measure of protection from the tribunal to protect evidence. It may be argued that its context is therefore somewhat different to the present discussion, but it is a useful starting point. It is evident that the definition above is not limited to what might be described as the stock standard traditional understanding of the word 'document', i.e. a tangible piece of paper on which information has been written or drawn.

68. The definition of 'documents' found in the 2010 IBA Rules on the Taking of Evidence is narrower, but still goes beyond a tangible piece of paper:

> 'Document' means a writing, communication, picture, drawing, program or data of any kind, whether recorded or maintained on paper or by electronic, audio, visual or any other means.

69. There is very little in the *travaux préparatoires* that provides guidance on whether electronic documents were intended to be included within

[103] *Railroad Development Corporation* v. *Guatemala*, Decision on Provisional Measures, ICSID Case No. ARB/07/23 (15 October 2008) 6, and footnoted as 'Exhibit C-1 to the Request'.

the scope of this sub-article. Textual arguments – both quite weak – can be made for either conclusion. On the one hand, paragraphs 1 and 2 refer to traditionally tangible documents; on the other hand, the Secretariat proposes in the *travaux préparatoires* that the WG may wish to consider whether emails are captured within the phrase 'written statements or written submissions' – arguably demonstrating an understanding that these were to be captured by the article in some way.[104]

70. While it seems likely that the term documents should be read broadly to include those in the electronic domain – or at least not to exclude the possibility – there have been numerous commentaries about the difficulties that electronic documents pose from the discovery perspective.[105]

5.7.5 *What documents are included?*

71. Even assuming the widest possible definition of documents, the next question to be considered is what types of documents have not already been covered by paragraphs 1 and 2. One set of documents that might immediately spring to mind for consideration are those comprising or reflecting the tribunal's deliberations. Examples of these documents would include draft awards or orders exchanged among the members of the tribunal; emails or other correspondence regarding those draft awards or orders shared between the tribunal; or notes taken by the secretary of the tribunal for use by the tribunal. Correspondence and notes exchanged between an arbitral institution and the tribunal where the applicable arbitral rules include a scrutiny of the award procedure[106] should be similarly encompassed into this set of 'deliberation documents'.

72. The *travaux préparatoires* do not offer any guidance on whether the tribunal's deliberations were to be encompassed by paragraph 3. In the absence of any such clear direction, it seems almost certain that

[104] UNCITRAL, 'Settlement of commercial disputes: preparation of a legal standard on transparency in treaty-based investor-State arbitration: Note by the Secretariat regarding the establishment of a repository of published information ('registry')' (2012) UN Doc. A/CN.9/WG.II/WP.177 [22].

[105] See, for general discussion, Gary B. Born, 'Chapter 16: Disclosure in International Arbitration' in *International Commercial Arbitration* (2nd edn., Kluwer Law International, 2014) 2368–73, noting in particular the references listed in footnote 245.

[106] See e.g. ICC Rules, Article 33.

deliberations were not intended to be within the scope, and indeed convincing arguments can be made as to why they should not be.

73. The first argument against the inclusion of the 'deliberation documents' is a textual one. On the plain words of the paragraph, deliberation documents are not encompassed because they are not '*documents provided to, or issued by, the arbitral tribunal*'. They are generated by the tribunal, hence not provided to; and they are retained confidentially by the tribunal, hence not issued by. The second argument against the inclusion is that it is a 'cardinal principle' of deliberations that they be kept confidential and are not communicated to the parties.[107] The integrity of the arbitral process requires this confidentiality. If deliberation documents were to be made public during the course of the proceedings, there would be a significant risk of prejudice. Publication after the award, would, in one sense, defeat the purpose of reasoning in an award, which is to provide insight into how the tribunal reached its decision.

74. There are of course limits to the obligation to keep the deliberations confidential, especially after the arbitration has concluded. This position is also reflected in Rule 9 of the IBA's Rules of Ethics for International Arbitrators, which states:

> The deliberations of the arbitral tribunal, and the contents of the award itself, remain confidential in perpetuity unless the parties release the arbitrators from this obligation. An arbitrator should not participate in, or give any information for the purpose of assistance in, any proceedings to consider the award unless, exceptionally, he considers it his duty to disclose any material misconduct or fraud on the part of his fellow arbitrators.

75. The third argument is that international investment arbitration already has an instrument that has expressly made a statement on how

[107] Greenberg, Kee and Weeramantry (n. 83) [8.6]. See also Gary B. Born, *International Commercial Arbitration* (2nd edn., Kluwer Law International, 2014) § 20.06. See also e.g. Supreme Court decision of 29 January 2010, LJN BK 2007, discussed by E. Meerdink and N. Dekker, 'Supreme Court Rules Arbitral Tribunal Not Required to Disclose Hearing Notes', (2010) 15(1) *IBA Arbitration News* 131; and see A. Redfern, 'The 2003 Freshfields Lecture: Dissenting Opinions in International Commercial Arbitration: The Good, the Bad and the Ugly' (2004) 20(3) *Arbitration International* 229. See as further examples *Noble China Inc* v. *Lei Kat Chong* [1998] CanLII 14708 (Ontario Supreme Court) (4 November 1998); *Jung Science Information Technology Co Ltd* v. *ZTE Corporation* [2008] HKCU 1127 (22 July 2008) (Hong Kong High Court, Court of First Instance).

deliberations are to be treated. Even where Rule 15 of the ICSID Arbitration Rules is not directly applicable, it can be considered persuasive practice. ICSID Rule 15 states:

Deliberations of the Tribunal

(1) The deliberations of the Tribunal shall take place in private and remain secret.
(2) Only members of the Tribunal shall take part in its deliberations. No other person shall be admitted unless the Tribunal decides otherwise.

76. One might argue that there is an element of folly in relying on the ICSID Arbitration Rules in this way, given that the Rules are newer and provide greater transparency. However, while appreciable, that argument on this specific point can be distinguished and defended. As noted above, and demonstrated in many of the arbitral decisions already discussed, the ICSID Arbitration Rules do not contain a requirement of confidentiality on the part of the parties. Rule 15 is, however, a very clear statement of a confidentiality obligation on the part of the arbitrators. The requirement that the deliberations remain secret goes beyond the requirement of privacy – a point made in the text of the rule itself.

5.7.6 Documents available at a specified site

77. The documents made available pursuant to paragraph 3 need not be published or sent to the Repository. There is very little comment on this sentence in the *travaux préparatoires*. These reveal '[t]he last sentence of paragraph (3) is meant to provide guidance to the arbitral tribunal as to alternative measures for making such documents public at a certain location'.[108]

78. It is evident from a holistic consideration of the drafting history, that this sentence is not intended to promote the idea that arbitral tribunals should establish their own websites or use other forms of media. Wherever and whenever possible, documents should be published through the repository. The sentence refers only to documents published pursuant to paragraph 3. The permission to make this limited class of

[108] UNCITRAL, 'Settlement of commercial disputes: preparation of a legal standard on transparency in treaty-based investor-State arbitration' (2012) UN Doc. A/CN.9/WG.II/WP.176 [32].

documents available at a site other than the repository is recognition of the practical reality that it may be particularly costly, time consuming and simply difficult to provide the documents to the repository. The need for this can be seen in the WG's discussion when it decided to merge what were then paragraphs 2 and 3. The report notes 'the Working Group considered that there were some categories of documents or information which would not lend themselves to publication, such that a right of access, rather than publication *per se*, would be more appropriate'.[109]

5.8 Article 3(4): Timing arrangements and the repository

> 4. The documents to be made available to the public pursuant to paragraphs 1 and 2 shall be communicated by the arbitral tribunal to the repository referred to under Article 8 as soon as possible, subject to any relevant arrangements or time limits for the protection of confidential or protected information prescribed under Article 7. The documents to be made available pursuant to paragraph 3 may be communicated by the arbitral tribunal to the repository referred to under Article 8 as they become available and, if applicable, in a redacted form in accordance with Article 7. The repository shall make all documents available in a timely manner, in the form and in the language in which it receives them.

5.8.1 'To be made available . . . pursuant to paragraphs 1 and 2 shall be'

79. Article 3(4) imposes an obligation on the arbitral tribunal to provide all documents that are to be made available pursuant to paragraphs 1 and 2 to the repository. The tribunal must do this as soon as possible. However, that timing obligation is tempered by any actions needed to protect confidential or protected information pursuant to Article 7.[110] Although the paragraph itself handles paragraphs 1 and 2 jointly, it would appear potentially advantageous for arbitral tribunals to address them separately. The tribunal could direct that redacted versions of the documents listed within paragraph 1 should be prepared and submitted simultaneously with the version to be used by the tribunal itself. This approach may not be as appropriate to documents to be

[109] UNCITRAL (n. 76) UN Doc. A/CN.9/760 [27].

[110] See the discussion of Article 7, Thierry P. Augsburger, 'Article 7', [149]–[176].

published pursuant to paragraph 2, as it is not a *fait accompli* that those documents will be published.

5.8.2 *'To be made available pursuant to paragraph 3 may be'*

80. There is not, by the strict wording, an obligation on the tribunal to communicate to the repository the documents made available pursuant to paragraph 3. The use of the word 'may' as opposed to the 'shall' seen earlier in the paragraph is a necessary and logical consequence of the last sentence of paragraph 3 itself. As noted above, that sentence allows publication of documents at a site other than the repository.[111] It would be contrary to the spirit of the Rules to interpret this sentence as providing the arbitral tribunal any real discretion. For example, this paragraph and paragraph 3 should not be interpreted as allowing a tribunal to set up its own website and choosing to publish paragraph 3 documentation there. Documents made available pursuant to paragraph 3 should, to the greatest extent possible, be made available through the repository.

5.8.3 *The repository, form and language*

81. The final sentence of paragraph 4 obliges the repository to make all documents available in a timely manner. The repository does this in the form and language in which the documents are received. It is clear from this sentence that the repository has no responsibility to prepare the documents for presentation in any particular fashion. This is, however, perhaps not as advantageous for the repository as it may first seem. The Rules themselves do not provide the repository with the ability to require documents communicated to it to be in a particular form, the implication being that the repository must either make the documents available in the form in which they have arrived or, should it wish to make them available in a different way, the efforts of doing so fall upon the repository itself. In light of the obligations on both the repository and the arbitral tribunal to facilitate the publication as promptly as possible, it would be advisable for the arbitral tribunal to obtain early guidance from the repository as to the best form to be used. The arbitral tribunal can then take this into account when directing the parties such that the

[111] See above [77f].

arbitral tribunal receives the documents in the most appropriate fashion from the very beginning.

5.9 Article 3(5): Costs

> 5. A person granted access to documents under paragraph 3 shall bear any administrative costs of making those documents available to that person, such as the costs of photocopying or shipping documents to that person, but not the costs of making those documents available to the public through the repository.

82. There will naturally be a variety of costs associated with the access and/or publication of documents. It was considered as going against the principle of transparency if these costs were to be borne by the persons to whom publication was being made – and even if that was not felt to be the case, it would seem unreasonable that the first person requesting the documents bear all the costs.[112] The position that was ultimately adopted by the WG was that the parties should be responsible for the costs of preparing the documents for publication, but that the person requesting them pay any incidental administrative costs such as photocopying and postage.

83. Consistent with this position, paragraph 5 therefore only addresses document publication or access that arises pursuant to Article 3(3) at sites other than the repository.

84. As noted above, the arbitral tribunal has an obligation to the parties to avoid unnecessary expense.[113] Pursuant to Article 3(3), the arbitral tribunal will need to decide how documents are made available. When making this decision, the tribunal will almost certainly have options that, on the one hand, keep the parties' expenses to a minimum but increase the likely administrative costs, versus options that are more costly to the parties in the first instance but reduce the likely administrative expense. In the absence of factors such as an applicable law, the arbitral tribunal's primary duty is to the parties and thus, notwithstanding the underlying principle regarding the allocation of costs, the tribunal's decision about the way documents are to be made available should not be influenced by considerations of the costs of anyone other than the party required to make the publication.

[112] UNCITRAL (n. 76) UN Doc. A/CN.9/760 [130].

[113] See above [17].

5.10 Evaluation

85. The penultimate draft of Article 3 was presented to the WG at its New York 2013 session. With the vast majority of the principles in the Article having already been agreed, the WG appears to have concentrated on clarity of drafting issues, save for one important issue that had been raised at the fifty-sixth session but does not appear to have been fully ventilated then.[114] That issue concerned what was to happen once the tribunal had completed its mandate and become *functus officio*. If an interested person wished for access to or publication of a document pursuant to paragraph 2 or 3, to whom, if anyone, would such a request be directed? This issue was not limited, however, to access and publication; it pertained also to the determination of confidentiality requests and redactions.

86. The WG report indicates that a clear decision of principle on this matter was taken:[115]

> 91. The Working Group considered how the registry would deal with requests for documents after the arbitral tribunal has discharged its function and its mandate terminated. It was clarified that requests for documents would have to be made before the arbitration terminated, as in any case, documents published by the registry could only be communicated to the registry by the arbitral tribunal. It was suggested that disputing parties should be encouraged to work out an arrangement to deal with requests for documents after the arbitral tribunal had discharged its functions.

87. This is a simple and straightforward position for the Rules to adopt, but it does seem to sidestep an issue on which one might have expected to find more proscriptive direction from the Rules. Purely as a matter of speculation, one may wonder about the extent to which the stage of the process at which this issue was finally raised led to the solution that was ultimately adopted. While it is not unreasonable that the Rules do not address these questions, it is nevertheless in the interest of parties and arbitral tribunals to turn their minds to them in advance.

88. Paragraph 4 states that the documents for publication are to be communicated to the repository by the arbitral tribunal. Paragraphs 1 and 2 are subject to Article 7, which involves the tribunal taking steps to

[114] UNCITRAL (n. 76) UN Doc. [29].

[115] UNCITRAL, 'Report of Working Group II (Arbitration and Conciliation) on the work of its fifty-eighth session' (2013) UN Doc. A/CN.9/765 [91].

protect confidential information. The entire Article therefore depends on the existence of the arbitral tribunal. This observation must also extend to the very nature of the transparency obligation contained in the Article itself.

89. The timing of when documents are disclosed, combined with the nature or manner in which that publication is made, is likely to be of real practical importance to State parties. The notice of arbitration, and the response to the notice of arbitration, are both likely to exist prior to the arbitral tribunal being composed. The statement of claim, and the statement of defence may also have been exchanged, though this seems less likely. The repository referred to in Article 8 already exists within UNCITRAL. However, even if the investor party were to simply send the notice of arbitration to the repository, the repository is under no obligation to publish it, nor should it publish it.[116] Equally, there is nothing in Article 3 that suggests in the absence of a tribunal, that the State party should be obliged to publish the notice of arbitration or any other document.

90. There is, of course, nothing preventing an investor party from publishing its own notice of arbitration. However, this must be clearly and carefully set against the popular legitimacy that may be gained from publication by the repository. Once details of a claim are published by the repository – or by the State party – the claim is likely to gain a certain level of popular legitimacy. In this particular respect State parties potentially face real risks from spurious claims and vexatious litigants. An apparently legitimate claim (as in the sense of genuine and not spurious) could prompt an untold number of responses from financial markets. Investment arbitration is sometimes criticised for the value of the awards that have been delivered, and the spectre of a very large claim against a financially vulnerable country may simply compound that country's difficulties. The country's credit rating may be adversely affected, as may the interest rate at which it can borrow money. The tribunal, therefore, notwithstanding the mandatory language of Article 3, stands as an important check and balance.

[116] Article 2 on a plain reading could impose on the repository a duty to publish the Notice of Arbitration if a record of its transmission to the respondent is also provided to it. This would, however, require the repository to determine the legitimacy of the record of transmission – both for its completeness (i.e. does it actually show the full path of transmission from dispatch to receipt?) and its accuracy (i.e. does it actually show that the receipt was at the right destination?). This sits uneasily with the intended role of the repository. See further Giuseppe Bianco's comments on Article 2 of the Rules, Giuseppe Bianco, 'Article 2', [4]–[12], [16]–[18] and see also Kathleen Claussen, 'Article 8', [6]–[13].

91. Similarly, once the tribunal has executed its duty, the question of publication of documents reverts to the parties. It is quite likely that a confidentiality order will have been issued during the proceedings and the effect of this order may last well past the end of the hearings. Any order may, and probably would, state a procedure to be followed should either party following the conclusion of the arbitration intend the disclosure or publication of documents.

92. However, the UNCITRAL Secretariat had invited the WG to consider what should happen in the period of time just before the arbitration concludes:[117]

> 21. The Working Group may wish to consider how the registry would deal with requests for documents after the arbitral tribunal has discharged its function and its mandate is terminated. Issues arising from a post-proceeding request include but are not limited to access to documents, decisions regarding redactions, and determination of confidentiality under draft Article 7.
>
> . . .
>
> **Draft Article 3(2)**
>
> 23. Under draft Article 3(2), expert reports and witness statements are provided to the registry by the tribunal and published, upon request, and are not subject to a discretionary decision regarding their publication by the arbitral tribunal (unlike the documents in draft Article 3(3)). This provision thus raises the following questions:
>
> . . .
>
> (b) Because such documents may require redaction, which redaction may be contentious and subject to a final determination by a tribunal, what would happen if the tribunal is still acting but the request is made, for example, at a late stage in proceedings (such as just before the rendering of a final award) where the parties or tribunal are unable to spend time redacting, in the case of the former, or to make a determination regarding redactions, in the case of the latter?
>
> (c) In light of the above, is the intention that the parties be required to provide expert reports and witness statements to the tribunal (and consequently the tribunal to the registry) in redacted form, in order that they are available upon request pursuant to draft Article 3(2), such that the parties and tribunal bear the cost of publicizing these documents even if these documents might never be requested or publicized?

[117] UNCITRAL (n. 104) UN Doc. A/CN.9/WG.II/WP.177 [21]–[24]: ‘Draft article 3’.

93. The *travaux préparatoires* do not suggest that these questions were actually considered by the WG, and as such offer no particular answers. The solution, it seems, is simply to promote an awareness of these potential issues to individual tribunals. While it may be unlikely, an intriguing and conceivable scenario can be imagined. A tribunal is usually considered to be *functus officio* after delivering the final award.[118] These rules must extend the mandate of the tribunal at least until the tribunal has sent the award to the repository for publication. If a tribunal were to deliver a final award and then pass it to the repository for publication prior to the expiration of the period for interpretations (Article 37 of the Arbitration Rules (2010)), omissions (Article 38 of the Arbitration Rules (2010)) or an additional award (Article 39 of the Arbitration Rules (2010)), and one of the parties were to seek redress under one of those articles, the tribunal could in theory be revived for this purpose and remain competent for nearly ninety days after the publication of the award. The award might indicate or reveal the existence of documents that did not fall under paragraph 1 or 2. An interested third person might then seek access to those documents under paragraph 3. On the one hand, the tribunal is in existence and so could hear and consider such a request. On the other, the functions under those particular rules are exceptional additions to the tribunal's mandate, and it could be argued therefore that the tribunal now only exists for that purpose and none other.

5.11 Conclusion

94. Although trite, it is nevertheless true to say that the effectiveness of Article 3 can only be judged in its actual operation and that is yet to be seen. It is first and foremost a process article. As such, the effectiveness of the article will be measured by the extent to which it does not impact negatively on the running of the arbitration. Ideally the article aids maximum transparency with minimal disruption. The drafters of the Rules faced a number of choices about the approaches that could have been adopted to achieve this aim. While this assessment is necessarily taken in the abstract, the approach taken does appear to reflect a well-considered balance.

[118] Julian D. M. Lew, Loukas A. Mistelis and Stefan Kröll, *Comparative International Commercial Arbitration* (Kluwer Law International, 2003) [24]–[26].

6

Article 4. Submission by a third person

MARIEL DIMSEY*

1. After consultation with the disputing parties, the arbitral tribunal may allow a person that is not a disputing party, and not a non-disputing Party to the treaty, ("third person(s)") to file a written submission with the arbitral tribunal regarding a matter within the scope of the dispute.
2. A third person wishing to make a submission shall apply to the arbitral tribunal, and shall, in a concise written statement, which is in a language of the arbitration and complies with any page limits set by the arbitral tribunal:
   (a) describe the third person, including, where relevant, its membership and legal status (e.g., trade association or other non-governmental organization), its general objectives, the nature of its activities, and any parent organization (including any organization that directly or indirectly controls the third person);
   (b) disclose any connection, direct or indirect, which the third person has with any disputing party;
   (c) provide information on any government, person or organization that has provided to the third person (i) any financial or other assistance in preparing the submission; or (ii) substantial assistance in either of the two years preceding the application by the third person under this article (e.g. funding around 20 per cent of its overall operations annually);
   (d) describe the nature of the interest that the third person has in the arbitration; and
   (e) identify the specific issues of fact or law in the arbitration that the third person wishes to address in its written submission.
3. In determining whether to allow such a submission, the arbitral tribunal shall take into consideration, among other factors it determines to be relevant:

* Mariel Dimsey, Dr iur (University of Basel), LLM (University of Cologne) is an associate based in the Cologne office of Cleary Gottlieb Steen & Hamilton LLP. Dr Dimsey is an Australian lawyer and specialises in international arbitration matters. The author would like to thank Giancarlo Capurro, Melanie Kaspers and Martin Köppen for their help in preparing this article. All opinions expressed herein are the author's own and she bears sole responsibility for the content of this contribution.

(a) whether the third person has a significant interest in the arbitral proceedings; and
(b) the extent to which the submission would assist the arbitral tribunal in the determination of a factual or legal issue related to the arbitral proceedings by bringing a perspective, particular knowledge or insight that is different from that of the disputing parties.

4. The submission filed by the third person shall:
(a) be dated and signed by the person filing the submission on behalf of the third person;
(b) be concise, and in no case longer than as authorized by the arbitral tribunal;
(c) set out a precise statement of the third person's position on issues; and
(d) only address matters within the scope of the dispute.
5. The arbitral tribunal shall ensure that any submission does not disrupt or unduly burden the arbitral proceedings, or unfairly prejudice any disputing party.
6. The arbitral tribunal shall ensure that the disputing parties are given a reasonable opportunity to present their observations on any submission by the third person.

6.1 Introduction

1. No modern rules of investor-State arbitration procedure would be complete without the possibility of allowing submissions by third persons. Indeed, it is the concerns surrounding the (lack of) transparency in investment arbitration that prompted the development by UNCITRAL, through UNCITRAL Working Group II (Arbitration and Conciliation) (WG), of the Rules.[1] Central to making investor-State arbitral proceedings more transparent is the role of *amici curiae*, or 'friends of the court'.[2]

2. The concept of *amicus curiae* allows third party participation by means of offering assistance to the court under certain circumstances. The underlying rationale for allowing such submissions is to provide the

[1] UNCITRAL 'Report of Working Group II (Arbitration and Conciliation) on the work of its fifty-third session' (20 October 2010) UN Doc. A/CN.9/712 [1].

[2] See generally Brigitte Stern, 'Civil Society's Voice in the Settlement of International Economic Disputes' (2007) *ICSID Review – Foreign Investment Law Journal* 280; Lucas Bastin, 'The Amicus Curiae in Investor-State Arbitration' (2012) 1(3) *Cambridge Journal of International and Comparative Law* 208; Eugenia Levine, 'Amicus Curiae in International Investment Arbitration: The Implications of an Increase in Third-Party Participation' (2011) 29(1) *Berkeley Journal of International Law* 200; Mariel Dimsey, 'Foreign Direct Investment and the Alleviation of Poverty' in Krista Nadakavukaren Schefer (ed.), *Poverty and the International Economic Legal System: Duties to the World's Poor* (Cambridge University Press, 2013) 167–8.

decision-making body with additional information falling outside its expertise or which would otherwise not have been adequately considered.[3]

3. *Amicus* briefs as a legal instrument for non-disputing party intervention are frequently found in common law jurisdictions. The concept was presumably first employed by common law courts as a means of compensating for the adversarial procedures that did not allow independent fact-gathering by the court.[4] Civil law jurisdictions with inquisitorial court structures and more extensive options for third party intervention generally have traditionally been more reluctant to allow *amici curiae*.[5] Depending on which procedural 'style' is followed in investor-State disputes, these historical motives can still be relevant.[6]

4. Before international panels, *amicus* briefs have developed to become widely accepted and used instruments. Over the past decade, tribunals constituted under the North American Free Trade Agreement (NAFTA), bilateral investment treaties (BITs) and Free Trade Agreements (FTAs) have received numerous requests from non-governmental organisations (NGOs), industry bodies, other groups, and individuals seeking participation in investor-State arbitral proceedings. The content of such requests has differed, but generally petitioners have sought leave to file written submissions, access case documents, and both passively and actively participate in oral hearings.[7] Third person participation is a concept largely confined to disputes involving matters of a greater public interest, which frequently arise in the context of investor-State arbitral proceedings on the basis of the types of projects that are covered by BIT and other treaty protections, because third persons often represent such public interests.

5. What started as a rather ambitious attempt to represent public interests in an environment of hostility towards and suspicion of non-disputing parties has progressed to a more liberal attitude towards third person participation in investment arbitral proceedings. In recent years,

[3] See Levine (n. 2) 8.

[4] Samuel Krislov, 'The Amicus Curiae Brief: From Friendship to Advocacy' (1962–63) 72(4) *Yale Law Journal* 694, 696.

[5] Samuel Krislov, 'Amici Curiae in Civil Law Jurisdictions' (2012–2013) 122 *Yale Law Journal* 1653.

[6] Cf. *Suez, Sociedad General de Aguas de Barcelona S.A. and InterAguas Servicios Integrales del Agua S.A.* v. *Argentina*, ICSID Case No. ARB/03/17, Order in Response to a Petition for Participation as Amicus Curiae (17 March 2006) www.italaw.com/sites/default/files/case-documents/ita0803.pdf [13]. Cf. UNCITRAL (n. 1) [50].

[7] See generally Bastin (n. 2) 212.

investment arbitral tribunals have shown increasing willingness to provide third parties with a limited mandate to participate as *amici curiae* in investment disputes.[8] Indeed, the Rules have been signed off in an environment of momentum and diversification concerning both the number and types of third parties seeking participation in investor-State arbitral proceedings.

6. The increase in third party attempts to participate raises challenging questions concerning the scope of interests that such third parties represent, the advantages and disadvantages of their involvement in proceedings and, in the context of their ultimate utility, the extent to which regard is had to such submissions in a tribunal's evaluation of the case. Article 4 of the Rules represents the most recent step in a long, slowly developing trend of increased acceptance of third person participation in investor-State arbitral proceedings.

7. NAFTA paved the way for the role of third persons as early as 2003 when, in the wake of the *Methanex* v. *USA*[9] and *UPS* v. *Canada*[10] statements, the NAFTA Free Trade Commission (FTC) issued a statement on non-disputing party participation setting out a detailed procedure by which non-disputing party submissions could be made to an investment arbitral tribunal (NAFTA FTC Statement). This breakthrough development at NAFTA was followed, in 2006, by the amendments to the International Centre for the Settlement of Disputes (ICSID) Rules, which now provide in Rule 37(2) for third party submissions to an investment arbitral tribunal.

8. These initiatives have been corroborated by new provisions in various FTAs and BITs, together with the development of investment treaty jurisprudence in the area. As such, Article 4 of the Rules constitutes a consolidation of the developments in this area and set up best practice rules for addressing this issue.

6.2 Background and purpose

9. Third person submissions are not a new beast in the context of investor-State arbitration. Investment arbitration often, indeed almost always, affects issues of public interest, and representatives of third party interests have now sought participation in the investor-State arbitral process for just over a decade. Indeed, discussion of the 'public' nature

[8] See Levine (n. 2). [9] See discussion below in section 6.5.2.
[10] See discussion below in section 6.5.3.

of investor-State arbitration and the need for public accountability in cases involving the public interest is long-standing and ongoing, and has resulted in several initiatives at a bilateral and regional level. With these Rules, the issue has finally reached the UNCITRAL realm.

10. In the fifty-third session of the WG, the first session devoted to expounding rules on transparency, there was widespread support among the delegation for allowing third person submissions in investor-State arbitral proceedings. At the outset, the WG stated that the purpose of including rules on third person submissions was their usefulness to the arbitral tribunal and the promotion of legitimacy of the arbitral process.[11]

11. Indeed, 'legitimacy' is the reason perhaps most often cited in the context of proclaiming a need for transparency in investment arbitration. In the words of Professor Stern:

> the participation of the *amici curiae* in investor-State arbitration is ... consistent with the changing nature of investor-State arbitrations and the complex issues of public policies that tribunals are increasingly being called upon to address ... [T]his system, which was traditionally based on private legitimacy arising from the consent of the parties, seems to now be in search of public legitimacy, which it is thought can be obtained from a certain degree of openness to civil society.[12]

12. The WG protocols confirm the generally accepted need for a uniform standard on transparency in the investor-State arbitration area. As will be seen in the discussion of existing case law throughout the commentary to this article, the approach to addressing issues of third person participation in arbitral proceedings is inherently haphazard, due largely to the fact-specific circumstances of each case and the large degree of discretion granted to tribunals. However, this area is now generally characterised by a growing acceptance of a limited role for third person participants in specific circumstances.[13]

[11] UNCITRAL (n. 1) UN Doc. A/CN.9/712 [46]ff.

[12] Stern (n. 2) 347. Cf. also Joachim Delaney and Daniel Barstow Magraw, 'Procedural Transparency' in Peter Muchlinski, Federico Ortino and Christoph Schreuer (eds.), *The Oxford Handbook of International Investment Law* (Oxford University Press, 2008) 780; Katia Fach Gomez, 'Rethinking the Role of Amicus Curiae in International Investment Arbitration: How to Draw the Line Favorably for the Public Interest' (2012) 35 *Fordham International Law Journal* 510, 545.

[13] Cf. generally Christian Schliemann, 'Requirements for Amicus Curiae Participation in International Investment Arbitration. A Deconstruction of the Procedural Wall Erected in Joint ICSID Cases ARB/10/25 and ARB/10/15' (2013) 12 *The Law and Practice of International Courts and Tribunals* 365.

13. When drafting this Article 4 on submissions by third persons, the WG was faced with two options in terms of approach.[14]

14. Option 1 was based on a provision found in some BITs that embodied the general principle that submissions by third parties to the arbitral proceedings should be permitted, without giving details for such a procedure.

15. However, it was widely held that more guidance on this matter was needed in the Rules and Option 2, which provided such guidance, was the option preferred by the WG.[15]

16. The WG relied on material already available in the investment arbitration context. A proposal was ultimately accepted to draft a provision along the lines of Rule 37(2) ICSID Rules, complemented by elements in paragraph B.2 of the NAFTA FTC Statement.[16] The WG decided that rules on third person participation should contain a detailed procedure on the information to be provided, matters to be considered by the arbitral tribunal and the submission itself.[17]

17. The approach chosen was not intended to be limiting – and indeed it is not, as the tribunal retains a large degree of discretion. Instead, it was intended to be facilitative; the need to give active guidance on the issue of third person participation, rather than simply leaving it to the tribunal, which would be the default position in any case, was a specific purpose driving the development of the Rules. Indeed, the differing approaches taken in case law up until this point had the benefit of highlighting the need for a flexible approach, able to be adapted to a variety of different circumstances.

18. The purpose of allowing third persons to participate in arbitral proceedings is that the tribunal and the parties should benefit from the special knowledge of the third person and its perspective on the issues. As stated in the case of *Suez/Vivendi* v. *Argentina*,[18] 'the purpose of

[14] UNCITRAL 'Report of Working Group II (Arbitration and Conciliation) on the work of its fifty-fifth session' (17 October 2011) UN Doc. A/CN.9/736 [68]ff.

[15] *Ibid.* [70].

[16] UNCITRAL 'Report of Working Group II (Arbitration and Conciliation) on the work of its fifty-fourth session' (25 February 2011) UN Doc. A/CN.9/717 [121].

[17] UNCITRAL (n. 14) UN Doc. A/CN.9/736 [70].

[18] *Aguas Argentinas, S.A., Suez, Sociedad General de Aguas de Barcelona, S.A. and Vivendi Universal, S.A.* v. *Argentina ('Suez/Vivendi* v. *Argentina')*, ICSID Case No. ARB/03/19, Order in Response to a Petition for Transparency and Participation as *Amicus Curiae* (19 May 2005) www.italaw.com/sites/default/files/case-documents/ita0815.pdf; see summary of this case in section 6.5.5.

amicus submissions is to help the Tribunal to arrive at a correct decision by providing it with arguments, expertise, and perspectives that the parties may not have provided'.[19] The intention of allowing third person participation is one of 'added value': the third person should add something to the proceedings, otherwise there is no perceivable need to grant them access.[20] Any submission made by a third person must be done in such a way as to ensure that the proceedings are not disrupted and, importantly, that the benefit of such submission outweighs any concerns of efficiency, since a third person submission would usually be associated with a delay to the proceedings. As with the NAFTA FTC Statement and the amended ICSID Rules, the Rules aim at ensuring that third person submissions genuinely assist the tribunal's work and do not undermine the parties' interests and the efficiency of the proceedings.[21]

19. The status of third persons in the investment arbitral process is uncertain; while it is generally agreed that they are not akin to a party to the dispute,[22] the limits of matters on which they can opine is more uncertain. Generally, however, third persons may address the broader policy concerns associated with the dispute in their submissions, but will usually not be given access to documents that would not be otherwise publicly available. Third person submissions enable individuals and organisations that have expertise in relation to the broader public, environmental or socio-political issues that may arise in investment arbitration to provide the tribunal and the parties with the benefit of such expertise.

20. Guidance concerning the limitations of matters on which third persons can opine under Article 4 of the Rules is set out in more detail in this article.

21. One of the concerns surrounding the participation of third persons in the investment arbitral process is that they are often regarded not so much as a 'friend of the court' than as a 'friend of one of the parties' and are thereby often not perceived as neutral advisors, but as advisors

[19] *Suez/Vivendi* v. *Argentina* (n. 18) [24]. [20] Cf. Fach Gomez (n. 12) 559.

[21] Cf. Avidan Kent, 'The Principle of Public Participation in NAFTA Chapter 11 Disputes' www.cec.org/Storage/150/17636_Avidan_Kent_Public_Participation_in_NAFTA_Chapter_11_18_june_2013.doc, 17.

[22] Cf. e.g. *Biwater Gauff (Tanzania) Ltd* v. *Tanzania*, ICSID Case No. ARB/05/22, Award (24 July 2008) www.italaw.com/sites/default/files/case-documents/ita0095.pdf [64].

pursuing a sometimes more, sometimes less obvious political objective.[23] For example, particularly in the context of development or infrastructure projects, third persons have, in practice, often promulgated views in support of the State's defence of its actions or have expressed views and perspectives otherwise sympathetic to the State's arguments.[24] For that reason, investors often regard third persons with scepticism and, to the extent that consent of both parties is required for any element of third person participation, are likely to veto it.[25]

22. The role of third persons is usually limited by tribunals to providing written submissions of pre-defined scope, as shown in the case analysis below. Moreover, in very limited circumstances, third person participation has been extended to viewing documents in the arbitration, such as in the case of *Glamis Gold* v. *United States*,[26] discussed below.[27]

23. The scope of Article 4 of the Rules is to be clearly delimited from Article 5. Although initially dealt with in one Article in the WG drafting process, the WG decided that it was prudent to address regular third persons in one article and non-disputing parties to an underlying treaty in a separate article.[28] The scope of Article 5 will be dealt with in Chapter 7.

[23] A concern that has been challenged by Meg Kinnear: cf. Meg Kinnear, 'Transparency and Third Party Participation in Investor-State Dispute Settlement' Presentation, Symposium co-organised by ICSID, the OECD and UNCTAD, 'Making the Most of International Investment Agreements' (Paris, 12 December 2005) www.oecd.org/dataoecd/6/25/36979626.pdf, 7/ § G.

[24] Cf. Lucas Bastin, 'Amici Curiae in Investor-State Arbitration: Eight Recent Trends' (2014) 30(1) *Arbitration International* 125, 134; Bastin cites a number of examples in which *amici curiae* participation has favoured States.

[25] E.g. the Revised ICSID Arbitration Rules, which came into force in 2006, provide for the possibility of third persons to attend hearings. However, since the right to attend hearings is subject to a veto right by the parties, this possibility is probably, at least in the near future, of limited practical significance. Cf. also Dimsey (n. 2) 267.

[26] *Glamis Gold, Ltd* v. *United States of America*, Procedural Order No. 11 (9 July 2007) www.italaw.com/sites/default/files/case-documents/ita0376.pdf [15]. For a case summary, see also section 6.5.8 below.

[27] However, requests to access parties' submissions were denied in *Biwater Gauff* and *Suez/Vivendi* v. *Argentina* (discussed below in the case summaries at sections 6.5.7 and 6.5.5, respectively). See *Biwater Gauff (Tanzania) Ltd* v. *Tanzania*, Procedural Order No. 5 (2 February 2007) www.italaw.com/sites/default/files/case-documents/ita0091_0.pdf [68]; *Suez/Vivendi* v. *Argentina*, Order in Response to a Petition by Five Non-Governmental Organizations for Permissions to Make an Amicus Curiae Submission (12 February 2007) http://italaw.com/sites/default/files/case-documents/ita0823.pdf [25].

[28] UNCITRAL (n. 14) UN Doc. A/CN.9/736 [80]ff.

6.3 A note on terminology

24. The Rules are somewhat unique in their reference to 'third persons' in Article 4. In other instruments, parties making submissions to arbitral tribunals as third persons as they are interpreted under Article 4 have been referred to variously as *amici curiae*, third parties, non-disputing parties and other similar terms. In the WG discussions, a conscious decision was made not to use the phrase '*amicus curiae*' because of its historical background of use in court proceedings in certain jurisdictions, and instead to use a term that 'would be understood in the same manner in all legal systems'.[29] 'Third persons' was suggested based on its use in Article 17(5) of the Arbitration Rules (2010)[30] and ultimately received consensus.

25. In this paper, when discussing case law or particular rules, the author generally refers to the designation of the third person as it appears in the original text concerned. When commenting directly on this Article 4 of the Rules, the author intends to consistently refer to 'third persons'. In any case, there is no intended difference in meaning between the terms used to refer to third person participants within the meaning of Article 4 of the Rules.

6.4 International instruments containing provisions concerning third person submissions

6.4.1 Relevance of other instruments

26. As detailed above, when drafting the Rules, the WG gave substantial consideration to existing international provisions governing third person intervention. As a result,[31] the instruments used as points of reference by the WG are important for understanding and correctly applying Article 4 of the Rules. This holds true especially for Rule 37(2) of the ICSID Rules and paragraph B.2 of the NAFTA FTC Statement, which together form the fundament of Article 4.[32]

6.4.2 NAFTA FTC Statement 2003

27. The NAFTA FTC Statement on non-disputing party participation of 7 October 2003 was a response to the issues raised in two NAFTA cases,

[29] *Ibid.* [71]. [30] *Ibid.* [72].

[31] See drafting history and background in section 6.2 above.

[32] UNCITRAL (n. 16) UN Doc. A/CN.9/717 [121].

Methanex v. *Canada* and *UPS* v. *Canada*. Both of these cases discussed the issue of *amici* submissions in detail[33] and the NAFTA FTC felt a need to clarify NAFTA practice concerning these issues. Importantly, the NAFTA FTC Statement brought Mexico into a consensus of the three NAFTA parties that amicus submissions are a legitimate part of the NAFTA investor-State arbitration process.[34] The relevant wording of the NAFTA FTC Statement reads as follows:

B. Procedures

1. Any non-disputing party that is a person of a Party, or that has a significant presence in the territory of a Party, that wishes to file a written submission with the Tribunal (the "applicant") will apply for leave from the Tribunal to file such a submission. The applicant will attach the submission to the application.
2. The application for leave to file a non-disputing party submission will:
   (a) be made in writing, dated and signed by the person filing the application, and include the address and other contact details of the applicant;
   (b) be no longer than 5 typed pages;
   (c) describe the applicant, including, where relevant, its membership and legal status (e.g., company, trade association or other non-governmental organization), its general objectives, the nature of its activities, and any parent organization (including any organization that directly or indirectly controls the applicant);
   (d) disclose whether or not the applicant has any affiliation, direct or indirect, with any disputing party;
   (e) identify any government, person or organization that has provided any financial or other assistance in preparing the submission;
   (f) specify the nature of the interest that the applicant has in the arbitration;
   (g) identify the specific issues of fact or law in the arbitration that the applicant has addressed in its written submission;
   (h) explain, by reference to the factors specified in paragraph 6, why the Tribunal should accept the submission; and
   (i) be made in a language of the arbitration.

[33] See the case summaries in sections 6.5.2 and 6.5.3 below.
[34] Cf. also Howard Mann, 'The Free Trade Commission Statements of October 7, 2003, on NAFTA's Chapter 11: Never-Never Land or Real Progress?' www.iisd.org/pdf/2003/trade_ftc_comment_oct03.pdf.

3. The submission filed by a non-disputing party will:
   (a) be dated and signed by the person filing the submission;
   (b) be concise, and in no case longer than 20 typed pages, including any appendices;
   (c) set out a precise statement supporting the applicant's position on the issues; and
   (d) only address matters within the scope of the dispute.
4. The application for leave to file a non-disputing party submission and the submission will be served on all disputing parties and the Tribunal.
5. The Tribunal will set an appropriate date by which the disputing parties may comment on the application for leave to file a non-disputing party submission.
6. In determining whether to grant leave to file a non-disputing party submission, the Tribunal will consider, among other things, the extent to which:
   (a) the non-disputing party submission would assist the Tribunal in the determination of a factual or legal issue related to the arbitration by bringing a perspective, particular knowledge or insight that is different from that of the disputing parties;
   (b) the non-disputing party submission would address matters within the scope of the dispute;
   (c) the non-disputing party has a significant interest in the arbitration; and
   (d) there is a public interest in the subject-matter of the arbitration.
7. The Tribunal will ensure that:
   (a) any non-disputing party submission avoids disrupting the proceedings; and
   (b) neither disputing party is unduly burdened or unfairly prejudiced by such submissions.
8. The Tribunal will render a decision on whether to grant leave to file a non-disputing party submission. If leave to file a non-disputing party submission is granted, the Tribunal will set an appropriate date by which the disputing parties may respond in writing to the non-disputing party submission. By that date, non-disputing NAFTA Parties may, pursuant to Article 1128, address any issues of interpretation of the Agreement presented in the non-disputing party submission.
9. The granting of leave to file a non-disputing party submission does not require the Tribunal to address that submission at any point in the arbitration. The granting of leave to file a non-disputing party submission does not entitle the non-disputing party that filed the submission to make further submissions in the arbitration.

28. The NAFTA FTC Statement sets out a clear procedure for making non-disputing party submissions to an ongoing arbitration. At the time,

and following on from developments in WTO law,[35] the NAFTA FTC Statement was the first instrument of its kind to acknowledge that third person participation is not necessarily predicated on the consent of the parties. Moreover, the NAFTA FTC Statement acknowledges that non-disputing party participation can assist the tribunal and enhance the quality of decisions.[36] Many of the ideas set out in the NAFTA procedure provided inspiration for the wording of the Rules.[37] Although the NAFTA FTC Statement is not binding upon tribunals as such, the consistent reliance on its content by investment arbitral tribunals and compliance with its procedures by third persons evinces the impact that the Statement has had on investment arbitration practice.[38]

6.4.3 ICSID Arbitration Rule 37(2)

29. The ICSID Rules were amended in 2006 in response to developments in investment treaty arbitration jurisprudence and above all in response to cries for increased transparency in ICSID arbitration. One of the changes was the inclusion of a rule concerning third person participation in the arbitral process. The rule arose as a response to, among other things, the tribunals' approach to third person submissions in the *Methanex* and *UPS* v. *Canada*[39] arbitrations.[40] An ICSID Discussion Paper in 2004 stated as follows:

> There may well be cases where the process could be strengthened by submissions of third parties, not only civil society organizations but also for instance business groups or, in investment treaty arbitrations, the other States parties to the treaties concerned. It might therefore be useful to make clear that the tribunals have the authority to accept and consider submissions from third parties ... The amendments could set out conditions for the submissions – for example, as to financial and other

[35] Cf. Stern (n. 22) 285ff; Fach Gomez (n. 12) 522.
[36] Cf. Kent (n. 21) 15.
[37] UNCITRAL (n. 16) UN Doc. A/CN.9/717 [121].
[38] Cf. Christina Knahr, 'Transparency, Third Party Participation and Access to Documents in International Investment Arbitration' (2007) 23(2) *Arbitration International* 327, 346.
[39] For case summaries, see sections 6.5.2 and 6.5.3 below.
[40] ICSID Secretariat, 'Possible Improvements of the Framework for ICSID Arbitration' (22 October 2004) https://icsid.worldbank.org/ICSID/FrontServlet?requestType=CasesRH&actionVal=OpenPage&PageType=AnnouncementsFrame&FromPage=NewsReleases&pageName=Archive_%20Announcement14 [13].

disclosures by aspiring friends of the court – or more flexibly to leave such conditions for determination by the tribunals in each case.[41]

30. Amended Rule 37(2), which arose in response to such comments, reads as follows:

> After consulting both parties, the Tribunal may allow a person or entity that is not a party to the dispute (in this Rule called the 'non-disputing party') to file a written submission with the Tribunal regarding a matter within the scope of the dispute. In determining whether to allow such a filing, the Tribunal shall consider, among other things, the extent to which:
>
> (a) the non-disputing party submission would assist the tribunal in the determination of a factual or legal issue related to the proceeding by bringing a perspective, particular knowledge or insight that is different from that of the disputing parties;
> (b) the non-disputing party submission would address a matter within the scope of the dispute;
> (c) the non-disputing party has a significant interest in the proceeding.
>
> The Tribunal shall ensure that the non-disputing party submission does not disrupt the proceeding or unduly burden or unfairly prejudice either party, and that both parties are given an opportunity to present their observations on the non-disputing party submission.

31. Given the number of common elements between the NAFTA FTC Statement and the amended ICSID Rule, one begins to discern trends in the approach to this issue. Although the ICSID Rule, unlike the NAFTA FTC Statement, does not contain details concerning the application process, the criteria to be considered by a tribunal when considering whether to allow non-disputing party participation are identical to the first three criteria in section B.6 of the NAFTA FTC Statement. Noticeably absent in the ICSID Rule, however, is the requirement that there is a public interest in the subject matter of the arbitration, although ICSID tribunals usually consider the public nature of a dispute in deciding whether to allow third party participation.[42]

[41] *Ibid.*; cf. also Peter Malanczuk, 'Confidentiality and Third-Party Participation in Arbitration Proceedings under Bilateral Investment Treaties' (2008) 1(2) *Contemporary Asia Arbitration Journal* 183, 200.

[42] Cf. e.g. *Suez/Vivendi* v. *Argentina* (n. 18) [19]ff. For a case summary, see section 6.5.5 below.

6.4.4 BITs and FTAs

32. Following this trend, some more recent BITs and FTAs specifically contemplate the use of non-disputing party participation in the resolution of investment disputes. For example, in the US Model BIT published in 2004, Article 28(3) sets out that '[t]he tribunal shall have the authority to accept and consider *amicus curiae* submissions from a person or entity that is not a disputing party'.[43] This provision was maintained without change in the recently released 2012 US Model BIT, enforcing the State's commitment to transparency in investor-State arbitration.[44]

33. An increasing number of FTAs also specifically contemplate third person participation. For example, the Australia–Chile FTA provides tribunals with the power to accept and consider *amicus curiae* submissions in Article 10.20(2). The relevant provision reads:[45]

> The tribunal shall have the authority to accept and consider amicus curiae written submissions that may assist the tribunal in evaluating the submissions and arguments of the disputing parties from a person or entity that is not a disputing party (the 'submitter'). The submissions shall be provided in both Spanish and English, and shall identify the submitter and any Party, other government, person, or organisation, other than the submitter, that has provided, or will provide, any financial or other assistance in preparing the submission. Where such submissions are admitted by the tribunal, the tribunal shall provide to the parties an opportunity to respond to such written submissions.

34. Moreover, at a regional level, the EU Commission released a Communication Paper on 7 July 2010 entitled 'Towards a comprehensive European international investment policy', which lists transparency, including *amicus curiae* submissions, as one of the challenges in arriving at state-of-the-art investor-State dispute resolution mechanisms.[46]

[43] Cf. Article 28(3) of the 2004 US Model BIT www.state.gov/documents/organization/117601.pdf.

[44] Article 28(3) of the 2012 US Model BIT www.ustr.gov/sites/default/files/BIT%20text%20for%20ACIEP%20Meeting.pdf. Cf. also Article 39 Canada Model Foreign Investment Promotion and Protection Agreement ('FIPA') (2004) http://italaw.com/documents/Canadian2004-FIPA-model-en.pdf; Fach Gomez (n. 12) 529ff.

[45] Australia–Chile FTA (entered into force 6 March 2009) www.dfat.gov.au/fta/aclfta/Australia-Chile-Free-Trade-Agreement.pdf. See also Article 10.20(3) CAFTA-DR (2004) www.ustr.gov/sites/default/files/uploads/agreements/cafta/asset_upload_file328_4718.pdf.

[46] European Commission Communication, 'Towards a comprehensive European international investment policy' COM(2010)343 final http://trade.ec.europa.eu/doclib/docs/2011/may/tradoc_147884.pdf, 10.

6.4.5 *UNCITRAL Arbitration Rules*

35. In addition to the explicit rules referred to above, tribunals subject to the Arbitration Rules have allowed third person participation pursuant to their general discretionary power under former Article 15 of the Arbitration Rules (1976).[47] In the context of revising the Arbitration Rules, discussions were held concerning the possible incorporation of a rule on non-disputing party participation into the revised Rules. The proposed new Article 15(5) read as follows:

> Unless the parties have agreed otherwise, the Arbitral Tribunal may, after having consulted with the parties, and especially in cases raising issues of public interest, allow any person who is not a party to the proceedings to present one or more written statements, provided that the Tribunal is satisfied that such statements are likely to assist it in the determination of a factual or legal issue related to the proceeding by bringing a perspective, particular knowledge or insight which the parties are unable to present. The Arbitral Tribunal shall determine the mode and number of such statements after consulting with the parties.[48]

36. This proposal was ultimately not incorporated into the revisions to the Arbitration Rules (2010). Nonetheless, the considerations held to be relevant in the drafting process can certainly be said to have influenced the drafting of Article 4 of the Rules, since it was the same WG responsible for the drafting of both instruments.[49] Regardless of the failure to include a specific provision on non-disputing party participation in the revised rules, the scope of what is now Article 17(1) of the Arbitration Rules (2010) is broad enough to allow non-disputing party submissions in the arbitral process.[50]

[47] See *Methanex Corporation* v. *United States of America*, UNCITRAL, 'Decision of the Tribunal on Petitions from Third Persons to Intervene as 'Amici Curiae" (15 January 2001) www.italaw.com/sites/default/files/case-documents/ita0517_0.pdf [31], [32], relying on what was then Article 15 UNCITRAL Arbitration Rules.

[48] Jan Paulsson and Georgios Petrochilos, 'Revision of the UNCITRAL Arbitration Rules', a report commissioned by the UNCITRAL Secretariat (2006) www.uncitral.org/pdf/english/news/arbrules_report.pdf, 72.

[49] Cf. explanation in UNCITRAL (n. 1) UN Doc. A/CN.9/712 [1].

[50] Article 17(1) UNCITRAL Arbitration Rules (2010) states: 'Subject to these Rules, the arbitral tribunal may conduct the arbitration in such manner as it considers appropriate, provided that the parties are treated with equality and that at an appropriate stage of the proceedings each party is given a reasonable opportunity of presenting its case. The arbitral tribunal, in exercising its discretion, shall conduct the proceedings so as to avoid unnecessary delay and expense and to provide a fair and efficient process for resolving the parties' dispute' www.uncitral.org/pdf/english/texts/arbitration/arb-rules-revised/arb-rules-revised-2010-e.pdf.

6.5 Case law concerning third person submissions

6.5.1 Relevance and overview of case law development

37. During the drafting process of Article 4,[51] the WG took account not only of existing instruments, but also of case law interpreting those instruments.[52] Especially in light of the deliberate decision to adopt an approach similar to established instruments,[53] cases interpreting the role of third persons in investor-State proceedings prior to the introduction of the Rules continue to be relevant to the interpretation of Article 4.

38. As mentioned briefly above, the case law concerning the role of third person submissions in investment arbitration has not developed in an entirely consistent manner, which is not something that is likely to change, due to the inherent discretion retained by the tribunal and the fact that situations in which third person submissions will be allowed are highly fact-specific. As a general matter, however, and bolstered by the possibilities created in the BIT and FTA framework, there has been increasing acceptance of third person submissions in investor-State arbitral proceedings, although it would be premature to describe the practice as 'widespread'. There has been a number of cases in which the utility of third person submissions has been discussed.

6.5.2 Methanex *v.* USA

39. The participation of third persons in investor-State arbitration first arose in the NAFTA context.

40. In the case of *Methanex* v. *USA* ('*Methanex*'),[54] Methanex, a Canadian manufacturer of the additive MTBE, brought arbitration proceedings against the USA under Chapter 11 of NAFTA.[55] Since the case concerned the potential effect of MTBE on Californian drinking water, the case attracted

[51] See section 6.2 above.

[52] Cf. UNCITRAL 'Comments by the International Centre for Settlement of Investment Disputes (ICSID)' (8 August 2011) UN Doc. A/CN.9/WG.II/WP.167 [15]–[23]. The comments were invited by the Working Group in preparation for its fifty-fifth session, and contain an extensive discussion of case law on third persons.

[53] UNCITRAL (n. 16) UN Doc. A/CN.9/717 [121].

[54] *Methanex Corporation* v. *United States of America*, UNCITRAL www.italaw.com/cases/documents/692.

[55] NAFTA Chapter 11, Article 1120(1)(c) https://www.nafta-sec-alena.org/Default.aspx?tabid=97&ctl=SectionView&mid=1214&sid=539c50ef-51c1-489b-808b-9e20c9872d25&language=en-US.

significant public attention and several NGOs applied to the tribunal for non-disputing party status. The International Institute for Sustainable Development (IISD) submitted an individual application for *amicus curiae* status and three other NGOs submitted a joint application.[56] All non-disputing party petitioners supported the position of the USA[57] concerning the banning of the additive. Methanex opposed all of the requests.[58]

41. The tribunal held that it had the power to accept *amicus curiae* submissions and that the issues concerned extended beyond the commercial interests of the parties. Whilst the tribunal was at pains to state that it 'can set no legal precedent',[59] it found for the first time in the NAFTA/UNCITRAL context that, under its broad procedural powers in what was then Article 15(1) of the Arbitration Rules (1976), 'it has the power to accept *amicus* written submissions from the Petitioners'[60] but that it was minded to allow the third persons to make such submissions at a later stage of the arbitral proceedings.[61] By the time of the award in 2005, the NAFTA FTC Statement had been issued. The award referenced that the tribunal accepted and considered a written submission from IISD and from the other NGOs, but the award did not elaborate on the perspectives or interests of the third persons in the proceeding, other than to state that the tribunal appreciated 'the scholarship and industry which ... the amici have deployed'.[62]

6.5.3 UPS *v.* Canada

42. *United Parcel Service of America Inc* v. *Canada* ('*UPS*'),[63] also a NAFTA case decided under the Arbitration Rules (1976), was the second

[56] *Methanex*, Final Award of the Tribunal on Jurisdiction and Merits (3 August 2005) http://italaw.com/sites/default/files/case-documents/ita0529.pdf, § II(C)(28).

[57] For IISD submissions see Amicus Curiae Submissions (9 March 2004) www.state.gov/documents/organization/30475.pdf; for the three other NGOs, see Submission of Non-Disputing Parties Bluewater Network, Communities for a Better Environment and Center for International Environmental Law (9 March 2004) www.state.gov/documents/organization/30472.pdf.

[58] *Methanex*, Claimant Methanex Corporation's Reply to the Amicus Curiae Submissions of Earthjustice and the International Institute for Sustainable Development (23 April 2004) www.state.gov/documents/organization/31979.pdf.

[59] *Methanex* (n. 47) [51]. [60] *Ibid.* [53]. [61] *Ibid.*

[62] *Methanex* (n. 56) § I (Preface)(11).

[63] *United Parcel Service of America Inc ('UPS')* v. *Canada*, UNCITRAL www.international.gc.ca/trade-agreements-accords-commerciaux/topics-domaines/disp-diff/parcel.aspx?lang=eng.

recorded investment arbitration proceedings to discuss third party participation in the arbitral process. In this case, two external organisations, the Canadian Union of Postal Workers and the Council of Canadians (together the 'Petitioners'), requested 'standing as parties' to the proceedings or, in the alternative, among other requests, 'the right to intervene as amicus curiae' in the proceedings.[64] The Petitioners claimed that they both had a direct interest in the subject matter of the claim, and may have been adversely affected by the award of the arbitral tribunal. They also claimed an interest in the broader public policy implications of the dispute, and claimed to offer a unique and distinct perspective, as well as expertise concerning issues raised by the claim that would be of assistance to the tribunal.[65]

43. While acknowledging the general jurisdiction of the tribunal to grant *amicus curiae* status to third parties to the arbitration, UPS submitted that the application to provide an *amicus* brief should be dismissed at the time, but that the tribunal might determine that the Petitioners could be granted leave to reapply in the future.[66] Canada's position was not dissimilar to UPS' in that it also acknowledged the tribunal's discretion to receive *amicus* briefs, but stated that such discretion should only be exercised at the merits phase of the arbitration.[67]

44. While rejecting the Petitioners' request to be granted standing as parties, the tribunal found that the powers conferred by Article 15(1) of the Arbitration Rules (1976) could be used to facilitate the tribunal's 'process of inquiry into, understanding of, and resolving, that very dispute which has been submitted to it in accordance with the consent of the disputing parties'.[68] The tribunal found that within this scope was

[64] *UPS*, Amicus Petitions by the Canadian Union of Postal Workers and the Council of Canadians (8 November 2000) http://www.international.gc.ca/trade-agreements-accords-commerciaux/topics-domaines/disp-diff/parcel.aspx?lang=eng; Amended Amicus Petitions by the Canadian Union of Postal Workers and the Council of Canadians (10 May 2001) http://www.international.gc.ca/trade-agreements-accords-commerciaux/topics-domaines/disp-diff/parcel.aspx?lang=eng; Response to Canada's Submissions by the Canadian Union of Postal Workers and the Canadian Union of Postal Workers (18 June 2001) http://www.international.gc.ca/trade-agreements-accords-commerciaux/topics-domaines/disp-diff/parcel.aspx?lang=eng; and Response to UPS and Mexico's Submissions by the Canadian Union of Postal Workers and the Council of Canadians (20 June 2001) http://www.international.gc.ca/trade-agreements-accords-commerciaux/topics-domaines/disp-diff/parcel.aspx?lang=eng.

[65] *UPS*, Decision on Petitions for Intervention and Participation as Amici Curiae (17 October 2001) http://italaw.com/sites/default/files/case-documents/ita0883.pdf [3].

[66] *Ibid.* [5]. [67] *Ibid.* [8]. [68] *Ibid.* [60].

the discretion to receive submissions offered by third parties with the purpose of assisting the tribunal[69] and acknowledged the cogency of the Petitioners' arguments concerning the important public character of the matters in dispute. Such discretion was, however, not to be used in a way that was unduly burdensome for the parties or which unnecessarily complicated the process.[70]

45. The tribunal subsequently directed the parties to provide the Petitioners with their pleadings[71] and permitted the Canadian Union of Postal Workers and the Council of Canadians to submit a joint brief at the merits phase of the proceedings.[72] During the merits phase, the US Chamber of Commerce also sought permission to make a submission as an additional *amicus curiae*;[73] its written submission was also allowed.[74]

6.5.4 Aguas del Tunari SA *v.* Bolivia

46. The issue of authority to permit third persons to participate in arbitration proceedings under the ICSID Rules arose for the first time in *Aguas del Tunari* v. *Bolivia* ('*Aguas del Tunari*').[75] In the *Aguas del Tunari* case, the project at the centre of the dispute was a 40-year concession granted to a foreign investor to operate Cochabamba's sewerage and water system. The foreign concession operators claimed under the Netherlands–Bolivia BIT for loss of anticipated profits. Eight petitioners applied for *amicus curiae* status in the proceedings, basing their request on the grounds of unique expertise, direct interest in the subject matter of the claim, and for reasons of transparency.[76]

[69] *Ibid.* [61]–[65]. [70] *Ibid.* [69].

[71] *UPS*, Procedural Directions for Amicus Submissions (4 April 2003) http://www.international.gc.ca/trade-agreements-accords-commerciaux/topics-domaines/disp-diff/parcel.aspx?lang=eng.

[72] *UPS*, Amicus Submissions of the Canadian Union of Postal Workers and of the Council of Canadians (20 October 2005), and 3 November 2005 http://www.international.gc.ca/trade-agreements-accords-commerciaux/topics-domaines/disp-diff/parcel.aspx?lang=eng.

[73] *UPS*, Amicus Submissions of the US Chamber of Commerce (20 October 2005) http://www.international.gc.ca/trade-agreements-accords-commerciaux/topics-domaines/disp-diff/parcel.aspx?lang=eng.

[74] *UPS*, Award (24 May 2007) http://www.international.gc.ca/trade-agreements-accords-commerciaux/topics-domaines/disp-diff/parcel.aspx?lang=eng [3].

[75] *Aguas del Tunari SA* v. *Republic of Bolivia*, ICSID Case No. ARB/02/3 www.italaw.com/cases/57.

[76] *Aguas del Tunari*, Petition of La Coordinadora para la Defensa del Agua y Vida, La Federación Departamental Cochabambina de Organizaciones Regantes, Semapa Sur, Friends of the Earth-Netherlands, Oscar Olivera, Omar Fernandez, Father Luis Sánchez,

47. Referring to the Singapore–USA FTA, which includes express provisions on *amicus curiae* participation, the tribunal appeared to conclude that the absence of similar express provisions in the Netherlands–Bolivia BIT restricted its authority to allow *amicus curiae* participation.[77] The tribunal rejected their application, stating that there was 'not at present a need ... to seek supplementary non-party submissions at the jurisdictional phase of its work. We hold this view without in any way prejudging the question of the extent of the Tribunal's authority to call witnesses or receive information from non-parties on its own initiative'.[78]

6.5.5 Suez/Vivendi *v.* Argentina

48. In the case of *Suez/Vivendi* v. *Argentina* ('*Suez/Vivendi*'),[79] the project at the centre of the dispute was a concession for the provision of water and sewerage systems to the greater Buenos Aires area, which had been organised and managed by the claimants. Five NGOs applied for *amici curiae* status. The *Suez/Vivendi* tribunal found that it was generally appropriate for *amici curiae* to participate in the case,[80] but that it did not require assistance in the jurisdictional phase.[81] In the merits phase, the tribunal did consider *amicus curiae* participation appropriate and granted leave to submit a joint brief.[82] In its first order, the tribunal reasoned:[83]

> The factor that gives this case particular public interest is that the investment dispute centers around the water distribution and sewage systems of a large metropolitan area ... Those systems provide basic public services to millions of people and as a result may raise a variety of complex public and international law questions, including human rights considerations. Any decision rendered in this case, whether in favor of the Claimants or the Respondent, has the potential to affect the operation of those systems and thereby the public they serve.

and Congressman Jorge Alvarado to the Arbitral Tribunal (29 August 2002) www.italaw.com/sites/default/files/case-documents/ita0018.pdf [2].

77 See also in general Boris Kasolowsky and Caroline Harvey, 'Amici curiae in investment treaty arbitrations: authority and procedural fairness' www.sccinstitute.com/filearchive/4/40616/ARTICLE_Amici%20Curiae%20in%20Investment%20Treaty%20Arbitrations_Har%E2%80%A6.pdf, [17]ff.

78 *Aguas del Tunari*, Letter from President of Tribunal Responding to Petition (29 January 2003) www.italaw.com/sites/default/files/case-documents/ita0019_0.pdf, 2.

79 *Suez/Vivendi* (n. 18) http://italaw.com/cases/documents/1063.

80 *Ibid.* [22]–[23].

81 *Ibid.* [28].

82 *Suez/Vivendi* (n. 27) [27].

83 *Suez/Vivendi* (n. 18) [19]–[20], partially quoted in Order in Response to a Petition by Five Non-Governmental Organizations for Permissions to Make an Amicus Curiae Submission (n. 27) [3].

> These factors lead the Tribunal to conclude that this case does involve matters of public interest of such a nature that have traditionally led courts and other tribunals to receive amicus submissions from suitable nonparties. This case is not simply a contract dispute between private parties where nonparties attempting to intervene as friends of the court might be seen as officious intermeddlers.

49. The tribunal's decision here was made before the 2006 amendments to the ICSID Rules. As such, the tribunal had no specific power to allow *amici curiae* briefs, but instead relied on its 'residual power'[84] in Article 44 of the ICSID Convention.[85] The tribunal reasoned that acceptance of an *amicus curiae* submission should be based on:

(i) the appropriateness of the subject matter of the case;
(ii) the suitability of the non-party to act as *amicus curiae*; and
(iii) the procedure to apply to the submission.[86]

On suitability to make a non-party submission, the tribunal stated that it would 'only accept amicus submissions from persons who establish to [its] satisfaction that they have the expertise, experience, and independence to be of assistance in this case'.[87]

50. Although the new amended ICSID Arbitration Rule 37(2) did not apply, the tribunal nevertheless found that the new Rule accorded with the three criteria set out in its initial decision of 19 May 2005.[88]

6.5.6 Suez/Interaguas *v.* Argentina

51. The case of *Suez/Interaguas* v. *Argentina* ('*Suez/Interaguas*')[89] was decided by an identical tribunal to that of *Suez/Vivendi* and the tribunal

[84] *Suez/Vivendi* (n. 18) [10].

[85] Article 44 ICSID Convention: 'If any question of procedure arises which is not covered by this Section or the Arbitration Rules or any rules agreed by the parties, the Tribunal shall decide the question' https://icsid.worldbank.org/ICSID/StaticFiles/basicdoc/CRR_English-final.pdf. Cf. also Christoph Schreuer, Loretta Malintoppi, August Reinisch and Anthony Sinclair, *The ICSID Convention: A Commentary* (2nd edn., Cambridge University Press, 2009), Article 44 [97]ff.

[86] *Suez/Vivendi* (n. 18) [17], quoted in the later Order (n. 27) [12]. Cf. also the summary in Bastin (n. 2) 215–16; Campbell McLachlan, Laurence Shore, and Matthew Weiniger, *International Investment Arbitration: Substantive Principles* (Oxford University Press, 2007) [3.44].

[87] *Suez/Vivendi* (n. 18) [24].

[88] *Suez/Vivendi* (n. 27) [15]. See also Kasolowsky and Harvey (n. 77) [19]ff.

[89] *Suez, Sociedad General de Aguas de Barcelona S.A., and InterAguas Servicios Integrales del Agua S.A.* v. *Argentina*, ICSID Case No. ARB/03/17 www.italaw.com/cases/documents/1049.

stated that the issues raised were 'virtually identical'.[90] However, although the tribunal applied the same three criteria as in the *Suez/Vivendi* case, the tribunal declined the would-be third persons' request to make submissions as they had not shown that their 'experience, expertise and perspectives will assist the Tribunal in arriving at its decision', and had 'not provided ... sufficient information and reasons to [demonstrate] that they qualify as *amici curiae*'.[91]

6.5.7 Biwater Gauff *v.* Tanzania

52. The *Biwater Gauff* v. *Tanzania* case ('*Biwater*')[92] concerned a World Bank-funded project to repair, update and expand Dar es Salaam's water and sewerage infrastructure. Problems arose in the implementation of the project. Biwater Gauff commenced ICSID arbitration under the United Kingdom–Tanzania BIT. Here, five petitioners filed for *amici curiae* status in the proceedings, claiming their interest to be, among other things, that 'this arbitration process goes far beyond merely resolving commercial or private conflicts, but rather has a substantial influence on the population's ability to enjoy basic human rights'.[93]

53. The arbitral tribunal in this case was the first to apply revised ICSID Arbitration Rule 37(2). Relying on this Rule, the tribunal allowed written submissions from the *amici curiae* despite Biwater Gauff's opposition, on the basis that any decision by the arbitral tribunal would have the potential to impact upon 'wider interests',[94] and that a written submission may potentially assist the tribunal in bringing a perspective, knowledge and insight different from that of the parties.[95] However, in order to ensure that the parties were not unduly burdened, the tribunal imposed a number of procedural safeguards, including that the five petitioners submit one joint memorial with a limit of 50 pages.[96]

54. In its final award, the tribunal further stated that the *amici curiae* submissions had offered 'expertise and perspectives that have been demonstrated to materially differ from those of the two contending parties, and as such have provided a useful contribution to these

[90] *Suez/Interaguas* (n. 6) [4]. [91] *Ibid.* [33]–[34]. Cf. also Bastin (n. 2) 216.

[92] *Biwater Gauff (Tanzania) Ltd.* v. *Tanzania*, ICSID Case No. ARB/05/22 www.italaw.com/cases/documents/158.

[93] *Biwater* (n. 27) [14]. [94] *Ibid.* [53].

[95] *Ibid.* [50]. Cf. also ICSID Commentary (n. 85) Art 44 [128]. [96] *Ibid.* [60(a)].

proceedings' and that it had relied on the *amici curiae* submissions to inform its decision-making.[97]

6.5.8 Glamis Gold *v.* USA

55. In *Glamis Gold* v. *USA* ('*Glamis Gold*'),[98] a dispute arose between Glamis, a Canadian mining company, and the USA, concerning mining rights in California. Glamis commenced proceedings under NAFTA Chapter 11. The Quechan Indian Nation (QIN) was the first third person to apply for *amicus* status. In its application, QIN cited a unique and different approach to that of the disputing parties and its significant interest in the arbitration.[99] The tribunal accepted the request from QIN, while acknowledging that it 'is important . . . to avoid undue burden on the Parties and delay in the proceedings'.[100]

56. Subsequently, three additional non-disputing parties applied to file submissions. The tribunal stated that it would consider each submission, as appropriate, in accordance with the principles of the NAFTA FTC Statement and with particular reference to whether they offered 'a perspective, particular knowledge or insight that is different from that of the disputing parties'.[101] The tribunal emphasised that the requirements specified in the NAFTA FTC Statement should be applied strictly, such as by restricting the length of the submission or limiting the matters to be addressed, but that, in light of the public and remedial purposes of non-disputing submissions, leave to make third person submissions should be granted liberally. The tribunal noted that the granting of leave to make *amicus* submissions did not require the tribunal to actually address the submission at any point in the arbitration, nor did it entitle a non-disputing party to make subsequent submissions at a later stage of the arbitration.[102]

97 *Biwater*, Award (n. 22) [355], [359], [392].

98 *Glamis Gold, Ltd* v. *United States of America*, NAFTA/UNCITRAL www.italaw.com/cases/documents/488.

99 Referred to in Stern (n. 2) 302ff.

100 *Glamis Gold*, Decision on Application and Submission by Quechan Indian Nation (16 September 2005) www.italaw.com/sites/default/files/case-documents/ita0366.pdf, [11]–[12].

101 *Glamis Gold, Ltd.* v. *United States of America*, NAFTA/UNCITRAL Award (8 June 2009) www.italaw.com/sites/default/files/case-documents/ita0378.pdf, [286], quoting its decision of 15 February 2007 and NAFTA FTC Statement § B.6(a).

102 *Ibid.* [286].

57. QIN applied to file a second submission, which included an expert report that QIN requested remain confidential. The tribunal rejected this request, explaining that 'transparency of Chapter Eleven tribunals is of particular importance to the [NAFTA] member states'.[103] QIN was, however, allowed to redact its report before publication.

6.5.9 Grand River Enterprises Six Nations, Ltd et al. *v.* USA

58. In *Grand River Enterprises Six Nations, Ltd et al.* v. *United States* ('*Grand River*'),[104] the parties agreed with the tribunal at the first session that 'the Tribunal should later adopt a process for receiving and considering *amicus* submissions, as necessary (but not at this stage) by having recourse to the recommendations of the [NAFTA FTC Statement]'.[105] Upon receiving an unsolicited submission from the Office of the National Chief of the Assembly of First Nations, the tribunal stated that it would be guided by the NAFTA FTC Statement in considering whether to accept and consider the submission.[106] The submission was ultimately included by the claimants as a supporting exhibit to their March 2009 reply. The tribunal stated that the submission was read in that context.[107]

6.5.10 Merrill & Ring Forestry *v.* Canada

59. Merrill & Ring Forestry (MRF) brought an arbitration claim against Canada under the Arbitration Rules pursuant to NAFTA Chapter 11.[108] The Communication, Energy and Paperworkers Union of Canada, the United Steelworkers and the British Columbia Federation of Labour applied for leave to intervene in the proceedings. In its decision on the application, the tribunal confirmed that it had jurisdiction under Article 15(1) of the

[103] *Ibid.* [282].

[104] *Grand River Enterprises Six Nations, Ltd et al.* v. *United States of America*, NAFTA/UNCITRAL www.italaw.com/cases/documents/511.

[105] *Grand River*, Minutes of the First Session of the Tribunal (31 March 2005) www.state.gov/documents/organization/45017.pdf, § II(1).

[106] *Grand River*, Letter from the Tribunal to the Parties Concerning the Amicus Curiae Submission (27 January 2009) www.state.gov/documents/organization/117813.pdf, 1–2.

[107] *Grand River*, Award (12 January 2011) www.italaw.com/sites/default/files/case-documents/ita0384.pdf [60].

[108] *Merrill & Ring Forestry LLP* v. *Canada*, UNCITRAL, ICSID Administered Case.

Arbitration Rules (1976) to consider a request for *amicus curiae* participation in the proceedings.[109] Nonetheless, the tribunal pointed out that the applicants still must meet the requirements set out in the NAFTA FTC Statement and directed the applicants to make any such compliant submission by a certain date.[110] The petitioners filed their application and *amicus curiae* submissions on 26 September 2008[111] and the parties were given the opportunity to comment on these submissions. The tribunal's award did not state whether, and, if so, to what extent, the *amici* submissions influenced its decision-making.[112]

6.5.11 Piero Foresti *v.* South Africa

60. In the case of *Piero Foresti* v. *South Africa* ('*Piero Foresti*'),[113] the tribunal granted two South African and two international human rights groups[114] the right to participate in the arbitral proceedings, which concerned mining interests in South Africa.

61. In the petition for participation as non-disputing parties, which the four groups made jointly in order to reduce the potential burden on the tribunal and the parties,[115] the petitioners relied on Article 41(3) of the ICSID Additional Facility Arbitration Rules (AFR), which had been included to allow for third party submissions when the Rules were revised in 2006.

[109] *Merrill & Ring Forestry LLP* v. *Government of Canada*, Letter (31 July 2008) from the Tribunal to Steven Shrybman regarding submission of an application on behalf of the Communication, Energy and Paperworkers Union of Canada, the United Steelworkers and the British Columbia Federation of Labour www.international.gc.ca/trade-agreements-accords-commerciaux/assets/pdfs/disp-diff/merrill-13.pdf.

[110] *Ibid.*

[111] *Merrill & Ring Forestry LLP* v. *Canada*, Application to File a Written Submission by the United Steel Workers, Communications, Energy and Paperworkers Union of Canada, and the British Columbia Federation of Labour (26 September 2008) www.international.gc.ca/trade-agreements-accords-commerciaux/assets/pdfs/disp-diff/merrill-14.pdf.

[112] *Merrill & Ring Forestry LLP* v. *Canada*, Award (31 March 2010) http://italaw.com/sites/default/files/case-documents/ita0504.pdf. This document only discusses the amici submissions in the context of the procedural history: [22]–[25].

[113] *Piero Foresti, Laura di Carli and Others* v. *South Africa*, ICSID Case No. ARB/(AF)/07/1 http://italaw.com/cases/446.

[114] And one additional petition by the International Commission of Jurists (19 August 2009), which was not made publicly available.

[115] *Piero Foresti* (n. 113), Petition for Limited Participation as Non-Disputing Parties in terms of Articles 41(3), 27, 39, and 35 of the Additional Facility Rules (17 July 2009) http://italaw.com/sites/default/files/case-documents/ita0333.pdf [3.7].

62. The petitioners referred to the public interest of the human rights and sustainable development dimensions of the dispute in their reasons for making the petition.[116] Drawing on both the wording of Article 41(3) of the ICSID AFR and previous ICSID tribunals in order to establish what information they needed to provide to describe their suitability as non-disputing parties,[117] the petitioners provided detailed descriptions of each petitioner to underline their expertise and experience in this area. The petitioners asserted that they brought a 'perspective, particular knowledge or insight that differs from that of the disputing parties', but also stated that this criterion was difficult to ascertain without access to certain documents in the proceedings, for which the petitioners also applied.[118]

63. For the first time in the ICSID context, in addition to allowing the petitioners to make submissions, the tribunal also ordered the parties to the arbitration to disclose to the petitioners their key legal filings in the case. In ordering this, the tribunal kept two basic principles in mind:

> (1) NDP [Non-disputing party] participation is intended to enable NDPs to give useful information and accompanying submissions to the Tribunal, but is not intended to be a mechanism for enabling NDPs to obtain information from the Parties.
> (2) Where there is NDP participation, the Tribunal must ensure that it is both effective and compatible with the rights of the Parties and the fairness and efficiency of the arbitral process.[119]

64. Although the case was ultimately discontinued, the tribunal's statements about third person participation and the petitioners' detailed petition provide interesting insights into the development of this area of law.

6.5.12 Achmea (formerly Eureko) *v.* Slovak Republic

65. In the first dispute[120] between Achmea (formerly Eureko) and the Slovak Republic ('*Achmea*'),[121] the development of the practice of employing third person submissions in investment arbitration reached

[116] *Ibid.* [4.7]ff. [117] *Ibid.* [5.7]ff. [118] *Ibid.* [5.16]ff.

[119] *Piero Foresti* (n. 113), Letter (5 October 2009) http://italaw.com/cases/446.

[120] For the second set of proceedings between Achmea and the Slovak Republic, see *Achmea BV* v. *The Slovak Republic*, UNCITRAL, PCA Case No. 2013-12 (Number 2) (Achmea II) www.italaw.com/cases/2564.

[121] *Achmea BV* v. *The Slovak Republic*, PCA Case No. 2008-13, UNCITRAL (Achmea I; hereinafter referred to as '*Achmea*') http://italaw.com/cases/documents/418.

a significant milestone: the tribunal *invited* third person submissions from two entities, the European Commission and the Kingdom of the Netherlands.[122] It was the second of three publicly accessible investor-State arbitral proceedings in which the European Commission made submissions as *amicus curiae*.[123]

66. The claim in *Achmea* was brought by Eureko under the Dutch–Slovak BIT, after the Slovak Republic changed legislation that restricted Eureko's operations as an insurance company on the Slovak market. Slovakia challenged the jurisdiction of the tribunal by submitting that the EC Treaty superseded the Dutch–Slovak BIT. In its jurisdictional objections, the Slovak Republic requested that the European Commission participate as *amicus curiae*.[124] The claimant initially objected to this request on the grounds that a potential intervention of the European Commission would be irrelevant and solely disruptive to the proceedings.[125] However, after the tribunal consulted with the parties, an agreement was reached to extend an invitation to make third person submissions to the European Commission and the Netherlands on the condition that 'tight deadlines' would be implemented to limit the additional costs and delay associated with third party submissions.[126]

67. The tribunal based its invitation on the view that the third persons would assist the tribunal in making a decision on jurisdiction in the context of an intra-EU BIT.[127] Their participation was focused on a specific interest in the development of Community law and the potential conflict with the tribunal's jurisdiction.[128]

68. The third persons' submissions to the tribunal have not been published; notably, in a decision made on 13 July 2010, the tribunal

[122] *Achmea*, Award on Jurisdiction, Arbitrability and Suspension (26 October 2010) http://italaw.com/sites/default/files/case-documents/ita0309.pdf, [31]–[32]. See also Bastin (n. 24), 129. The submission for the Netherlands would now probably be analysed under Article 5 of the Rules, see Martins Paparinskis and Jessica Howley, 'Article 5', [6]–[7].

[123] See also *AES Summit Generation Limited and AES-Tisza Erömü Kft* v. *The Republic of Hungary*, Award (23 September 2010) www.italaw.com/sites/default/files/case-documents/ita0014_0.pdf, [3.18], [3.22]; *Electrabel S.A.* v. *Republic of Hungary*, Award on Jurisdiction, Applicable Law and Liability (30 November 2012) www.italaw.com/sites/default/files/case-documents/italaw1071clean.pdf, [1.18].

[124] *Achmea* (n. 122) [151]. [125] *Ibid.* [152]–[153]. [126] *Ibid.* [154].

[127] *Ibid.* [154].

[128] *Ibid.* [176]ff; cf. also *Electrabel SA* v. *Hungary* (n. 123) [4.91]ff, in particular [4.92]. Cf. detailed discussion in Séverine Menétrey, 'La participation "amicable" de la Commission européenne dans les arbitrages lies aux investissements intracommunautaires' (2010) 137 *Journal du droit international* 1127 [14].

explicitly declined a request of the Slovak Republic to disclose the submission of the European Commission to another tribunal.[129]

6.5.13 Bernard von Pezold *v.* Zimbabwe; Border Timbers Ltd *v.* Zimbabwe

69. In 2010, Bernhard von Pezold as well as Border Timbers Limited, Border Timbers International (Private) Limited and Hangani Development Co (Private) Limited initiated two claims against the Republic of Zimbabwe ('*von Pezold*').[130] The disputes, which were ultimately conjoined by agreement of the parties and administered by the identically-constituted tribunals, arose out of Zimbabwe's alleged breach of its obligations under its BITs with Switzerland and Germany by failing to provide fair and equitable treatment in conjunction with Zimbabwe's Land Reform Programme.

70. In these two ICSID cases, the tribunals denied the participation of two third persons. The two petitioners, the European Center for Constitutional and Human Rights (ECCHR) and a group of indigenous communities in Zimbabwe, applied to present submissions on the interdependence of investment treaty law and human rights law, and to submit that human rights law was directly applicable to the dispute. In their submissions, the petitioners stated that they had a significant interest in the outcome of the proceedings since they impacted on alleged rights over or in relation to the ancestral lands of the indigenous communities[131] and the ECCHR's mission to develop the strategic use of legal actions for corporate human rights responsibilities.[132]

71. The tribunals, applying ICSID Arbitration Rule 37(2), considered that a requirement of independence was implicit in the ICSID Rules, which mandated that the third persons bring a perspective to the proceedings that was different from that of the disputing parties.[133] Although the tribunals rejected the claimants' argument that because the chiefs of the indigenous communities were appointed by the

[129] *Achmea* (n. 122) [40].

[130] *Bernhard von Pezold and Others* v. *Zimbabwe*, ICSID Case No. ARB/10/15; *Border Timbers Limited, Border Timbers International (Private) Limited and Hangani Development Co (Private) Limited* v. *Zimbabwe*, ICSID Case No. ARB/10/25 ('*von Pezold*') www.italaw.com/cases/1472.

[131] *Von Pezold*, Procedural Order No. 2 (26 June 2012) www.italaw.com/sites/default/files/case-documents/ita1044.pdf, [21].

[132] *Ibid.* [22]. [133] *Ibid.* [49].

Zimbabwean president, they were not independent,[134] it rejected the non-disputing party request on another ground of independence: the tribunals stated that because the indigenous communities sought to occupy parts of the Border estate, the land at issue in the proceedings, this suggested that they were not independent but rather supportive of the respondent's land reform policies.[135]

72. The tribunals thus found that the petitioners did not appear to be 'independent' of the Zimbabwean State.[136] Moreover, it stated that the petitioners were seeking to make submissions 'on legal and factual issues that are unrelated to the matters before the Arbitral Tribunals'[137] and that neither party had put the international human rights law issues concerned in issue in the proceedings.[138] They also found that a consideration of indigenous rights was not within the scope of their mandate under either the ICSID Convention or the applicable BITs[139] and that the ECCHR's mission and expertise were not relevant to the issues at stake and, as such, the ECCHR had no significant interest in the case.[140]

73. This case has been criticised by commentators for its departure from the 'consolidated standard' set forth in the NAFTA FTC Statement and the ICSID Rules, bolstered by reasonably consistent application in case law.[141] It remains to be seen how future investment arbitral tribunals will deal with the *von Pezold* approach when faced with the question of third person participation, particularly in the context of human rights concerns.

6.5.14 Pac Rim Cayman *v.* El Salvador

74. On 30 April 2009, Pac Rim Cayman commenced arbitral proceedings against El Salvador under the Dominican Republic–Central America–United States Free Trade Agreement (CAFTA-DR).[142]

75. On 2 February 2011, the tribunal issued a Procedural Order inviting any person or entity other than the disputing parties to make a written application to the tribunal for permission to file written submissions as an *amicus curiae*.[143] On 2 March 2011, member organisations of Mesa

[134] *Ibid.* [52]ff. [135] *Ibid.* [55]ff. [136] *Ibid.* [50]. [137] *Ibid.* [57]. [138] *Ibid.*
[139] *Ibid.* [59]. [140] *Ibid.* [61]. [141] Cf. e.g. Schliemann (n. 13); Bastin (n. 24), 137–9.
[142] *Pac Rim Cayman LLC* v. *El Salvador*, ICSID Case No. ARB/09/12 www.italaw.com/cases/783.
[143] *Pac Rim Cayman LLC* v. *El Salvador*, Procedural Order, ICSID News Release regarding Amicus Curiae www.italaw.com/sites/default/files/case-documents/ita0608.pdf.

Nacional Frente a la Minería Metálica de El Salvador (La Mesa) made an application to the tribunal for permission to proceed as *amici curiae*.[144]

76. On 23 March 2011, the tribunal issued an order granting La Mesa permission to file a written submission as *amici curiae* under Article 10.20.3 of CAFTA-DR and ICSID Arbitration Rule 37(2).[145] The tribunal limited the scope of its permission to submissions made on jurisdictional issues. Submissions on the merits of the case were expressly excluded. Moreover, the tribunal demanded that the written submission should not risk the disruption of the arbitration proceedings or otherwise unduly burden or unfairly prejudice any party or non-disputing party.[146]

77. La Mesa's submission asserted that it was assisting the tribunal in its determination of jurisdiction, although La Mesa's arguments 'closely track[ed] the arguments raised by the parties'.[147] La Mesa asserted that the tribunal's decision could impact on the communities that La Mesa represented and that it had 'particular knowledge' of the issues at the core of the arbitration.[148]

78. Although the tribunal set out the submissions of the third person in the award on jurisdiction, it did not rely on them directly.[149]

6.5.15 Chevron and Texaco *v.* Ecuador

79. In a second round of proceedings[150] in the case of *Chevron and Texaco* v. *Ecuador* ('*Chevron*'),[151] a long-running, complex dispute

[144] *Pac Rim Cayman LLC* v. *El Salvador*, Application for Permission to Proceed as *Amici Curiae* (2 March 2011) www.italaw.com/sites/default/files/case-documents/ita0609.pdf.

[145] *Pac Rim Cayman LLC* v. *El Salvador*, Procedural Order No. 8 (23 March 2011) www.italaw.com/sites/default/files/case-documents/ita0615.pdf.

[146] *Ibid.*

[147] *Pac Rim Cayman LLC* v. *El Salvador*, Submission of Amicus Curiae Brief (20 May 2011) www.italaw.com/sites/default/files/case-documents/italaw1208.pdf, 1.

[148] *Ibid.* 2.

[149] With respect to the abuse of process issue, the tribunal relied on the claimant's submissions and stated that it did 'not accept the arguments made to the contrary in the Amicus Curiae Submission', Decision on the Respondent's Jurisdictional Objections (1 June 2012) www.italaw.com/sites/default/files/case-documents/ita0935.pdf, [2.41]ff. With respect to the denial of benefits argument, the tribunal did not expressly accept the *amicus curiae* argument, but stated in passing that a statement by the *amicus curiae* was in support of its findings, *ibid.* [4.85].

[150] For the first arbitration between Chevron/Texaco and Ecuador see *Chevron Corporation (USA) and Texaco Petroleum Company (USA)* v. *Ecuador*, UNCITRAL (Chevron I), PCA Case No. 34877 www.italaw.com/cases/251.

[151] *Chevron Corporation and Texaco Petroleum Company* v. *Ecuador*, PCA Case No. 2009-23 (Chevron II; hereinafter referred to as '*Chevron*') www.italaw.com/cases/257.

arising out of Chevron and its affiliates' oil operations in Ecuador, two third persons made a joint application to the tribunal for *amicus* status in the proceedings. A case administered by the PCA, it was subject to the Arbitration Rules (1976) and the order for *amicus* status was, as in earlier cases, sought pursuant to the tribunal's general procedural powers under Article 15. However, the *amici* referred to both ICSID Arbitration Rule 37(2) and the NAFTA FTC Statement as 'two objective sets of criteria which may be useful to the Tribunal and which the Petitioners have consequently sought to apply in this Petition'.[152] The petitioners relied on their experience and perspectives in making their application and declared that they were independent of the parties. In rejecting the petitioners' application, the tribunal appeared to rely on the fact that both parties had agreed that the *amicus* submissions would not be helpful to the tribunal.[153] Thus, while, under the NAFTA FTC Statement and ICSID Arbitration Rule 37(2), the parties cannot exercise a 'veto right' against third person participation, it would appear that in cases where both parties are against the participation of the third person, the tribunal will give this due weight in making its decision.

6.5.16 Apotex Holdings et al. *v.* USA

80. On 29 February 2012, Apotex Holdings Inc., a Canadian pharmaceuticals corporation, for the second time[154] initiated an arbitral proceeding against the USA under NAFTA (*Apotex*). As Canada was not an ICSID Convention Member State at this time (it has since become one), the arbitration was conducted under the ICSID AFR.[155]

81. On 31 January 2013, the tribunal invited written applications for permission to file submissions as *amicus curiae* by 8 February 2013 in compliance with the requirements of the NAFTA FTC Statement and ICSID AFR 41(3).[156] The tribunal received applications from two petitioners.

[152] *Chevron* (n. 151), Petition for Participation as Non-Disputing Parties (22 October 2010) http://italaw.com/cases/documents/266, [2.2].

[153] *Chevron* (n. 151), Procedural Order No. 8 (11 April 2011) http://italaw.com/cases/documents/266 [18].

[154] For the first Apotex case see *Apotex Inc.* v. *United States of America*, UNCITRAL www.italaw.com/cases/documents/2156.

[155] *Apotex Holdings Inc and Apotex Inc* v. *United States of America* ('*Apotex*'), ICSID Case No. ARB(AF)/12/1 www.italaw.com/cases/documents/1700.

[156] *Apotex*, Invitation to Amici Curiae (31 January 2013) www.italaw.com/sites/default/files/case-documents/italaw1253.pdf.

82. The first petitioner, Mr Appleton, a Canadian attorney, sought leave to present arguments as *amicus curiae* to the arbitral tribunal on the basis that he 'has particular experience with the challenge of providing fairness in regulatory conduct and with ensuring that governments provide equality of competitive opportunities to foreign and domestic investors alike. He can assist the Tribunal with the consequences of conduct that can distort international trade and investment flows and undermine market access benefits'.[157] What Mr Appleton did not disclose – to which the US Government drew attention – was that he was representing claimants in three current cases under NAFTA, at least one of which addressed the same issues as Mr Appleton's application. On this basis, the US Government alleged that Mr Appleton could have a financial interest in the outcome of the case.[158]

83. The second petitioner, BNM, stated that its interest was in the development of new financial services to build a more ethical legal framework for the global pharmaceutical market. With reference to its interest in creating a 'litigation venture capital fund', BNM stated that its submission was intended to clarify the scope of definition of 'investment' under Article 1139 (g) NAFTA.[159]

84. The tribunal followed the parties' submissions and applied the NAFTA FTC Statement criteria to find that both Mr Appleton's and BNM's applications:

(a) would not be of any assistance to the tribunal in the arbitration;
(b) did not address matters within the scope of the dispute;
(c) did not demonstrate a *significant* interest in the arbitration; and
(d) did not explain why the subject matter of the arbitration was of public interest.[160]

85. In rejecting Mr Appleton's application, the tribunal was not convinced that Mr Appleton's expertise, despite him being an international lawyer, could provide a different perspective or insight from that of the counsel already engaged in the case. Further, with respect to whether

[157] *Apotex*, Procedural Order on the Participation of Applicant Mr Barry Appleton as a Non-Disputing Party (4 March 2013) www.italaw.com/sites/default/files/case-documents/italaw3001.pdf, [11]ff.

[158] *Apotex* (n. 157) [18]ff.

[159] *Apotex* Procedural Order on the Participation of the Applicant, BNM, as a Non-Disputing Party (4 March 2013) www.italaw.com/sites/default/files/case-documents/italaw1320.pdf, [8]ff.

[160] *Apotex* (n. 157) [23]ff; (n. 159) [15]ff.

Mr Appleton had a 'significant interest' in the case, the tribunal stated as follows:[161]

> It seems that the Applicant's 'significant interest' in this arbitration lies only in having this Tribunal adopt legal interpretations of NAFTA that he favours that could be advantageous to his clients in his pending and possible future NAFTA cases. Although it may be an interest, the Tribunal concludes that it is not a significant interest under Section B(6)(c) NAFTA FTC Statement. The contrary interpretation would lead to absurd results; and that cannot possibly be what was intended with the admission of amicus curiae briefs in NAFTA arbitrations.

86. Finally, the tribunal found that Mr Appleton's *amicus* application was driven by a particular professional interest, rather than a public interest affecting him as a member of the community.[162] With respect to disclosure requirements, the tribunal noted that applicants in Mr Appleton's shoes should clarify from the outset their involvement in other pending NAFTA cases, even if such information is publicly available elsewhere.[163]

87. In rejecting BNM's application,[164] the tribunal held that BNM had failed to satisfy several aspects of the NAFTA FTC Statement's test, including a showing of special expertise and a significant interest.[165]

6.6 Article 4(1)

6.6.1 *'After consultation with the disputing parties'*

88. A key requirement for the ongoing success of third person participation in investor-State arbitration is, of course, the involvement of the disputing parties themselves.

89. It is noteworthy here that the Rules do not require the consent of the parties; the requirement is deliberately limited to an obligation to consult with the parties. Of course, if one party were to make strong objections to the participation of third persons in the proceedings, the tribunal would be obliged to give these due weight and then to exercise its

[161] Apotex (n. 157) [40]. [162] *Ibid.* [43]. [163] *Ibid.* [46].

[164] This entity was also refused amicus status, for similar reasons (it made the same submission in both cases), in the earlier NAFTA case of *Apotex Inc* v. *USA*, UNCITRAL (NAFTA), Procedural Order No. 2 (11 October 2011) www.italaw.com/sites/default/files/case-documents/ita0033.pdf.

[165] *Apotex* (n. 159) [20]ff.

discretion. On the other hand, the tribunal's obligation to merely consult with the parties represents a clear stance to the effect that it will not be the parties, but the tribunal, that will determine the participation of third persons in the proceedings.[166] Indeed, this was discussed in detail by the WG when drafting the Rules. Ultimately, it was decided that leaving the decision to the parties would not be advisable due to the often one-sided nature of third person submissions, or instances where the submission will not decidedly favour either side. In light of the purpose of third person submissions to enlighten the arbitral tribunal in its decision-making process, the WG decided that the arbitral tribunal should play the role of 'gate-keeper' and decide on whether to allow the submissions.[167]

90. In the case of *Achmea*,[168] the respondent's request to invite the intervention of the European Commission as *amicus curiae* was opposed by the claimant.[169] Although the claimant, after consultation with the respondent and the tribunal, eventually agreed to extend an *amicus* invitation to the European Commission,[170] the question *Achmea* leaves open is whether there is an obligation on tribunals to consider *requests to invite* potential *amici curiae* in the same way as it should consider a party's objections to a third person *application*. Moreover, had the claimant in *Achmea* refused to agree to inviting the European Commission's participation, it may have arguably been a stretch of the tribunal's discretion to actively seek third person participation in the proceedings in circumstances in which no application was actually pending.

91. In practice, the third person seeking participation will usually request permission in the form of a letter or other written document. Consequently, the parties should usually be given the opportunity by the tribunal to review why the third person wants to participate and to make submissions on whether or not participation should be allowed. In effect, therefore, what 'consultation' will mean in most cases is that the parties will be given the opportunity to comment, and the tribunal will then make a ruling as to whether a third person submission will be allowed into the proceedings.

[166] Cf. e.g. *Biwater*, case summary at section 6.5.7 above, in which the tribunal allowed third person submissions despite the claimant's objections.

[167] UNCITRAL (n. 1) UN Doc. A/CN.9/712 [47].

[168] See case summary at section 6.5.12 above.

[169] *Achmea* (n. 122) [152]–[153].

[170] *Ibid.* [154].

6.6.2 *'the arbitral tribunal may allow'*

92. The wording in this provision leaves no room for doubt that the arbitral tribunal is entitled to exercise its discretion when deciding whether to admit third person submissions. Guidance in the exercise of the tribunal's discretion is provided by paragraphs 3 and 5.[171] This is congruent with the inherent discretion of the arbitral tribunal to conduct the proceedings in an efficient manner as it best sees fit. If all parties to an arbitration are in agreement in favour of – or against[172] – the participation of a third person, it is difficult to conceive of a situation in which the tribunal would decide to ignore the will of the parties. As a general rule, the tribunal will, absent unanimous agreement between the parties, seek a middle road that accommodates the parties' wishes to the greatest extent possible.

93. Article 4 of the Rules leaves open the question to what extent, if any, the tribunal's decision on the admissibility of an *amicus* submission requires reasoning. A decision on third person submissions would usually be in the form of a procedural order.[173] Thus, the various requirements for awards do not find direct application.[174]

94. On the one hand, the argument could be made that the third person application does not affect the parties' rights and obligations in, and is indeed 'external' to, the arbitral proceedings concerned, with the consequence that a decision on such an application does not need to be reasoned.

95. On the other hand, the Rules have been drafted specifically for the purpose of establishing legitimacy of investment arbitration proceedings by increasing transparency standards in investor-State disputes. Legitimacy concerns must require that decisions on third person submissions be reasoned – at least rudimentarily – and be communicated not only to the parties, but to the third person applicants.

6.6.3 *'a person that is not a disputing party'*

96. The wording 'a person that is not a disputing party' seeks to clarify the scope of potential third person applicants. This goes back to the

[171] UNCITRAL, 'Report of Working Group II (Arbitration and Conciliation) on the work of its fifty-seventh session (12 October 2012) UN Doc. A/CN.9/760 [40].

[172] See *Chevron*, section 6.5.15 above.

[173] See generally section 6.5 above.

[174] Cf. also Gary Born, *International Commercial Arbitration* (2nd edn. Kluwer, 2014) §22.02[B][d].

object and purpose of this article: namely, to provide third persons in the form of NGOs, other interest groups, and even individuals[175] with the opportunity to present information or provide a perspective that may be 'useful' to the resolution of a dispute.

97. Article 4(2)(b), discussed below, states that any third person seeking to participate in investor-State arbitral proceedings must disclose any connection to any party to the dispute. Reading these two paragraphs together, this means that a third person seeking participation in investor-State arbitral proceedings cannot be a disputing party, but must disclose any connection it may have to a disputing party.

6.6.4 *'and not a non-disputing Party to the treaty'*

98. This phrase seeks to establish delineation to Article 5 of the Rules, which addresses separately the involvement of a party to the underlying treaty that is not party to the dispute. Article 5 establishes a separate regime for third persons that are a party to the underlying treaty.

99. The final wording of this section of Article 4 of the Rules, notably, does not include a reference to 'non-disputing *State* parties'. This deliberate omission was in recognition of the fact that parties to an investment treaty do not necessarily have to be States.[176] Supranational bodies, such as the European Commission, now fall within the scope of application of Article 5 as an individual and independent party of the underlying treaty.[177]

6.6.5 *'written submission'*

100. In terms of the form of the submission, the Rules are unambiguous that the submissions covered by Article 4 are to be in the form of written submissions only. This term is broad enough to cover memorials, but also less formal documents such as emails or letters. Oral statements in the form of, for example, participation at oral hearings are not covered by this article.[178]

[175] Cf. *Apotex* (n. 157). [176] UNCITRAL (n. 14) UN Doc. A/CN.9/736 [95].

[177] Martins Paparinskis and Jessica Howley, 'Article 5', [6].

[178] For a third person's potential involvement in hearing, cf. Krista Nadakavukaren Schefer, 'Article 1', [69]–[73] and Klint Alexander, 'Article 6', [17]–[20].

6.6.6 *'matter within the scope of the dispute'*

101. It will be the task of the tribunal, aided by the parties, to determine whether the matter intended to be submitted falls within the scope of the dispute. The burden thereby also lies on the third person itself to define the relevance of its concerns precisely and with clear reference to the context of the matter in dispute.

102. For example, as early as the case of *UPS* v. *Canada*,[179] the tribunal stated that third person submissions 'are to relate to issues raised by the disputing parties and cannot introduce new issues in the litigation or go beyond the scope of the case as defined by the disputing parties'.[180] The reference may seem to be obvious since, as Professor Stern has pointed out in the context of the revised ICSID Arbitration Rule 37(2),[181] 'it is difficult to envision a friend of the court intervening in a matter that is unrelated to the dispute'.[182] In the case of *Piero Foresti*, the petitioners interpreted this criterion to mean that 'they will not introduce new contested issues that could expand the dispute'.[183]

103. This criterion is also subject to the limitation that the role of third persons in one of assistance to the tribunal: to aid in the resolution of the dispute.[184] Care should be taken to ensure that third person participation is not abused as a means of following a political, environmental or other goal that clearly goes beyond the scope of the dispute at hand.[185]

6.7 Article 4(2)

6.7.1 *Purpose of Article 4(2)*

104. Article 4(2) as a whole is concerned with a third person's suitability to make a submission to the tribunal. As stated in the *Suez/Vivendi* case,[186] the tribunal should be satisfied that a potential third person has the expertise, experience and independence to be of assistance to the tribunal.[187] As set out in that case, and reflected in the wording of the

[179] See case summary at section 6.5.3 above.

[180] *UPS* v. *Canada*, Direction of the Tribunal on the Participation of Amici Curiae (1 August 2003) www.international.gc.ca/trade-agreements-accords-commerciaux/assets/pdfs/disp-diff/ups-52.pdf, [5].

[181] For discussion of ICSID Rule 37(2), see section 6.4.3 above.

[182] Stern (n. 2) 341.

[183] *Piero Foresti* (n. 115) [5.20].

[184] See section 6.8.3 below.

[185] For a discussion on *ex officio* duties of tribunals to examine certain claims brought before them (e.g. corruption), cf. section 6.9.3 below.

[186] See case summary at section 6.5.5 above.

[187] *Suez/Vivendi* v. *Argentina* (n. 18) [24].

NAFTA FTC Statement,[188] the potential third person needs to include in its petition certain information in order for the tribunal to assess its suitability,[189] and indeed, to assess the motivations of the third person and any potential conflicts of interest.[190] This information has been incorporated into Article 4(2) Rules.

6.7.2 *'apply to the arbitral tribunal'*

105. The wording of Article 4(2) clarifies that any third person wishing to participate in a proceeding must first apply to the tribunal. Similar to ICSID Arbitration Rule 37(2)[191] and the procedure set out in the NAFTA FTC Statement, the process of submitting a third person brief is divided into two stages: an application to the tribunal (Article 4(2)); and the actual submission (Article 4(4)), if the tribunal grants the application. Unlike the NAFTA FTC Statement, however, Article 4 leaves open the question of whether the submission should be made simultaneously with the application or whether the application and the submission should be kept separate; in practice, the precise modalities will be left to the tribunal in exercise of its discretion.[192]

106. The wording of this Article does not, however, exclude the possibility that the tribunal may, within the scope of its discretion, invite third persons to participate in the proceedings if the tribunal is of the view that such third persons can aid it in resolving the dispute.[193]

[188] For discussion of NAFTA FTC Statement, see section 6.4.2 above.

[189] *Suez/Vivendi* v. *Argentina* (n. 18) [25]; NAFTA FTC Statement (n. 18).

[190] Cf. Delaney and Magraw (n. 12) 783.

[191] For discussion of ICSID Rule 37(2), see section 6.4.3 above.

[192] § B.1 of the NAFTA FTC Statement sets out that submissions have to be filed simultaneously with the application. See e.g. *Glamis Gold* (NAFTA/UNCITRAL Rules), Application for Leave to File a Non-Party Submission and Non-Party Submission (Submission of the Quechan Indian Nation) (19 August 2005) www.state.gov/documents/organization/52531.pdf. In non-NAFTA claims governed by rules which do not contain provisions to this effect, the third persons submitted their statements only after leave was granted by the tribunal, cf., e.g., *Aguas del Tunari* (ICSID) (n. 76); *Biwater* (ICSID) (n. 233). Similarly, in the pre-2003 FTC Statement NAFTA case of *UPS*, the application for amicus status was filed without the submissions themselves. See Petition to the Arbitral Tribunal/Canadian Union of Postal Workers and of the Council of Canadians (10 May 2001) www.international.gc.ca/trade-agreements-accords-commerciaux/assets/pdfs/disp-diff/ups-13.pdf.

[193] Cf. *Achmea* v. *Slovak Republic* discussed at section 6.5.12 above.

6.7.3 *'concise written statement'; 'complies with any page limits set by the arbitral tribunal'*

107. Similar to the 'written submission' limitation set out in Article 4 (1),[194] this requirement makes clear that the appropriate form of application for third person participation is in writing. Here, however, the requirement has been added that the written statement must be concise and comply with any page limits set by the arbitral tribunal. There was discussion in the WG during the drafting of this article as to whether a page limit should be included directly into the Rules. This proposal was ultimately rejected by the WG in favour of granting more discretion to the tribunal in determining how long such an application should be.[195] Conciseness accords with a central goal of third person participation, namely that such participation should not unduly disrupt or burden the proceedings.[196] Long-winded, extensive applications would usurp the time and resources of both the parties and the tribunal. This is undesirable and should be avoided.

108. In the *Glamis Gold* and *UPS* v. *Canada* cases,[197] the tribunal stated that the third person submissions were not to exceed twenty pages, in line with the NAFTA FTC Statement's guidelines.[198] In the *Suez/Vivendi* case[199] under ICSID, the tribunal ordered that the third person submissions 'shall not be longer than 30 double-spaced pages in 12 point font'.[200]

109. Moreover, in several cases, tribunals have ensured conciseness through requiring multiple third persons to make joint submissions. For example, in *Biwater*,[201] the tribunal ordered that the various third persons make one joint submission not exceeding fifty pages.[202]

6.7.4 *'in a language of the arbitration'*

110. Where an investor-State arbitral proceeding is being conducted in more than one official language (this will usually be set out specifically in the dispute resolution clause or, at the latest, in the terms of reference or

194 See section 6.6.5 above.

195 UNCITRAL (n. 14) UN Doc. A/CN.9/736 [75].

196 Cf. in this respect the discussion in section 6.10 below.

197 See sections 6.5.3 and 6.5.10 above.

198 *Glamis Gold* (n. 100) [2]; *UPS* (n. 180) [8].

199 See section 6.5.5 above.

200 *Suez/Vivendi* (n. 82) [27(b)].

201 See section 6.5.7 above.

202 *Biwater* (n. 93) [60(a)]. Cf. also *Suez/Vivendi* v. *Argentina* (n. 82) [27(b)].

the first procedural order), a third person can submit an application in any language of the arbitration.[203]

6.7.5 *Disclosure requirements under Article 4(2)(a)–(e)*

111. Section 2 of Article 4 sets out detailed provisions regarding the information to be provided by the third person when making its application. These requirements accord in large part with those set out in paragraph B.2 of the NAFTA FTC Statement.

112. The scope of information to be brought to the tribunal's attention by the potential third person participant under Section 2 extends even to information already in the public domain. This applies all the more so to information that could bear relevance on the investment arbitral proceedings in question. In the *Apotex* case,[204] for example, the tribunal criticised the third person applicant Mr Appleton for failing to disclose his involvement in other NAFTA cases. The tribunal noted that applicants in Mr Appleton's shoes should clarify from the outset their involvement in other pending NAFTA cases, even if such information is publicly available elsewhere.[205]

6.7.6 *Article 4(2)(a)*

6.7.6.1 'describe the third person including, where relevant, its membership and legal status (e.g., trade association or other non-governmental organization)'

113. The basic rule for applying to make a third person submission to investor-State arbitral proceedings is that the application should comprehensively describe who, or what, the third person is. This includes providing information including its full name, legal status, general objectives, the nature of its activities and who it is controlled by. For individuals, increasingly in the role of third person interventionists, detailed *curricula vitae* should be provided.[206] Such a comprehensive

[203] In the bilingually conducted cases of *Aguas del Tunari* (see Petition of La Coordinarora para La Defensa Del Agua y Vida et al. (29 August 2009) www.italaw.com/sites/default/files/case-documents/ita0018.pdf) and *Suez/Interaguas* (see Order in Response to a Petition for Participation as Amicus Curiae (17 March 2006) www.italaw.com/sites/default/files/case-documents/ita0803.pdf, [1], [4]), the petitions filed to participate as *amicus curiae* were filed in one language only.

[204] See above case summary at section 6.5.10 above.

[205] *Apotex* (n. 157) [46].

[206] Cf. *Suez/Interaguas* (n. 6) [30]; Stern (n. 2) 322.

description is essential for a tribunal to determine the potential utility of any submissions to be made by the third person and whether the third person's profile is one which is likely to be of benefit to the arbitral proceedings as a whole.[207] This responds to criticism made in the past in the context of third person participation that it is often difficult to determine exactly what the intentions of the third person are and whose interests it represents.[208]

114. Until recently, the question of 'who' in the context of third person submissions to an investment arbitration tribunal was confined largely to the realm of NGOs.[209] This is not surprising when one considers that the subject matter of the overwhelming majority of investment arbitrations concern the public interest; as such, NGOs have regularly sought permission to represent the public's interests as third persons in such disputes.

115. However, the field of potential third persons has been steadily expanding to include a broader range of entities. In recent years, third persons have included the QIN who, rather than representing a somewhat more idealistic notion of public interest, had a direct interest in the outcome of the dispute because it was the land that it claimed a right to that was in question in the dispute. Similarly, in *Achmea*,[210] the European Commission was granted permission to participate as a third person based on its ability to provide useful information on the interaction between EU law and the provisions of the applicable BIT.[211]

116. Tribunals will also be careful to ensure that third persons have a certain gravitas before admitting them to the proceedings. Whilst there is no 'threshold' to speak of, a tribunal presiding over investor-State arbitral proceedings of considerable public interest would be prudent to ensure that potential third person participants stand in some sensible proportion in the context of the issues at stake. Entities that have been permitted to participate as third persons further include workers' unions (Canadian Union of Postal Workers in the *UPS* case[212]), environmental interest

[207] Cf. Schliemann (n. 13) 378. [208] Cf. Knahr (n. 38) 327.

[209] Cf. in general Levine (n. 2) 209ff; Bastin (n. 24) 127, citing *Methanex*, Decision of the Tribunal on Petitions from Third Persons to Intervene as 'Amici Curiae' (n. 47); *UPS*, Decision of the Tribunal on Petitions for Intervention and Participation as Amici Curiae (n. 65); *Aguas del Tunari*, Letter from the President of the Tribunal (n. 78); *Suez/Vivendi*, Order in Response to a Petition for Transparency and Participation as Amicus Curiae (n. 18); *Suez/Interaguas*, Order in Response to a Petition for Participation as Amicus Curiae (n. 6); *Biwater*, Procedural Order N. 5 (n. 27).

[210] See section 6.5.12 above. [211] See *Achmea* summary at section 6.5.12 above.

[212] See case summary at section 6.5.3 above.

groups (e.g. International Institute for Sustainable Development and the Center for International Environmental Law in several cases including *Methanex*,[213] *Biwater*,[214] *Suez/Vivendi*[215] and *Piero Foresti*[216]) and business federations (US Chamber of Commerce in *UPS*).

6.7.6.2 'its general objectives, the nature of its activities'

117. The general objectives and activities of the third person seeking 'access' to the proceedings will usually be particularly relevant. The arbitral tribunal will be required to examine whether the third person has a genuine reason to participate in the proceedings and that it is not otherwise patently unsuitable to make third person written submissions. The onus is on the third person to provide the tribunal with adequate information for the tribunal to determine that the third person's experience and expertise is such that allowing them to participate in the arbitration will be an effective exercise.[217]

118. In the *Suez/Interaguas* case,[218] the tribunal criticised that the third person had not provided information on the nature and size of its membership, the qualifications of its leadership, the expertise of its staff and the activities in which it was engaged. According to the tribunal, this information would have been necessary for it to assess whether the third person possessed the expertise and experience to qualify as an appropriate third person participant.[219]

6.7.6.3 'any parent organization (including any organization that directly or indirectly controls the third person)'

119. Direct or indirect control of a third person seeking participation in investor-State arbitral proceedings is a significant issue. There has been criticism in the past of *amici curiae* as not so much 'friends of the court' as 'friends of the state'.[220] It should thus be of primary concern to tribunals to ensure that they are not confronted with shadow organisations, in which the true controlling entity is not apparent.[221]

120. The Rules must, as far as possible, ensure that any measures that are designed and intended to enhance transparency in investor-State

[213] See case summary at section 6.5.2 above.
[214] See case summary at section 6.5.7 above.
[215] See case summary at section 6.5.5 above.
[216] See case summary at section 6.5.11 above.
[217] Cf. Stern (n. 2) 322.
[218] See case summary at section 6.5.6 above.
[219] *Suez/Interaguas* (n. 6) 30; cf. also Knahr (n. 38) 350–1; Stern (n. 2) 321ff.
[220] Cf. Kinnear (n. 23) 7; Dimsey (n. 2) 167.
[221] Cf. also section 6.7.7 below.

arbitration, such as third person participation, actually are transparent in and of themselves. Hence, the obligation is on third person applicants themselves to be sufficiently transparent in order for the tribunal to be able to assess whether such third person participation is legitimate and will provide a valuable, necessary contribution to the dispute at hand.[222]

6.7.7 *Article 4(2)(b): 'disclose any connection, direct or indirect, which the third person has with any disputing party'*

121. Article 4(2)(b) requires that the third person applicant disclose any connection that it has with any disputing party. This principle is crucial for the long-term credibility of submissions by third persons in investor-State arbitration and goes to the heart of legitimacy of third person submission in investor-State arbitration. In order to establish a lasting, viable role, it is imperative that such submissions remain truly 'third' person, rather than as an extended arm of the party's legal counsel. Third persons must be seen to be offering, and must actually be offering, added value to the resolution of the dispute.

122. Implicit in this requirement is that a third person should not be (economically) dependent on any of the disputing parties.[223] Any economic dependency would presumably impact on a third person's motivations for making an application and could raise questions as to the third person's suitability to offer assistance in the proceedings.[224] If third person applicants are not independent, transparency and fair treatment of the parties[225] (Article 4(5)) demand that any connection to any party to the proceedings be disclosed at the outset.[226] This is a positive duty on the third person; it is not the task of the tribunal or the parties to 'uncover' connections of the third person. Such connections should be disclosed by the third person voluntarily. Moreover, the scope of this subparagraph places an obligation on the third person to not only disclose whether a relationship exists with a disputing party, but also to specify the nature of the relationship.[227]

[222] For example, the tribunal in *Suez/Vivendi* held that for potential third persons to be 'suitable', they have to 'establish to the Tribunal's satisfaction that they have the expertise, experience and independence to be of assistance' (n. 18) [24].

[223] Cf. *von Pezold* (n. 131) [49]; *Suez/Interaguas* (n. 6) [32].

[224] See section 6.8 below.

[225] For discussion of fairness standard in treatment of the parties, see section 6.10.3 below.

[226] Cf. Fach Gomez (n. 12) 557.

[227] UNCITRAL (n. 171), [45]ff.

123. One can imagine that, were a scenario to occur in which the third person failed to disclose a connection, but such connection was discovered later by one of the parties or the arbitral tribunal, the third person's submission would, on the basis of such behaviour, be devoid of any credibility. In such a case, the tribunal would have the power within its discretion to exclude the third person submission from the proceedings.[228]

124. What a tribunal makes of such a connection to one of the parties is left to its discretion. Case law shows that disclosure of a connection to a disputing party is not necessarily fatal to a would-be third person participant's cause.[229]

125. In *Grand River*,[230] as stated above, the third person submission was ultimately attached to the claimants' submission as an exhibit. The tribunal in that case stated that the submission was read in that context.[231] The implication was, therefore, that the tribunal attached little weight to the submission as a third person submission, and instead treated it as essentially a party submission.

126. By way of contrast, the Tanzanian NGO in the *Biwater* case[232] was granted certain rights of third person participation even though the petitioners had explicitly stated that they sought to work with the government and governmental agencies in their area of expertise.[233] In *UPS*,[234] the US Chamber of Commerce openly stated that it was supporting one of its members, UPS, in making its third person application.[235] The tribunal granted the application.

127. The connection to any disputing party need not be direct; the provision is unambiguous in its extension to 'indirect' connections.

6.7.8 *Article 4(2)(c)*

6.7.8.1 General obligation to disclose financial assistance

128. Article 4(2)(c) is to be regarded, broadly speaking, as an obligation to disclose assistance of any kind that the third person has received.[236]

[228] Cf. also section 6.7.11 below.
[229] For reasons for accepting a third person application, see section 6.8 below.
[230] See case summary at section 6.5.9 above. [231] *Grand River* (n. 107) [60].
[232] See case summary at section 6.5.7 above.
[233] *Biwater* (n. 92); The Lawyers' Environmental Action Team and others, Petition for Amicus Curiae Status (27 November 2006) http://italaw.com/sites/default/files/case-documents/ita0090.pdf, 3.
[234] See section 6.5.3 above. [235] *UPS* (n. 73).

This phrase clarifies the scope of entities from which assistance will be considered relevant, i.e., from anyone, and is intended to aid the tribunal in assessing the suitability of the applicant to make a third person submission. Due to the unique nature of investor-State arbitration, where public interests play a significant role, it is not only connections to the parties that could be relevant, but also connections to governments and other entities.

129. The role of third persons in investor-State arbitral proceedings is also to be considered in the context of this rule. Unlike tribunal-appointed experts, who could conceivably be engaged to fulfil the same role as third persons, third persons are not usually remunerated by anyone involved in the dispute. It was noted in the drafting of this provision that third persons here do not have the quality of an expert. They are neither 'appointed' by the arbitral tribunal (or the parties), nor are they required to be independent and impartial.[237] By the same token, however, what they cannot be are 'hired guns', financed or otherwise supported by a party to provide a certain view on aspects of the case that will give that party an advantage. Since third persons also cannot be granted party status in the proceeding, it may be fair to question their motives. It is thus justified to 'pierce' the public face of the third person in order to ascertain what, if any, financial and/or other support may be motivating the third person to intervene in the proceedings.

130. Of note in Article 4(2)(c) is the absence of consequences with respect to the third person submission where assistance is disclosed; it will be for the tribunal to decide on whether to allow a third person submission, perhaps in spite of disclosed assistance, and on the weight to be given to it.[238]

131. It is interesting to note that this provision is not limited to governments involved in the dispute (or parties to the underlying BIT), but applies to 'any government, person or organization'. This reflects the wide-reaching nature of the issues regularly at stake in investor-State arbitration, whereby the impact is likely to extend beyond the realm of simply the BIT in question.

[236] UNCITRAL (n. 171) UN Doc. A/CN.9/760 [49].

[237] UNCITRAL (n. 1) UN Doc. A/CN.9/712 [50].

[238] In *UPS*, the US Chamber of Commerce disclosed in its amicus application that it received payments from UPS amounting to 12% of its annual budget. However, the tribunal still granted the application; cf. Schliemann (n. 13) 379, referencing *UPS* (n. 73) § B(IV)(9).

6.7.8.2 Article 4(2)(c)(i): 'provide any information on any government, person or organization that has provided to the third person – any financial or other assistance in preparing the submission'

132. Subsection (i) is a reference to direct assistance or influence concerning the third person's potential role in the dispute. The reasoning behind such a rule is, of course, that if someone has financed or otherwise assisted in the preparation of a submission, e.g. by providing support in the drafting of the third person application or submissions, they may have been able to exert a degree of pressure in determining the content of the submission. A third person's submission to investor-State arbitral proceedings should be an accurate statement of that person's concerns and interests, and cannot be a puppet for another entity, be it a government or other organisation, who is actually pulling the strings of the submission for their own purposes.[239]

6.7.8.3 Article 4(2)(c)(ii): 'substantial assistance in either of the two years preceding the application by the third person under this article (e.g. funding around 20 per cent of its overall operations annually)'

133. This subsection concentrates on the issue of assistance generally and thereby addresses the issue of indirect support in the preparation of the third person submission. Pursuant hereto, petitioners must not only disclose support given specifically for the preparation of the submission itself (which, in practice, it will often not be), but also support of the third person in general for the two years leading up to the application to make a submission.

134. The assistance need not be only financial in nature, although this is certainly the most common type of assistance that will be relevant in this context. Conceivable is also assistance through the provision of office space, photocopying facilities, secretarial support and the like, all of which will have a value to the third person and thereby a potential impact on the content of a submission.

135. According to this subsection, the support must be 'substantial'. Guidance as to what might constitute substantial assistance is

[239] Similarly, in *Biwater*, a Tanzanian NGO was accepted as *amicus curiae*, despite stating in its application that it seeks to cooperate with the government; cf. Schliemann (n. 13) 379, referencing *Biwater* (n. 233) [3].

provided by the example of 'around 20 per cent of its overall operations annually'.[240] According to the WG documents, 20 per cent was not intended as a threshold, but provided by way of illustrative example. Whether assistance is substantial will always depend on the particular facts.[241]

136. In the *von Pezold* case,[242] both petitioners had received assistance with their non-disputing party applications from the Nyahode Union Learning Centre (NULC), which, although described as a Zimbabwean NGO, was characterised by the claimants as being a political vehicle led by Mr Sacco, a known political activist who was opposed to the claimants' ownership of the land at issue. Funding for the NULC was provided primarily through private donation (75 per cent), with only 10 per cent coming from the Government of Zimbabwe. The tribunal found that the NULC did not appear to be closely linked with either party.[243] Similarly, in the case of *UPS*,[244] a payment by UPS to the US Chamber of Commerce, a third person in the arbitration, of US$100,000, which was 12 per cent of its annual budget, was not considered by the tribunal to be a sufficient ground on which to reject the petitioner for lack of independence.[245]

137. In the *Suez/Interaguas case*,[246] the non-disputing party stated that it did not receive support from either the claimants or the respondent and that it got financial support from members' contributions. This was, however, insufficient for the tribunal, who stated that it would require additional information on the non-disputing party's membership in order to evaluate its independence.[247]

6.7.9 Article 4(2)(d): 'nature of interest that the third person has in the arbitration'

138. The interest that the third person has in the arbitration should ideally be apparent from the type of entity that the third person represents. However, in order to avoid ambiguity and to obtain a clear statement from the third person, this provision requires the third person to describe the nature of its interest in the arbitration. A myriad of

[240] UNCITRAL (n. 171] UN Doc. A/CN.9/760 [49]. [241] *Ibid.* [50].
[242] See case summary at section 6.5.13 above. [243] *Von Pezold* (n. 131) [54].
[244] See section 6.5.3 above. [245] *UPS* (n. 73) [9].
[246] See case summary at section 6.5.6 above. [247] *Suez/Interaguas* (n. 90) [32].

different interests has been presented in case law to date, including the right to (clean) water, rights of indigenous peoples, environmental interest groups and rights of business unions such as that in *UPS*.[248]

139. Case law indicates that the third person must provide evidence of a relatively specific interest and not simply a general interest in human rights, the environment or other general causes.[249] For instance, in the *Suez/Interaguas* case,[250] the tribunal stated:

> [i]t is not enough for a nongovernmental organization to justify an amicus submission on general grounds that it represents civil society or that it is devoted to humanitarian concerns. It must show the Tribunal in specific terms how its background, experience, expertise or special perspectives will assist the Tribunal in the particular case.[251]

140. Further, whether the third person's interest is political or not will usually be a significant factor for the tribunal in assessing whether to accept a submission from such third persons.[252] Investor-State arbitration has evolved precisely as a means of de-politicising this kind of dispute. To re-introduce a political interest, particularly an external one, often runs counter to the very aims that the proceedings seek to pursue. As Yves Fortier stated:

> Returning to the point I made earlier in respect of the de-politicization of disputes through use of the arbitral model of dispute resolution, a concern with 'pre-award transparency', that is the participation of *amici curiae*, the publication of pre-award decisions, and open hearings, among other measures, is that both claimants and respondents can use this kind of access as a weapon, contrary to the very principle of neutral, non-political dispute resolution.[253]

141. Despite this, it was precisely a political interest that the European Commission claimed, and the tribunal allowed, in the case of *AES* v.

[248] See case summary at section 6.5.3 above.

[249] Cf. *Suez/Interaguas* (n. 6) [31]; Stern (n. 2) 322.

[250] See case summary at section 6.5.3 above. [251] *Suez/Interaguas* (n. 6) [33].

[252] For factors in deciding to accept submissions, see section 6.8.1 below.

[253] L. Yves Fortier, 'Investment Protection and the Rule of Law: Change or Decline?', lecture given on 17 March 2009 at the British Institute of International and Comparative Law www.arbitration-icca.org/media/0/12392785460140/0732_001.pdf, 15, quoting Noah Rubins, 'Opening the Investment Arbitration Process: At What Costs, for What Benefit?' in Rainer Hoffman and Christian Tams (eds.), *The International Convention on the Settlement of Investment Disputes (ICSID): Taking Stock after 40 Years* (Nomos, 2007) 179, at 217–22. Cf. also Fach Gomez (n. 12) 558.

Hungary.[254] The Commission made submissions as to the relevance of its legally prescribed regulatory mandate, which has policy implications for the entire European Union, and as to a potential conflict between its mandate and the tribunal's jurisdiction.[255]

142. Under this paragraph of the Rules, the criteria relating to any 'interest' in the dispute refer to the interests of the third party applying to make a submission. Unlike the NAFTA FTC Statement, there is specifically no requirement that there be a public interest in the dispute.[256] However, the point is well made that most investor-State disputes in which third person participation is sought will, by their very nature, contain an element of public interest, which will be likely – even implicitly – to influence a tribunal's assessment of whether a third person application should be allowed.[257]

6.7.10 Article 4(2)(e): 'identify specific issues of fact or law in the arbitration that the third person wishes to address in its written submission'

143. In addition to describing its interest in the arbitration, the third person is required to go even further and identify specific issues of fact or law in the arbitration that it wishes to address in its submission. Contrary to the ruling in *von Pezold*,[258] while such facts or law must fall within the overall scope of the dispute,[259] they do not necessarily have to arise out of the parties' submissions but can also concern issues pertaining solely to the third person's interest in the proceedings.

144. In practice, when seeking to address matters of fact and law that have arisen in a particular investment arbitral proceeding, questions of confidentiality and access to information become relevant.

145. For a third person wishing to make a submission, the requirement of Article 4(2)(e) presupposes that the would-be third person has enough information about the case to identify specific issues of fact or law. The

[254] See n. 123 above. This case would probably be resolved today under Article 5 of the Rules.

[255] As the European Commission's submission is not publicly available; cf. Epaminontas Triantafilou, 'A More Expansive Role for Amici Curiae in Investment Arbitration?' Kluwer Arbitration Blog (11 May 2009) http://kluwerarbitrationblog.com/blog/2009/05/11/a-more-expansive-role-for-amici-curiae-in-investment-arbitration/.

[256] For NAFTA FTC Statement, see also section 6.4.2 above.

[257] Cf. Knahr (n. 38) 336, 347–8; Biwater (n. 27) [53].

[258] See summary at section 6.5.13 above. [259] See section 6.9.3 below.

means by which a third person can obtain such information have been discussed in other chapters of this commentary.[260] Due to increasing transparency, not only under the Rules but also under other instruments, access to information about a case for the purpose of identifying factual and legal issues in an arbitration is not likely to pose significant problems going forward. Under the Rules, information about the case shall be published,[261] enabling third persons, at the very least, to become aware of the existence of a dispute.

146. In practice, whether a third person's reference to issues of fact and law is specific enough will be left to the tribunal to decide at its discretion. Obviously, where the tribunal is of the view that the third person can make a valuable contribution to the proceedings, it is entitled to assess the specificity of the issues raised in this light.

6.7.11 Consequences of failure to comply with Article 4(2)

147. Article 4(2) does not expressly set out the consequences of a failure to provide all relevant information.

148. Due to the highly fact-specific nature of third person submissions, not every failure to disclose impacts the proceedings in the same way and to the same degree.

149. In *Apotex*,[262] which referred to the disclosure requirements under Section B(2) of the NAFTA FTC Statement, the tribunal was confronted with two issues of non-disclosure by the applicant Mr Appleton. The first was Mr Appleton's omission concerning an indirect affiliation with one of the claimants. On the basis of the claimants' clarification of the issue, the tribunal found such non-disclosure to be 'inconsequential'.[263] With respect to the requirement that the third person specify the nature of its interest in the arbitration, the tribunal stated that:

> from the outset Mr. Appleton should have disclosed his involvement in the pending NAFTA cases, even if this information is publicly available. In any event, the Tribunal has already drawn the consequences of the nature of Mr. Appleton's interest in this arbitration; and this non-disclosure (by itself) plays no part in the Tribunal's decision.'[264]

[260] See Christopher Kee, 'Article 3', [42]–[83] and Kathleen Claussen, 'Article 8', [31]–[38].
[261] *Ibid.* [262] See case summary at section 6.5.16 above. [263] *Apotex* (n. 157) [45].
[264] *Ibid.* [46].

150. The tribunal thereby implied that incomplete disclosure does not *per se* prevent the tribunal from granting a third person's application.

151. As a general rule, the tribunal should have discretion to determine whether the information provided by an applicant is sufficient and to request further information within the boundaries of Article 4(5). However, also conceivable are cases in which the non-disclosure, in and of itself, could be considered so egregious (such as, for example, the demonstrably deliberate failure to disclose affiliations to parties) as to justify a tribunal's rejection of a third person application without the need to request further information.

6.8 Article 4(3)

6.8.1 Introduction to Article 4(3): Consideration of relevant factors

152. Basically, Article 4(3) is the flip side of Article 4(2) of the Rules. It is under this section that factors are set out for the arbitral tribunal to guide it in deciding whether to allow the third person submission on the basis of the information provided under Article 4(2).

153. The reference to certain limiting criteria according to which the arbitral tribunal should make its decision was considered important to the tribunal's 'gate-keeping' role in deciding whether to allow third person submissions; the WG referred to the 'sufficient' experience of NAFTA with such criteria in the NAFTA FTC Statement and various model BITs.[265] While Article 4(3) sets out certain factors, it should be noted here that these are not exhaustive. It was deliberately left to the arbitral tribunal's discretion to determine other factors that it considers to be relevant.[266] Article 4(3) therefore constitutes a compromise between the detailed provision of the NAFTA FTC Statement[267] and the need for flexibility in deciding on whether to allow a submission. The ultimate consensus of the WG was to draft a regulation along the lines of the amended ICSID Arbitration Rule 37(2).[268] Regarding the relationship between the listed factors and unnamed 'other factors' the tribunal considers relevant, it would appear that those factors explicitly listed are of general importance and touch upon the essential function of third party submissions. Such factors need to be considered in every scenario.

[265] UNCITRAL (n. 1) UN Doc. A/CN.9/712 [47].

[266] UNCITRAL (n. 14) UN Doc. A/CN.9/736 [76].

[267] NAFTA FTC Statement, § B.3.

[268] UNCITRAL (n. 16) UN Doc. A/CN.9/717.

Implicit is that the listed criteria are also *a priori* of decisive importance. However, as part of the tribunal's inherent discretion, should there be further concerns based on the circumstances of the particular case, the purpose of the term 'among other factors' clarifies that the tribunal is free to adopt a flexible approach[269] and have regard to additional concerns.

154. The impact of a consideration of the factors set out in this section is also deliberately left open. Article 4(3) does not prescribe consequences; it simply states that the tribunal is to have regard to such factors when considering whether to allow a submission.

6.8.2 *Article 4(3)(a): 'significant interest'*

155. The standard of 'significant interest' reflects the standard set out by both the NAFTA FTC Statement and ICSID Arbitration Rule 37(2).[270] While Article 4(2)(d) prescribes that the third person state the nature of its interest in the proceedings, this 'interest' is further delineated by the present subsection, in which the tribunal is required to consider whether the third person's interest is 'significant'.

156. Whether a third person has a significant interest in the arbitral proceedings can be a double-edged sword.[271] On the one hand, the arbitral tribunal will only wish to allow those third persons access to the proceedings that have a genuine interest in contributing to the solution of the dispute. This genuine interest should be manifest in an ability to assist the arbitral tribunal to decide the dispute.

157. On the other hand, the arbitral tribunal will not wish for third persons to participate who are 'interested' in the dispute, i.e. who have an incentive or are otherwise motivated to influence the outcome through financial assistance or a close connection to one of the parties.[272]

158. Thus, a fine line must be trod: a party must have an interest in the subject matter of the dispute, but cannot be interested in its outcome.

159. In the early days of investment jurisprudence, characterised by cases like *Methanex*,[273] the role of third persons was confined predominantly to NGOs such as the IISD and the CIEL, whose 'significant interest' in the dispute was advocating issues of public concern.

[269] UNCITRAL (n. 14) UN Doc. A/CN.9/736 [76].

[270] For discussion of NAFTA FTC Statement and ICSID Arbitration Rule 37(2) see sections 6.4.2 and 6.4.3 above.

[271] Cf. Fach Gomez (n. 12) 558. [272] Cf. also sections 6.7.7 and 6.7.8 above.

[273] See case summary at section 6.5.2 above.

160. In such earlier cases, a petitioner's support for one side was openly stated and even, in some cases, confirmed by the tribunal. In *Methanex*, for example, the tribunal stated that 'amici are not experts; such third persons are advocates . . . and not 'independent' in that they advance a particular case to a tribunal'.[274]

161. By way of contrast, in the very recent *von Pezold* case,[275] the tribunal found that it was implicit in ICSID Arbitration Rule 37(2) that an *amicus curiae* must be independent of the parties. As stated by the tribunal in the *von Pezold* case, there is some 'latent tension in the Rule 37(2) criteria which require that an NDP be independent yet also possess a significant interest in the proceedings'.[276]

162. These two opposed views demonstrate that clarification is required to determine whether independence is a requirement for third persons and, if so, what the requirement actually means in this context. Under the *Suez/Vivendi* criteria,[277] independence was certainly one of the factors that the tribunal was required to consider when evaluating the suitability of a potential third person.[278] If one looks at the context of these criteria, however, the focus would appear to be on financial independence, alluding perhaps more to a criteria of 'free from influence' than true independence. Schliemann has described the issue as follows:

> The relevant question to assess whether an amicus petitioner remains independent is, therefore, whether a relationship of control or the determinative influence of a party to the dispute on the writing of an amicus brief and therefore on its content can be ascertained.[279]

163. At least with respect to the notion of 'ideological' independence, it would seem from the existing case law – *von Pezold* constituting an exception – that a third person applicant is not required to be ideologically independent from the parties; indeed, the nature of most investor-State arbitration necessarily dictates that a third person will be sympathetic to a particular party's arguments in a given set of circumstances, even though the party itself and the third person may be pursuing different goals. In the *UPS* case,[280] the US Chamber of Commerce, not an NGO representing a public interest but a business organisation, very frankly disclosed that it was intervening as *amicus* to support one of its members,

[274] *Methanex* (n. 47) [38]. [275] See case summary at section 6.5.13 above.
[276] *von Pezold* (n. 131) [62]. [277] See case summary at section 6.5.5 above.
[278] *Suez/Vivendi* (n. 18) [24]. [279] Schliemann (n. 13) 380.
[280] See case summary at section 6.5.3 above.

UPS, and that it had 'a significant interest in the international trade and investment implications' of the claim.[281] The tribunal allowed the submission, but did not make any statements on the Chamber's significant interest.[282]

164. In the case of *Apotex*,[283] the arbitral tribunal, in deciding whether to allow an *amicus curiae* application from a lawyer, decided the application by reference to the NAFTA criteria of 'significant interest'. The tribunal initially stated:

> To meet this requirement, the applicant needs to show that he has more than a 'general' interest in the proceeding. For example, the applicant must demonstrate that the outcome of the arbitration may have a direct or indirect impact on the rights or principles the applicant represents and defends.[284]

165. Applying this to Mr Appleton's application, the tribunal noted that 'it seems that the Applicant's 'significant interest' in this arbitration lies only in having this Tribunal adopt legal interpretations of NAFTA that he favours that could be advantageous to his clients in his pending and possible future NAFTA cases'.[285] Although the tribunal acknowledged that public interests might be at stake and, if so, that arbitrators should consider these, the tribunal held that Mr Appleton's application was driven by a particular professional interest, not a public interest affecting him personally.[286] Consequently, if the 'significant interest' is a purely selfish one on the part of the third person, this would appear to speak against allowing participation in the proceedings.

166. In the first arbitration between Apotex and the United States,[287] conducted under the Arbitration Rules (1976), BNM, a management consultancy firm, which at the time was considering founding a 'litigation venture capital fund', sought *amicus curiae* status. The tribunal rejected this on the grounds that the potential third party's professional considerations were insufficiently concrete and did not amount to a significant interest.[288]

281 *UPS* (n. 73) [A.4], [B.4], [10]. 282 *UPS* (n. 74) [3].
283 See case summary at section 6.5.16 above. 284 *Apotex* (n. 155) [38].
285 *Apotex* (n. 157) [40]. 286 *Ibid.* [39]. 287 *Apotex* (n. 154).
288 *Apotex* (n. 164) [27]–[28]. While the tribunal in this case did not go into detail concerning BNM's aspirations to become a litigation funder, it could be presumed that – as a general rule – third persons acting as third party funders in litigation finance or as insurers, which by their very definition are commercially affected by the pending dispute, should not be admitted as third persons under Article 4.

167. Furthermore, in light of both recent case law[289] and EU Regulations,[290] the European Commission will regularly have a significant 'systemic' interest[291] in the outcome of proceedings under treaties involving Member States.

168. The Rules leave the detailed analysis of this issue to tribunals' discretion by prescribing simply that the tribunal is to consider whether a third person has a significant interest in the proceedings – a significant interest cannot, therefore, be presumed[292] – without going so far as to say how such significant interest should affect the tribunal's decision on whether to allow a submission.

6.8.3 *Article 4(3)(b)*

6.8.3.1 Assisting the tribunal 'in the determination of a factual or legal issue related to the arbitral proceedings'

169. Article 4(3)(b) goes to the fundamental sense and purpose of third person submissions in investor-State arbitration: a non-party 'friend' must be of assistance to the proceedings.

170. The third person submission should actively assist the arbitral tribunal in the determination of a factual or legal issue. Discussions in the WG to limit this section to legal issues only were rejected on the basis that third parties frequently provide important factual information that satisfies the requirement to bring 'a perspective, particular knowledge or insight that is different from that of the disputing parties' and that to exclude such a role would be a disservice to the tribunal.[293] Consequently, it is implicit that the arbitral tribunal would not be able to decide

[289] See case summary of *Achmea* at section 6.5.12 above. For extra-EU BITs see amicus application of the European Commission in *Iberdrola Energía SA* v. *Guatemala*, ICSID Case No. ARB/09/5 www.italaw.com/cases/1518. Material on application only available at www.iareporter.com/articles/20140709_3. For intra-EU BITs see *AES Summit Generation Limited and AES-Tisza Erömü Kft* v. *Hungary*, ICSID Case No. ARB/07/22, Award (23 September 2010) www.italaw.com/sites/default/files/case-documents/ita0014_0.pdf [3.18]; *Electrabel SA* v. *Hungary*, Award on Jurisdiction, Applicable Law and Liability (30 November 2012). www.italaw.com/sites/default/files/case-documents/italaw1071clean.pdf.

[290] Cf. Regulation (EU) No. 1219/2012 http://eur-lex.europa.eu/LexUriServ/LexUriServ.do?uri=OJ:L:2012:351:0040:0046:En:PDF.

[291] See application of the European Commission in *Iberdrola Energía* (n. 289).

[292] Cf. Stern (n. 2) 341.

[293] Cf. UNCITRAL (n. 171) UN Doc. A/CN.9/760 [52]; *Aguas del Tunari* (n. 76) [35].

the factual or legal issue concerned properly without the input from the third person submission. This is a high standard to satisfy.

6.8.3.2 'by bringing a perspective, particular knowledge or insight different from that of the disputing parties'

171. The wording of what the third person should bring to the proceedings tracks verbatim the requirements of the NAFTA FTC Statement and ICSID Arbitration Rule 37(2).[294] That the perspective of the third person should be different from that of the disputing parties can be traced back to the original purpose of third party submissions: to assist the tribunal by providing information or insight that the parties to the proceedings were not in a position to do. It would be wasteful of the time and efforts of all concerned if a third person were permitted to make a submission containing information that had already been provided by one of the parties. With respect to information that could have been provided by one of the parties, but was not, the situation may be different. If the party concerned is not providing information because it could be harmful to its case, but necessary for the proper resolution of the dispute, the tribunal should allow the third party submission. For information 'innocently' omitted, the opportunity granted to the parties to comment on the third person's application should be used to clarify to the tribunal that the party concerned can provide the relevant information.

172. Moreover, in certain circumstances, in particular for arbitrations in which the European Commission comments as a third person,[295] there may be an obligation on the tribunal to examine its jurisdiction regardless of whether the parties have made submissions in this respect.[296]

173. As such, when considering whether to allow a third person submission, a tribunal should consider whether the submission would offer directly relevant, 'added value' to the proceedings.[297] It is a core feature of third person participation, which has been clarified by recent case law, that the third person participant should not be an extended arm

[294] For a discussion of the NAFTA FTC Statement and ICSID Rule 37(2), see sections 6.4.2 and 6.4.3 above.

[295] Given the new provisions of the Transparency Rules allowing non-State Treaty Member to intervene as third parties, see [97]–[98] above and Martins Paparinskis and Jessica Howley, 'Article 5', [6]–[7].

[296] Cf. *Electrabel SA* v. *Hungary* (n. 289) [4.115]. By way of contrast, in some cases such as *UPS*, the tribunal may regard third person submissions in the jurisdictional phase as inappropriate, cf. *UPS* (n. 65) [71].

[297] Cf. e.g. *UPS* (n. 65) [61]–[65].

of one of the parties, but should actually add something different, and useful, to the proceedings.

174. For example, in the *Apotex* case,[298] the tribunal was of the view that Mr Appleton was not in a position to offer a perspective different from that of the disputing parties. As discussed above, Mr Appleton had based his third person application on his particular knowledge as an investment arbitration specialist. The tribunal held the view that the knowledge claimed by Mr Appleton was already covered by the counsel to the parties in the dispute; as such, it was 'most unlikely' that Mr Appleton would provide a different perspective.[299]

175. In contrast, in the case of *Biwater*,[300] the tribunal noted the important role of the third persons in setting the context of the dispute. It stated:

> The five Petitioners comprise NGOs with specialized interests and expertise in human rights, environmental and good governance issues locally in Tanzania. They approach the issues in this case with interests, expertise and perspectives that have been demonstrated to materially differ from those of the two contending parties, and as such have provided a useful contribution to these proceedings.[301]

176. In the case of *Piero Foresti*,[302] the petitioners pointed out the inherent difficulty in providing a new and different perspective in cases in which the potential third person does not have access to the parties' pleadings. The petitioners stated that, in order to satisfy this criterion, '[t]he non-disputing party Petitioners must therefore possess a sufficient knowledge of the Parties' perspectives to focus their own submissions on the specific issues on which their perspectives and arguments differ most'.[303]

177. Consequently, in order to provide a 'different' perspective, case law would tend to indicate that would-be third persons should be appraised of the parties' perspectives. This, in turn, has implications for the transparency of the proceedings and the availability of information as a whole.[304]

178. An additional complexity has been added by the *von Pezold* case[305] which, if taken to its logical conclusion, would mean that in many cases the requirement of a new and different perspective would

[298] See case summary at 6.5.16 above. [299] *Apotex* (n. 155) [33].
[300] See case summary at section 6.5.7 above. [301] *Biwater* (n. 22) [359].
[302] See case summary at section 6.5.11 above. [303] *Piero Foresti* (n. 115) [6.17].
[304] See section 6.7.10 above. [305] See case summary at section 6.5.13 above.

be impossible to satisfy because the third person concerns – often revolving around other areas of international law, such as human rights and environmental issues – would be unrelated to the proceedings.[306] In *von Pezold*, the third persons made submissions on human rights issues which had apparently not been referenced by the parties. As a reaction to the parties' comments on the third person application, the tribunal appears to have simply accepted that the issues were unrelated to the proceedings because no party had made them 'in issue' in the proceedings.[307] Implicitly, the tribunal appears to be saying that submissions on human rights law would not have assisted it in deciding the dispute. More problematically, however, the tribunal appears to have curtailed the possibility of providing a 'different' perspective to that of the parties by stating that perspectives outside the scope of the parties' submissions are 'unrelated' to the proceedings and do not need to be considered by the tribunal. Such an interpretation of this criterion would cut off the right of third persons to participate in investor-State arbitrations in which their own rights do not 'coincide' with the interests of the parties pursued in their submissions.[308] Moreover, as discussed further below, the issue also arises as to whether the tribunal has a duty, *ex officio*, to examine human rights concerns.[309]

179. Some commentators have also noted that another way in which third persons could fulfil a role different to that of the parties is in the provision of useful statistics or background information concerning a case which would otherwise take years to collect.[310]

180. Connected with this notion that a third person should provide different information from that of the parties is also the principle that the third person submission should not unduly burden the parties or the arbitral proceeding itself,[311] for example, by providing duplicative or unnecessary information which could serve to complicate, rather than aid, the dispute.[312]

[306] Cf. Schliemann (n. 13) 384. [307] *Von Pezold* (n. 131) [57], [59].

[308] Cf. Bastin (n. 24) [138]. [309] See section 6.9.3 below.

[310] See Daniel Barstow Magraw and Niranjali Manel Amerasinghe, 'Transparency and Public Participation in Investor-State Arbitration' (2009) 15(2) *ILSA Journal of International and Comparative Law* 337, 346.

[311] Discussed below in section 6.10.1.

[312] Cf. also *Piero Foresti*, in which the petitioners claimed that access to the parties' pleadings was necessary to ensure that the information provided by petitioners would not be duplicative (n. 115) [5.19].

6.9 Article 4(4)

6.9.1 Formal requirements

181. The requirements of Article 4(4) concerning the submission itself are, to some extent, duplicative of other provisions of Article 4. Subsection (a) deals with the formal requirements of dating and signing the submission. The precise requirements for making submissions, for example by email, would be determined by the tribunal concerned when addressing the application under Article 4(3).

182. The wording of Article 4(4), which deals with submissions, reflects the formal provisions for applications found in Article 4(2), subsection (b) which requires the submission to be concise and secondly, requires it to be no longer than as authorised by the arbitral tribunal

6.9.2 'precise statement of the third person's position on issues'

183. That the third person is required to set out a precise statement of its position on issues directly reflects the wording used in the NAFTA FTC Statement. This wording goes to the clarity of the third person's statement; both the tribunal and the parties should be able to immediately recognise the third person's position.

184. Moreover, this provision is intended to distance the role of the third person from the role of the parties in the arbitral proceedings. In preparing a submission, third persons are not to adopt the format of a party memorial, which would usually include, among other things, background and procedural history, but are to confine themselves to a precise statement of their position.

6.9.3 'matters within the scope of the dispute'

185. Subsection (d) requires that the submission only address matters within the scope of the dispute. In effect, it is the tribunal's analysis of whether the third person has fulfilled the requirement of Article 4(1).[313] Similar to the requirement in Article 4(2)(e) that the third person identify the specific issues of fact or law that it wishes to address in its submission, subsection (d) limits the scope of the third person's submission and thereby attempts to minimise the risk that a third person uses

[313] See section 6.6.6 above.

the platform of the investor-State arbitral proceedings to improperly advocate a cause going beyond the scope of the proceedings.

186. The question arises as to whether third persons have a role to play in raising matters that may not have been raised by the parties, but are of such an important nature as to potentially give rise to an *ex officio* obligation on the tribunal to consider them. A detailed analysis of this question would go beyond the scope of this work, but two aspects that require brief attention are with respect to human rights and to corruption.

187. Many cases have allowed third persons to raise human rights concerns even though such concerns were not, strictly speaking, within the ambit of the parties' pleadings.[314] In the case of *von Pezold*,[315] however, submissions on international human rights law were not allowed because the tribunal found that they would not assist the tribunal.[316] This approach raises some serious questions as to the obligation on tribunals to instigate their own investigation where fundamental principles of law are at stake. Few would argue that international human rights law can be considered so important as to have attained *ius cogens* status;[317] consequently, the *von Pezold* tribunal approach of dismissing international human rights arguments as irrelevant requires clarification by future investment treaty tribunals. It is the author's view that allegations of breach of international human rights law give rise to a duty on the tribunal to investigate, even if such allegations may not ultimately be directly relevant to the findings in the dispute at hand.

188. Certain commentators have suggested that third persons in investor-State arbitration may have a role to play in bringing to light allegations of corruption.[318] In the case of *World Duty Free* v. *Kenya*,[319] both parties to the investment arbitration acknowledged that payment of a bribe had been made; scenarios are equally likely in which neither of the

[314] Cf. e.g. *Methanex*, case summary at section 6.5.2 above; *Biwater*, case summary at section 6.5.7 above; *Suez/Vivendi* v. *Argentina*, case summary at section 6.5.5 above; *Piero Foresti*, case summary at section 6.5.11 above.

[315] See case summary at section 6.5.13 above. [316] *Von Pezold* (n. 131) [57].

[317] Cf. also Schliemann (n. 13) 382.

[318] Cf. Levine (n. 2) 217 quoting Kenneth Kinyua, 'Assessing the Benefits of Accepting Amicus Curiae Briefs in Investor-State Arbitrations: A Developing Country's Perspective' (Stellenbosch University Faculty of Law, Working Paper Series No. 4, 2009), no longer publicly available.

[319] *World Duty Free Company Ltd.* v. *Kenya*, ICSID Case No. ARB/00/7, Award (4 October 2006) http://italaw.com/documents/WDFv.KenyaAward.pdf.

parties would consider it advantageous to make allegations of corruption. In such cases, the question arises as to whether an appropriate role for third persons could be to bring such corruption to the attention of the tribunal. In *World Duty Free*, the tribunal stated that there was 'a strongly held view within the arbitration community that an arbitral tribunal has the power and jurisdiction to consider issues of illegality and can do so of its own motion, if the issue has not been put before it by the parties'.[320]

6.10 Article 4(5)

6.10.1 Limits of transparency

189. The use of third person participants is both a consequence and a necessary requirement of a transparent forum for investor-State disputes. Going forward, third person submissions in investment arbitration will only be viable if the transparency standards are such as to allow would-be third parties to obtain enough information about pending proceedings to make a useful submission.[321]

190. Nonetheless, the benefits created by additional transparency have to be weighed against the burden such transparency may result in for the arbitral proceedings concerned. As can be inferred from Article 7 of the Rules,[322] investment arbitration has to guarantee 'a careful balancing between two competing interests: the need for transparency and the need to protect the procedural integrity of the arbitration'.[323] In this regard, one has to take into account that admission of non-disputing party submissions to an otherwise neutral forum may serve, in certain circumstances, to politicise a dispute in what was otherwise an apolitical environment,[324] thereby creating an additional, unanticipated burden on

[320] Cf. Levine (n. 2) 217, quoting Kenneth Kinyua (n. 318). Cf. also Gary Born, 'Bribery and an Arbitrator's Task', Kluwer Arbitration Blog (11 October 2011) http://kluwerarbitrationblog.com/blog/2011/10/11/bribery-and-an-arbitrator%E2%80%99s-task/. Born states that investigating claims of bribery where none has been raised by the parties may invite challenges to the tribunal's jurisdiction and the validity of the award, based on *ultra vires* or *ultra petita*.

[321] Cf. *Piero Foresti* (n. 115) [6.17].

[322] Thierry P. Augsburger, 'Article 7', [2]–[31].

[323] *Biwater*, Procedural Order No. 3 (29 September 2006) www.italaw.com/sites/default/files/case-documents/ita0089.pdf [112]. See also David Buntenbroich and Markus Kaul 'Transparenz in Investitionsschiedsverfahren – Der Fall Vattenfall und die UNCITRAL-Transparenzrregeln' (2014) *SchiedsVZ* 1, 5.

[324] Cf. *Biwater* (n. 27) [35]; Buntenbroich and Kaul (n. 323) 5; Bastin (n. 2) 226; Levine (n. 2) 21.

parties. Some commentators regard this as critical, especially considering the drastically lowered settlement chances connected with more public proceedings.[325] It will therefore be the task of the tribunal concerned, applying the guidelines of this Article 4, to ensure that third person submissions are not utilised as political vehicles.[326]

191. In a broader context, excessive use of third party submissions, particularly where such submissions tend to favour State arguments, could lead to less investor confidence in the long run with respect to the role of investor-State arbitration in providing for a 'stable and predictable investment environment'.[327]

6.10.2 *'disrupt or unduly burden the arbitral proceedings'*

192. This section constitutes a limitation on the tribunal's discretion to admit third person participation and constitutes what was often referred to as 'Procedural Safeguards' in the context of the same wording in ICSID Arbitration Rule 37(2).[328] The primary concern surrounding the admission of non-disputing party submissions is the increase in cost and delay for the parties.[329] In a system in which proceedings already run for years and lawyers' costs are great, the benefit of any potential non-disputing party submission must be carefully balanced against the delay and cost.

193. Concerns about disrupting the proceedings and burdening the parties were raised as early as the *Methanex* case,[330] in which the tribunal expressed concerns that accepting *amicus* submissions could significantly add to the overall cost of the proceedings and 'impos[e] an extra burden on one or both the Disputing Parties'.[331] This concern has been raised in most cases addressing the issue of third person participation since then.[332]

194. The arbitral tribunal has a duty to ensure that the proceedings are conducted with minimum delay. As the parties must be given an opportunity to respond to third person submissions, one of the considerations

[325] See Buntenbroich and Kaul (n. 323) 5. Cf. Fach Gomez (n. 12) 558.

[326] Cf. Fach Gomez (n. 12) 558; Levine (n. 2) 21. Cf. also *Biwater* (n. 323), [112] [135]ff.

[327] Aron Broches, cited in Noah Rubens, 'Opening the Investment Arbitration Process: At What Cost, for What Benefit?' (2009) *Austrian Arbitration Yearbook* 483, 486ff.

[328] Cf. e.g. *Biwater* (n. 27) [56].

[329] Cf. Delaney and Magraw (n. 12) 781; Bastin (n. 2) 225.

[330] See case summary at section 6.5.2 above.

[331] *Methanex* (n. 47) [35]ff, [50].

[332] Cf. the cases summarised in section 6.5 above.

in allowing third person submissions will be the impact on the procedural timetable. It would therefore be prudent, as a general rule, for arbitral tribunals to deal with third person submissions as early as possible in the proceedings. In the *Piero Foresti* case,[333] the petitioners made detailed arguments as to the timeliness of their petition, which they claimed had been made diligently and without undue delay, taking into account the procedural timetable and the previous developments in the arbitration.[334] In the *Glamis Gold* case,[335] QIN wanted to delay its submissions until after the parties had submitted their memorials. The tribunal refused to allow this and ordered an earlier deadline, relying on the principle of the NAFTA FTC Statement,[336] and emphasising the importance of not delaying or burdening the proceedings.[337] Despite the tribunal's efforts, it ended up with five submissions of roughly twenty pages each. Giving the parties an opportunity to respond, in addition to the tribunal's own review, places an additional burden on the arbitral proceedings.[338] This burden must therefore be weighed up against any potential benefit of having the third person(s) make submissions to the proceedings.

195. The general rule that third person submissions should be made as early as possible in the proceedings must be considered in light of the individual case. In some cases, submissions made prematurely in the proceedings may, if accepted, actually serve to disrupt an efficient course of proceedings. As seen in various cases discussed above,[339] many tribunals have rightly refused to deal with non-disputing party submissions prematurely, particularly at the stage of jurisdictional objections when submissions on the merits – and the matters referred to in the third person submissions – are not yet ripe for decision.

196. The concerns surrounding delay to the proceedings go hand-in-hand with the objective of minimising costs. Third person participation increases costs on the part of both the parties and the arbitral tribunal. Parties are to be given an opportunity to respond to third person submissions; tribunals are required to rule on the status of third persons and consider their submissions.[340]

[333] See case summary at section 6.5.11 above. [334] *Piero Foresti* (n. 115), [5.24ff].

[335] See case summary at section 6.5.8 above. [336] *Glamis Gold* (n. 100) [2]–[4].

[337] *Ibid.* [11]–[12]. [338] Cf. in this regard Stern (n. 2) 303; Kinnear (n. 23) 7.

[339] Cf. *Methanex*, case summary at section 6.5.3 above; *UPS*, case summary at section 6.5.3 above; *Suez/Vivendi* v. *Argentina*, case summary at section 6.5.2 above.

[340] Cf. also Magraw and Amerasinghe (n. 310) 352; Fach Gomez (n. 12) 553.

197. Some commentators have noted an additional dimension to the mandate of allowing non-disputing party submissions only where they do not unduly burden the parties: often, responding to such submissions will fall more heavily on one party, usually the party opposing the submission. Consequently, a non-disputing party submission has the potential to introduce inequality between the parties, which will be for the tribunal to manage and ameliorate.[341]

198. In practice, the objective of not disrupting or unduly burdening the arbitral proceedings should serve as no more than a clarification of other aspects of Article 4 of the Rules. Implicit in this duty on the tribunal is the setting of short time limits, and limiting any third person submission both in terms of length (requiring concise submissions and setting page limits, as referred to already in Article 4(2), (4)(b)) and content (matter within the scope of the dispute (Article 4(1), (4)(d)), specific issues of fact or law (Article 4(2)(e))), precise statement (Article 4 (4)(c)), such that minimal time and effort will be needed by the parties to respond to them.

6.10.3 'unfairly prejudice any disputing party'

199. Whether or not a third person submission would unfairly prejudice any disputing party has both a substantive and a procedural element.

200. With respect to substantive prejudice, one could imagine a situation in which a third person made a submission that was highly detrimental to the arguments being presented by one party to the case. In practice, any prejudice, if prejudice is the correct term, would be short-lived and extinguished by the opportunity given by the tribunal to the parties to respond to the third person submission, thereby, as it were, 'setting the record straight' for the affected party.

201. With respect to procedural prejudice, the author submits that this would, in most cases, follow on from substantive prejudice. One can imagine a situation in which the content of a third person submission would prompt, and indeed necessitate, a detailed and lengthy response by

[341] Cf. *Methanex* (n. 47) [37], [50]; Bastin (n. 2) 225, quoting Paul Friedland, 'The Amicus Rule in International Arbitration', Conference Paper at the School of International Arbitration, London, 12 April 2005, 10; and Andrew Newcombe and Axelle Lemaire, 'Should Amici Curiae Participate in Investment Treaty Arbitrations?' (2001) 5 *Vindobona Journal of International Commercial Law and Arbitration* 22, 32.

the party of whose case the third person submission had been critical, resulting in additional cost for that party.[342]

202. In practice, this situation often arises. By their very nature, third person submissions are often more favourable to one 'side' of an arbitration than to the other. Therefore, in reacting to such submissions, one side may have to do more to defend its case than the other side, which, for example, might be content to submit a two-liner stating that it agrees with the content of the third person submission. Ultimately, however, the burden should not result in one-sided prejudice as such. Whilst a submission may cost time and money, it is difficult to conceive of a situation in which such outlays would be so imbalanced between the parties that one could speak of prejudice.

203. Moreover, it is within a party's own control to determine how much it wishes to spend on commenting on a third person submission. If of the view that the cost implications of commenting on a third person submission would result in genuine prejudice, the party should communicate this to the tribunal. Further, Article 4 in itself already provides for a mechanism to reasonably limit additional cost from the outset by explicitly enabling the tribunal to set page limits for *amici* submissions. Both aspects described here illustrate that it is left to the tribunal to avoid any potential prejudice associated with submissions of third parties by efficiently conducting the proceedings and limiting the scope of any (financial) burden on the parties.[343]

204. To address such prejudice it will lie, firstly, in the discretion of the tribunal to construct a procedure in which prejudice is minimised. Secondly, subject to any constraints set by the tribunal concerned, each party is free – within any limits set by the tribunal – to write as much or as little in response to a third party submission as it chooses. In fact, a party that feels criticised by the content of a third person submission could even view the right to respond as another opportunity to present its case.

205. One case in which the tribunal found that a third person submission unfairly prejudiced a party substantively was *von Pezold*.[344] The tribunal did not elaborate on the prejudice further, but explained in

[342] See section 6.10.1 above.

[343] Cf. Kyla Tienhaara, 'Third Party Participation in Investment-Environment Disputes: Recent Developments' (2007) 16 *Review of European Community and International Law* 230, 240.

[344] For case summary, see generally section 6.5.13 above.

another context that the third persons appeared to be in conflict with the claimants' main position in the proceedings.[345] This interpretation of prejudice would appear to be unsupported by previous case law concerning this question, which has focused on (irreparable) procedural inequality as constituting a ground of prejudice,[346] rather than a substantive argument that can be rebutted by the parties, and which can even be ignored by the tribunal if it so wishes.

206. Consequently, provided that the tribunal upholds the principle of equal treatment with respect to each party, allegations of prejudice should not arise in practice.[347]

6.11 Article 4(6)

207. This rule has been engrained in tribunals' approaches to third person submissions since the NAFTA FTC Statement.[348] Investment arbitral tribunals should, for reasons of due process alone, but also to enhance the efficacy of third person participation, provide the parties with the opportunity to comment on whatever a third person has contributed to the proceedings. Article 4(6) makes it clear that the right of disputing parties to respond is not dependent on the discretion of the tribunal. In practice, if a third person submission is allowed, the procedural timetable will usually provide for the submission by the third person, followed by a reasonable deadline by which all parties are to comment on the third person's submission.[349]

208. Often tribunals are faced with the somewhat competing concerns of due process and the efficiency of the proceedings.[350] On the one hand, third person participation should not disrupt or delay the proceedings. On the other hand, the parties will demand ample opportunity to respond to any third person applications or submissions, thereby adding additional steps and deadlines to the procedural timetable. Consequently, in considering whether to accept a third person submission, the tribunal will need to keep the impact on the procedural timetable in mind and weigh this against the perceived benefit of any submission.

[345] *Von Pezold* (n. 131) [51]. [346] See Schliemann (n. 13) 387.

[347] This sentiment was echoed by the petitioners in *Piero Foresti*, who stated that 'the Tribunal is master of its own proceeding and is fully competent to take any necessary steps to prevent undue burden or unfair prejudice to the Parties' (n. 115) [5.29].

[348] See section 6.4 above. [349] Cf. also Fach Gomez (n. 12) 560–1.

[350] See section 6.4 above. See also, e.g., *Glamis Gold* (n. 100); *Suez/Vivendi* (n. 18) [29] and *Biwater* (n. 27) [56]ff.

6.12 Conclusion

209. The development of the Rules as a whole, and the inclusion of rules specifically concerning submissions by third persons, highlights the importance of transparency in investor-State arbitration. Article 4 of the Rules confirms the continuing importance of third person submissions in the investment arbitration process. At this stage of development of international investment arbitration, where it can no longer be called an 'infant' and has passed the stage of 'teething problems', it is significant that UNCITRAL has seen it necessary to engrain the participation of third persons within its transparency rules. On some views, this encroaches on the autonomy of the parties.[351] However, the preferred view is that it is precisely the public interests usually at stake in investor-State arbitration that make third person participation a necessary element, provided that such participation is useful and serves to assist the tribunal.

210. Article 4 of the Rules highlights the importance of the tribunal's involvement in ensuring that transparency does not result in an erosion of the cornerstones of party autonomy, efficiency and costs. As Canada said at the outset of the WG's draft, 'public participation in treaty-based investor-State arbitration can be effectively managed by a Tribunal to ensure that it benefits rather than burdens the process'.[352]

211. It remains critical that third person participation in the investment arbitration process remains confined to '[i]nstances where third-party involvement actually serves both to improve the legal quality of the award and to assist in the systemic development of international investment law as a whole'[353] and does not extend to, effectively, adding another advocate for one of the parties to the proceedings.

212. Ultimately, the ongoing viability of third party participation in investor-State arbitration will depend on the tribunals' approach to their involvement. As has been shown by previous initiatives, including by NAFTA and ICSID, there is no foolproof way of ensuring transparency in investment arbitration, and certainly no guarantees that third person participation will enhance such transparency. It will be up to the tribunals, when seized with requests for third person participation, to evaluate

351 Delaney and Magraw (n. 12) 780; Fach Gomez (n. 12) 549.

352 UNCITRAL, 'Working Group II (Arbitration and Conciliation) fifty-third session, Addendum' (4 August 2010) UN Doc. A/CN.9/WG.II/WP.159/Add.1 [14].

353 Levine (n. 2) 217.

these requests carefully, with a view to ensuring that only genuine 'friends of the court' are allowed to pervade a process otherwise determined by party autonomy. The third person's expertise and experience should be clear, and their 'added value' to the dispute beyond question. What Article 4 of the Rules seeks to achieve is to provide guidelines for this task of tribunals, in an effort to bolster consistency and confidence in the role of third parties in the investment arbitration process.

7

Article 5. Submission by a non-disputing Party to the treaty

MARTINS PAPARINSKIS* AND JESSICA HOWLEY**

1. The arbitral tribunal shall, subject to paragraph 4, allow, or, after consultation with the disputing parties, may invite, submissions on issues of treaty interpretation from a non-disputing Party to the treaty.
2. The arbitral tribunal, after consultation with the disputing parties, may allow submissions on further matters within the scope of the dispute from a non-disputing Party to the treaty. In determining whether to allow such submissions, the arbitral tribunal shall take into consideration, among other factors it determines to be relevant, the factors referred to in article 4, paragraph 3,[1] and, for greater certainty, the need to avoid submissions which would support the claim of the investor in a manner tantamount to diplomatic protection.
3. The arbitral tribunal shall not draw any inference from the absence of any submission or response to any invitation pursuant to paragraphs 1 or 2.
4. The arbitral tribunal shall ensure that any submission does not disrupt or unduly burden the arbitral proceedings, or unfairly prejudice any disputing party.
5. The arbitral tribunal shall ensure that the disputing parties are given a reasonable opportunity to present their observations on any submission by a non-disputing Party to the treaty.

* Martins Paparinskis is Lecturer at Faculty of Laws, University College London.
** Jessica Howley is a DPhil candidate at Magdalen College, University of Oxford. The authors are grateful to the editors for comments on an earlier draft.

1 This paragraph provides:

> 3. In determining whether to allow such a submission, the arbitral tribunal shall take into consideration, among other factors it determines to be relevant:
>   *(a)* Whether the third person has a significant interest in the arbitral proceedings; and
>   *(b)* The extent to which the submission would assist the arbitral tribunal in the determination of a factual or legal issue related to the arbitral proceedings by bringing a perspective, particular knowledge or insight that is different from that of the disputing parties.

7.1 Introduction

1. Chapter 6 considered the place of third person submissions in arbitral proceedings subject to the UNCITRAL Rules on Transparency in Treaty-based Investor-State Arbitration (the Rules).[2] As will be noted, this chapter is also concerned with submissions made by a third party to the relevant investment arbitration proceedings. However, it deals specifically with submissions made to an arbitral tribunal by a 'non-disputing party to the treaty', that is, by an entity that is not a party to the relevant arbitral proceedings, but is a Party to the treaty on investment pursuant to which those proceedings are brought.[3] This chapter will begin by outlining the background and purpose of Article 5, as well as the history of non-disputing Party submissions in State practice and case law, before analysing the text of Article 5 of the Rules and addressing a number of the key issues it raises.

7.2 Background and purpose

2. Article 5 is entitled 'Submission by a non-disputing Party to the treaty'. As noted, its purpose is to provide rules to govern submissions made to an arbitral tribunal by a Party to the relevant investment treaty that is not a party to the arbitration proceedings brought thereunder. Given that a non-disputing Party is, by definition, not a party to the relevant investment arbitration proceedings, Article 5 submissions may be considered to be a form of third person, or *amicus curiae*, intervention, as the UNCITRAL's Working Group II (Arbitration and Conciliation) (WG) on the Rules acknowledged.[4] Indeed, in its original form,

[2] UNCITRAL, *UNCITRAL Rules on Transparency in Treaty-based Investor-State Arbitration* (2014) www.uncitral.org/pdf/english/texts/arbitration/rules-on-transparency/Rules-on-Transparency-E.pdf.

[3] See e.g. UNCITRAL, 'Report of the Working Group II (Arbitration and Conciliation) on the work of its fifty-third session' (2010) UN Doc. A/CN.9/712 [49] (UNCITRAL, fifty-third session Report) (referring to an investment treaty Party that is not party to the relevant dispute as a 'non-disputing State'). Although the entity will usually be a State, there was a deliberate decision by the Working Group not to use the term 'State' in Article 5, as Parties to investment treaties were not necessarily always States: UNCITRAL, 'Report of the Working Group II (Arbitration and Conciliation) on the work of its fifty-fifth session' (2011) UN Doc. A/CN.9/736 [95] (UNCITRAL, fifty-fifth session Report).

[4] See e.g. UNCITRAL (n. 3) UN Doc. A/CN.9/712 [49]. See also Gabrielle Kaufmann-Kohler, 'Non-Disputing State Submissions in Investment Arbitration: Resurgence of Diplomatic Protection?' in Laurence Boisson de Chazournes, Marcelo G. Kohen, and Jorge E. Viñuales (eds.), *Diplomatic and Judicial Means of Dispute Settlement* (Martinus Nijhoff, 2013) 312.

Article 5 was one paragraph in what is now Article 4, which addresses third person submissions more generally.[5] Ultimately, non-disputing Party submissions were addressed separately in the Rules,[6] with Article 4(1) expressly excluding non-disputing Parties from its scope. As will be discussed in further detail below, there are important reasons for keeping the two distinct, especially insofar as the views of a non-disputing Party on questions of treaty interpretation are of particular legal significance for the proper interpretation of that treaty. The involvement of a non-disputing Party may also raise concerns of prejudice of a particular kind to the parties to the arbitral proceedings, namely the risk that a State of nationality engages in the diplomatic protection of one of its investors.[7] Nonetheless, in many other respects, the positions of non-disputing Parties and other third persons is similar and there remains a degree of overlap between Articles 4 and 5 of the Rules, relating respectively to third person and non-disputing Party submissions.[8] Article 5 therefore shares much in terms of purpose with Article 4, but additionally has the aim of addressing the particular role that non-disputing Parties play and the risks to which their submissions might give rise that warrant such submissions being addressed separately in the Rules.

7.3 State practice and case law

3. The history of submissions by non-disputing Parties to the treaty will be addressed in two parts. Submissions on the basis of explicit treaty rights constitute the largest and most significant part of the practice, and will be addressed first. The second section will address a number of

[5] For the two alternative original draft articles addressing third person submissions, second of which contained a provision in respect of non-disputing Party submissions, see UNCITRAL, 'Settlement of commercial disputes: preparation of a legal standard on transparency in treaty-based investor-State dispute settlement' (2011) UN Doc. A/CN.9/WG.II/WP.166 [43]. It may be noted that there was a view expressed that even this differentiation was unnecessary and that non-disputing Parties 'should enjoy the same rights as third parties': see UNCITRAL (n. 3) UN Doc. A/CN.9/736 [82].

[6] See UNCITRAL (n. 3) UN Doc. A/CN.9/736 [83]–[84].

[7] One reason for keeping third person and non-disputing Party submissions separate was 'the risk... of diplomatic protection', which was relevant for non-disputing Party submissions but for third persons more generally: *ibid.* [83]. See further below, section 7.5.3, and, on interpretation, sections 7.4.2 and 7.6.

[8] Thus, for example, it was noted that a number of the provisions now found in Article 4 warranted independent application to Article 5 submissions: *ibid.* [84]. See also below sections 7.5 and 7.7.

diverse strands of other practice, loosely connected as throwing some light on such submissions.

7.3.1 *Submissions by non-disputing Parties on the basis of explicit treaty rights*

4. Submissions by non-disputing Parties to a treaty have mostly taken place on the basis of explicit rights that are provided in certain multilateral investment treaties. Article 1128 of the 1994 North American Free Trade Agreement (NAFTA) provides the basis for most of the existing practice, stating that '[o]n written notice to the disputing parties, a Party may make submissions to a Tribunal on a question of interpretation of this Agreement'. NAFTA non-disputing Parties have made a number of submissions:[9] Canada has made submissions in nine cases,[10] Mexico has made submissions in eleven

[9] An overview of Article 1128 submissions is affected by their less-than-ideal distribution over the websites of the institutions of different States. The website of the US State Department on NAFTA Investor-State Arbitration www.state.gov/s/l/c3439.htm has sections on cases brought by investors against all NAFTA Parties, but cases against other Parties often have incomplete documents. The Department of Foreign Affairs, Trade, and Development of Canada provides documents, including submissions, for cases brought against Canada www.international.gc.ca/trade-agreements-accords-commerciaux/topics-domaines/disp-diff/nafta.aspx?lang=eng, and the Secretariat of Economy of Mexico for cases brought against Mexico www.economia.gob.mx/comunidad-negocios/comercio-exterior/solucion-controversias/inversionista-estado. On non-disputing Party practice under NAFTA and CAFTA-DR, see also Kaufmann-Kohler (n. 4) 313.

[10] *Metalclad Corp.* v. *Mexico*, Submission of Canada (28 July 1999) www.economia.gob.mx/files/comunidad_negocios/solucion_controversias/inversionista-estado/casos_concluidos/Metalclad_Corporation/1128_990728_Canada.pdf; *Marvin Roy Feldman Carpa (CEMSA)* v. *Mexico*, Submission of Canada (6 October 2000) www.economia.gob.mx/files/comunidad_negocios/solucion_controversias/inversionista-estado/casos_concluidos/Marvin_roy_Feldman_Karpa/001006_1128_Second_Canada_Feldman.pdf; *Methanex* v. *US*, Submission of Canada (10 November 2000) www.state.gov/documents/organization/3935.pdf; Second Submission of Canada (30 April 2001) www.state.gov/documents/organization/3946.pdf; *Marvin Roy Feldman Carpa (CEMSA)* v. *Mexico*, Second Submission of Canada (28 June 2001) www.economia.gob.mx/files/comunidad_negocios/solucion_controversias/inversionista-estado/casos_concluidos/Marvin_roy_Feldman_Karpa/010628_1128_First_Canada_Feldman.pdf; *Mondev International Ltd.* v. *US*, Second Submission of Canada (6 July 2001) www.state.gov/documents/organization/18271.pdf; *Loewen* v. *US*, Submission of Canada (19 November 2001) www.state.gov/documents/organization/6327.doc; *Methanex* v. *US*, Third Submission of Canada (8 February 2002) www.state.gov/documents/organization/8060.pdf; *ADF Group Inc.* v. *US*, Submission of Canada (18 January 2002) www.state.gov/documents/organization/142319.pdf; *Loewen* v. *US*, Second Submission of Canada (27 June 2002) www.state.gov/documents/organization/11748.pdf; *ADF Group Inc.* v. *US*, Second Submission of Canada (19 July 2002)

cases,[11] and the US has made submissions in fifteen cases.[12] Submissions have addressed a variety of legal issues. In the

www.state.gov/documents/organization/12224.pdf; *Fireman's Fund Insurance Company* v. *Mexico*, Submission of Canada (27 February 2003) www.economia.gob.mx/files/comunidad_negocios/solucion_controversias/inversionista-estado/casos_concluidos/Fireman_Fund_Insurance_Company/1128_canada.pdf; Fourth Submission of Canada (30 January 2004) www.state.gov/documents/organization/28854.pdf; *International Thunderbird Gaming Corp.* v. *Mexico*, Submission of Canada (21 May 2004) www.economia.gob.mx/files/comunidad_negocios/solucion_controversias/inversionista-estado/casos_concluidos/Thunderbird/040526_Escrito_canada.pdf; *Grand River Enterprises Six Nations, Ltd., et al.* v. *US*, Submission of Canada (19 January 2009) www.state.gov/documents/organization/115489.pdf.

11 *Ethyl Corporation* v. *Canada*, Submission of Mexico (11 March 1998), cited in the Award on Jurisdiction, 24 June 1998 [48]; *Pope & Talbot, Inc.* v. *Canada*, Submission of Mexico (2 December 1999) www.international.gc.ca/trade-agreements-accords-commerciaux/assets/pdfs/disp-diff/pope-05.pdf; *Loewen* v. *US*, Submission of Mexico (16 October 2000) www.state.gov/documents/organization/142099.pdf; *Methanex* v. *US*, Submission of Mexico (10 November 2000) www.state.gov/documents/organization/3936.pdf; *Methanex* v. *US*, Second Submission of Mexico (15 May 2001) www.state.gov/documents/organization/3959.pdf; *Loewen* v. *US*, Second Submission of Mexico (9 November 2001) www.state.gov/documents/organization/6362.pdf; *ADF Group Inc.* v. *US*, Submission of Mexico (18 January 2002) www.state.gov/documents/organization/142320.pdf; *Methanex* v. *US*, Third Submission of Mexico (11 February 2002) www.state.gov/documents/organization/8070.pdf; *Loewen* v. *US*, Second Submission of Mexico (2 July 2002) www.state.gov/documents/organization/11749.pdf; *ADF Group Inc.* v. *US*, Second Submission of Mexico (22 July 2002) www.state.gov/documents/organization/12504.pdf; *Methanex* v. *US*, Fourth Submission of Mexico (30 January 2004) www.state.gov/documents/organization/28829.pdf; *Canadian Cattlemen for Fair Trade* v. *US*, Submission of Mexico (1 March 2007) www.state.gov/documents/organization/81389.pdf; *Merrill & Ring Forestry Company LP* v. *Canada*, Submission of Mexico (2 April 2009) www.international.gc.ca/trade-agreements-accords-commerciaux/assets/pdfs/disp-diff/merrill-16.pdf; *Chemtura Corporation* v. *Canada*, Submission of Mexico (31 July 2009) www.international.gc.ca/trade-agreements-accords-commerciaux/assets/pdfs/disp-diff/chemtura-16.pdf; *Mobil Investments Inc. and Murphy Oil Corporation* v. *Canada*, Submission of Mexico (8 July 2010) www.international.gc.ca/trade-agreements-accords-commerciaux/assets/pdfs/disp-diff/mobil-08.pdf; Second Submission of Mexico (21 January 2011) www.international.gc.ca/trade-agreements-accords-commerciaux/assets/pdfs/disp-diff/mobil-15.pdf; *Apotex Holdings Inc. and Apotex Inc.* v. *US*, Submission of Mexico (8 February 2013) www.state.gov/documents/organization/212321.pdf; *Detroit International Bridge Company* v. *Canada*, Submission of Mexico (14 February 2014) www.international.gc.ca/trade-agreements-accords-commerciaux/assets/pdfs/disp-diff/detroit-11.pdf.

12 *Metalclad Corp.* v. *Mexico*, Submission of the US (9 November 1999) www.state.gov/documents/organization/4178.pdf; *Pope & Talbot, Inc.* v. *Canada*, Submission of the US (7 April 2000) www.state.gov/documents/organization/4097.pdf; Second Submission of the US (25 May 2000) www.state.gov/documents/organization/4176.pdf; Third Submission of the US (24 July 2000) www.state.gov/documents/organization/4101.pdf; *Marvin Roy Feldman Carpa (CEMSA)* v. *Mexico*, Submission of the US (6 October 2000) www.state.gov/documents/organization/4179.pdf; *Pope & Talbot, Inc.* v. *Canada*, Fourth

early *Pope & Talbot* v. *Canada* case, non-disputing Parties addressed procedural preconditions for arbitration, the interpretation of substantive obligations (national treatment, performance requirements, and fair and equitable treatment), the effect of agreed interpretation by States Parties, and the conditions and criteria for claiming damages.[13] In another early and important case, the *Methanex* v. *US* tribunal received non-disputing Parties' submissions on the concept of investment, the interpretation of substantive obligations, and its power to accept submissions from *amici curiae*.[14] In more recent cases, submissions have tended to focus on narrower points: for example, on the interpretation of reservations to the NAFTA in *Mobil* v. *Canada*, and on the procedure for waiving the right to pursue parallel domestic proceedings in *Detroit Bridge Company* v.

Submission of the US (1 November 2000) www.state.gov/documents/organization/4098.pdf; Fifth Submission of the US (1 December 2000) www.state.gov/documents/organization/4175.pdf; *United Parcel Service* v. *Canada*, First Submission of the US (11 June 2001) www.state.gov/documents/organization/4102.pdf; *S.D. Myers, Inc.* v. *Canada*, Submission of the US (18 September 2001) www.state.gov/documents/organization/6029.pdf; *Pope & Talbot, Inc.* v. *Canada*, Sixth Submission of the US (2 October 2001) www.state.gov/documents/organization/8250.pdf; Seventh Submission of the US (6 November 2001) www.state.gov/documents/organization/8251.pdf; Eighth Submission of the US (3 December 2001) www.state.gov/documents/organization/8252.pdf; *United Parcel Service* v. *Canada*, Second Submission of the US (13 May 2002) www.state.gov/documents/organization/10235.pdf; Third Submission of the US (23 August 2002) www.state.gov/documents/organization/13200.pdf; *Fireman's Fund Insurance Company* v. *Mexico*, Submission of the US (27 February 2003) www.state.gov/documents/organization/18210.pdf; *GAMI Investments Inc.* v. *Mexico*, Submission of the US (30 June 2003) www.state.gov/documents/organization/22212.pdf; *International Thunderbird Gaming Corp.* v. *Canada*, Submission of the US (21 May 2004) www.state.gov/documents/organization/32819.pdf; *Bayview Irrigation et al.* v. *Mexico*, Submission of the US (27 November 2006) www.state.gov/documents/organization/77667.pdf; *Merrill & Ring Forestry Company LP* v. *Canada*, Submission of the US (14 July 2009) www.state.gov/documents/organization/128851.pdf; *Chemtura Corporation* v. *Canada*, Submission of the US (31 July 2009) www.state.gov/documents/organization/128849.pdf; *Mobil Investments Inc. and Murphy Oil Corporation* v. *Canada*, Submission of the US (8 July 2010) www.state.gov/documents/organization/144850.pdf; Second Submission of the US (21 January 2011) www.state.gov/documents/organization/155736.pdf; *Clayton/Bilcon* v. *Canada*, Submission of the US (19 April 2013) www.state.gov/documents/organization/208140.pdf; *Detroit International Bridge Company* v. *Canada*, Submission of the US (14 February 2014) www.state.gov/documents/organization/223166.pdf; *KBR, Inc.* v. *Mexico*, Submission of the US (30 July 2014) www.state.gov/documents/organization/230291.pdf.

[13] See submissions by Mexico and the US in *Pope & Talbot* v. *Canada* at nn. 11–12.

[14] See submissions by Canada and Mexico in *Methanex* v. *US* at nn. 10–11.

Canada.[15] Article 10.20(2) of the 2004 Dominican Republic–Central America Free Trade Agreement (CAFTA-DR) expresses a similar rule in somewhat different terms: 'A non-disputing Party may make oral and written submissions to the tribunal regarding the interpretation of this Agreement'. It has already provided the basis for submissions in a number of cases:[16] submissions in one case by the Dominican Republic,[17] in two cases by Costa Rica,[18] El Salvador[19] and Honduras,[20] and in three cases by the US.[21] Similar rules allowing submissions by non-disputing Parties can be found in some recent model bilateral

[15] See submissions by Mexico and the US in *Mobil* v. *Canada* and *Detroit International Bridge Company* v. *Canada* at nn. 11–12.

[16] Just as with NAFTA, there is no single website that would provide access to all non-disputing Parties' submissions. The US submissions are available at the State Department website www.state.gov/s/l/c33165.htm. Submissions in cases against Guatemala are available at http://portaldace.mineco.gob.gt/casos-guatemala. Submissions in cases against El Salvador are available at www.minec.gob.sv/index.php?option=com_phocadownload&view=sections&Itemid=63.

[17] *TECO Guatemala Holdings Inc.* v. *Guatemala*, Submission of the Dominican Republic (5 October 2012) http://portaldace.mineco.gob.gt/sites/default/files/unidades/DefensaComercial/Casos/Controversias/Inversionista%20-%20Estado/Arbitraje%2010-23%20%28Teco%29/Escrito%20Parte%20No%20Contendiente/Submission%20of%20DR%20as%20non-disputing%20Party.pdf.

[18] *San Sebastián Gold Mines, Inc.* v. *El Salvador*, Submission of Costa Rica (20 October 2010) http://italaw.com/sites/default/files/case-documents/ita0204_0.pdf; *Pac Rim Cayman LLC* v. *El Salvador*, Submission of Costa Rica (13 May 2011) http://italaw.com/sites/default/files/case-documents/italaw1207.pdf.

[19] *Railroad Development Corp.* v. *Guatemala*, Submission of El Salvador (3 January 2012) http://italaw.com/sites/default/files/case-documents/ita0710_0.pdf; *TECO Guatemala Holdings Inc.* v. *Guatemala*, Submission of El Salvador (5 October 2012) http://portaldace.mineco.gob.gt/sites/default/files/unidades/DefensaComercial/Casos/Controversias/Inversionista%20-%20Estado/Arbitraje%2010–23%20%28Teco%29/Escrito%20Parte%20No%20Contendiente/Attachment%20Traducción%20al%20inglés%20de%20Escrito%20de%20Parte%20no%20contendiente%20de%20El%20Salvador%20-%20145226%20v3%20FHE-DC%20%282%29.pdf.

[20] *Pac Rim Cayman LLC* v. *El Salvador*, Submission of Honduras (1 January 2011) http://italaw.com/sites/default/files/case-documents/ita0711_0.pdf; *TECO Guatemala Holdings Inc.* v. *Guatemala*, Submission of Honduras (15 November 2012) http://portaldace.mineco.gob.gt/sites/default/files/unidades/DefensaComercial/Casos/Controversias/Inversionista%20-%20Estado/Arbitraje%2010–23%20%28Teco%29/Escrito%20Parte%20No%20Contendiente/Escrito%20Parte%20No%20Contendiente%20ante%20el%20Tribunal%20TECO.pdf.

[21] *Pac Rim Cayman LLC* v. *El Salvador*, Submission of the US (20 May 2011) www.state.gov/documents/organization/164308.pdf; *Railroad Development Corp.* v. *Guatemala*, Submission of the US (31 January 2012) www.state.gov/documents/organization/184681.pdf; *TECO Guatemala Holdings Inc.* v. *Guatemala*, Submission of the US (23 November 2012) www.state.gov/documents/organization/201834.pdf.

investment treaties (BITs),[22] and also investment treaties and free trade agreements of the US and Canada, which only recently have given rise to actual submissions.[23]

5. The practice in respect of non-disputing Party submissions pursuant to NAFTA and CAFTA-DR, while varying in subject matter and level of detail, permits a number of general observations. First, submissions by non-disputing Parties share some features with submissions by third persons more generally, but have the important distinction of being expressed in the treaty as a right of the submitting party to make, rather than the discretion of the tribunal to accept, the submission.[24] Second, it is usual to include a disclaimer in one of the first paragraphs of the

[22] 2004 Canada Model FIPA 2012 Article 35 http://italaw.com/documents/Canadian2004-FIPA-model-en.pdf; 2012 US Model BIT Article 28(2) www.ustr.gov/sites/default/files/BIT%20text%20for%20ACIEP%20Meeting.pdf; similarly Kaufmann-Kohler (n. 4) 312, fns 22–3.

[23] Kaufmann-Kohler (n. 4) 312–13 and fns 24–5. On the treaty practice and the earlier lack of case law, see more recent practice of Canada, see 2011 Canada–Latvia FIPA Annex B II.1; 2011 Canada–Romania FIPA Annex B II.1; 2012 Canada–Czech Republic FIPA Annex B II.1; 2012 Canada–Slovakia FIPA Annex B II.1; 2013 Canada–Tanzania FIPA Article 28(2) www.international.gc.ca/trade-agreements-accords-commerciaux/agr-acc/fipa-apie/index.aspx?lang=eng. In recent case law, US–Peru TPA Tribunal ordered disputing parties to jointly submit to the US an invitation to make submissions, a *The Renco Group, Inc.* v. *Peru*, Procedural Order No. 2 (31 July 2014), which the US subsequently made, Submission of the US (10 September 2014) www.state.gov/documents/organization/232051.pdf. See also *Adel A. Hamadi Al Tamimi* v. *Oman*, Submission of the US (22 September 2014) www.state.gov/documents/organization/232927.pdf.

[24] This distinction was raised in a rare example of diverging treaty Parties' submissions, when the admissibility of *amicus curiae*, or third person, submissions was discussed in the *Methanex* v. *US* case. Mexico argued against *amicus curiae* submissions by contrasting them with the rights of States under Article 1128. In its view, *amici* would not have access to necessary information that States will (under Articles 1127 and 1129), and acceptance of *amici* submissions would either give them broader rights than States have under Article 1128 or would make Article 1128 superfluous, since States could then themselves make *amici* submissions for issues going beyond Article 1128 (*Methanex* v. *US*, Submission of Mexico (10 November 2000) www.state.gov/documents/organization/3936.pdf [4]–[7]). Canada noted that only States Parties, and not non-Parties, have the right to make submissions on interpretation, while approving *amici* submissions in principle (Submission of Canada (10 November 2000) www.state.gov/documents/organization/3935.pdf [3]). The US similarly observed that the important distinction between submissions under Article 1128 and *amici curiae* procedures was that the right to make submissions existed only under the former rule (Statement of the US (22 November 2000) www.state.gov/documents/organization/3965.pdf 2 [I]). The NAFTA Free Trade Commission's 'Note of Interpretation on non-disputing Party participation' provides a without-prejudice rule to Article 1128 www.international.gc.ca/trade-agreements-accords-commerciaux/assets/pdfs/Nondisputing-en.pdf [A.2], and a right under Article 1128 to respond to *amici* submissions, *ibid.* [B.8].

submission that no position is taken regarding the application of the suggested interpretation to facts, and that 'n[o] inference should be drawn from the absence of' submissions on a particular point.[25] Third, despite the disclaimer, submissions on interpretation are usually not abstract, but made in light of issues that have arisen or that might arise in the case. Even if submissions do not themselves spell out how the suggested content of legal rules is to be applied in the particular case, the 'virtually inseparable link between interpretation and application' of international treaties[26] means that an argument on the former will be strongly suggestive about the approach to be adopted to the latter. Fourth, with rare exceptions, submissions by non-disputing Parties, including the home State of the investor, tend to be substantially in favour of the position taken by the respondent State and against the position taken by the investor.[27] It remains to be seen whether this trend is followed in other legal settings, particularly when non-disputing Party submissions are made pursuant to bilateral treaties, or whether it is a peculiarity of such multilateral treaties as NAFTA that there is a greater likelihood that treaty Parties *inter se*, rather than a particular non-disputing Party and its investor, share a similar

[25] For a recent example see *Detroit International Bridge Company* v. *Canada*, Submission of the US (14 February 2014) www.state.gov/documents/organization/223166.pdf [1]; similarly Kaufmann-Kohler (n. 4) 320–1.

[26] Frank Berman, 'International Treaties and British Statutes' (2005) 26 *Statute Law Review* 1, 10.

[27] See, e.g., Kaufmann-Kohler (n. 4) 314–315; UNCITRAL, 'Report of the Working Group II (Arbitration and Conciliation) on the work of its fifty-seventh session' (2012) UN Doc. A/CN.9/760 [60] ('arbitral experience showed that a non-disputing Party to a treaty rarely intervened simply to protect its investor's interests') (UNCITRAL, fifty-seventh session Report); and see similar comments in respect of NAFTA: UNCITRAL (n. 3) UN Doc. A/CN.9/736 [88]. Under NAFTA, States have made submissions regarding the scope of the treaty, procedural preconditions, scope and content of substantive rules, available remedies, and the effects of interpretation by the Free Trade Commission, *prima facie* supporting the position of the particular respondent State and rejecting the position of the particular investor, see nn. 10–12. Mexico's objection to the admissibility of *amicus curiae* submissions in the *Methanex* case (see n. 24) provides one possible exception. Kaufmann-Kohler also points to two US submissions in the early cases of *Feldman* and *Metalclad* as partially supporting investors (on issues of, respectively, nationality and attribution): Kaufmann-Kohler (n. 4) 314–15. In CAFTA-DR, States have made submissions regarding the operation of the denial of benefits clause, procedural preconditions, and the content of substantive rules, again *prima facie* supporting the respondent State, see nn. 17–22. It may be that a closer reading of particular submissions and cases could reveal greater nuances and perhaps even qualified support for particular aspects of investors' claims, but at the very least it is not a dominant impression.

perspective.[28] Fifth, in most cases non-disputing Parties make submissions of their own initiative, but in some cases submissions are made in response to an invitation or questions by the tribunal.[29] Overall, the point that one should take away from the existing practice is that non-disputing Parties' submissions repay careful reading: they are often extensive in scope and detailed in substance. They also provide unparalleled insights into Parties' thinking about legal issues that may be, for them, of importance in pending or future cases but are of less direct significance in the context of the particular dispute. In addition – as will be addressed in further detail below – submissions may also have possible interpretative effect.[30] Since, as will be seen below, Article 5 borrows in part from NAFTA Article 1128, the law and practice pursuant to that Article, as well as other treaty rules formulated in similar terms, may well be helpful in its interpretation and application.

7.3.2 Other instances of practice related to submissions

6. There are a number of other instances of practice regarding submissions that have little in common in positive terms, being rather united by amounting to a non-disputing Party actively making submissions based on a treaty right to do so. First, sometimes States make submissions regarding treaty interpretation in the absence of an express treaty right akin to those already discussed. One example is provided by the US

[28] See Kaufmann-Kohler (n. 4) 315–16 for possible explanations for the trend in the NAFTA context and querying the applicability of the NAFTA experience to BITs more generally.

[29] See e.g. *Fireman's Fund Insurance Company* v. *Mexico*, Submission of the US (27 February 2003) www.state.gov/documents/organization/18210.pdf; and *Mobil Investments Inc. and Murphy Oil Corporation* v. *Canada*, Second Submission of the US (21 January 2011) www.state.gov/documents/organization/155736.pdf. See also *Archer Daniels Midland Company et al.* v. *Mexico*, ICSID Additional Facility Case No. ARB (AF)/04/05, cited in Kaufmann-Kohler (n. 4) 313, fn 27, where the Tribunal invited submissions but none was forthcoming. In a recent case, the Tribunal ordered the disputing parties to jointly invite the non-disputing Party to make submissions: see *Renco Group Inc.* v. *Peru* discussed above at n. 23.

[30] It has been suggested that submissions by States may give rise to subsequent practice or even subsequent agreement: *Archer Daniels Midland Company et al.* v. *Mexico*, ICSID Additional Facility Case No. ARB(AF)/04/05, Award (21 November 2007) [175]–[176]; *Canadian Cattlemen for Fair Trade* v. *US*, UNCITRAL Case, Award on Jurisdiction (28 January 2008) [181]–[189]. See further below, section 7.6. and, generally, Anthea Roberts, 'Power and Persuasion in Investment Treaty Interpretation: The Dual Role of States' (2010) 104 *American Journal of International Law* 179, 180–1, 199–200, 217–20.

submission to the International Centre for Settlement of Investment Disputes (ICSID) Annulment Committee in the *Siemens* v. *Argentina* case.[31] Another example, albeit a less direct one, is the statement by Switzerland after the award in the *SGS* v. *Pakistan* case, criticising the interpretation of the umbrella clause in light of the presumed intentions of States Parties (since the award had been rendered, the submission was not made to the particular tribunal but addressed to ICSID).[32] The *SGS I* case also demonstrates why tribunals might wish to actively request submissions, in order to evade possibly erroneous interpretation. Submissions by the European Commission (EC) are both similar to, and importantly different from those of non-disputing Parties, and the substantive and procedural interplay of European Union law and investment treaty law raises different complex legal questions in different cases.[33] Tribunals have tended to accept these submissions under the applicable rules relating to third person submissions.[34] Second, tribunals sometimes

[31] *Siemens AG* v. *Argentina*, ICSID Case No. ARB/02/08, Annulment Proceedings, Submission of the US www.italaw.com/sites/default/files/case-documents/ita0792.pdf. The US submission was not directed at the interpretation of the underlying Germany–Argentina BIT but to that of the ICSID Convention, in response to a suggestion made by Argentina that the US shared its view as to the correct interpretation of the interplay between Articles 54 and 55. The US made its submission under the general ICSID rules for submissions by non-disputing parties, namely Rule 37(2) of the ICSID Arbitration Rules. On this case, and that in the following footnote, see further Kaufmann-Kohler (n. 4) 317–18, cases, among others, where submissions were made 'despite the absence of a provision in the treaty' (*ibid.* 316).

[32] 'Interpretation of Article 11 of the Bilateral Investment Treaty between Switzerland and Pakistan in the light of the decision of the Tribunal on Objections to Jurisdiction of ICSID in Case No. ARB/01/12 SGS Société Générale de Surveillance SA versus Islamic Republic of Pakistan' (2004) 1(3) Transnational Dispute Management 3–4. See further Martins Paparinskis, 'Inherent Powers of ICSID Tribunals: Broad and Rightly so' in Ian A. Laird and Todd J. Weiler (eds.), *Investment Treaty Arbitration and International Law* (JurisNet, 2012) 21.

[33] Philip Strik, *Shaping the Single European Market in the Field of Foreign Direct Investment* (Hart Publishing, 2014), particularly chapters 3, 5.

[34] In two cases brought under the Energy Charter Treaty, to which the European Union is a Party, ICSID Tribunals accepted EC submissions under ICSID Arbitration Rule 37(2), which deals with submissions by non-disputing parties generally: *AES Summit Generation Limited and AES Tisza Erömü Kft* v. *Hungary*, ICSID Case No. ARB/07/22, Award (23 September 2010) [8.2]; *Electrabel SA* v. *Hungary*, ICSID Case No. ARB/07/19, Decision on Jurisdiction, Applicable Law and Liability (30 November 2012) [4.89], [4.92]. In a case raising questions about the effect of European Union law on an intra-EU BIT, a UNCITRAL Tribunal invited submissions of the European Commission (and the home State of the investor) with the agreement of the disputing parties and without spelling out the nature of the legal interest of the Commission: *Eureko B.V.* v. *Slovakia*, PCA Case No. 2008-13, Award on Jurisdiction, Arbitrability and Suspension (26 October 2010) [154]. See further Kaufmann-Kohler (n. 4) 318–19.

do request submissions by non-disputing Parties regarding the interpretation of the treaty.[35] Third, while the focus of this chapter is on unilateral submissions by States, one should not forget that there are also other means by which States may express their views regarding the interpretation of the treaty, particularly by joint agreement on interpretation.[36] Finally, there may also be treaty rules that exclude particular types of submissions by non-disputing Parties.[37] The practice considered in this section is not heterogeneous, but demonstrates that there may be a number of other means, in addition to the possibility of making non-disputing Party submissions, through which States can express their views on issues arising in a particular dispute. The availability of such means and their effect depends on the rules applicable in a given situation, as well as on the broader legal framework.

7.4 Article 5(1)

7.4.1 Inherent powers of tribunals

7. Before addressing the text of Article 5, one initial question that may be asked is whether, in light of both the cases noted above, in which tribunals have sought the views of non-disputing Parties, and particularly given the role such Parties retain in respect of treaty interpretation, discussed further below, there is any need for a provision such as Article 5. As has already been noted, a number of tribunals have obtained information from States or institutions not party to arbitral proceedings

[35] See the examples from NAFTA cases at n. 29. In a number of cases, tribunals have asked for submissions from the home State of the investor: see e.g. *Aguas del Tunari S.A.* v. *Bolivia*, ICSID Case No. ARB/02/03, Decision on Respondent's Objections to Jurisdiction (21 October 2005) Appendix IV; *Eureko* (n. 34) [154]. See generally Part V of the award on the responses. See further Paparinskis (n. 32) 21–2; Kaufmann-Kohler (n. 4) 316, 318.

[36] Parties may agree on interpretation either under the general rules of the law of treaties, VCLT Article 31(3)(a) (see the Argentina–Panama exchange of diplomatic notes with an 'interpretative declaration' referred to in *National Grid PLC* v. *Argentina*, UNCITRAL Case, Decision on Jurisdiction (20 June 2006) [85]), or in accordance with procedures provided for in the particular instrument, either in an *ad hoc* manner (*CME* v. *Czech Republic*, UNCITRAL Case, Final Award (14 March 2003) [87]–[93]) or through an institution, most notably the Free Trade Commission in NAFTA. See further Kaufmann-Kohler (n. 4) 316–17; see below n. 40, section 7.6 [26] and n. 123.

[37] Thus, for example, Article 27(1) of the ICSID Convention suspends diplomatic protection during investor-State arbitration, not extending this suspension, however, as per Article 27(2), to 'informal diplomatic exchanges for the sole purpose of facilitating a settlement of the dispute'; see below n. 105.

notwithstanding the absence of explicit power, such as that contained in Article 5, to do so.[38] It could therefore be argued that the capacity to ask a non-disputing Party for its views is an 'inherent power' belonging to an arbitral tribunal.[39] Indeed, during the drafting of Article 5, there was some suggestion that States Party to a treaty already had the capacity to make comments in respect of that treaty, and that arbitral tribunals were able to request such submissions.[40] As the WG noted, Article 5 was nonetheless retained in a provision separate to that addressing third persons more generally, in part to help in 'clarifying the legal regime applicable to [non-disputing Party] submissions'.[41]

7.4.2 'submissions on issues of treaty interpretation'

8. The key difference between general third persons wishing to make submissions and a non-disputing Party is the latter's status as a Party to the treaty pursuant to which the relevant arbitral proceedings are brought. As a matter of public international law, the treaty obligations on which an investor relies in bringing investment arbitration proceedings come into being on the basis of the consent of the treaty Parties, usually two or more sovereign States, to be bound by such obligations.[42] It is also the consent of the treaty Parties, together with that of the relevant investors, that allows those investors to bring claims.[43] As Roberts has put it, States therefore

[38] E.g. the non-NAFTA cases noted above at n. 35 and accompanying text; similarly Kaufmann-Kohler (n. 4), 316; Roberts (n. 30) 220.

[39] See Paparinskis (n. 32) 31–3; similarly Roberts (n. 30) 220, arguing that the right of a non-disputing Party to intervene should be implied.

[40] UNCITRAL (n. 3) UN Doc. A/CN.9/736 [81] it was suggested as an example, that 'a State Party to a treaty might issue statements on treaty interpretation, or unilateral declarations on its understanding of a treaty provision'. See also UNCITRAL, 'Report of the Working Group II (Arbitration and Conciliation) on the work of its fifty-eighth session' (2013) UN Doc. A/CN.9/765 [46], suggesting that 'a non-disputing Party could make submissions on its own initiative' and the tribunal would 'deal with them as it deemed appropriate' (UNCITRAL, fifty-eighth session Report).

[41] UNCITRAL (n. 3) UN Doc. A/CN.9/736 [83].

[42] See Vienna Convention on the Law of Treaties, Articles 2(1)(a), (g) (definitions of 'treaty' and 'party'), and generally Part II Section 1 ('Conclusion of Treaties'); George Korontzis, 'Making the Treaty' in Duncan Hollis (ed.), *The Oxford Guide to Treaties* (Oxford University Press, 2012) 195–201.

[43] As the Working Group noted, the nature of treaty-based investment arbitration is that 'two different levels of consent' are relevant: not only the consent of the investor and respondent State, being parties to the arbitral proceedings in question, but also the consent of the two Parties to the treaty *inter se*: UNCITRAL (n. 3) UN Doc. A/CN.9/712 [23]; similarly Roberts (n. 30) 182.

have a 'dual role' in respect of investment treaties as both Parties to the treaty and 'potential respondents' to investment claims.[44] From these considerations flow two important points that are of relevance to the role of a non-disputing Party in respect of questions of treaty interpretation.

9. First, as already alluded to, all treaty Parties, whether or not they are also party to a particular set of arbitral proceedings, play an important role in determining the proper interpretation of the relevant treaty pursuant to which those proceedings are brought. The Vienna Convention on the Law of Treaties (VCLT) provides that a treaty is to be interpreted 'in good faith in accordance with the ordinary meaning to be given to the terms of the treaty in their context and in the light of its object and purpose',[45] with the 'context' including agreements between the Parties related to the treaty, or instruments accepted by all Parties as so related, and made in connection with the treaty's conclusion.[46] A term is given a 'special meaning' a if it is apparent that this was intended,[47] 'any subsequent agreement' of the Parties relating to the treaty's interpretation and application, or 'any subsequent practice' establishing such agreement, is to 'be taken into account',[48] and reference may be made to 'supplementary means of interpretation', which includes the *travaux préparatoires*, 'to confirm the meaning' or to clarify it in the event that the result is ambiguous, obscure, unreasonable or 'manifestly absurd'.[49] The important point to note is that the focus of treaty interpretation is on the Parties' intention, as reflected in the words used and as elucidated by any other relevant considerations.[50] Moreover, any agreement of the treaty Parties as to the interpretation and application of the relevant treaty, particularly as expressed through subsequent agreement or practice, is authoritative as to that intention.[51]

[44] Roberts (n. 30) 180. [45] Article 31(1). [46] Article 31(2)(a) and (b).

[47] Article 31(4).

[48] Articles 31(3)(a) and (b). Pursuant to Article 31(3)(c), 'any relevant rules of international law applicable in the relations between the parties' are also to be taken into account.

[49] Article 32.

[50] *Dispute Regarding Navigational and Related Rights (Costa Rica* v. *Nicaragua), Judgment* [2009] ICJ Rep 213 [48]. See also ILC, 'Draft Articles on the Law of Treaties with commentaries' in (1966) *Yearbook of the International Law Commission*, Vol. II, 223 (text 'presumed to be the authentic expression of the intentions of the parties'); James Crawford, *Brownlie's Principles of Public International Law* (8th edn., Oxford University Press, 2012) 379.

[51] Roberts (n. 30) 200, citing particularly *Kasiliki/Sedudu Island (Botswana/Namibia)* [1999] ICJ Rep 1045, 1075–6, in turn citing ILC, 'Draft Articles on the Law of Treaties' (n. 50)

10. Given the importance for the proper interpretation of the relevant treaty of the intention and agreement of the Parties, a non-disputing Party's views can be of significance for an arbitral tribunal. As will be discussed further below, if the views of the treaty Parties coincide, this may be demonstrative of an agreement as to the treaty's proper interpretation.[52] But even in the absence of such agreement, a non-disputing Party may well have an alternative perspective on the treaty than that put forward by the respondent State.[53] It may also, on a more practical level, have materials available to it that are relevant to the treaty's interpretation, such as documents relating to the drafting history, but to which the parties to the arbitration proceedings do not have access.[54] As the WG noted, allowing non-disputing Party submissions can therefore help to avoid treaty interpretation being 'one-sided'.[55]

221–2. The ILC noted, in particular (as Roberts, citing the ICJ, observes), that about a treaty's interpretation subsequent agreement interpretation 'represents an authentic interpretation by the parties' and that subsequent practice 'constitutes objective evidence of the understanding of the parties as to the meaning of the treaty' (*ibid.* 221). As the ILC noted more recently, though not conclusively, 'the common will of the parties, from which any treaty results, possesses a specific authority regarding the identification of the meaning of the treaty, even after the conclusion of the treaty': ILC, 'Report of the International Law Commission on the work of its sixty-fifth session' (2013) UN Doc. A/68/10, 21 (ILC, sixty-fifth session Report). See also Jean-Marc Sorel and Valérie Boré Eveno, 'Article 31 Convention of 1969' in *The Vienna Convention on the Law of Treaties: A Commentary*, Vol. I (Oxford University Press, 2011) [42]. As was noted in another context, it is the States Parties that are 'masters' of the relevant treaty: see UNCITRAL, 'Settlement of commercial disputes: preparation of a legal standard on transparency in treaty-based investor-State dispute settlement' (2010) UN Doc. A/CN.9/WG.II/WP.162 [28]; similarly Mark E. Villiger, *Commentary on the 1969 Vienna Convention on the Law of Treaties* (Martinus Nijhoff, 2009) 429, cited in Roberts (n. 30) 202.

52 See below [26]; Roberts (n. 30) 217.

53 UNCITRAL (n. 3) UN Doc. A/CN.9/736 [86]; also Kaufmann-Kohler (n. 4) 322. See also UNCITRAL (n. 40) UN Doc. A/CN.9/765 [44], on obtaining 'balanced and comprehensive information' and ensuring 'all views would be on record'; UNCITRAL (n. 27) UN Doc. A/CN.9/760 [60], noting that the non-disputing Party's insights might assist 'the tribunal's understanding of the treaty'.

54 See UNCITRAL (n. 3) UN Doc. A/CN.9/736 [78], [86]; Kaufmann-Kohler (n. 4) 322; and see similarly UNCITRAL (n. 3) UN Doc. A/CN.9/712 [49]; UNCITRAL, 'Report of the Working Group II (Arbitration and Conciliation) on the work of its fifty-fourth session' (2011) UN Doc. A/CN.9/717 [124] (UNCITRAL, fifty-fourth session Report); UNCITRAL, 'Settlement of commercial disputes: Preparation of a legal standard on transparency in treaty-based investor-State dispute settlement' (2010) UN Doc. A/CN.9/WG.II/WP.162/Add.1 [20].

55 UNCITRAL (n. 3) UN Doc. A/CN.9/736 [78], [86]; Kaufmann-Kohler (n. 3) 322; similarly UNCITRAL (n. 3) UN Doc. A/CN.9/712 [49]; UNCITRAL (n. 54) UN Doc. A/CN.9/717 [124]; UNCITRAL (n. 54) UN Doc. A/CN.9/WG.II/WP.162/Add.1 [20].

11. Second, even if non-disputing Parties do not have a particular interest in the outcome of the arbitral proceedings in question, they may be regarded as having 'a legitimate interest in the interpretation of the treaty to which they are a party'[56] in the sense that such an interpretation could affect the scope of their legal obligations under that treaty. Although there is no doctrine of precedent in international law, including in international investment law, a decision by an arbitral tribunal may impact the interpretation of the treaty under consideration by other tribunals.[57] It follows that the non-disputing Party's rights may be affected in respect of any proceedings that are brought against it in the future.[58] It may be for this reason that State practice indicates that non-disputing Parties are concerned about questions of interpretation in relation to a particular treaty even where they are not directly involved in the relevant proceedings.[59] Indeed, it is not uncommon outside the field of investment law for non-disputing Parties to be given a right of

[56] Roberts (n. 30) 182.

[57] *Ibid.* 188–9. The author notes that along with the sources of international law are listed 'judicial decisions' which are a 'subsidiary means, for the determination of the rules of law' law (citing Article 38(1)(d) of the Statute of the International Court of Justice), and that international courts have a law-making function, with their decisions 'routinely looked to' in establishing the content of the law: 188, also referring to the previous edition of Christine Chinkin, 'Article 63' in Andreas Zimmerman, Christian Tomuschat, Karin Oellers-Frahm and Christian J. Tams (eds.), *The Statute of the International Court of Justice: A Commentary* (2nd edn., Oxford University Press, 2012), see particularly on this point 1575, 1596. See generally as to the question of precedent in international investment law, Christoph Schreuer, 'Diversity and Harmonization of Treaty Interpretation in Investment Arbitration' in Malgosia Fitzmaurice, Olufemi Elias and Panos Merkouris (eds.), *Treaty Interpretation and the Vienna Convention on the Law of Treaties: 30 Years On* (Martinus Nijhoff, 2010) 139–43.

[58] See UNCITRAL (n. 27) UN Doc. A/CN.9/760 [60], noting that the State's rights might be affected 'in future proceedings'; also [69], noting that a State could be 'directly affected by issues of treaty interpretation'.

[59] See Roberts (n. 30) 188 (fn 43), making the same point in relation to rights of intervention, and see the practice noted above, particularly in respect of NAFTA and CAFTA-DR. For another example, in *Sovereignty over Pulau Ligitan and Pulau Sipadan (Indonesia/Malaysia)*, Application for Permission to Intervene, Judgment [2001] ICJ Rep 575, the Philippines sought, unsuccessfully, to intervene pursuant to Article 62 of the Court's Statute, arguing that it had 'an interest of a legal nature' in the dispute in respect of the findings the Court might make vis-à-vis treaties that were in issue in other disputes (see [46]); discussed in Christine Chinkin, 'Article 62' in Andreas Zimmerman, Christian Tomuschat, Karin Oellers-Frahm and Christian J. Tams (eds.), *The Statute of the International Court of Justice: A Commentary* (2nd edn., Oxford University Press, 2012) 1549–50. Another reason for making submissions may be the inferences that could be drawn from the conduct of non-disputing Parties as a matter of subsequent practice, a matter addressed in further depth below. The proper reaction to arguably incorrect judgments in third party disputes is

intervention in cases where the construction of a treaty by which they are bound is in issue.[60] However, such rights of intervention often extend the binding effect of the resulting interpretation given by the tribunal to the intervening Party,[61] whereas a non-disputing Party under the Rules is not bound by interpretation of a treaty in an investment dispute even if it has made submissions in respect thereof.

12. It is therefore apparent that a non-disputing Party, even if not directly involved in particular arbitral proceedings, has an interest in interpretation and application of that treaty that is of a different nature to the interests that other third persons might have in a given dispute. It is not surprising, then, that provision was made in what became Article 5 (1) for the tribunal to accept submissions from a non-disputing Party on issues of treaty interpretation.

7.4.3 *'shall, subject to paragraph 4, allow'*

13. Insofar as treaty interpretation is concerned, the debate in the WG about whether the non-disputing Party should have a right to make submissions or whether this ought to be at the discretion of the tribunal[62] was resolved in favour of requiring the tribunal to accept such submissions if the non-disputing Party wished to make them.[63] This can be contrasted with the Article 4 position, which makes the acceptance of

not a straightforward matter: Daniel Bethlehem, 'The Secret Life of International Law' (2012) 1 *Cambridge Journal of International and Comparative Law* 23, 32–3.

[60] See Roberts (n. 30) 188 (fn. 43), referring to Article 63 of the Statute of the International Court of Justice, which provides a State Party to a given Convention with a 'right to intervene' in a dispute relating to the construction of that Convention, with the caveat that the construction will then be binding for it, and to the previous edition of Chinkin (n. 57), see particularly 1575–6, 1596–7, where similar provisions in other instruments are noted. Cf. Article 36 of the European Convention on Human Rights, which only allows intervention by right to the State of nationality of the applicant, while other States Party may be allowed to intervene at the Court's discretion 'in the interest of the proper administration of justice': for discussion, see Roberts (n. 30) 203.

[61] See e.g. Article 63(2) of the Statute of the International Court of Justice, discussed in the previous footnote.

[62] See UNCITRAL (n. 40) UN Doc. A/CN.9/765 [42]–[51]; UNCITRAL (n. 27) UN Doc. A/CN.9/760 [59]–[62]; UNCITRAL (n. 3) UN Doc. A/CN.9/736 [90]. See also UNCITRAL, 'Settlement of commercial disputes: preparation of a legal standard on transparency in treaty-based investor-State dispute settlement' (2011) UN Doc. A/CN.9/WG.II/WP.169 [39]; UNCITRAL, 'Settlement of commercial disputes: preparation of a legal standard on transparency in treaty-based investor-State dispute settlement' (2012) UN Doc. A/CN.9/WG.II/WP.176 [40].

[63] See UNCITRAL (n. 40) UN Doc. A/CN.9/765 [51].

third person submissions a matter for the tribunal's discretion.[64] Given the legal significance of a Party's views to the interpretation of a treaty, the existence of a right to make submissions on such questions is understandable. In any event, it would be unusual for a tribunal to ignore submissions expressing such views, as was observed in the WG.[65] Whether submissions from a non-disputing Party on questions of treaty interpretation are made as a matter of right under particular rules or not may therefore not make a significant difference.[66] Nonetheless, Article 5 provides non-disputing Parties with such a right, though it is important to note that this right is subject to the requirement in Article 5(4) that the submissions do not 'disrupt or unduly burden the arbitral proceedings, or unfairly prejudice any disputing party',[67] a point that will be addressed in further detail below.

7.4.4 'or, after consultation with the disputing parties, may invite'

14. In addition to being required to accept non-disputing Party submissions made in respect of issues of treaty interpretation, the tribunal was also given the power, after consultation,[68] to invite such submissions.[69] There is no such power contained in Article 4 in respect of submissions by other third persons. However, the views of non-disputing Parties may be particularly important on questions of treaty interpretation and, as has already been noted, there is some practice in which tribunals have sought such views in order to assist their

[64] Mariel Dimsey, 'Article 4', section 6.6.2.

[65] UNCITRAL (n. 40) UN Doc. A/CN.9/765 [44] (rejection 'unusual or unlikely'). See also n. 32 and accompanying text on *SGS I* at.

[66] UNCITRAL (n. 40) UN Doc. A/CN.9/765 [46]. As has already been noted, there are instances of practice where non-disputing Parties have made submissions to tribunals not by right but pursuant to general provisions for third person submissions and subject to the discretion of the tribunal: see e.g. *Siemens* v. *Argentina*, discussed above at n. 31 and generally section 7.4.1.

[67] See e.g. UNCITRAL (n. 40) UN Doc. A/CN.9/765 [51].

[68] The idea of consulting with the parties in respect of third person submissions generally was regarded as flowing from the 'consensual' nature of arbitration: UNCITRAL (n. 3) UN Doc. A/CN.9/712 [48]. Nonetheless, as has been noted, consultation is not the same as requiring the parties' consent: Mariel Dimsey, 'Article 4', section 6.6.1.

[69] UNCITRAL (n. 3) UN Doc. A/CN.9/736 [91]; UNCITRAL (n. 40) UN Doc. A/CN.9/765 [51], despite a concern that a power to invite submissions might 'prejudice the rights of the other Party to [the] treaty' ([50]). While there had been a suggestion that the State should only be able to make a submission in response to an invitation, this 'received little support': UNCITRAL (n. 3) UN Doc. A/CN.9/736 [92].

decision-making.[70] This power may prove important in circumstances in which the non-disputing Party is unaware of the intricacies of a given dispute, perhaps because of confidentiality restrictions.[71]

7.5 Article 5(2)

7.5.1 'further matters within the scope of the dispute'

15. The previous sections have established that non-disputing Parties have a clear interest, and a role to play, in respect of questions of treaty interpretation, warranting their having a right to make submissions on such issues. However, those same considerations do not arise in respect of other issues, and it is therefore less clear that non-disputing Parties should have such a right in respect of matters other than treaty interpretation.[72]

16. Initially, the WG limited the subject matter of non-disputing Parties' submissions to questions of law and treaty interpretation, and not factual matters.[73] Thus, the original proposed draft in respect of non-disputing Party submissions, based on Article 1128 of NAFTA,[74] provided:

> The arbitral tribunal may accept or request submission from a non-disputing State Party to the treaty, provided that such submission shall be restricted to issues of law and of treaty interpretation and shall not include submission on the factual aspects of the dispute.[75]

17. Debates in the WG raised questions whether the non-disputing Party should be restricted to making submissions on 'matters of treaty interpretation',[76] whether the State of nationality of the investor might, to the

[70] See nn. 29, 35 above.

[71] In one pending case, the manner of balancing the access by non-disputing Parties to pleadings and confidentiality restrictions has become a contentious issue, *Detroit International Bridge Company* v. *Canada*, UNCITRAL, PCA Case No. 2012-25, Procedural Order No. 9 (5 June 2014) [19]–[24].

[72] See below n. 83.

[73] See UNCITRAL (n. 3) UN Doc. A/CN.9/736 [79], [85]; UNCITRAL (n. 5) UN Doc. A/CN.9/WG.II/WP.166 [51]. As will be noted in further detail below, the particular concern here was in respect of diplomatic protection.

[74] UNCITRAL (n. 5) UN Doc. A/CN.9/WG.II/WP.166 [51].

[75] *Ibid.* [43].

[76] See UNCITRAL (n. 3) UN Doc. A/CN.9/736 [87]. See also UNCITRAL (n. 62) UN Doc. A/CN.9/WG.II/WP.169 [40], noting that whether non-disputing Party submissions could go further than treaty interpretation to issues of law, fact or other matters was 'extensively discussed' and left as an 'open question' at that stage.

contrary, have valuable factual information to provide,[77] and whether it was even feasible to separate out questions of law and fact.[78] It was ultimately accepted that non-disputing Parties could make submissions with respect to 'matters within the scope of the dispute'.[79] This align[s] the right of non-disputing Parties, in respect of matters other than questions of treaty interpretation to those of other third persons in Article 4.[80] As with Article 4, the tribunal is not obliged to accept such submissions,[81] and it may not invite them.[82] In respect of matters other than treaty interpretation, a non-disputing Party is therefore in a position that is not 'more privileged' than that of other third person interveners.[83]

7.5.2 'arbitral tribunal shall take into consideration, among other factors it determines to be relevant, the factors referred to in article 4, paragraph 3'

18. As in respect of other third person submissions,[84] the WG considered that there needed to be criteria restricting the participation of

[77] UNCITRAL (n. 3) UN Doc. A/CN.9/736 [88], where it was noted, for example, that 'the arbitral tribunal might need information on the nationality or corporate status of the investor, or the policy of the investor's home State, and the non-disputing State Party to the treaty, as home State of the investor, might be best placed to provide such information that belonged to the realm of domestic law or factual matters'. In this respect, it may also be noted that Article 4 relating to third person submissions allows for the provision of factual information: see the discussion in UNCITRAL (n. 27) UN Doc. A/CN.9/760 [52]–[53].

[78] UNCITRAL (n. 3) UN Doc. A/CN.9/736 [89], [98]. It was noted, for example, that 'records of treaty negotiations' might be considered legal or factual issues: *ibid.* [89]. See also UNCITRAL (n. 27) UN Doc. A/CN.9/760 [65].

[79] UNCITRAL (n. 62) UN Doc. A/CN.9/WG.II/WP.176 [41]. As to this language generally, see Mariel Dimsey, 'Article 4', [101]–[103].

[80] see also UNCITRAL (n. 3) UN Doc. A/CN.9/736 [98]; see also UNCITRAL (n. 27) UN Doc. A/CN.9/760 [67].

[81] Indeed, during debates, the view was expressed that 'the arbitral tribunal's discretion would serve as a filter to determine which submissions would be useful to it': UNCITRAL (n. 27) UN Doc. A/CN.9/760 [65].

[82] See *ibid.* [68]–[70]. Although initially included in the draft, the power to invite such submissions was removed, it having been suggested that it risked 'a politicization of disputes' and the introduction of 'aspects of diplomatic protection', as well as to avoid the non-disputing Party being 'put ... in a more privileged position than any third person to the dispute, which was said not to be justified in relation to issues outside the scope of treaty interpretation': *ibid.* [69]. However, this was not intended to 'impact on any power the tribunal might otherwise have under the arbitration rules or otherwise': *ibid.* [70].

[83] See *ibid.* [69], cited in the previous footnote.

[84] See e.g. UNCITRAL (n. 3) UN Doc. A/CN.9/712 [47], on restrictions on third person submissions generally.

non-disputing Parties in relation to matters that were not questions of treaty interpretation.[85] Thus, in determining whether to accept such submissions, the tribunal is to give consideration to, among other things it considers relevant, those mentioned in respect of Article 4.[86] As in respect of Article 4(3), those factors are non-exhaustive, and the tribunal is able to consider others when it regards them as relevant.[87] In addition, there was a particular concern in respect of the risk of diplomatic protection, considered in the following section, which warranted a specific reference in Article 5(2) to 'the need to avoid' a State making submissions supporting an investor's claim 'in a manner tantamount to diplomatic protection'.

7.5.3 'the need to avoid submissions which would support the claim of the investor in a manner tantamount to diplomatic protection'

19. The major concern in respect of allowing non-disputing Parties to make submissions on matters outside the limited scope of treaty interpretation was the risk of these amounting to diplomatic protection.[88] It is accepted in international law that:

> diplomatic protection consists of the invocation by a State, through diplomatic action or other means of peaceful settlement, of the responsibility of another State for an injury caused by an internationally wrongful act of that State to a natural or legal person that is a national of the former State with a view to the implementation of such responsibility.[89]

20. The concern was that if the non-disputing Party is the home State of the investor and is able to make broad factual and legal submissions,

[85] See e.g. UNCITRAL (n. 3) UN Doc. A/CN.9/736 [84], [96]; UNCITRAL (n. 27) UN Doc. A/CN.9/760 [72].

[86] These requirements are discussed in detail elsewhere in this volume: see Mariel Dimsey, 'Article 4', [152]–[180].

[87] See Mariel Dimsey, 'Article 4', [153]. For a concern that the criteria should not be restricted to those listed in Article 4(3), 'but would also include discretion of the arbitral tribunal to take account of other possible criteria', see UNCITRAL (n. 3) UN Doc. A/CN.9/736 [98].

[88] See e.g. UNCITRAL (n. 5) UN Doc. A/CN.9/WG.II/WP.166 [51]; UNCITRAL (n. 3) UN Doc. A/CN.9/736 [79], [85]. See also on non-disputing Party submissions and the risk of diplomatic protection, Kaufmann-Kohler (n. 4) 320–1; Roberts (n. 30) 219–20.

[89] *Ahmadou Sadio Diallo (Guinea* v. *DRC)* [2007] ICJ Rep 582 [39], citing ILC; ILC, 'Draft Articles on Diplomatic Protection with Commentaries' in *Report of the International Law Commission on the Work of its 61st Session*, UN Doc. A/61/10 15, Article 1.

this could essentially enable that State to engage in diplomatic protection with respect to its nationals.[90] As has been noted, this concern prompted the inclusion of Article 5(2) second sentence *in fine*, which provides that '[i]n determining whether to allow' submissions from a non-disputing Party on 'matters within the scope of the dispute' other than issues of treaty interpretation, the Tribunal shall give consideration to 'the need to avoid submissions which would support the claim of the investor in a manner tantamount to diplomatic protection'.

21. To understand the impact of Article 5(2), one has to consider two issues: first, whether the home State would, in the circumstances, otherwise be able to exercise diplomatic protection properly so-called regarding investors and investments; and second, what the meaning of the phrase 'tantamount to diplomatic protection' is. The first issue relates to the right of a State to invoke responsibility through diplomatic protection for the breach of primary (treaty) obligations regarding the treatment of its nationals and their investment, and whether this right is affected by the existence of procedures for investor-State arbitration. The starting point of analysis is that, in technical terms, a breach of a primary obligation, bilateral in form or bilateralisable in substance, *prima facie* injures the other party to the obligation;[91] therefore an additional legal argument has to be introduced to demonstrate why the normal consequences of the right to invoke responsibility do not follow. In other words, a breach by a State of its obligations regarding the treatment of investments and investors under investment protection treaties (and customary international law) *prima facie* gives the right of diplomatic protection to the State of nationality of the investor.[92] Sometimes, the issue is explicitly dealt with by treaty rules: for example, Article 27(1) of the ICSID Convention suspends diplomatic protection in relation to disputes that investors and States have either 'consented to submit or... have submitted to arbitration', unless the State has failed to 'comply

[90] See e.g. UNCITRAL (n. 3) UN Doc. A/CN.9/736 [87]–[88]; UNCITRAL (n. 3) UN Doc. A/CN.9/712 [49], noting that 'issues of diplomatic protection [were] to be given careful consideration'; see also UNCITRAL (n. 27) UN Doc. A/CN.9/760 [61], noting the possible 'effect of facilitating diplomatic protection', and [66], noting the 'danger of opening the door to diplomatic protection'. See also Kaufmann-Kohler (n. 4) 321.

[91] ILC, 'Draft Articles on Responsibility of States for Internationally Wrongful Acts with Commentaries', in *Report of the International Law Commission on the Work of its 56th Session*, UN Doc. A/56/10 31, Article 42 Commentaries 5–8.

[92] Martins Paparinskis, 'Investment Arbitration and the Law of Countermeasures' (2008) 79 *British Yearbook of International Law* 264, 281–97.

with the award'.[93] The legal situation is less clear in those situations where special treaty rules do not apply, and the general reluctance of States to engage in diplomatic protection of their investors makes it challenging to distinguish between the silence signifying the lack of a right to protection and the discretionary choice not to exercise this right.[94] There is considerable support for the proposition that diplomatic protection cannot coexist with investment arbitration, if with widely differing reasoning.[95] Still, the better view *de lege lata* is that the right of diplomatic protection of investments and investors by the home State still exists, despite the presence and exercise of investor-State arbitration, unless it has been waived or suspended by a treaty or a unilateral act.[96]

22. The second issue relates to the legal effect of 'tantamount'. Article 5(2) is *prima facie* not directed at diplomatic protection in the technical sense of that term noted above, but rather at support of the claim of the investor in a manner 'tantamount to' diplomatic protection. In international investment law, the term 'tantamount' has been discussed in the context of measures 'tantamount to expropriation', with some tribunals reading 'tantamount' as 'equivalent' (and referring to the traditional customary law of indirect

[93] *Ibid.* 305–17; Christoph Schreuer and others, The *ICSID Convention: A Commentary* (2nd edn., Cambridge University Press, 2009) 414–27.

[94] As to the discretionary nature of diplomatic protection, see *Barcelona Traction, Light and Power Company, Limited (Belgium* v. *Spain)* [1970] ICJ Rep 3 [78]–[80]; ILC, 'Draft Articles on Diplomatic Protection (n. 89) Article 19.

[95] See e.g. *Italy et Cuba* (Sentence preliminaire) (2005) http://italaw.com/sites/default/files/case-documents/ita0434_0.pdf [65]; *Italy et Cuba* (Sentence finale) (2008) http://italaw.com/sites/default/files/case-documents/ita0435_0.pdf, [141] (Article 27 of the ICSID Convention can be applied by analogy); Chittharanjan and F. Amerasinghe, *Diplomatic Protection* (Oxford University Press, 2008) 341 (duplication of claims must be avoided by reading invocation of investment arbitration as excluding diplomatic protection); Zachary Douglas, *The International Law of Investment Claims* (Cambridge University Press, 2009) 94–5 (breach of an investment treaty does not injure the home State in the first place); Anthea Roberts, 'State-to-State Investment Treaty Arbitration: A Hybrid Theory of Interdependent Rights and Shared Interpretative Authority' (2014) 55 *Harvard International Law Journal* 1, 30–52 (rights of investors and their home States are interdependent, and therefore the first claim against the host State, whichever it is, precludes the second one). See also ILC, 'Draft Articles on Diplomatic Protection' (n. 89) Article 17 and Commentary 3 (noting that the articles do not apply to investment arbitration insofar as they are inconsistent with BIT provisions and addressing investment arbitration separately from the general Article 16 rule that approved parallel invocation of responsibility); Kaufmann-Kohler (n. 4) 324.

[96] Paparinskis (n. 93) 281–300; Martins Paparinskis, 'Investment Treaty Arbitration and the (New) Law of State Responsibility' (2013) 24 *European Journal of International Law* 617, 640–1, 643.

expropriation, which focuses on substance rather than form), and others leaving open the possibility that the treaty rule might have a broader scope than the customary rules.[97] A rule like indirect expropriation might indeed be usefully addressed by focusing on the substance, rather than the form, of the underlying conduct by the State. However, it may be more challenging to apply the 'substance over form' approach to diplomatic protection, where it is precisely the form of the invocation of responsibility with a view to its implementation – namely the presentation of an international claim by a State of nationality to another State in respect of injury done to the former State's national – that makes diplomatic protection what it is.[98] Nonetheless, this seems to be what Article 5(2) requires, with the concern being to identify submissions that resemble those that might be made in respect of a diplomatic protection action.[99]

23. It follows that Article 5(2) will apply to submissions being made by a non-disputing Party even where these do not amount to diplomatic protection properly so-called. This means, for instance, that even if a non-disputing Party does not invoke the responsibility of the other State for injury done to its national by making a claim,[100] its actions may be captured by Article 5(2). There may, however, be a difficult distinction to draw in this respect between submissions that are 'tantamount to diplomatic protection' and those that are not. On the one hand, a non-disputing Party may be making abstract submissions about treaty interpretation without any direct relevance for the investor-State dispute.[101] Indeed, as has already been noted, non-disputing Parties are entitled,

[97] See the discussion of different decisions in *Waste Management* v. *Mexico (II)*, ICSID Additional Facility Case ARB(AF)/00/3, Award (30 April 2004) [142]–[155]. The authors benefited here from discussion with participants at the Transparency Workshop, held in Cambridge on 18 January 2014.

[98] See the definition at n. 89 above.

[99] See e.g. UNCITRAL (n. 3) UN Doc. A/CN.9/736 [87] (risk that submissions 'might come very close to diplomatic protection'); see similarly Kaufmann-Kohler (n. 4) 321 ('A home State submission defending a position on factual issues in aid of its own national would *de facto* equate, or at least come very close to, diplomatic protection').

[100] For which claim it would, presumably, need to invoke jurisdiction, as the right of home States to make submissions could not be used as a basis for inter-State claims. The claim would have to be made on some other jurisdictional basis, such as under the inter-State arbitration clause in the relevant treaty, if available: see e.g. the claim in *Ecuador* v. *US* (2012) http://pca-cpa.org/showpage.asp?pag_id=1455; *Italy et Cuba* (Sentence finale) (n. 95), though cf. the reasoning regarding the availability of diplomatic protection in that case.

[101] Roberts makes a similar distinction to that made herein between States 'advancing their investor's claims directly' and their 'express[ing] general views on interpretation' that 'might indirectly affect' such claims: Roberts (n. 30) 220; see also Kaufmann-Kohler (n. 4) 321.

pursuant to Article 5(1), to make submissions relating to questions of treaty interpretation. Importantly, this is a right not subject to evaluation by the Tribunal taking account of the considerations contained in Article 5(2) and must therefore be taken to be excluded from being 'tantamount to diplomatic protection'. Only submissions in respect of other matters are potentially caught by Article 5(2). However, as noted above,[102] there is a close link between the interpretation and application of treaties, and an interpretation of the relevant treaty put forward by a non-disputing Party is likely – if accepted – to affect the investor's claim to some degree and could in fact be favourable to it.[103] Still, this alone should not deprive a non-disputing Party's submissions of having the character of treaty interpretation and render them of the nature of diplomatic protection.[104] On the other hand, as noted at the end of the previous paragraph, a non-disputing party could make submissions in the context of a particular dispute that are related to the facts, and supportive of its national's claim, akin to those that may have otherwise been made in a diplomatic protection claim. Such submissions may well, depending on the circumstances, be regarded as 'tantamount to diplomatic protection'. More difficult questions are likely to arise regarding situations that fall between these extremes, where a non-disputing Party makes submissions that combine characteristics of interpretation and application, regarding both the content of rules as well as their application to facts in the context of the particular dispute. It will be for the tribunal to determine whether the submissions of a non-disputing Party are sufficiently similar to the exercise of diplomatic protection to warrant their not being allowed.

24. There may also be other reasons why actions of a particular State cannot be regarded as diplomatic protection as such but may nonetheless be captured by Article 5(2). For instance, Article 5(2) can operate without prejudice to the complex debates about the availability of diplomatic protection noted previously. It would therefore be capable of application even if one took the view that diplomatic protection was not available, or was excluded, in the context of a particular investor-State arbitration (and therefore the relevant non-disputing Party submissions could not amount to diplomatic protection properly so-called).[105] Alternatively, there might be particular situations in which diplomatic protection

[102] See n. 26 above and accompanying text.
[103] See similarly Roberts (n. 30) 219–20.
[104] *Ibid.* 220.
[105] Cf Kaufmann-Kohler (n. 4) 321 (potential for non-disputing Party submissions to breach the Article 27 ICSID prohibition on diplomatic protection).

would be technically unavailable because one or more of its legal procedural requirements are not met and where, if there were no reference to submissions being 'tantamount to diplomatic protection', home States might be able to argue plausibly that what they were engaging in was not diplomatic protection *per se*.[106] They might also be able to abuse the right to make submissions in order to get around the restrictions of diplomatic protection. For example, diplomatic protection usually requires exhaustion of local remedies before the claim becomes admissible, while investor-State arbitration often does not.[107] A State might be tempted to present its arguments on law and fact, taken from a possible diplomatic protection claim, as a non-disputing Party submission so as to evade the requirement of exhaustion of local remedies. However, submissions made pursuant to such a strategy could plausibly be characterised as 'tantamount to diplomatic protection' and fall under Article 5(2). Finally, even if a non-disputing Party endeavours to characterise its submissions as relating to 'direct' injury to itself (in respect of which no local remedies need be exhausted)[108] rather than a diplomatic protection claim regarding 'indirect' injury (where local remedies have to be exhausted),[109] it may be that these would be caught by Article 5(2). Cases regarding alleged injury to identifiable investors have generally been viewed as – perhaps even, by implication, presumed to be – diplomatic protection ('indirect') claims,[110] but even if a State focuses on aspects of 'direct' injury to itself, if its submissions are sufficiently related to the facts of cases involving particular nationals, Article 5(2) may nonetheless apply.

[106] One could imagine situations where aspects of the customary law of diplomatic protection – on, say, double or continuous nationality, or effective link – preclude a proper diplomatic protection claim, see ILC, 'Draft Articles on Diplomatic Protection' (n. 89) Article 4 Commentary 5, Articles 5–7, 10; therefore the home State presents it as a non-disputing Party submission. The practice of submissions under NAFTA and CAFTA-DR provides very little support for concerns about diplomatic protection, since home States' submissions overwhelmingly have been directed against their investors: see n. 27.

[107] Zachary Douglas, *The International Law of Investment Claims* (Cambridge University Press, 2009) 28–30.

[108] As noted above, if the State were actually to make a claim in this respect, jurisdiction would need to be demonstrated: see n. 100.

[109] On the direct indirect claims distinction, see ILC, 'Draft Articles on Diplomatic Protection' (n. 89) Article 14, Commentaries 9–12.

[110] See e.g. *Interhandel Case (Switzerland* v. *US)* [1959] ICJ Rep 6, 28–9; *Elettronica Sicula SpA (ELSI) (US* v. *Italy)* [1989] ICJ Rep 15 [51]–[52]; *Italy et Cuba* (Sentence preliminaire) (2005) (n. 95) [141]–[142], [154], [174], [222]–[245]. See also ILC, 'Draft Articles on Diplomatic Protection' (n. 89) Article 14, Commentaries 9–12.

25. It remains to be seen what effect the formulae of Article 5(2) will have. It is probable that the language employed will enable tribunals to address abusive elements in submissions of non-disputing Parties that would not be caught by more precisely drafted rules. However, the key difficulty will lie in distinguishing those kinds of submissions that are sufficiently close to a diplomatic protection claim to be regarded as 'tantamount' thereto from those that are not, including distinguishing submissions on questions of interpretation from broader submissions on other legal and factual matters.

7.6 Article 5(3): Inferences to be drawn from non-disputing Party submissions on treaty interpretation

26. As has already been noted, subsequent agreement by treaty Parties – which may be established through subsequent practice – is indicative of their agreed understanding as to the interpretation of the relevant treaty.[111] In some cases, it has been argued that coinciding treaty Party submissions are demonstrative of agreement between those Parties as to the treaty's correct interpretation within the meaning of Article 31(3)(a) of the VCLT.[112] In addition, the pleadings of States Parties may be regarded as amounting to subsequent practice establishing agreement within the meaning of Article 31(3)(b).[113] Importantly, such agreement does not need to be express, but may be the result of acquiescence in an interpretation adopted by another treaty Party.[114] As a result, if a non-disputing Party does not object to a statement relating to treaty interpretation

[111] See [9] above, particularly n. 51 and accompanying text; also Roberts (n. 30) 217.

[112] See e.g. *ADF Group* v. *United States*, Final Post-Hearing Submission of Respondent on Article 1105(1) and *Pope & Talbot* www.state.gov/documents/organization/12591.pdf, 2–3, where the US argued that there was agreement, within the meaning of Article 31(3)(a), between the NAFTA parties, as expressed through their submissions, 'as to the proper interpretation of the treaty'. See also *Canadian Cattlemen for Fair Trade* v. *US* (n. 30) [186]–[187]; generally Roberts (n. 30) 216–17.

[113] See generally Roberts (n. 30) 217–19, on the use to be made of pleadings as subsequent practice, both in respect of respondents and non-disputing Parties, and discussion of relevant case law.

[114] See Roberts (n. 30) 199–200 and authorities cited therein, particularly ILC, 'Draft Articles on the Law of Treaties' (n. 50) 222. See also ILC, sixty-fifth session Report (n. 51) 41, noting that subsequent practice can include 'tacit acceptance of statements or acts by other parties', and I. C. MacGibbon, 'The Scope of Acquiescence in International Law' (1954) 31 *British Yearbook of International Law* 143, discussed further at n. 116 below.

contained within the pleadings of a respondent State, the former may arguably be regarded as having agreed to that interpretation.[115]

27. It is in this light that one can examine Article 5(3) of the Rules, which provides that no inference is to be drawn from any failure by a State to make a submission with respect to treaty interpretation or other matters. This reflected a concern that, because a State could not be obliged to make submissions, nothing should be taken from its not doing so.[116] There may of course be a variety of reasons why a State does not make submissions in respect of a particular dispute, and it should not be assumed that such an omission necessarily arises from agreement with the interpretation proposed.[117] Nonetheless, the inclusion of this paragraph in the Rules may acknowledge the possibility of submissions by treaty Parties to tribunals evidencing subsequent practice or agreement as to the interpretation or application of the treaty. While Article 5(3) prevents any such inferences arising from a failure by a non-disputing Party to make submissions from being taken into account by an arbitral tribunal applying the Rules, this does not exclude the possibility that such actions might be of relevance more broadly to the interpretation of the treaty as a matter of international law.

[115] See further the discussion in n. 116 below. The Appellate Body of the World Trade Organization did 'not exclude that, in specific situations, the "lack of reaction" or silence by a particular treaty party may, in the light of attendant circumstances, be understood as acceptance of the practice of other treaty parties': *EC-Customs Classification of Frozen Boneless Chicken Cuts*, Appellate Body Report, WTO/DS269/AB/R, WTO/DS286/AB (12 September 2005) [272].

[116] UNCITRAL (n. 3) UN Doc. A/CN.9/736 [100]. The lack of obligation to make submissions was at issue in the recent *Ecuador* v. *US* arbitration (n. 91), where the Tribunal accepted the argument that there was no dispute between Ecuador and the US (and consequently no jurisdiction) when the US did not respond to Ecuador's submission regarding the interpretation of the treaty (the decision is not publicly available), www.state.gov/s/l/c53491.htm. Whatever the merits of this decision, it still leaves open the question of whether the silence of the US, even if perfectly lawful, had any interpretative effect. MacGibbon suggests that if a treaty Party fails to protest against another's clear assertion as to the interpretation of a given treaty, this amounts to acquiescence: MacGibbon (n. 114) 146. If this is correct, the US may have won the case against Ecuador through its silence, but has potentially lost any interpretative battle in the long run, 'with the silence contributing to subsequent practice that reflects the content of Ecuador's position': see Martins Paparinskis, 'On the Love of Hybrids and Technicalities' (31 March 2014) *Opinio Juris* http://opiniojuris.org/2014/03/31/hilj-online-symposium-love-hybrids-technicalities/; Anthea Roberts, 'Anthea Roberts Responds to Martins Paparinskis' (31 March 2014) *Opinio Juris* http://opiniojuris.org/2014/03/31/hilj-online-symposium-anthea-roberts-responds-martins-paparinskis/.

[117] Roberts (n. 30) 195–6, particularly fn. 78, also 224, noting *inter alia* that States may be unaware of proceedings or without the resources for a response.

7.7 Articles 5(4) and 5(5): Procedural issues

28. The final point to be made here is that while there are some key differences between Articles 4 and 5 of the Rules, important questions of procedural fairness are common to both non-disputing Party submissions and third person submissions more generally.[118] Third persons generally pose the risk of delaying proceedings and increasing their cost, and submissions may be made that go against the interests of either or both of the parties to the proceedings.[119] The same may be said of non-disputing Party submissions. Therefore, the capacity of a non-disputing Party to make submissions, including in respect of treaty interpretation, is subject to the requirement that they not 'disrupt or unduly burden' the proceedings, nor 'unfairly prejudice any disputing party'.[120] Additionally, the parties to the arbitral proceedings are to be given 'a reasonable opportunity to present their observations on any submission by a non-disputing Party'.[121] These provisions are the same as those to be found in Article 4 and the comments made regarding their application in respect of Article 4 apply with equal force in respect of Article 5.

29. However, one particular issue arises in respect of non-disputing Party submissions and potential unfairness that might result during the relevant arbitral proceedings that does not arise in respect of third person submissions more generally. This relates to the role that non-disputing

[118] Indeed, as has been noted, one of the reasons for addressing third person and non-disputing Party submissions in separate articles was that the provisions now contained in Article 4(3), (5) and (6) were equally relevant to non-disputing Party submissions: see UNCITRAL (n. 3) UN Doc. A/CN.9/736 [84].

[119] UNCITRAL (n. 3) UN Doc. A/CN.9/712 [47]. See also Meg Kinnear, 'Transparency and Third Party Participation in Investor-State Dispute Settlement' Symposium: Making the Most of International Investment Agreements (12 December 2005) www.oecd.org/investment/internationalinvestmentagreements/36979626.pdf, 5; and generally Mariel Dimsey, 'Article 4', sections 6.2, 6.10.1.

[120] See UNCITRAL (n. 40) UN Doc. A/CN.9/765 [51]. For example, concern was expressed during the drafting of Article 5 about the possibility of a non-disputing Party causing disruption or prejudice by, for example, making submissions late in the proceedings: *ibid.* [46], [48]. These requirements, as they apply to third person submissions more generally, are discussed in Mariel Dimsey, 'Article 4', sections 6.10.2–6.10.3.

[121] As the Working Group noted in respect of third person submissions generally, there are both procedural and substantive matters of fairness to be considered: the former is given effect in the requirement that submissions not 'disrupt or unduly burden' proceedings; the latter seemingly in the requirement that parties be able to comment on the submissions made: see UNCITRAL (n. 3) UN Doc. A/CN.9/736 [77]; Mariel Dimsey, 'Article 4', [192]–[206] to [199]–[200], also noting the potential for further 'procedural prejudice' flowing from the substantive: [201].

Parties play in respect of questions of treaty interpretation. As noted above, treaty Parties – including non-disputing Parties – are able to speak to the intention behind, and to agree with other treaty Parties as to the correct interpretation of, a given text.[122] The possibility therefore arises that treaty Parties could interfere with the arbitral process by making use of their powers to interpret the treaty under consideration to the disadvantage of the investor while proceedings are ongoing.[123] As has been noted, the capacity of a non-disputing Party to make submissions in respect of treaty interpretation is not exempt from the requirements of procedural fairness contained in Article 5(4). It will therefore be for the arbitral tribunal to try to reach an appropriate balance should such a situation arise.

7.8 Conclusion

30. Submissions by a non-disputing Party to the treaty occupy a somewhat unusual place in the Rules. Article 5 borrows from Article 1128 of NAFTA, and its interpretation can therefore draw on the rich practice of submissions in that multilateral context. At the same time, on many of the procedural issues Article 5 refers back to the practice developed in the context of *amici curiae* and expressed in Article 4. In its future application, Article 5 will present a challenge of combining these two concepts: on the one hand, the rights of treaty Parties to make submissions on interpretation (with the danger of both pro-investor *de facto* diplomatic protection and anti-investor *de facto* reinterpretations);

[122] See [9]–[10] above. See also n. 36.

[123] See Roberts (n. 30) 179–81, 212–15, 217. See also Schreuer (n. 57) 148. In respect of the NAFTA Free Trade Commission Statement of 31 July 2001, see further e.g. Gabrielle Kaufmann-Kohler, 'Interpretative Powers of the Free Trade Commission and the Rule of Law' in Emmanuel Gaillard and Frederic Bachand (eds.), *Fifteen Years of NAFTA Chapter 11 Arbitration* (JurisNet, 2011) 181–5. This is a point on which reasonable people might disagree. For one Whewell Professor, the powers of interpretation of the Free Trade Commission reflect the elementary proposition that 'the parties to a treaty own the treaty and can interpret it': James Crawford, 'A Consensualist Interpretation of Article 31(3) of the Vienna Convention on the Law of Treaties' in Georg Nolte (ed.), *Treaties and Subsequent Practice* (Oxford University Press, 2013) 31. For one of his predecessors, '[t]his is surely against the most elementary rules of the due process of justice': *Methanex* v. *US*, Second Opinion of Sir Robert Jennings (6 September 2001) http://italaw.com/sites/default/files/case-documents/ita0983.pdf 6. See Martins Paparinskis, 'Analogies and Other Regimes of International Law' in Z. Douglas, J. Pauwelyn and J. Viñuales (eds.), *The Foundations of International Investment Law* (Oxford University Press, 2014) 86–90.

and on the other hand, the balance between effectiveness and due process common to all types of non-party submissions in investment treaty arbitration. This, of course, is not a new challenge, and the similarities and differences between different non-parties have been at the heart of the debate since the very first acceptance of third person submissions in the *Methanex* v. *US* case.[124] It remains to be seen how the practice will develop.

[124] See n. 24.

8

Article 6. Hearings

KLINT ALEXANDER*

1. Subject to article 6, paragraphs 2 and 3, hearings for the presentation of evidence or for oral argument ("hearings") shall be public.
2. Where there is a need to protect confidential information or the integrity of the arbitral process pursuant to article 7, the arbitral tribunal shall make arrangements to hold in private that part of the hearing requiring such protection.
3. The arbitral tribunal shall make logistical arrangements to facilitate the public access to hearings (including where appropriate by organizing attendance through video links or such other means as it deems appropriate). However, the arbitral tribunal may, after consultation with the disputing parties, decide to hold all or part of the hearings in private where this becomes necessary for logistical reasons, such as when the circumstances render any original arrangement for public access to a hearing infeasible.

8.1 Introduction

1. In July 2013, the United Nations Commission on International Trade Law (UNCITRAL)[1] adopted a new set of rules aimed at promoting greater openness and transparency of the arbitral process in investor-State

* Klint Alexander is Professor/Dean and Professor of Law at the University of Wyoming College of Law.

[1] The United Nations Commission on International Trade Law (UNCITRAL) is the core legal body of the United Nations system in the field of international trade law. Its mandate is to remove legal obstacles to international trade by progressively modernising and harmonising trade law. It prepares legal texts in a number of key areas such as international commercial dispute settlement, electronic commerce, insolvency, international payments, sale of goods, transport law, procurement and infrastructure development. UNCITRAL also provides technical assistance to law reform activities, including assisting Member States to review and assess their law reform needs and to draft the legislation required to implement UNCITRAL texts. The UNCITRAL Secretariat is located in Vienna, Austria.

arbitration (the Rules).[2] The Rules represent a shift away from secrecy and confidentiality towards greater openness in treaty-based investor-State arbitrations. Increased transparency has become the 'new normal' in international investment arbitration as more investor-State disputes involve challenges to generally applicable regulatory measures – environmental laws, human rights and public health measures – enacted by host State governments. Resolution of cases involving these issues can impact investor interests, the public interest and the regulatory powers of the State. The Rules establish a process and an institutional framework to ensure that transparency is clearly and consistently applied in arbitration.

2. Article 6 of the Rules provides for public access to hearings in investor-State arbitration, subject to certain exceptions.[3] Under the previous Arbitration Rules (1976), hearings were kept confidential unless the parties agreed to waive confidentiality, even where important public policies were at issue. Article 6 alters the landscape of dispute resolution under bilateral investment treaties (BITs) and other multilateral treaties by making the arbitration process more open to public participation and scrutiny. Article 6 applies to all disputes under UNCITRAL as the default rule; however, the previous standard of closed hearings applies to disputes fully within treaties concluded before 1 April 2014.[4]

3. This chapter discusses the implications of open hearings under the Rules and examines some of the benefits and concerns of conducting arbitral hearings in this manner. Investors, States and the general public need to better understand how the idea of 'open hearings' will affect their interests and the decision to arbitrate claims under these rules in future investor-State disputes.

[2] See UNCITRAL Rules on Transparency in Treaty-based Investor-State Arbitration, Pre-Release Draft (2 October 2013). An earlier Pre-Release draft was available as of 30 July 2013 (A/CN.9/XLVI/CRP.3 (9 July 2013) (as modified in negotiations)).

[3] Greater transparency arguably will result in increased stability, predictability and legitimacy of the international investment law regime and provide for more accountability in investor-State arbitrations. See Stephan W. Schill, 'Enhancing the Legitimacy of International Investment Law: Conceptual and Methodological Foundations of a New Public Law Approach' 52 *Va. J. Int. L.* 57 (2011).

[4] Efforts continue by reformers to make the transparency rules apply to matters brought under existing treaties. The hope is that some disputants will choose to use the new standard voluntarily, that some treaties will be renegotiated and that an overriding new international convention will include the transparency reforms.

8.2 Background and purpose

4. International investment law has neither a centralised legal framework nor a hierarchy of rules to govern investor-State relations. In the absence of a single set of rules or standards for investment disputes, it is difficult to develop a consistent set of transparency norms for this area of dispute resolution. The fact that most international investment cases take place behind closed doors, with little or no information provided to the public, exacerbates this issue, making it difficult for scholars, lawyers and the general public to ascertain information about the development of substantive investment law. Transparency matters, advocates say, because of the growing importance of 'investor-State' matters being arbitrated and the decisions that result from these matters.

5. The expectation of a closed hearing has long been the centrepiece of the arbitration system. Under various sets of procedural rules, the parties to an arbitral proceeding can rely on confidentiality at hearings unless they consent to waive it.[5] The American Arbitration Association (AAA) enforces strict rules on privacy and confidentiality and ensures both at hearings.[6] The Judicial Arbitration and Mediation Services (JAMS) International Arbitration Rules and International Chamber of Commerce (ICC) rules also require hearings to remain confidential unless parties consent to transparency.[7] The International Centre for the Settlement of Investment Disputes (ICSID),[8] the London Court of International Arbitration (LCIA),[9] the Paris Court of International Arbitration (PCIA),

[5] The rules of ICSID, UNCITRAL (1976 and 2010), the ICC and the SCC all require the consent of both disputing parties for hearings to be open to those not involved in the proceedings. Other than the ICSID Arbitration Rules, the rules used in investor-State arbitrations, including the UNCITRAL Arbitration Rules, have largely been crafted to apply to commercial disputes between private parties.

[6] See International Dispute Resolution Procedures (Including Mediation and Arbitration Rules) Article 20.

[7] JAMS International Arbitration Rules, Article 16.

[8] The ICSID Arbitration Rules are the only arbitration rules established exclusively for disputes arising between investors and States and in recognition of the fact that resolution of these disputes implicates matters of international law relating to the treatment of investments. Even though these Arbitration Rules rely heavily on arbitral rules established for commercial disputes, the ICSID system nevertheless distinguishes itself in various ways from other mechanisms, including in relation to its approach to transparency.

[9] Article 30 of the LCIA Rules imposes the general duty of confidentiality towards the parties (Article 30.1), the arbitral tribunal (Article 30.2) and the LCIA Court (Article 30.3). Article 30.3 allows the Court to publish an award or any part of an award only if the parties and the arbitral tribunal submit written consent.

the World Intellectual Property Organization (WIPO),[10] and the Stockholm Chamber of Commerce (SCC), among others, also impose a duty of privacy and confidentiality during arbitration hearings. Because most BITs are silent on the subject of transparency, neither mandating confidentiality nor requiring disclosure,[11] the parties to an investor-State dispute look to the various arbitration institutions for procedural guidance.

6. In the last decade, international tribunals have allowed for expanded public access to information in investor-State disputes and, in some cases, have ordered open hearings. The World Trade Organization (WTO), which has traditionally been a strong proponent of confidentiality in dispute resolution, has begun to explore ways to promote more transparency and openness in its procedures. In 2005, a WTO panel ordered that hearings be opened to the public at the request of the European Communities (EC) in the *US – Continued Suspension of Obligations of Canada Dispute.*[12] In 2012, another WTO panel granted a request to allow the public to observe hearings through closed-circuit TV in a WTO meeting room.[13]

7. ICSID tribunals have also been reconsidering the idea of confidentiality in investment disputes in an effort to strike the right balance between the need for transparency and the need to protect procedural integrity in arbitration. In the *Biwater Gauff* case, the tribunal denied the Government of Tanzania's request to open the hearing to the

[10] Article 75 of the WIPO Rules allows the award to be disclosed if: (i) the parties consent; (ii) it falls into the public domain as a result of an action before a national court or other competent authority; or (iii) it must be disclosed in order to comply with a legal requirement imposed on a party or in order to establish or protect a party's legal rights against a third party.

[11] Hearings in treaty-based investor-State disputes will only be open when required by the underlying treaty.

[12] In the *United States – Continued Suspension of Obligations in the EC and Canada* v. *Continued Suspension of Obligation*, the Tribunal accepted the European Community's request for an open hearing. The EC based its argument on public policy grounds which affected the entire membership of the WTO. It also stated that secret deliberations were not required to protect the integrity of the judicial process where the case related to 'an important individual treaty and questions of public concern, such as the legitimacy of a law protecting the health of citizens'. See *United States – Continued Suspension of Obligations in the EC – Hormones Dispute* and *Canada – Continued Suspension of Obligations in the EC – Hormones Dispute*, WT/DS320/AB/R, WT/DS321/AB/R, adopted 14 November 2008.

[13] *Ibid.*

public, but allowed for disclosure of memorials and the tribunal's procedural orders. According to the Tribunal:[14]

> Given the treatment of awards and the treatment of such materials in investment arbitration generally, the presumption should be in favour of allowing the publication of the Tribunal's Decisions, Orders and Directions. Publication of the Tribunal's decisions also, as a general matter, will be less likely to aggravate or exacerbate a dispute, or to exert undue pressure on one party, than publication of parties' pleadings or release of other documentary materials. (Paragraph 152)
>
> The Tribunal considers itself responsible to ensure that the hearing is conducted in an efficient manner, to resolve the parties' dispute fairly and impartially. The publication of minutes or records of hearings has at least the potential to affect the procedural integrity and efficiency of the hearing itself. Indeed:
>
> (a) Regulation 22(2) of the Administrative and Financial Regulations provides that the Secretary-General of ICSID shall only arrange for the publication of the minutes and other records of proceedings if both parties to a proceeding so consent, and
> (b) Rule 32(2) of the new ICSID Arbitration Rules provides that the hearing may not be opened by the Tribunal to third parties if a party objects.
>
> Accordingly, it is appropriate that minutes or records of hearings should not be disclosed unless the parties so agree, or the Tribunal so directs. (Paragraph 155)

8. ICSID, which is a leading investor-State arbitration venue,[15] publishes its awards and provides to some degree access to the proceedings. ICSID tribunals' decisions largely affect the world of investor-State arbitration due to persuasiveness. Even though the draft versions of the ICSID Arbitration Rules and the Additional Facility Rules in 2005 contained a provision that changed the default rule from *in camera* to public hearings,[16] ICSID eventually decided to require hearings *in camera* if one of the disputing parties objects to a public hearing.

[14] See *Biwater Gauff (Tanzania) Limited* v. *Tanzania*, Procedural Order No. 3 (Confidentiality), ICSID Case No. ARB/05/22, IIC 31 (2006), 29 September 2006, International Centre for Settlement of Investment Disputes (ICSID).

[15] In 2013, ICSID registered 40 new cases and the website in April 2014 showed 187 active cases.

[16] See Rule 32 Arbitration Rules and Rule 39 Additional Facility Rules in ICSID, Working Paper of the ICSID Secretariat, 12 May 2005, icsid.worldbank.org/ICSID/FrontServlet?requestType=ICSIDPublicationsRH&actionVal=ViewAnnouncePDF&AnnouncementType=archive&AnnounceNo=25_1.pdf.

9. The Arbitration Rules contain a similar provision that requires hearings *in camera*. However, they are more transparent than ICSID's. In 2002, under Arbitration Rules (1976), the arbitral tribunal in the *United Parcel Service (UPS)* case against Canada emphasised the broader public policy implications of anti-competitive conduct in the use of courier and parcel services to make hearings open to the public, subject to the protection of confidential information.[17] The arbitral tribunal based its decision on Article 15(1) of the Arbitration Rules (1976), which provides:

> Subject to these rules the arbitral tribunal may conduct the arbitration in such a manner as it considers appropriate, provided that the parties are treated with equality and that at any stage of the proceedings each party is given a full opportunity of presenting his case.

The public hearing in the *UPS* case was broadcast live in the World Bank Headquarters.

10. Some tribunals acting under certain bilateral and multilateral investment agreements have also begun to open the door to greater transparency. The Model United States and Canadian BITs, for example, expressly allow for greater transparency, including access to public hearings and case documents.[18] The North American Free Trade Agreement (NAFTA) investment dispute settlement mechanism under Chapter 11 is becoming one of the more transparent institutional arbitration frameworks for resolving investor-State disputes.[19] The 2001 'Note of Interpretation' issued by the NAFTA parties made transparency a priority, requiring the disclosure of memorials and pleadings, the composition of panels, decisions on challenges to arbitrators, and arbitral orders and awards.[20] Since 2001, several NAFTA tribunal decisions have expanded transparency obligations to cover public access to documents and hearings, and to allow for the submission of *amicus* briefs by third parties in environmentally sensitive cases.[21]

[17] *United Parcel Service of America Inc.* v. *Canada*, NAFTA (UNCITRAL), Procedural Directions for Amicus Submissions, 4 April 2003.

[18] More than 3,000 BITs and regional treaties today grant substantive and procedural protections to foreign investors, including greater transparency in the arbitral process.

[19] Chapter 11 – Investment, North American Free Trade Agreement (NAFTA), 17 December 1992, Can-Mex-US, 32 ILM 605, 32 ILM 289 (1993).

[20] NAFTA Free Trade Commission, 'Notes of Interpretation of Certain NAFTA Chapter 11 Provisions', 31 July 2001 www.naftaclaims.com/, part A.

[21] In *Methanex Corporation* v. *United States of America*, Order on Amicus and Article 1128 Submissions, 6 April 2004, the International Institute for Sustainable Development (IISD)

11. The trend in favour of more transparency was later extended to the Dominican Republic–Central America–United States Free Trade Agreement (CAFTA-DR), which mandates open hearings under Article 10.21 (2).[22] In 2010, ICSID for the first time webcast a hearing in the *Pac Rim Cayman LLC* v. *El Salvador* case.[23] Noteworthy is the fact that the hearing was webcast in both English and Spanish, which allowed citizens in El Salvador the opportunity to be informed of the efforts to halt harmful metals mining in their country and the private sector's response to those efforts in their own language. ICSID reported that on the first day of the hearing, there were 150 hits during the live webcast. Out of the 150 hits, 120 of them viewed the hearings in English, and 30 in Spanish. These hearings have since been archived on ICSID's website for further viewing.

12. The call for more transparency and open hearings was also reinforced by influential non-arbitral institutions. The International Institute of Sustainable Development (IISD), a Canadian-based, international public policy research institute for sustainable development, stresses the importance of aligning international arbitration rules with public interests calling for increased public access to hearings.[24] The Washington-based

and Earthjustice requested permission to submit written *amicus curiae* briefs, public hearings, the disclosure of all documents for purposes of making the submissions to the IISD and the allowance to make oral arguments. Communities for a Better Environment and the Earth Island Institute also submitted a joint request for permission to appear as *amici curiae*. The Tribunal noted the importance of the public interest due to the subject matter of the arbitration and the benefits of openness and transparency. Based on these findings, the Tribunal allowed the submission of *amicus curiae* briefs and open hearings. The Tribunal, however, did not recognise that *amici* have any authority to participate in oral arguments. This decision was issued in January 2004, and the open hearing was conducted via closed circuit TV in June 2004.

[22] Article 10.21(2) of CAFTA-DR reads: 'The tribunal shall conduct hearings open to the public and shall determine, in consultation with the disputing parties, the appropriate logistical arrangements'. The article also requires disclosure of the notice of intent, the notice of arbitration, pleadings, memorials, and briefs submitted to the tribunal by a disputing party minutes or transcripts of hearings of the tribunal, where available, and orders, awards and decisions of the tribunal.

[23] *Pac Rim Cayman LLC.* v. *El Salvador*, ICSID Case No. ARB/09/12.

[24] Howard Mann of the International Institute for Sustainable Development said: 'These investment arbitrations often involve important public interest issues and have resulted in individual awards against governments as much as USD 100 million and higher'. Secret arbitrations make decisions about public interest issues that include the environment, public health, mineral exploitation, forests, water and other natural resources, and the delivery of public services. Such awards can have a considerable impact on public finances, especially for developing countries. See CIEL, 'CIEL and IISD call for an end to

Centre for International Environmental Law has called for open hearings and was deeply involved in the UNCITRAL changes. Moreover, the Office of the US Trade Representative (USTR) recognises and welcomes the growing global interest in arbitration transparency.[25] These and other institutions have helped to facilitate support for more transparency in arbitration hearings, now enunciated in Article 6 of the Rules.

8.3 Article 6(1): Requirement to hold public hearings

> 1. Subject to article 6, paragraphs 2 and 3, hearings for the presentation of evidence or for oral argument ("hearings") shall be public.

13. Article 6 requires that, as a rule, hearings should be open. '[A]s a matter of principle, hearings should always be open where they were substantive (including jurisdictional hearings and hearings in which evidence by witnesses or experts, or oral arguments, were presented), but not where mere matters of procedure were to be addressed'.[26] Only parts of UNCITRAL's Working Group II (Arbitration and Conciliation) (WG) wished to link the term to the understanding of hearing under Article 17(3) of the Arbitration Rules (2010) or to Article 24(1) of the UNCITRAL Model Law on International Commercial Arbitration.[27]

14. Article 6 represents a shift in direction towards openness, rather than confidentiality, in treaty-based investor-State arbitrations. Article 6(1) states that hearings for the presentation of evidence or for oral argument ('hearings') 'shall be open to the public'. The disputing parties – individually or collectively – cannot veto open hearings. Article 6(1) overrides Article 28(3) of the Arbitration Rules (2010), which required *in camera* hearings.

15. At the beginning of the debate, one part of the WG fostered an approach similar to that under the Arbitration Rules.[28] Two groups proposed the wording '[i]n the event of oral hearings, the Tribunal shall

an era of secrecy in investor-State arbitration: UN body must support transparency in new arbitration rules', The Centre for International Environmental Law, 26 June 2008.

[25] The USTR released its Statement on Open Hearings in NAFTA Chapter Eleven Arbitration on 7 October 2003. In this statement, the USTR recommends some methods for open hearings such as the use of closed-circuit television systems, internet webcasting, or 'other forms of access'.

[26] UNCITRAL, 'Report of the Working Group II (Arbitration and Conciliation) on the work of its fifty-seventh session' (2012) UN Doc. A/CN.9/760 [86].

[27] *Ibid.* [87].

[28] UNCITRAL, 'Report of the Working Group II (Arbitration and Conciliation) on the work of its fifty-fourth session' (2011) UN Doc. A/CN.9/717 [101].

conduct hearings open to the public',[29] but one group in favour of slight transparency suggested an inclusion of the phrase 'unless either party objects'.[30] One option of this draft suggested right of veto for the disputing parties.[31] Another group in favour of broad transparency and the civil society suggested deleting this proposed wording. The disputing parties should not be involved in the determination of whether to hold a public hearing.[32] The WG finally adopted the option that provided no right of veto for the disputing parties in Article 6(1).[33] The WG emphasised that this paragraph establishes 'a good balance and allowing the arbitral tribunal to exercise its discretionary powers in accordance with article 1 (3)'.[34] The tribunal has to give due consideration to Article 3(1) while exercising its discretion under Article 6(1).

16. Under the Arbitration Rules (2010) third persons and other members of the public lack a right to access to the hearings. Whether non-disputing State parties may participate remains unclear and largely depends on the non-disputing State parties' rights established under the treaty. NAFTA Arbitral Tribunals either allowed or refused access to non-disputing State parties whenever any of the disputing parties objected to the non-disputing State parties' participation or access.

17. There seems to be a practice that non-disputing State parties may participate at oral hearings.[35] In *SD Myers* v. *Canada* the tribunal held hearings *in camera* but accepted the participation of the non-disputing State parties even though the investor objected to the tribunal's position on the issue.[36] Similarly, in *Pope & Talbot* v. *Canada* the tribunal held

[29] UNCITRAL, 'Settlement of commercial disputes: Preparation of a legal standard on transparency in treaty-based investor-State dispute settlement' (2010) UN Doc. A/CN.9/WG.II/WP.162/Add.1 [50].

[30] *Ibid.*

[31] UNCITRAL, 'Settlement of commercial disputes: preparation of a legal standard on transparency in treaty-based investor-State dispute settlement' (2011) UN Doc. A/CN.9/WG.II/WP.166 [54].

[32] UNCITRAL (n. 28) UN Doc. A/CN.9/717 [104].

[33] UNCITRAL, 'Report of the Working Group II (Arbitration and Conciliation) on the work of its fifty-fifth session' (2011) UN Doc. A/CN.9/736 [77]–[82].

[34] UNCITRAL, 'Settlement of commercial disputes: preparation of a legal standard on transparency in treaty-based investor-State dispute settlement' (2011) UN Doc. A/CN.9/WG.II/WP.169 [42].

[35] *Detroit Bridge International Company* v. *Canada*, PCA Case No. 2012–25, Letter to the Tribunal, 19 March 2010.

[36] *S.D. Myers Inc.* v. *Canada*, UNCITRAL (NAFTA) Procedural Order No. 11, 11 November 1999 at 2, [1] and *S.D. Myers Inc.* v. *Canada*, UNCITRAL (NAFTA), 'Investor's Reply to the Submissions of the United Mexican States', 28 January 2000, [1].

hearings *in camera* but accepted that the non-disputing parties could participate in the hearings, despite the investor's objections.[37] In *GAMI* v. *Mexico* the hearings were *in camera* but non-disputing State parties participated in the hearings.[38] In *Chemtura* v. *Canada* the procedural order failed to mention the rights of non-disputing State parties, and the hearings were held *in camera*, but non-disputing State parties formed part of the hearings.[39] In *ADF* v. *United States of America* the tribunal repeated this principle 'that the Governments of Canada and Mexico have the right to make written and oral submissions pursuant to NAFTA Article 1128'.[40]

18. Not every NAFTA tribunal provided access to hearings of non-disputing State parties. In *Detroit International Bridge Company (DIBC)* v. *Canada*, under NAFTA, the investor vetoed open hearings. Dealing with confidentiality in hearings in accordance with NAFTA, the FTC Statements and the Arbitration Rules (2010),[41] the tribunal stated that hearings would be held *in camera* under Article 28(3) of the Arbitration Rules (2010).[42] This excluded everyone not expressly listed under the Arbitration Rules. The public, third persons and non-disputing State parties have the same rights to participate in the hearings,[43] unless otherwise established under the applicable law. The disputing State parties alleged that the right to participate in hearings arises out of NAFTA Article 1128. The tribunal stated, however, that this provision allows written submissions of non-disputing State parties but lacks a reference that grants a right of physical participation to non-disputing

[37] *Pope & Talbot Inc.* v. *Canada*, UNCITRAL (NAFTA), Procedural Order on Confidentiality No. 5, 17 December 1999, [1] and *Pope & Talbot Inc.* v. *Canada*, UNCITRAL (NAFTA), 'Investor's Reply to the Post-hearing Submission of Mexico and the United States', 1 June 2000 [32].

[38] *GAMI Investments, Inc.* v. *Mexico*, UNCITRAL (NAFTA), Procedural Order No. 1, 31 January 2003, [12.1]; *GAMI Investments, Inc.* v. *Mexico*, UNCITRAL (NAFTA) Transcript of Jurisdictional Hearing, 17 September 2003 at 44; *GAMI Investments, Inc.* v. *Mexico*, UNCITRAL (NAFTA), Procedural Order No. 5, 7 April 2004; *GAMI Investments, Inc.* v. *Mexico*, UNCITRAL (NAFTA), Final Award, 15 November 2004.

[39] *Chemtura Corporation* v. *Canada*, UNCITRAL (NAFTA), Confidentiality Order, 21 January 2008, [5], [10].

[40] *ADF Group Inc.* v. *United States of America*, ICSID Case No. ARB(AF)/00/1, Minutes of the First Session of the Tribunal, Feb. 3, 2001, [15].

[41] *Detroit International Bridge Company* v. *Canada*, UNCITRAL, PCA Case No. 2012–25, Confidentiality Order, 27 March 2013 and Procedural Order 3, 27 March 2013, [10]–[11].

[42] *Ibid.* [14].

[43] See Procedural Order 3, [28] and Procedural Order 4, 27 March 2013 [5].

State parties at the hearings.[44] Similarly, *UPS* v. *Canada* refused access to non-disputing State parties.[45]

19. Outside NAFTA tribunals, few cases are known that have accepted non-disputing State party or third person participation in *in camera* hearings.[46] Comparable situations may occur under multilateral investment treaties, for example under the Energy Charter Treaty, in which the European Commission requests to participate in hearings involving members of the European Union.[47]

20. Article 6(1) changes the default from *in camera* to public hearings. Anyone has a right to sit in the hearing physically subject to paragraphs 2 and 3. Where there is a need to protect confidential information or the integrity of the arbitral process, the arbitral tribunal may make arrangements to hold the part of the hearing requiring such protection in private.[48] However, the paragraph lacks reference to the form of submissions or whether any persons attending the hearings can make oral submissions at all. These are questions answered in Articles 4, 5 and Article 1(5).[49]

8.4 Article 6(2): Protection of information and the integrity of the process

2. Where there is a need to protect confidential information or the integrity of the arbitral process pursuant to article 7, the arbitral tribunal shall make arrangements to hold in private that part of the hearing requiring such protection.

[44] See Procedural Order 6, 27 March 2013, [5]; see also NAFTA 1128 ('on written notice to the disputing parties, a [non-disputing State] Party may make submissions to a Tribunal on a question of interpretation of [NAFTA]').

[45] *United Parcel Service of America Inc.* v. *Canada*, UNCITRAL (NAFTA) Decision of the Tribunal on Petitions for Intervention and Participation as Amici Curiae, 17 October 2001, [67]; *United Parcel Service of America Inc.* v. *Canada*, UNCITRAL (NAFTA) Award on Jurisdiction, 22 November 2002, [5].

[46] *Mr A. J. O.* v. *Slovak Republic*, UNCITRAL (The Netherlands–Czech/Slovak BIT) Final Award, 23 April 2012, [57].

[47] It is not clear from the award if the European Commission requested access to the hearings in recent intra EU disputes such as *Electrabel S.A.* v. *Hungary*, ICSID Case No. ARB/07/19, Decision on Jurisdiction, Applicable Law and Liability, 30 November 2012; *Eastern Sugar B.V.* v. *Czech Republic*, SCC No. 088/2004, Final Award Concerning the Arbitration Costs of the Arbitral Tribunal, 12 April 2007; *Eureko B.V.* v. *Slovak Republic*, UNCITRAL, Award on Jurisdiction, Arbitrability and Suspension, 26 October 2010.

[48] With respect to confidential information and issues relating to the 'integrity of the process', Article 6(2) refers to Article 7, which further defines these concepts.

[49] Mariel Dimsey, 'Article 4', [100], [104]–[151]; Martins Paparinskis and Jessica Howley, 'Article 5', [7]–[19]; and Krista Nadakavukaren Schefer, 'Article 1', [69]–[73].

21. Article 6(2) represents a departure from other arbitration rules in that it requires hearings to be open, subject to the need to protect confidential information and the 'integrity of the arbitral process'. In order to protect information, the WG suggested a reference to Article 7 in the draft of the article concerning the hearings:[50]

> Where a hearing is to be [public] [held openly] and there is a need to protect confidential and sensitive information or the integrity of the arbitral process pursuant to article 7, the arbitral tribunal shall make arrangements for all or part of the hearing to be [held in private][closed].

The chapter concerning Article 7[51] describes the circumstances that give rise to making arrangements to hold in private that part of the hearing requiring such protection. According to Article 7(2), confidential or protected information consists of the following:

(1) confidential business information;
(2) information that is protected against being made available to the public under the treaty;
(3) information that is protected against being made available to the public, in the case of the information of the respondent, under the law of the respondent, and in the case of other information, under any law or rules determined by the arbitral tribunal to be applicable to the disclosure of such information; or
(4) information the disclosure of which would impede law enforcement.

22. These arrangements may require the refusal of or delay to access to the proceedings. It may be that it is appropriate for some information to be made accessible after the hearing in the form of transcripts, even though the tribunal treats the information as confidential during the proceedings. Tribunals can refuse access to public hearings under Article 6(2) while delaying the publication of information, whereas the same information will be available under Article 3(1).[52] Thus, the scope of information to be made available may be deferred even though both articles refer to Article 7. In particular, with regard to 'information the disclosure of which would impede law enforcement' the Tribunal may refuse access to the proceedings but allow delayed access in the form of

[50] UNCITRAL (n. 31) UN Doc. A/CN.9/WG.II/WP.166 [52].
[51] To date, there has been no decision elaborating on the meaning of confidential business information under the Rules. See Thierry P. Augsburger, 'Article 7', [99]–[106].
[52] Article 3(1) provides access to the transcript subject to Article 7.

transcripts. The investor objected to access in *DIBC* v. *Canada*.[53] In this case the Tribunal *inter alia* emphasised that the attendance of non-disputing State parties at the hearings will affect one of the disputing parties' position in other proceedings. These ongoing litigations were deemed to be understandable grounds for excluding the non-disputing State party and for opting to hold hearings *in camera*.[54] The tribunal, however, stated that the non-disputing State parties could apply for access to the transcripts once the hearings had taken place, in order to be able to make written or oral submissions on issues of interpretation.[55] In slightly different circumstances, Australia objected to access to the documents in *Philip Morris Asia Limited* v. *Australia*, because it would have impeded their position in other proceedings, such as in cases before the WTO.[56]

23. Article 6 gives arbitral tribunals more flexibility to decide whether to conduct open or closed hearings in full or in part. The arbitral tribunal, after consultation with the disputing parties, establish procedures for the designation and redaction of certain confidential information in documents[57] presented at the hearing, suggest technical solutions, available under Article 6(3), or, as an ultimate solution, impose time limits on party notification that it seeks protection for such information in documents.

24. In light of its attempts to foster transparency, the arbitral tribunal has to consider all other options first before ordering that hearings shall be held in private. This will be the case if the tribunal determines that the information should be kept from the public eye[58] and the tribunal lacks

[53] *Detroit Bridge International Company* v. *Canada*, PCA Case No. 2012–25.

[54] *Ibid.*, Procedural Order 7, 25 March 2014, 4, [4].

[55] *Ibid.*, 6 ('The non-disputing NAFTA Parties may request to have access to the transcripts of hearings or part of it in order to be able to make written or oral submissions on issues of interpretation of the NAFTA').

[56] Disputing parties' submissions concerning the freedom of information act plus the decision of the tribunal, *Philip Morris Asia Limited* v. *Australia*, UNCITRAL, PCA Case No. 2012–12, Procedural Order No. 5, 30 November 2012 (Regarding Confidentiality) [51ff].

[57] Where the arbitral tribunal determines that information should not be redacted from a document, or that a document should not be prevented from being made available to the public, any disputing party, non-disputing party to the treaty or third person that voluntarily introduced the document into the record shall be permitted to withdraw all or part of the document from the record of the arbitral proceedings.

[58] The applicability of the confidential business information exception would only become relevant if the allegedly confidential or protected information were (1)(a) ordered to be provided by the respondent State to the investor/claimant by the tribunal or court, or

an appropriate logistical solution under Article 6(3).[59] Such a determination will be made on a case-by-case basis based on the nature of the information before the tribunal and the applicable law.[60]

25. The arbitration panel may also close hearings where the disclosure of information, if made available to the public, would jeopardise the integrity of the arbitral tribunal.[61] Specifically, the arbitral tribunal may prevent disclosure where the information could hamper the collection or production of evidence, lead to the intimidation of witnesses, lawyers, or arbitrators, or members of the arbitral tribunal, or in comparably exceptional circumstances. Because the 'integrity of the process' concept can be read broadly, UNCITRAL inserted additional language in Article 7(7) clarifying that this exception should be narrowly applied.

8.5 Article 6(3): Logistical arrangements to facilitate action

3. The arbitral tribunal shall make logistical arrangements to facilitate the public access to hearings (including where appropriate by organizing attendance through video links or such other means as it deems appropriate). However, the arbitral tribunal may, after consultation with the disputing parties, decide to hold all or part of the hearings in private where this becomes necessary for logistical reasons, such as when the circumstances render any original arrangement for public access to a hearing infeasible.

26. Article 6(3) explicitly provides the tribunal with the discretion to switch from physical hearings to online or to partially closed hearings. In case of limited space in the room, or where demonstrations most likely disrupt the proceedings, the tribunal may decide to facilitate public access through video links, online tools or other such means, as it deems

otherwise already in the possession of the investor/claimant, and (b) later submitted by the investor/claimant to the tribunal; or (2) voluntarily submitted to the tribunal by the respondent State.

59 UNCITRAL (n. 33) UN Doc. A/CN.9/736 [105].

60 The rules allow the tribunal discretion to determine how parties and non-parties should proceed when designating information as confidential or protected. Designations are subject to the tribunal's review on its own motion or the motion of a disputing party. The substantive law governing the question of whether information is confidential or protected is likewise largely left open, giving the tribunal the power to determine questions regarding that preliminary issue on its own motion or on the motion of a party. See Thierry P. Augsburger, 'Article 7', [36]–[80].

61 Rules, Article 7.

appropriate. In some instances, it may be necessary to videotape a hearing if a live feed is impractical. The WG stated from the very beginning of the debate that webcast or other technological solutions may be an alternative in order to facilitate public access to the hearings even where physical attendance was impossible.[62]

27. Article 6 provides for the tribunal's discretion to close all or part of the hearings for logistical reasons, such as technical problems or public disruption after consultation with the parties.[63] To ensure that the authority to close hearings for logistical reasons is not abused, the WG inserted language in the provision indicating that logistical issues should be arranged in advance of the hearing in order to facilitate public access and avoid practical challenges. For example, technical glitches with video or online technology may delay a proceeding, thus prompting a tribunal to order more limited access. The hearing later could be posted online. Only if (a) unforeseen or unexpected circumstances later arise, and (b) those circumstances make closure necessary (as opposed to merely inconvenient) should hearings be closed under Article 6(3). When the hearings are closed for any of the three reasons listed in Articles 6(2) and 6(3), they should only be closed to the extent necessary.

28. One NAFTA investor-State arbitration case reveals the philosophy behind Article 6(3). In *Glamis Gold Limited* v. *United States of America*, the disputing parties accepted the tribunal's measures in arranging closed-circuit hearings for the public in a room other than the one where the arbitral tribunal was in session.[64] The tribunal requested that all interested third persons supply their email addresses to the Secretariat in order to inform them about logistical arrangements.[65] The tribunal arranged procedures whereby the disputing parties were to explain their assertions of privileged information and challenge those of the other party behind closed doors.[66] The tribunal also made arrangements to

[62] UNCITRAL (n. 29) UN Doc. A/CN.9/WG.II/WP.162/Add.1 [29].

[63] See the 1999 Seattle Round of WTO Negotiations where civil society disruptions caused a breakdown and failure of the negotiations to initiate a Development Round of multilateral trade talks.

[64] *Glamis Gold Limited* v. *United States of America*, UNCITRAL (NAFTA), Procedural Order No. 1, 3 March 2005, [5(d)].

[65] *Glamis Gold Limited* v. *United States of America*, UNCITRAL (NAFTA), Award, 8 June 2009, [189] and [290].

[66] *Glamis Gold Limited* v. *United States of America*, UNCITRAL (NAFTA), Procedural Order No. 7, 10 November 2005, [1], Procedural Order No. 8, 31 January 2006, [2].

protect the cultural heritage of the QIN, who were affected third parties in this proceeding, by holding hearings *in camera*.[67]

8.6 Deliberations and transcripts

29. Article 6 does not speak to the public's access to deliberations at hearings. Most arbitral rules treat the deliberations as confidential. In Paris, the home of the ICC, the deliberations of the arbitrators are determined by the relevant provisions of the Civil Code to be confidential. In England, there is no relevant legislation: the Arbitration Act 1996 is completely silent on confidentiality regarding deliberations.[68] However, Article 30 of the LCIA Rules includes a specific agreement that the award, disclosed materials and the deliberations of the Tribunal be confidential. Under UNCITRAL, discretion remains with the arbitral tribunal to provide public access to deliberations.

30. Article 6 provides no reference to the transcripts. The WG suggested, in the early version of Article 6, the inclusion of two paragraphs that established a right to access the transcripts.[69] The WG transferred this paragraph to Article 3(1) of the Rules.[70]

8.7 Evaluation

8.7.1 Clarify the role of third persons and non-disputing State parties

31. There are certain advantages to opening up arbitration hearings to the public eye. First and foremost, granting the public access to hearings is important for the perceived legitimacy of investor-State arbitration. Under previous versions of the Arbitration Rules, disputes between investors and States were often criticised by public interest groups for being too secretive, especially where vital public concerns were involved. Open hearings remove the veil of secrecy and invite public participation in the process of resolving disputes that may have implications for the

[67] *Glamis Gold Limited* v. *United States of America*, UNCITRAL (NAFTA), Procedural Order No. 11, 9 July 2007; Award, [290]–[296].

[68] Under the Arbitration Act of 1996, there is an implied obligation of confidentiality which arises in arbitration, but this duty of confidentiality is subject to the exceptions of consent, court order, reasonable necessity and public interest.

[69] UNCITRAL (n. 31) UN Doc. A/CN.9/WG.II/WP.166, [52].

[70] UNCITRAL (n. 33) UN Doc. A/CN.9/736 [109]; See also Christopher Kee, 'Article 3', [42]–[86].

public. In addition, for proceedings involving third parties, open hearings give the public the ability to observe and scrutinise third party arguments and positions. In *Glamis Gold Ltd.* v. *United States*, a NAFTA dispute submitted under the Arbitration Rules (1976), the tribunal believed that the diverse interests of environmentalists, mining interests and Native American groups outweighed commercial interests in deciding that the public would be allowed to view the hearings by closed-circuit television.[71] *Glamis* was a major step forward in reconciling the public's interest in transparency with the parties' interest in a fair and efficient resolution of their dispute. Although Article 6 does not specifically require the arbitral panel to undertake a public interest analysis, open hearings give the general public an opportunity to observe the arbitral process without secrecy concerns. Thus, Article 6 not only opens the door to the public to observe hearings, it recognises the importance of transparency in resolving private commercial disputes that have public policy effects.

32. Furthermore, open hearings may or may not work in favour of the investor's interest or the State's interest in arbitration. On the one hand, the increased visibility of UNCITRAL actions 'may constitute an advantage' by assisting investors in determining their rights,[72] and assessing more accurately the real risk to their investment in host States and the merits of commencing arbitration if a dispute arises.[73] At the same time, public exposure of a controversial commercial practice can have a deleterious effect on investor interests, perhaps yielding a decline in performance of the company's stock on international markets. Moreover, counsel for the host State might take advantage of the opportunity during public hearings to 'act up' and make pronouncements on behalf of the State to score political points, knowing that the public is watching. It depends on the nature of the dispute, the parties involved and the

[71] Glamis, a Canadian corporation, claimed that certain federal government actions and California measures with respect to open-pit mining operations resulted in the expropriation of its investment. The hearings were open to the public and on 8 June 2009, the Tribunal released the Award, dismissing Glamis' claim in its entirety. *Glamis Gold Ltd.* v. *United States*, Award (NAFTA Arb. Trib. 2009) www.state.gov/documents/organization/125798.pdf.

[72] See Clayton Utz and Mark Gillard, 'Transparency is the New Black in Investor-State Arbitration: UNCITRAL's New Transparency Rules', *Lexology*, 1 August 2013 www.claytonutz.com/publications/edition/01_august_2013/20130801/transparency_is_the_new_black_in_investor-state_arbitration_uncitrals_new_transparency_rules.page.

[73] *Ibid.*

public policy issues at hand in order to better assess whether open hearings will benefit one party or the other.

33. Finally, public hearings may encourage consistent decisions and reasoning in arbitral awards.[74] Although the decisions are not precedential, access to them would assist lawyers in arguing cases and guide arbitrators when writing their opinions, possibly providing more coherence to the decisions. According to Argentinian diplomat, Ignacio Toterola, public access to decisions helps to create a body of case law 'that brings more certainty' to the arbitration system, 'precludes future inefficiencies and contingencies for the parties involved' and 'raises the professional standards to be met by the arbitrators in their decisions'.[75] With the increase in cases that potentially affect the public interest, he said, UNCITRAL transparency should reflect national transparency and participation laws.[76]

34. In sum, good governance, accountability and democratic participation are important goals that underpin the Rules, and open hearings are an important mechanism to promote these goals. Articles 6 and 7 take into account the challenge of opening the door to public participation without compromising the parties' rights to confidentiality or the integrity of the arbitral process. Important exceptions are built in to the new rules to ensure that the parties' interests are protected, and the arbitral tribunal retains its authority to determine the manner and scope of transparency during hearings. This flexibility offers numerous benefits for the parties, the public and the arbitration process. More transparency will bring greater understanding about the work of arbitration bodies and improve the arbitration system overall.

8.7.2 Steer parties away from using the Rules

35. There are several concerns with open hearings that may steer parties away from using the Rules. Investors, in particular, may find that their interest in maintaining confidentiality outweighs the public's interest in the disclosure of information about a dispute. For example, an investor may wish to shield from disclosure certain confidential information,

[74] *Ibid.*

[75] See Toby McIntosh, 'Trade Dispute Body Adopts Limited Transparency Rules', 7 January 2014 www.freedominfo.org/2014/01/trade-dispute-body-adopts-limited-transparency-rules.

[76] *Ibid.*

trade secrets or business strategies that may compromise the company's image or give competitors an advantage. This concern may affect the way that counsel for the investor drafts pleadings, presents documentary evidence, prepares witnesses or argues the case in a public hearing. In addition, more transparency at hearings may prevent open discussion between the parties, making it more difficult for the parties to settle disputes. Governments may be tactically limited, knowing that their statements might be misperceived. The consequences of open hearings, thus, may have a chilling effect on disclosure of information leading up to and during the hearings.

36. Moreover, open hearings may dictate whether an investor decides to pursue an investment claim under a treaty (where open hearings would apply) or a contract (where open hearings would not apply). This might upend the recent trend in favour of qualifying commercial disputes as investment disputes in investor-State arbitration.

37. Open hearings may also present challenges for State parties to a dispute. Increased exposure to the public may be used by investors as a 'scare tactic' or a means to force a settlement with a State party. Argentina, for example, recently agreed to settle five separate investment treaty arbitration claims at a cost of approximately US$500 million in a historic departure from the State's refusal to comply with awards made by international investment treaty arbitration bodies.[77] Whilst each of the arbitration awards was based on a different set of facts, the claims all arose in the context of Argentina's financial crisis in the late 1990s and early 2000s, and the privatisation of many industry sectors.[78] Increased

[77] See Daniel Cancel, 'Argentina Settles $677 million Arbitration Cases with Bonds', *Bloomberg News*, 18 October 2013 www.bloomberg.com/news/2013-10-18/argentina-settles-677-million-of-arbitration-cases-paying-bonds.html; see also Paul Hodges, Christian Leathley and Louise Barber, 'Argentina Settles Five Outstanding Investment Treaty Arbitration Claims in Historic Break with its Anti-Enforcement Stance', Lexology, 14 October 2013 www.lexology.com/library/detail.aspx?g=5546cffa-46d3-4421-a47d-e86817aee4e5.

The settlements relate to the French media conglomerate Vivendi SA, British electricity and gas utility National Grid PLC, Continental Casualty Company (a subsidiary of the American financial and insurance products provider CNA Financial Corp), the American water company Azurix, and Blue Ridge Investments, the wholly owned subsidiary of Bank of America Corp. These companies were each successful in bringing claims against Argentina through ICSID over the past twelve years, with the exception of National Grid which brought its claim under the UNCITRAL Arbitration Rules and Blue Ridge Investments, which acquired the ICSID award from the original claimant, CMG Gas Transmission.

[78] *Ibid.* The claims were brought under bilateral investment treaties between Argentina and each of the respective countries of origin of the claimant entities:

public scrutiny of these disputes involving sensitive public issues and difficult economic times reflected negatively on the State and exposed public officials to criticism.

38. Regarding the public perspective, logistical issues may undermine the goal of transparency at hearings. For example, the location and format of the hearing may have a direct impact on the public's access to the hearing. Most investor-State arbitrations take place in a conference room in an office building or hotel at or near the investor's residence in a developed country. This makes it difficult for the general public from the host State, often a developing country, to attend a hearing and observe first-hand the arguments of counsel and the presentation of evidence. Moreover, during the hearing, arbitrators usually accept two types of proof: oral testimony by witnesses and documentary evidence. Should the parties choose to submit mostly documentary evidence as proof, the public may glean very little useful information at a public hearing other than opening and closing statements. In the end, the parties still control the process and can limit the public's access to hearings through procedural manoeuvring to undermine the purpose of Article 6.

39. Article 6 also fails to address certain concerns regarding the arbitral tribunal itself. One specific concern is the degree of public accountability for the arbitrators who tend to be private citizens rather than public

- In *Suez, Sociedad General de Aguas de Barcelona, S.A., and Vivendi Universal, S.A.* v. *Argentina*, ICSID Case No. ARB/03/19 , the claimant's water and sewerage concession was subject to forced tariff reductions and termination of the concession contract by the provincial authorities of Tucuman.
- The *Azurix* award also concerned a water concession which was prevented by local authorities from applying the tariffs to which it was entitled: *Azurix Corp.* v. *Argentina*, ICSID Case No. ARB/01/12.
- In the award due to Blue Ridge Investments LLC, the original claimant (CMS Gas Transmission) purchased a 25 per cent stake in the Argentine gas transportation utility, the terms of which provided for a periodic tariff increase in line with inflation. The award concerned the unilateral removal by the Argentine government of this right to adjust the tariffs: *CMS Gas Transmission Company* v. *Republic of Argentina*, ICSID Case No. ARB/01/8 (former Blue Ridge Investment case).
- In *National Grid PLC* v. *Argentina*, the claimant purchased a significant stake in the local electricity transmission sector, only to have its investment vastly devalued by emergency measures taken during the financial crisis.
- The award made to Continental Casualty Company concerned the forcible conversion of the claimants' investments from US dollars into pesos at a time when the Argentine peso was dramatically losing value, combined with a prohibition on transferring assets out of the State: *Continental Casualty Company* v. *Argentina*, ICSID Case No. ARB/03/9.

officials. As many judges are elected officials, their conduct is subject to public scrutiny in open court, which can have direct personal and professional consequences. Increasing transparency through open hearings in arbitration, however, does little to foster accountability among private arbitrators. Private arbitrators are incentivised differently than judges and are motivated more by financial concerns and the parties' expectations than public opinion.

40. Finally, investors and States should be aware that the introduction of the Rules could materially change the nature of the dispute resolution clauses in BITs or other investment treaties which provide for UNCITRAL arbitration. To address this concern, UNCITRAL adopted a draft convention in relation to the application of the Rules to such disputes. With more than 3,000 investment treaties in existence, this convention will hopefully bring further clarity to the application of the new rules without States having to renegotiate these treaties. These concerns make the idea of open hearings more difficult to conceptualise in practice. In the end, whether the balance of interests favours a party or the general public depends on the facts and circumstances of each case.

8.8 Conclusion

41. The Rules' call for open hearings represents a huge step in the direction of increasing transparency and openness in investor-State arbitration. For those seeking full transparency for investor-State treaty-based arbitrations, open hearings are an innovative approach to balancing the public interest with the interests of the disputing parties in a fair and efficient way. For those concerned about the future of confidentiality in arbitration, the implications are less clear and may, in the end, have a chilling effect on the use of the Rules, or the use of arbitration altogether, to resolve investment disputes. Striking the right balance is not an easy task, and one of the consequences of favouring the public's interest in transparency is to run the risk of driving the parties to choose another form of alternative dispute resolution. Perhaps, then, the most significant achievement with the Rules is the shift in the underlying presumption towards openness even if the practical application of these new rules remains in question.

42. Article 6 has been received with mixed reactions. While advances in technology have made open hearings more feasible through the use of video and online communications, concerns remain about how open hearings will impact litigation strategy and tactics, the protection of

confidential information and trade secrets, and accountability, among other issues. Moreover, it remains to be seen how arbitral tribunals will exercise their discretion under the new rules to order closed hearings when technology fails or public access threatens to disrupt a hearing. Thus, UNCITRAL's call for open hearings signals progress in the effort to increase transparency in treaty-based investor-State arbitrations, but there are still issues that must be addressed to ensure that the integrity of the arbitral process is not compromised.

9

Article 7. Exceptions to transparency

THIERRY P. AUGSBURGER*

Confidential or protected information

1. Confidential or protected information, as defined in paragraph 2 and as identified pursuant to the arrangements referred to in paragraphs 3 and 4, shall not be made available to the public pursuant to articles 2 to 6.
2. Confidential or protected information consists of:
   (a) Confidential business information;
   (b) Information that is protected against being made available to the public under the treaty;
   (c) Information that is protected against being made available to the public, in the case of the information of the respondent State, under the law of the respondent State, and in the case of other information, under any law or rules determined by the arbitral tribunal to be applicable to the disclosure of such information; or
   (d) Information the disclosure of which would impede law enforcement.
3. The arbitral tribunal, after consultation with the disputing parties, shall make arrangements to prevent any confidential or protected information from being made available to the public, including by putting in place, as appropriate:
   (a) Time limits in which a disputing party, non-disputing Party to the treaty or third person shall give notice that it seeks protection for such information in documents;
   (b) Procedures for the prompt designation and redaction of the particular confidential or protected information in such documents; and
   (c) Procedures for holding hearings in private to the extent required by article 6, paragraph 2.

* Thierry P. Augsburger, LLM, is a Swiss-qualified attorney-at-law specialised in international arbitration (both commercial and treaty-based and litigation). He wishes to thank Cynthia Winkelmann and Mike Han for their help in researching for this chapter. Of course all opinions expressed herein are his own – the same applies to any errors in law or in fact.

Any determination as to whether information is confidential or protected shall be made by the arbitral tribunal after consultation with the disputing parties.

4. Where the arbitral tribunal determines that information should not be redacted from a document, or that a document should not be prevented from being made available to the public, any disputing party, non-disputing Party to the treaty or third person that voluntarily introduced the document into the record shall be permitted to withdraw all or part of the document from the record of the arbitral proceedings.
5. Nothing in these Rules requires a respondent State to make available to the public information the disclosure of which it considers to be contrary to its essential security interests.

Integrity of the arbitral process

6. Information shall not be made available to the public pursuant to articles 2 to 6 where the information, if made available to the public, would jeopardize the integrity of the arbitral process as determined pursuant to paragraph 7.
7. The arbitral tribunal may, on its own initiative or upon the application of a disputing party, after consultation with the disputing parties where practicable, take appropriate measures to restrain or delay the publication of information where such publication would jeopardize the integrity of the arbitral process because it could hamper the collection or production of evidence, lead to the intimidation of witnesses, lawyers acting for disputing parties or members of the arbitral tribunal, or in comparably exceptional circumstances.

9.1 Introduction

9.1.1 Scope and purpose

1. Article 7 of the Rules is the provision limiting the principle of transparency as promulgated in Articles 2 to 6 of the Rules.

2. In view of the mandatory nature of the Rules,[1] the inclusion of certain limitations seems not only appropriate, but a mere necessity to strike a balance between the public interest in transparency and the interest of the parties in a fair and efficient resolution of their dispute.[2]

[1] For a discussion on the level of consent see Krista Nadakavukaren Schefer, 'Article 1', [60]–[68].

[2] See Article 1(4) of the UNCITRAL Transparency Rules; also, Julia Salasky and Corinne Montineri, 'UNCITRAL Rules on Transparency in Treaty-Based Investor-State Arbitration' (2013) 4 *ASA Bulletin* 774, 793.

Publishing all information without taking into consideration their nature or possible impact when made public would mean ignoring justified party or public interests to keep certain information confidential. Transparency can neither be an end in itself, nor absolute. Where concrete and substantial interests outbalance the general public interest in transparency, the latter has to step back.[3]

3. Article 7 defines such substantial interests colliding with the principle of transparency and gives procedural guidance on how to deal with them.

4. As a principle, Article 7 deals only with exceptions to the flow of information from within a specific arbitration procedure into the public sphere.[4]

5. The Rules do not deal with information (only) in the sphere of a party to the proceedings and the mechanisms under which such information comes into the arbitration proceeding. This is an issue of evidence. Article 7 of the Rules is no guide when it comes to issues of discovery, document production and evidentiary privilege claims, i.e., which information has to be disclosed by a party in such a procedure or under an order pursuant to Article 27(3) of the Arbitration Rules (2010).[5]

6. The case of *Apotex Holdings Inc. and Apotex Inc.* v. *United States of America* is illustrative: its Confidentiality Agreement and Order dated 24 July 2012 deals only with public access issues.[6] Even after it was amended on 24 October 2013 by an addendum providing for a category of documents not to be disclosed to the other party, but only its counsel, the difference between the issue of public access to documents and the matters of evidence remained.[7] This difference is also to be respected when applying Article 7 of the Rules.

[3] For a discussion on the balance of interest, see Article 1(4) UNCITRAL Transparency Rules, discussed above, Krista Nadakavukaren Schefer, 'Article 1', [69]–[73].

[4] And vice versa, when it comes to public participation in the proceeding.

[5] Waincymer speaks of 'inter-party confidentiality' vs. 'confidentiality vis-à-vis the rest of the world', cf. Jeffrey Waincymer, *Procedure and Evidence in International Arbitration* (Kluwer Law International, 2012) 799.

[6] *Apotex Holdings Inc. and Apotex Inc.* v. *United States of America*, ICSID Case No. ARB (AF)/12/1, First Procedural Order (29 November 2012) [11] www.state.gov/documents/organization/203094.pdf; and Confidentiality Agreement and Order (24 July 2012), accessible via the case search function on the ICSID homepage https://icsid.worldbank.org/ICSID/Index.jsp.

[7] *Apotex Holdings Inc.* (n. 6), Amended Confidentiality Agreement and Order (24 October 2013) http://italaw.com/sites/default/files/case-documents/italaw3064.pdf.

9.1.2 *Background*

7. Article 7 of the Rules did not come out of the void. Where multilateral treaties and model BITs foresee procedural transparency for investor-State arbitration, they regularly also provide for exceptions. This is the case, for example, in NAFTA, CAFTA-DR, the US Model BIT 2012, the Canadian Model BIT 2004 and the (withdrawn) Norwegian Model BIT 2007.[8] These forbearers of Article 7 will be briefly discussed hereinafter.

8. The NAFTA FTC Note of Interpretation dated 31 July 2001,[9] which is binding for NAFTA Chapter 11 tribunals according to Article 1131(2) NAFTA, contains the following exceptions to public access to documents:

> 2. . . .
> b. Each Party agrees to make available to the public in a timely manner all documents submitted to, or issued by, a Chapter Eleven tribunal, subject to redaction of:
> i. confidential business information;
> ii. information which is privileged or otherwise protected from disclosure under the Party's domestic law; and
> iii. information which the Party must withhold pursuant to the relevant arbitral rules, as applied.
>
> . . .
>
> 3. The Parties confirm that nothing in this interpretation shall be construed to require any Party to furnish or allow access to information that it may withhold in accordance with Articles 2102 or 2105.

9. In the aftermath of the opening of NAFTA Chapter 11 arbitration to the public, another bilateral treaty was concluded that influenced the wording of Article 7: CAFTA-DR.[10] Article 10.21 CAFTA-DR, entitled 'Transparency of Arbitral Proceedings',[11] provides not only for a high

[8] Other examples are ASEAN Comprehensive Investment Agreement (2009), COMESA Common Investment Areas (2007) and a small number of BITs, see Joachim Pohl, Kekeletso Mashingo and Alexis Nohen, 'Dispute Settlement Provisions in International Investment Agreements – A Large Sample Survey', *OECD Working Papers on International Investment* (OECD Publishing, 2012) 37.

[9] Cf. NAFTA Free Trade Commission, 'North American Free Trade Agreement Notes of Interpretation of Certain Chapter 11 Provisions' (31 July 2001) www.sice.oas.org/tpd/nafta/Commission/CH11understanding_e.asp.

[10] Today seven countries are members of CAFTA-DR: the United States of America, El Salvador, Honduras, Nicaragua, Guatemala, the Dominican Republic and Costa Rica, cf. www.sice.oas.org/Trade/CAFTA/CAFTADR_e/CAFTADRin_e.asp.

[11] Cf. www.sice.oas.org/Trade/CAFTA/CAFTADR_e/chapter6_12.asp#Article10.21.

degree of transparency, but also both for certain exceptions to this principle and the procedure to be applied:

2. The tribunal shall conduct hearings open to the public and shall determine, in consultation with the disputing parties, the appropriate logistical arrangements. However, any disputing party that intends to use information designated as protected information in a hearing shall so advise the tribunal. The tribunal shall make appropriate arrangements to protect the information from disclosure.
3. Nothing in this Section requires a respondent to disclose protected information or to furnish or allow access to information that it may withhold in accordance with Article 21.2 (Essential Security) or Article 21.5 (Disclosure of Information).
4. Any protected information that is submitted to the tribunal shall be protected from disclosure in accordance with the following procedures:
   (a) Subject to subparagraph (d), neither the disputing parties nor the tribunal shall disclose to any non-disputing Party or to the public any protected information where the disputing party that provided the information clearly designates it in accordance with subparagraph (b);
   (b) Any disputing party claiming that certain information constitutes protected information shall clearly designate the information at the time it is submitted to the tribunal;
   (c) A disputing party shall, at the same time that it submits a document containing information claimed to be protected information, submit a redacted version of the document that does not contain the information. Only the redacted version shall be provided to the non-disputing Parties and made public in accordance with paragraph 1; and
   (d) The tribunal shall decide any objection regarding the designation of information claimed to be protected information. If the tribunal determines that such information was not properly designated, the disputing party that submitted the information may (i) withdraw all or part of its submission containing such information, or (ii) agree to resubmit complete and redacted documents with corrected designations in accordance with the tribunal's determination and subparagraph (c). In either case, the other disputing party shall, whenever necessary, resubmit complete and redacted documents which either remove the information withdrawn under (i) by the disputing party that first submitted the information or redesignate the information consistent with the designation under (ii) of the disputing party that first submitted the information.
5. Nothing in this Section requires a respondent to withhold from the public information required to be disclosed by its laws.

10. The US Model BIT 2012's provision regulating transparency of the proceedings and the limits thereto, Article 29,[12] is an exact copy of Article 10.21 CAFTA-DR reproduced above.

11. Canada's Model BIT 2004 also regulates public access to hearings and documents of investor-State arbitrations under the BIT.[13] First, Article 1 provides that 'confidential information means confidential business information and information that is privileged or otherwise protected from disclosure'.[14] Second, Article 38 states:

> 1. Hearings held under this Section shall be open to the public. To the extent necessary to ensure the protection of confidential information, including business confidential information, the Tribunal may hold portions of hearings in camera.
> 2. The Tribunal shall establish procedures for the protection of confidential information and appropriate logistical arrangements for open hearings, in consultation with the disputing parties.
> 3. All documents submitted to, or issued by, the Tribunal shall be publicly available, unless the disputing parties otherwise agree, subject to the deletion of confidential information.
> 4. Notwithstanding paragraph 3, any Tribunal award under this Section shall be publicly available, subject to the deletion of confidential information.
>
> ...
>
> 7. As provided under Article 10(4) and (5), the Tribunal shall not require a Party to furnish or allow access to information the disclosure of which would impede law enforcement or would be contrary to the Party's law protecting Cabinet confidences, personal privacy or the financial affairs and accounts of individual customers of financial institutions, or which it determines to be contrary to its essential security.

[12] United States Government, '2012 US Model Bilateral Investment Treaty' (2012) www.state.gov/documents/organization/188371.pdf.

[13] The Model BIT has seen some amendments since 2004, see Catharine Titi, 'The Evolving BIT: A Commentary on Canada's Model Agreement', *IISD Investment Treaty News* (26 June 2013) www.iisd.org/itn/2013/06/26/the-evolving-bit-a-commentary-on-canadas-model-agreement/. Its provisions regulating transparency and limitations thereto have not, however, fundamentally changed, cf. e.g. Article 30 of the Canada–Tanzania BIT, in force since 9 December 2013 www.international.gc.ca/trade-agreements-accords-commerciaux/agr-acc/fipa-apie/tanzania-text-tanzanie.aspx?lang=eng.

[14] Foreign Affairs, Trade and Development Canada, 'Canada Model Foreign Investment Promotion and Protection Agreement' (2004) http://italaw.com/documents/Canadian2004-FIPA-model-en.pdf.

12. In contrast to the above-cited examples, the Norwegian Draft Model BIT, published in December 2007, provides for a very lean framework regulating the transparency and confidentiality of the proceeding in its Article 19.[15] Article 19(2) of the Norwegian Model BIT limits the otherwise full transparency of all documents and hearings:

> When submitting information to the Tribunal, a Party to the dispute may designate specific information as confidential if the information
>
> i. is not generally known or accessible to the public, and
> ii. if disclosed would cause or threaten to cause prejudice to an essential interest of any individual or entity, or to the interest of a Party.
>
> Such information shall be treated as confidential and shall only be made available to the parties to the dispute and to the other Party.

13. According to Article 19(3) of the Norwegian Model BIT, the arbitral tribunal will have to decide on the designation of the information as confidential if the other party objects thereto. Should the arbitral tribunal find that the information does not meet the criteria of Article 19(2), the party that submitted the information can withdraw it.

14. In view of the above examples, it is hard to ignore the similarity of the framework provided in Article 7 of the Rules and in particular the respective provisions in NAFTA, CAFTA-DR and the US and Canadian Model BITs, which all provide for a high degree of transparency, paired with a couple of exceptions in relation to certain information.[16] It seems,

[15] www.italaw.com/sites/default/files/archive/ita1031.pdf. See also the comments on Norway's draft BIT 2007, published at the same time: Norwegian Draft Model BIT 2007: Comments on the model for future investment agreements (19 December 2007) www.italaw.com/sites/default/files/archive/ita1029.pdf. In 2009 the Norwegian government decided to withdraw the draft Model BIT, cf. Damon Vis-Dunbar, 'Norway Shelves its Draft Model Bilateral Investment Treaty', *IISD Investment Treaty News* (8 June 2009) www.iisd.org/itn/2009/06/08/norway-shelves-its-proposed-model-bilateral-investment-treaty/.

[16] It must be said, however, that the BITs concluded do not always retain the high degree of transparency provided for in the Model. For example, the recent Canada–China BIT deviates from the Canada Model BIT's policy of transparency insofar as it restricts publication of documents to the award only and does not provide for open hearings if the respondent State does not explicitly wish so; cf. Articles 28(1) and (2) of the Agreement Between the Government of Canada and the Government of the People's Republic of China for the Promotion and Reciprocal Protection of Investments (signed on 9 September 2012) www.international.gc.ca/trade-agreements-accords-commerciaux/agr-acc/fipa-apie/china-text-chine.aspx?lang=eng.

therefore, that Article 7 of the Rules has been largely influenced by a Canadian approach to both treaty drafting and transparency in treaty-based investor-State arbitration. The simple Norwegian Model was not retained.

9.1.3 Use of case law

15. Case law based on the above (and other) treaties can be a valuable source for the interpretation of Article 7 of the Rules. This is particularly true for issues where Article 7 lacks a comprehensive definition (for example, as to the meaning and scope of 'confidential business information'[17]) or leaves to the arbitral tribunal a large degree of discretion (such as in the arrangements of the procedure to detect, redact and protect confidential or protected information[18]).

16. However, reliance on such case law in the application of Article 7 of the Rules should be made with care for several reasons:

- First, the Rules enclose a general principle of transparency unknown to most treaties and all arbitration rules commonly used to resolve investor-State disputes.[19]
- Second, past arbitral tribunals did often only have a say on matters relating to exceptions to transparency if the parties disagreed on a particular issue. In the case of a mutual agreement of the parties on confidentiality, the arbitral tribunal was bound by it.[20] Under the Rules this is different: the arbitral tribunal is *de officio* the sole decision maker on all matters of exceptions to transparency, notwithstanding the parties' position.[21]
- Third, the Rules sometimes limit or guide the discretion of the arbitral tribunal in a very unique way.[22]

[17] Article 7(2)(a) UNCITRAL Transparency Rules; see below, section 9.3.1.

[18] Article 7(4) of the Rules, see below, section 9.4.

[19] For the general principle of transparency in the Rules, see Article 1(3)(b), (4)(a), (5), (6) of the Rules and their discussion in Krista Nadakavukaren Schefer, 'Article 1', [60ff]; in contrast, for the (few) treaties containing transparency provisions, see Joachim Pohl, Kekeletso Mashingo and Alexis Nohen (n. 8), and for provisions on confidentiality in arbitration rules Articles 28(3), 34(5) UNCITRAL Arbitration Rules; and Rules 32(2), 48 (4) ICSID Arbitration Rules; Articles 27(3), 46 SCC Rules.

[20] See the arbitration rules provisions cited *ibid.*

[21] Article 7(3) of the Rules, see below, section 9.4 (in particular section 9.4.7).

[22] See e.g. Article 7(2)(c), below section 9.3.3.1, Article 7(4), below section 9.6, or Article 7(7), below section 9.9.4.

17. For the above reasons, case law which would be pertinent for the Rules is scarce: arbitral tribunals did not have to decide on this matter. In addition, the assumption of transparency underlying the Rules makes it difficult to draw on the decisions of past tribunals in arbitrations where transparency was not the underlying principle. It is this author's view that this paradigm shift is a compelling ground for future arbitral tribunals to adopt solutions different from the ones established in past investment arbitrations.[23] Pertinent case law is slightly more frequent for exceptions to safeguard the integrity of the arbitral process (Articles 7(6) and 7(7)), as arbitral tribunals have used their powers to conduct the proceedings to regulate party behaviour in the context of information dissemination due to procedural integrity considerations.[24]

9.1.4 WG's deliberations

18. In order to understand Article 7 of the Rules, it is necessary to have a certain understanding of how the provision came to be. A grasp of the thoughts and discussions during the making of the provision is particularly important at this early stage of the Rules, where no case law on their interpretation exists.

19. The discussion about exceptions to transparency is as old as the discussion about transparency itself.

20. During the revision of the Arbitration Rules (1976), the WG considered the inclusion of a transparency provision for investment arbitration in the Arbitration Rules themselves, but dismissed the idea in favour of a generic approach to fit all kinds of arbitration under the Rules.[25] Already at that time the WG was aware that even if the principle ought to be one of transparency, public access and openness, such

[23] *Saipem SpA* v. *The People's Republic of Bangladesh*, ICSID Case No. ARB/05/07, Decision on Jurisdiction and Recommendation on Provisional Measures (21 March 2007) [67], www.italaw.com/sites/default/files/case-documents/ita0733.pdf.

[24] For such case law see below, section 9.7 Article 7(6) and 7(7): Integrity of the arbitral process.

[25] UNCITRAL, 'Report of the Working Group on Arbitration and Conciliation on the work of its forty-sixth session (New York, 5–9 February 2007)' (2007) UN Doc. A/CN.9/619 [61]–[62]; UNCITRAL, 'Report of the Working Group on Arbitration and Conciliation on the work of its forty-eighth session (New York, 4–8 February 2008) (2008) UN Doc. A/CN.9/646 [54]–[69]; Annexes I–III. On the other hand, the UNCITRAL Working Group II also rejected the inclusion of a generic duty of confidentiality into the UNCITRAL Arbitration Rules: cf. UNCITRAL UN Doc. A/CN.9/619 [127]–[133].

principle ought to have to be limited, at the arbitral tribunal's discretion, by exceptions to protect 'truly confidential information'.[26]

21. The Government of Canada, a strong supporter of the inclusion of a transparency provision in the Arbitration Rules, wrote to the UNCITRAL Commission, setting out several objectives of such inclusion, including:

> preserving the existing power of an arbitral tribunal to allow closed proceedings and restrict access to documents, or portions thereof, when necessary to protect confidential business information and/or information that is privileged or otherwise protected from disclosure under the domestic law of the disputing State.[27]

22. At the outset of the deliberations of the WG of a possible standard of transparency in treaty-based investor-State arbitration, the UNCITRAL Secretariat addressed a Note to the WG, observing that any such standard will have to balance 'the public interest and the need to protect confidentiality'.[28] The following points were judged as important for the WG to consider in this respect:

- who would 'be in charge of conveying information to the public';[29]
- clarification of 'the extent to which the parties may engage in general discussions about the case in public, or make disclosures';[30]
- 'whether publication should be automatic, left to the parties' discretion or subject to prior permission by the arbitral tribunal';[31]
- guidance as to 'whether and to what extent documents, revealing business secrets or other confidential information should be exempt from the possible public disclosure';[32] and
- the organisation of open hearings, 'taking account of the possible need to protect, to the extent required, confidential information'.[33]

23. The WG started discussing the exceptions to transparency in its fifty-third session, after having agreed on the principle of transparency

[26] UNCITRAL (n. 25) UN Doc. A/CN.9/646 [64].

[27] UNCITRAL 'Note by the Secretariat – Observation by the Government of Canada – Revision of the UNCITRAL Arbitration Rules – Settlement of commercial disputes' (12 June 2008) UN Doc. A/CN.9/662, Annex [17].

[28] UNCITRAL, 'Settlement of commercial disputes: Preparation of rules of uniform law on transparency in treaty-based investor-State dispute settlement' (2010) UN Doc. A/CN.9/WG.II/WP.160/Add.1 [11] *in fine*.

[29] *Ibid.* [14]. [30] *Ibid.* [31] *Ibid.* [32] *Ibid.* [17]. [33] *Ibid.* [19].

in the different stages of the arbitral procedure.[34] The idea was that these carve-outs would be 'drafted in a generic manner, thus circumventing the need to envisage all possible circumstances, but rather leaving a large degree of discretion to the arbitral tribunal'.[35] It was considered that it might be difficult to find a comprehensive definition of confidential information and that it would thus be useful to provide examples.[36] The WG considered that the arbitral tribunal should handle the determination of information to be protected: the parties would identify the information they considered to be sensitive, and such identification would then trigger the consideration and decision by the arbitral tribunal.[37] Overall, the provision on the 'exceptions to transparency to protect confidential or sensitive information should provide clarity and guidance, in order to avoid disputes between the parties on that matter'.[38]

24. Despite these simple initial ideas, the issue of exceptions to transparency turned out to be one of the most debated and discussed aspects of the Rules.[39]

25. At the wake of the second last session of the WG on the Rules, the draft of Article 7 had developed into a provision with eleven paragraphs[40] – more than double the number of the previous draft.[41] Part of the WG found that the draft had become 'too detailed and risked over-regulating the powers of an arbitral tribunal, while at the same time failing to enumerate every circumstance that may arise'.[42] The same part of the WG presented a new, concurring proposal, embracing 'a more flexible and simplified drafting approach ... in order to permit an arbitral tribunal to adjust its procedures to individual situations'.[43] The WG decided to continue its deliberation based on this concurring draft,[44]

34 UNCITRAL, 'Report of Working Group II (Arbitration and Conciliation) on the work of its fifty-third session (Vienna, 4–8 October 2010)' (2010) UN Doc. A/CN.9/712 [67]–[72].

35 *Ibid.* [67]. 36 *Ibid.* 37 *Ibid.* [69]. 38 *Ibid.* [70].

39 Julia Salasky and Corinne Montineri, 'UNCITRAL Rules on Transparency in Treaty-Based Investor-State Arbitration' (2013) 4 *ASA Bulletin* 774, 793.

40 UNCITRAL, 'Settlement of commercial disputes: preparation of a legal standard on transparency in treaty-based investor-State arbitration' (2011) UN Doc. A/CN.9/WG.II/WP.169 [45].

41 UNCITRAL, 'Settlement of commercial disputes: preparation of a legal standard on transparency in treaty-based investor-State arbitration' (2011) UN Doc. A/CN.9/WG.II/WP.166/Add.1 [1].

42 *Ibid.* [91].

43 UNCITRAL, 'Report of Working Group II (Arbitration and Conciliation) on the work of its fifty-seventh session' (2012) UN Doc. A/CN.9/760 [92].

44 Except for paragraphs 8(2)(c), 8(10) and 8(11), which were retained from the Secretariat's draft, cf. UNCITRAL (n. 43) UN Doc. A/CN.9/760 [93], [118]–[119].

thus departing from the draft that had been discussed before. During that same session, the WG discussed three further propositions:

- first, various wordings of Article 8(2)(c), addressing the extent to which an exception shall be made for information protected against being made available to the public according to a choice of law determination by the arbitral tribunal and the extent of such a determination;[45]
- second, the possibility of a new Article 8(2)(d), which would provide for an exception for information the parties had agreed should not be made public;[46] and
- third, a newly presented Article 8(2)(bis), providing for self-judging exceptions for the publication of information a respondent State unilaterally could consider 'would impede law enforcement or would be contrary to the public interest or its essential security interests' if made public.[47]

26. All these issues arose at a very late stage of the deliberations: there was only one session left during which the WG was supposed to revise and adopt the final version of the Rules, in spite of the number and importance of these newly brought up questions and issues.

27. During that last session, the WG's 58th, two of the issues introduced in the previous session could not be resolved:

- first, there was no agreement as to which one of the propositions of Article 8(2)(c) should govern the arbitral tribunal's determination of exceptions based on conflict of laws considerations;[48] and
- second, there was disagreement over whether the self-judging exceptions brought before the WG during the last session should be retained.[49]

28. A solution was included in the compromise proposal, with which all issues of disagreement throughout the Rules were to be resolved.[50] Although some of the other unresolved issues were of a far more fundamental nature,[51] it was the disagreement on exception provisions which

[45] UNCITRAL (n. 43) UN Doc. A/CN.9/760 [104].
[46] UNCITRAL (n. 43) UN Doc. A/CN.9/760 [117].
[47] UNCITRAL (n. 43) UN Doc. A/CN.9/760 [105]. [48] *Ibid.* [59]–[62].
[49] *Ibid.* [65]–[66]. [50] *Ibid.* [69].
[51] Such as the field of application of the Rules as such or the degree of openness of the hearings, cf. *ibid.* [67]–[68].

averted an agreement on the compromise proposal, incited the presentation of a counter-proposal (considerably reducing the arbitral tribunal's discretion by, first, a self-judging exception for essential security information and, second, the mandatory application of the respondent State's law for information of the respondent State (Articles 7(5) and 7 (2)(c) of the Rules, respectively),[52] and endangered the adoption of the complete Rules.[53] In the end, the adopted version of Article 7 was the one suggested in the counter-proposal.[54]

29. The restrictive versions of Articles 7(5) and 7(2)(c) of the Rules are, therefore, not the solutions a majority of the WG had preferred. Their adoption is the result of a tenacious minority able to impose on the rest of the WG its more restrictive preferences in view of a lingering risk that as an alternative no Rules at all would be adopted.

30. In any event, these amendments have changed the spirit of Article 7 of the Rules: while the initial premise was that the arbitral tribunal would have full and sole control over the exceptions to transparency, the respondent State now has considerable influence on their scope and content. A majority of the WG feared that this shift in control had the potential of being abused by respondent States.[55]

31. Finally, the substitution of the Secretariat's draft by a concurring draft of Article 7, the late introduction of new proposals for additional provisions in the WG's second last session and the tug-of-war on the different proposals in the WG's last session left the WG little time to deliberate on several aspects of the adopted version of Article 7. The result is twofold. First, Article 7 might at some places lack the clarity and guidance which the WG had contemplated at the start of the deliberations. Second, the *travaux préparatoires* do not always contain the desirable degree of explanation an arbitral tribunal would wish to find in them when having to interpret Article 7 of the Rules.

[52] *Ibid.* [70]–[71].

[53] *Ibid.* [73]: 'It was said that in relation to both proposals, delegations had made important concessions and in so doing had moved from their original positions. In particular, it was said that in considering the counter-proposal, the concessions agreed by some delegations in the initial compromise proposal were open to re-negotiation only on a non-comprehensive, article-by-article basis.'

[54] *Ibid.* [75], [78].

[55] UNCITRAL (n. 43) UN Doc. A/CN.9/760 [103], [106]–[109]; UNCITRAL, 'Report of Working Group II (Arbitration and Conciliation) on the work of its fifty-eighth session' (2013) UN Doc. A/CN.9/765 [61].

9.1.5 Structure

32. Article 7 is divided into two parts:

- The first part, entitled 'Confidential or protected information', paragraphs 1 to 5, consists of provisions dealing with exceptions to transparency due to the confidential or protected nature of information. Hence, this part considers information that shall not be made public due to the very nature of the information itself.
- The second part, entitled 'Integrity of the arbitral process', paragraphs 6 and 7, consists of provisions dealing with exceptions to transparency in order to safeguard the integrity of the arbitral process, i.e., information not to be disclosed to the public because this could have a disruptive effect on the arbitration.

33. Both of these parts contain (i) material provisions that identify the information giving rise to an exception; and (ii) procedural provisions that define by whom and how decisions about the materiality of an exception shall be made and what the consequences of such a decision are.

34. This division is slightly misleading, as there exists in reality a third category of information, for which the procedures set forth in the rest of Article 7 (and the whole Rules) do not apply: information the publication of which a respondent State unilaterally considers to be contrary to its essential security interests (paragraph 5).

35. Therefore, the following commentary on the different provisions of Article 7 will first discuss the exceptions due to confidential or otherwise protected information (Articles 7(1) to 7(4)), then turn to the essential security exception (Article 7(5)), and end with comments on the exceptions to safeguard the integrity of the arbitral process (Articles 7(6) and 7(7)).

9.2 Article 7(1)

9.2.1 'Confidential or protected information'

36. The WG chose the term 'confidential or protected' over the term 'privileged', as the latter 'might not be understood in the same manner in all jurisdictions'.[56]

[56] UNCITRAL, Report of Working Group II (Arbitration and Conciliation) on the work of its fifty-fourth session' (2011) UN Doc. A/CN.9/717 [132].

37. The reference to 'information' makes clear that what gives rise to an exception is a particular protected information, and not a particular document, type of document or certain author. For every piece of information, it will have to be established if it falls under an exception or not. Why the WG made this choice is not exposed in the *travaux préparatoires*. In *Biwater Gauff (Tanzania) Limited* v. *Tanzania*, for example, the arbitral tribunal preferred to link confidentiality to the type of document.[57] The latter solution implies, however, that information will be kept from the public based on the fact that it is contained in a certain type of document and not that there was a preponderant interest in keeping the very information confidential. The *Biwater* approach, therefore, protects more than what is necessary. This is inconsistent with the Rules' underlying principle of transparency, i.e. that the arbitration should be as accessible as possible. This being said, the solution retained by the *Biwater* tribunal was simple, clear and efficient. Costs and effort for the tribunal and the parties in connection to sensitive information were minimal. The solution in the Rules – while being more precise and providing for a higher level of transparency – has the potential to generate important costs and delays when undertaking the necessary work to identify, redact and protect information. It will be the arbitral tribunal's duty to limit this burden as far as possible and in scope with the transparency principle underlying the Rules.[58]

9.2.2 'as defined in paragraph 2'

38. The reference to paragraph 2 clarifies that only the circumstances listed in Article 7(2) of the Rules call for an exception. The arbitral tribunal is not free to define additional circumstances under which an exception shall be granted.

9.2.3 'and identified pursuant to the arrangements referred to in paragraphs 3 and 4'

39. This part of the provision refers to the procedure according to which the information is identified as potentially protected information and

[57] *Biwater Gauff (Tanzania) Limited* v. *Tanzania*, ICSID Case No. ARB/05/22, Procedural Order No. 3 (29 September 2006) [163(a)] www.italaw.com/sites/default/files/case-documents/ita0089.pdf.

[58] See Articles 1(3)(b) and 1(4) of the Rules, Krista Nadakavukaren Schefer, 'Article 1', [60]–[70].

decided upon by the arbitral tribunal. This implies that the arbitral tribunal has to put in place such arrangements.

9.2.4 'shall not be made available to the public'

40. This part of the provision states the core principle of Article 7: where the arbitral tribunal decides to protect certain information, all parties involved have to keep that information confidential. The wording of Article 7 does not limit this duty to the arbitral tribunal and/or the body administering an arbitration, but includes all parties involved.

41. The duty to keep information confidential does not only kick in when the arbitral tribunal has made its decision to protect certain information. If the exceptions in Article 7 of the Rules are to have any practical meaning, the prohibition to disseminate any information has to include the time up to such a decision. Otherwise Article 7 of the Rules would remain idle, as a party could undermine it by publishing any information as long as no decision to keep it confidential has been issued. This is obviously not the objective of Article 7, and a party acting in such way violates the Rules and its duty to act in good faith.

9.2.5 'pursuant to Articles 2 to 6'

42. Article 7(1) explicitly refers to Articles 2 to 6, but not to Article 1. This clarifies that Article 7 does not overrule the general principles laid down in Article 1 of the Rules. On the contrary, Article 1 has to be respected when applying Article 7.

43. When defining what kind of information shall be protected and in way such protection shall be executed, Article 7 confers on the arbitral tribunal a large degree of discretion. When exercising this discretion, Article 1(4) of the Rules directs the arbitral tribunal to take into account:

- the public interest in transparency in treaty-based investor-State arbitration in general, and in the arbitration at hand in particular; and
- the disputing parties' interest in a fair and efficient resolution of their dispute.

44. The use of the word 'shall' in Article 1(4) of the Rules means that the arbitral tribunal must take into account these two issues when exercising the discretion vested in it by Article 7 of the Rules.

9.3 Article 7(2): 'Confidential or protected information consists of'

45. Article 7(2) contains the list of information that shall give rise to an exception to transparency. This list is exhaustive.[59]

9.3.1 Article 7(2)(a): 'Confidential business information'

46. Article 7(2)(a) of the Rules forms the basis for exceptions based on confidential business information.

47. This subparagraph remained almost unchanged throughout the deliberations by the WG. Its wording did, however, raise some concerns. Parts of the WG found that it was not sufficiently broad and suggested including a definition or list of what kind of information shall fall under the term of confidential business information.[60] It was suggested that such a list could include 'business, political, institutional sensitive information, personal data and legal impediments under a law',[61] or enclose 'industrial or financial information, or personal data'.[62]

48. In the end, however, the WG did not retain any definition of the term 'confidential business information', nor provide for any guidance as to which type of information would fall under this term. It will remain the arbitral tribunal's duty to define the meaning of 'confidential business information' within an arbitral proceeding.

49. Several past arbitral tribunals have defined the term of confidential business information in their respective confidentiality orders. In various NAFTA Chapter 11 arbitrations, confidential business information has been defined in the form of a list enclosing:[63]

- trade secrets;
- financial, commercial, scientific or technical information that is treated consistently in a confidential manner by the disputing party or third

[59] Article 7(1) of the Rules, see above section 9.2 Article 7(1).

[60] UNCITRAL, 'Report of Working Group II (Arbitration and Conciliation) on the work of its fifty-fifth session' (2011) UN Doc. A/CN.9/736 [118], [125]; UNCITRAL (n. 43) UN Doc. A/CN.9/760 [96], [99].

[61] UNCITRAL (n. 60) UN Doc. A/CN.9/736 [118]; UNCITRAL (n. 43) UN Doc. A/CN.9/760 [99].

[62] UNCITRAL (n. 60) UN Doc. A/CN.9/736 [118].

[63] Inspired by *William Ralph Clayton, William Richard Clayton, Douglas Clayton, Daniel Clayton and Bilcon of Delaware Inc.* v. *Canada*, PCA Case No. 2009–04, Procedural Order No. 2 (Confidentiality Order) (4 May 2009) [1]; *Mercer International Inc.* v. *Government of Canada*, ICSID Case No. ARB(AF)/12/3, Confidentiality Order (24 January 2013) [1].

party to which it relates, including pricing and costing information, marketing and strategic planning documents, market share data, or detailed accounting or financial records not otherwise disclosed in the public domain;
- information the disclosure of which could result in financial loss or gain to the disputing party or third party to which it relates;
- information the disclosure of which could interfere with contractual or other negotiations of the disputing party or third party to which it relates; and
- other communications treated as confidential in furtherance of settlement between the disputing parties.

50. A further example can be found in *Philip Morris Asia Limited* v. *Australia*:[64]

> information relating to past, present or contemplated future business activities of the Claimant; the financial affairs of the Claimant or any of its affiliates; the past, present, or contemplated future management or operational policies, procedures, or practices of the Claimant or any of its affiliates; the manufacturing, supply, or distribution process and techniques of the Claimant or any of its affiliates; the value of the Claimant or any of its affiliates or any of their respective assets; the granting of licenses or the provision of goods or services to or by the Claimant or any of its affiliates; and any other information that is proprietary or competitively sensitive and the public disclosure of which may cause competitive injury[65]

51. Although these examples provide guidance and inspiration to future arbitral tribunals, every definition will have to take into account the particular circumstances of a case. The arbitral tribunal has, therefore, full discretion to define the scope of 'confidential business information' pursuant to Article 7(2)(a) of the Rules.

9.3.2 *Article 7(2)(b): 'Information which is protected against being made available to the public under the treaty'*

52. The provision clarifies that any information, for which the treaty provides protection from publication, is also protected in the scope of the

[64] *Philip Morris Asia Limited* v. *Australia*, PCA Case No. 2012–12, Procedural Order No. 5 (Regarding Confidentiality) (30 November 2012) [53].

[65] *Ibid.*

Rules. Article 7(2)(b) is thus an application of Article 1(7) (providing that where the Rules conflict with a treaty provision, the latter prevails[66]). Information protected directly by the treaty often relate to information in connection with:

- national security;[67]
- law enforcement;[68]
- public interest;[69]
- essential security interests;[70]
- cabinet and government confidence;[71]
- personal privacy;[72]
- legitimate commercial interests of particular public or private enterprises;[73] or
- the financial affairs and accounts of individual customers of financial institutions.[74]

53. Some of these treaty-based exceptions are also restated in the Rules: Article 7(2)(d), for example, contains an exception for information the disclosure of which could impede law enforcement, and Article 7(5) provides for an exception for information relating to essential security interests.

9.3.3 *Article 7(2)(c) – Information protected under the applicable law*

54. Article 7(2)(c) of the Rules contains an exception arising from various laws applicable to the information to be protected.

55. This exception was the most discussed issue throughout the deliberation of Article 7. It only found its final form in the scope of the compromise proposal, counter-proposal and revised compromise proposal at the very end of the deliberations of the Rules.[75]

56. The discussion started with the WG's statement that the provision dealing with exceptions should also consider 'information otherwise

[66] See Krista Nadakavukaren Schefer, 'Article 1', [74]–[80].
[67] E.g. Article 2102 NAFTA.
[68] E.g. Article 2105 NAFTA; Articles 10.21(3) and 21(5) CAFTA-DR; Article 38(7) Canada Model BIT 2004.
[69] E.g. Articles 10.21(3) and 21(5) CAFTA-DR.
[70] E.g. Articles 10.21(3) and 21(2) CAFTA-DR; Article 38(7) Canada Model BIT 2004.
[71] E.g. Canada Model BIT 2004.
[72] E.g. Article 38(7) Canada Model BIT 2004.
[73] E.g. Articles 10.21(3) and 21(5) CAFTA-DR.
[74] E.g. Article 38(7) Canada Model BIT 2004.
[75] See above, section 9.1.4.

protected from disclosure by the law of a party'.[76] The WG directed the Secretariat to take into account the question of applicable law as 'there often was national legislation to protect certain information',[77] and mentioned the NAFTA FTC 'Notes of Interpretation of Certain Chapter 11 Provisions' and its reference to 'information which is privileged or otherwise protected' from disclosure under the party's domestic law to the public.[78] The first draft of this provision, therefore, simply stated: 'Confidential and sensitive information consists of . . . information which is protected against disclosure under the treaty or the applicable law'.[79] This was found to be too vague.[80] At this point emerged what would become the central question not only for this provision, but for all of Article 7: how much discretion should be given to the arbitral tribunal in deciding on an exception? Until the very end, the delegations struggled to find a consensus: one part of the WG wanted to grant the arbitral tribunal 'discretion to determine whether the law of a disputing party or any other law or rules were applicable to the disclosure of confidential information'.[81] On the other hand, some delegates found that at least for the information provided by the respondent State, 'the arbitral tribunal should be under an obligation to apply the laws of a disputing party in that regard'.[82] The second view prevailed, making it mandatory for the arbitral tribunal to apply 'in the case of the information of the respondent . . . the law of the respondent'.[83]

57. Article 7(2)(c) thus directs the arbitral tribunal to apply two different standards when evaluating the law applicable to exceptions to transparency. If the information was provided by the respondent State, the arbitral tribunal must apply the law of that State. If, on the other hand, the information was provided by any other party, e.g., the claimant, a non-disputing party to the treaty or a third party, the arbitral tribunal has the discretion to determine which law is applicable to the exception.

58. The *travaux préparatoires* reveal that the term 'information of the respondent State' refers to information that has been provided in the arbitration by the responding State, i.e., the responding State introduced

[76] UNCITRAL (n. 34) UN Doc. A/CN.9/712 [67].
[77] UNCITRAL (n. 56) UN Doc. A/CN.9/717 [131]. [78] *Ibid.* [132].
[79] UNCITRAL (n. 41) UN Doc. A/CN.9/WG.II/WP.166/Add.1 [1].
[80] UNCITRAL (n. 60) UN Doc. A/CN.9/736 [119].
[81] *Ibid.* [127]; UNCITRAL (n. 43) UN Doc. A/CN.9/760 [102].
[82] UNCITRAL (n. 60) UN Doc. A/CN.9/736 [121], [127]; UNCITRAL (n. 55) UN Doc. A/CN.9/765 [61].
[83] UNCITRAL (n. 55) UN Doc. A/CN.9/765 [75].

the information into the arbitration.[84] So, the term does not refer to any information that has a connection with or concerns the responding State (which in an investor-State arbitration would direct to the respondent State's law for almost all information).

9.3.3.1 'in the case of the information of the respondent State, under the law of the respondent State'

59. The arbitral tribunal has to apply the law of the respondent State to information provided by the respondent State. This means that the arbitral tribunal has no discretion as to the choice of the applicable law. In the past, arbitral tribunals had at times rejected the application by the responding State of its own national laws in order to resist the production of documents because the arbitral tribunal found it not appropriate to allow such recourse to national law.[85] Such an approach is not possible within the scope of Article 7(2)(c) of the Rules.[86] The Arbitral Tribunal, however, retains discretion as to the interpretation – the content – of the respondent State's law. This is consistent with the goal of the mandatory application of the respondent State's law discussed within the WG, i.e., preventing a respondent State from being put in a situation in which it breaches its own laws because it has to make available to the public information that, according to its national law, it has to keep confidential.[87] Beyond that goal, the arbitral tribunal still has discretion in the application of the law of the respondent State and can use this discretion 'in order to equalize the protection of confidential information that might differ between the home State of the investor and the State party to the dispute'.[88]

[84] UNCITRAL (n. 43) UN Doc. A/CN.9/760 [102]–[103]; UNCITRAL (n. 55) UN Doc. A/CN.9/765 [61].

[85] See e.g. *Pope & Talbot Inc.* v. *Canada*, Decision by the Arbitral Tribunal (6 September 2000) [1.2]–[1.4] http://italaw.com/sites/default/files/case-documents/ita0676.pdf; or *Biwater Gauff (Tanzania) Limited* v. *Tanzania*, ICSID Case No. ARB/05/22, Procedural Order No. 2 (24 May 2006) 8 www.italaw.com/sites/default/files/case-documents/ita0088.pdf.

[86] The Rules do not, however, preclude the arbitral tribunal from persisting with such a view in the scope of document production: Article 7(2)(c) of the Rules is only applicable for the issue of an exception to public access and does not interfere with the determination by the arbitral tribunal of the applicable law for evidentiary privileges, i.e., the protection of documents from having to produce them to the other disputing party.

[87] UNCITRAL (n. 43) UN Doc. A/CN.9/760 [102].

[88] UNCITRAL (n. 60) UN Doc. A/CN.9/736 [121].

60. But even considering the above-mentioned use by the arbitral tribunal of its remaining discretion as a corrective tool, the mandatory application of the law of the respondent State remains a double-edged sword: keeping in mind all the possibilities that might arise during an arbitration, the law of the respondent State is not necessarily the best solution for every single such case.[89] This configuration does not, for example, take into consideration systems in which the respondent State's legal system attaches the protection of client–counsel correspondence to the country of residence or practice of the counsel and not of the client. If, under such a system, the respondent State retains foreign legal counsel, the information would not be protected from being made public under the laws of the respondent State and, therefore, neither under Article 7(2)(c) of the Rules.

61. Finally, the mandatory application of the respondent State's law might, as discussed during the WG's deliberations, open the door 'to abuse and . . . dilute the objective of the rules' as it would 'permit a State to circumvent the object of the Rules by introducing legislation precluding the disclosure of all information in investor-State disputes'.[90] It is, however, evident – and the WG unanimously affirmed this twice – that it is not permissible for a State to adopt the Rules in its investment treaties, and 'then use its domestic law to undermine the spirit (or the letter) of such rules'.[91]

62. Such behaviour would trigger Article 1(6) of the Rules, directing the arbitral tribunal to ensure the supremacy of the transparency objectives of the Rules 'in the presence of any conduct, measure or other action having the effect of wholly undermining' these objectives.[92]

63. The question remains, however, how an arbitral tribunal shall react if a respondent State not 'wholly' but only partially undermines the transparency objective of the Rules in its endeavour to maintain

[89] UNCITRAL (n. 55) UN Doc. A/CN.9/765 [60].

[90] UNCITRAL (n. 43) UN Doc. A/CN.9/760 [103]; UNCITRAL (n. 55) UN Doc. A/CN.9/765 [61].

[91] UNCITRAL (n. 43) UN Doc. A/CN.9/760 [103]; UNCITRAL (n. 55) UN Doc. A/CN.9/765 [65].

[92] And might well – should the UNCITRAL Transparency Rules indeed be incorporated into an investment treaty – put the respondent State in breach of its duties under Articles 26 and 27 of the Vienna Convention on the Law of Treaties (signed 23 May 1969, entered into force on 27 January 1980), which states that every treaty must be performed in good faith and that a State may not invoke its domestic law to justify a failure to execute its treaty obligations. In addition this could also constitute a breach of the respondent State's fair and equitable treatment obligation under the treaty.

secrecy. For instance, what if a State tried to exclude information pertaining to a certain sector or issued by a certain entity from publication?

64. How arbitral tribunals react to such behaviour by a respondent could be an important test of the effectiveness of the Rules.[93]

65. It is submitted that the test should be the same as for the essential security exception, discussed below:[94] the arbitral tribunal is to conduct a good faith test. In other words: the arbitral tribunal will have to determine if the main purpose of the respondent State's domestic law protecting certain information is to circumvent the publication of information otherwise not protected from being made public by the Rules or if the respondent State can bring forward reasonable justifications for the protection of such information other than preventing their openness to the public in an investment arbitration.

66. In summary, the arbitral tribunal is obliged to apply the respondent State's law when establishing if information provided by the respondent State is protected from being made available to the public or not, but:

- retains discretion in interpreting the content of such applicable laws; and
- retains the right to conduct a good faith test as to the purpose of the respondent State's applicable law.

67. Finally, the direction to the respondent State's laws in Article 7(2)(c) does not lower the protection otherwise provided by the Rules. In other words, while Article 7(2)(c) of the Rules has the goal of preventing the respondent State from having to act against its own law because the arbitral tribunal orders the disclosure of information that the respondent State has to keep confidential under its domestic law, it does not at the same time allow a State to disclose information protected under the Rules because under its national law it can be compelled to do so. For example, if any particular information has been accorded protection because it is confidential business information pursuant to Article 7(2)(a), the responding State would violate the Rules if it makes it accessible to the public because the protection in its national freedom of information law does not deem the same information protection-worthy. The reference to the responding State's national laws in Article 7(2)(c) does not allow the responding State to put its own national laws before the Rules.

[93] Ian A. Laird, 'Transparency in Investor-State Arbitration', OUPblog (3 March 2014) http://blog.oup.com/2014/03/transparency-in-investor-state-arbitration/.

[94] See below, section 9.6.3.

9.3.3.2 'and in the case of other information, under any law or rules determined by the arbitral tribunal to be applicable to the disclosure of such information'

68. For all information not coming from the respondent State, the arbitral tribunal has to determine the law applicable to the disclosure of the information in question.

69. The arbitral tribunal is free, in the limits set by the treaty, to determine which laws or rules it deems the most appropriate to apply.

70. The reference to 'rules' does not only enclose the applicable arbitration rules, but also other types of complementary rules, such as the IBA Rules for the Taking of Evidence in International Arbitration. Inspiration by the IBA Rules seems appropriate insofar as the exercise to be undertaken by the arbitral tribunal when applying Article 7(2)(c), second possibility, bears a strong resemblance to the analysis it has to make when determining the applicable law for evidentiary privileges.

71. Many arbitral tribunals have conducted such an analysis, which necessarily has to be made on a case-by-case basis.[95] Often arbitral tribunals have tried to find a standard that evens out the sometimes important differences between different national laws. For any information coming from the investor, a third party or a non-disputing party to the treaty, the arbitral tribunal is free to do so.

72. In order to avoid any discussion at a later time about the laws and rules on which the arbitral tribunal may rely in this respect, it might be appropriate for the arbitral tribunal to include the laws and rules it will take into consideration in an eventual transparency order.

[95] See e.g. *Vito G. Gallo* v. *Canada*, Procedural Order No. 3 (8 April 2009) www.international.gc.ca/trade-agreements-accords-commerciaux/assets/pdfs/disp-diff/gallo-po-12.pdf; *Abaclat and Others* (case formerly known as *Giovanna A Beccara and Others*) v. *Argentina*, ICSID Case No. ARB/07/5, Procedural Order No. 3 (Confidentiality Order) (27 January 2010); *William Ralph Clayton, William Richard Clayton, Douglas Clayton, Daniel Clayton and Bilcon of Delaware Inc.* v. *Canada*, Procedural Order No. 12 (2 May 2012) www.pca-cpa.org/showfile.asp?fil_id=2034 and Procedural Order No. 13 (11 July 2012) www.pca-cpa.org/showfile.asp?fil_id=2035; *Glamis Gold Ltd.* v. *United States of America* (NAFTA, UNCITRAL Arbitration Rules 1976), Decision on Parties' Requests for Production of Documents Withheld on Grounds of Privilege (17 November 2005) www.state.gov/documents/organization/57342.pdf and Decision on Requests for Production of Documents and Challenges to Assertions of Privilege (21 April 2006) www.state.gov/documents/organization/75784.pdf.

73. In any event, the arbitral tribunal will of course always have to weigh the protection conferred by the applicable law against the public interest for transparency.

9.3.4 *Article 7(2)(d): Protection of law enforcement*

74. The exception in Article 7(2)(d) of the Rules, relating to information 'the disclosure of which would impede law enforcement' had not been included in any of the earlier drafts discussed by the WG, but emerged from within the WG towards the end of the deliberation of the Rules as part of a new 'self-judging' exception:[96]

> Nothing in these rules shall require a party to make available information [to the public] the disclosure of which it considers would impede law enforcement or would be contrary to the public interest or its essential security interests.

75. The provision was heavily criticised.[97] The WG did not discuss the meaning of 'information the disclosure of which would impede law enforcement' or how information relating to 'law enforcement' would have to be delimited from information relating to 'security interests' and/or 'public interest'. The reason for this may well have been that Article 7 (2)(d) was completely dropped in the compromise proposal put before the WG to resolve the outstanding differences, and only reintroduced at the very last moment in the revised compromise proposal, although not as a self-judging exception, but as a regular exception under Article 7(2) of the Rules.[98] The *travaux préparatoires* do not provide for any further discussion as to why this was done, nor give the arbitral tribunal any guidance as to the interpretation of 'information the disclosure of which would impede law enforcement'.

76. In treaties, information regarding law enforcement is mostly referred to in the same breath as essential security interests and/or public interest. Neither treaty language nor case law give any autonomous definition or meaning to it.

[96] UNCITRAL (n. 43) UN Doc. A/CN.9/760 [105].

[97] In fact parts of the WG criticised the overly broad wording of 'would impede law enforcement', found that the same protection was already carried for in national laws and treaties and, therefore, found it unworthy to form a separate exception, see UNCITRAL (n. 43) UN Doc. A/CN.9/760 [106]–[109].

[98] For the compromise proposal and the revised compromise proposal, see UNCITRAL (n. 55) UN Doc. A/CN.9/765 [67]–[78].

77. It is therefore suggested that law enforcement relates to institutions, principles, operations and arrangements with the duty to enforce the application of the laws of a State and engage with the pursuit and prosecution of crime.

78. A more detailed definition is included in the US Freedom of Information Act, which contains a publication exception for information compiled for law enforcement purposes, when such information:

(a) could reasonably be expected to interfere with enforcement proceedings;
(b) would deprive a person of a right to a fair trial or an impartial adjudication;
(c) could reasonably be expected to constitute an unwarranted invasion of personal privacy;
(d) could reasonably be expected to disclose the identity of a confidential source, including a State, local, or foreign agency or authority or any private institution which furnished information on a confidential basis, and, in the case of a record or information compiled by a criminal law enforcement authority in the course of a criminal investigation or by an agency conducting a lawful national security intelligence investigation, information furnished by a confidential source;
(e) would disclose techniques and procedures for law enforcement investigations or prosecutions, or would disclose guidelines for law enforcement investigations or prosecutions if such disclosure could reasonably be expected to risk circumvention of the law; or
(f) could reasonably be expected to endanger the life or physical safety of any individual.[99]

79. The scope of the exception is closely linked to the functioning of the State and the ways it upholds the rule of law. Considering its scope, the law seems tailored to be invoked by the respondent State.

80. The exception is regularly included in treaties (and thus covered by Article 7(2)(b) of the Rules[100]). In addition, national law will regularly preclude the publication of information which, if made public, could impede law enforcement (thus meaning that such information is protected under Article 7(2)(c) of the Rules). It is therefore difficult to imagine a situation in which Article 7(2)(d) of the Rules carries weight

[99] The Freedom of Information Act, 5 USC § 552(b)(7) www.law.cornell.edu/uscode/text/5/552.

[100] See above, section 9.3.2.

of its own. One of the possible situations might be that a non-disputing party to the treaty invokes it.

9.4 Article 7(3)

81. Article 7(3) of the Rules clarifies both the 'gateway function' of the arbitral tribunal and the process to detect, decide on and enforce an exception under Article 7(2) of the Rules within the arbitral procedure. The paragraph also stipulates that the sole decision maker on an exception to transparency for information based on an exception under Article 7(2) of the Rules is the arbitral tribunal, and not the parties.

9.4.1 'The arbitral tribunal, after consultation with the disputing parties'

82. Before making any arrangements to prevent the publication of confidential or protected information, the arbitral tribunal is held to consult with the disputing parties. Other possible parties to the arbitration, such as non-disputing parties to the treaty or third parties, are not part of the consultation process. This includes, for example, that they have neither any veto right, nor any right to be heard when it comes to the arrangements made.

83. The leadership role of the arbitral tribunal intended by the Rules does not mean that the parties shall not be involved in the setting-up of the arrangements. On the contrary, including and considering the parties' comments or input will enhance the acceptance of such a framework. Possible ways for the arbitral tribunal to do so are, for example: (i) to circulate a procedural draft order regulating transparency; or (ii) to ask the parties to confer, and if possible agree on a possible framework. The arbitral tribunal might, however, have to remind the parties that they are not allowed, not even by joint agreement, to deviate from the Rules, and that even the arbitral tribunal is bound to the transparency objective of the same,[101] in particular if the propositions of the parties are undermining the purpose or functioning of Article 7 of the Rules.

84. In addition, the arbitral tribunal will have to consider how to balance and distribute the additional work made necessary by the transparency arrangements required under the Rules. In any event the Rules

[101] Articles 3(a) and 3(b) UNCITRAL Transparency Rules.

are likely to (further) increase the administrative and logistical burden going along with the arbitration procedure for both disputing parties, the arbitral tribunal and its secretary/clerk – and thus create higher costs for an investment arbitration procedure.[102]

9.4.2 'shall make arrangements to prevent any confidential or protected information from being made available to the public'

85. This part of the provision includes a positive and a negative duty: first, the arbitral tribunal has the (positive) duty to put in place a system to detect, process and protect confidential or protected information. Second, the parties have a (negative) duty to refrain from disseminating any information obtained in the arbitration before such arrangements are in place. This relates in particular to possible exchanges and/or submissions regarding interim measures, which, due to their urgent nature, might often be discussed before the arrangements to prevent the publication of protected information are in place.

86. Under the Rules, the information is channelled through the arbitral tribunal, not the parties.[103] This creates a duty of the parties to adhere to the prohibition to disseminate information unilaterally–even if no explicit prohibition to do so is contained in Article 7.[104]

87. In any event, the arbitral tribunal should endeavour to put in place the necessary arrangements rapidly and, if necessary, in several steps if the consultation process for a comprehensive solution takes too long.

9.4.3 'including putting in place, as appropriate'

88. The wording 'as appropriate' clarifies three things. First, it emphasises the vast discretion of the arbitral tribunal when it comes to putting

[102] E.g. Australia based its refusal to make accessible its Statement of Defence in *Philip Morris Asia Limited* v. *Australia*, PCA Case No. 2012–12, upon a request made under the Australian Freedom of Information Law, *inter alia*, on the 'significant cost' it would have to bear related to the designation and redaction of confidential information, cf. Jarrod Hepburn, 'Australia denies access to its "plain packaging" arbitration defence under freedom of information law' (12 May 2014) *Investment Arbitration Reporter* www.iareporter.com/articles/20140512_1.

[103] UNCITRAL (n. 60) UN Doc. A/CN.9/736 [112].

[104] *The Loewen Group, Inc. and Raymond L. Loewen* v. *United States of America*, ICSID Case No. ARB(AF)/98/3, Decision on hearing of Respondent's objection to competence and jurisdiction (5 January 2001) [25] www.state.gov/documents/organization/3921.pdf.

in place the arrangements in connection with confidential and protected information. The examples listed in Article 7(3)(a) to (c) of the Rules are neither exhaustive nor mandatory. The arbitral tribunal is free to adapt them or to replace them by measures it considers more appropriate. The WG wanted a flexible wording, 'in order to permit an arbitral tribunal to adjust its procedures to individual situations'.[105] Second, the words 'as appropriate' are also a reminder of Article 1(4)(b) of the Rules, which makes reference to the parties' interest in an efficient resolution to their dispute, and to Article 17(1) of the Arbitration Rules (2010), directing the arbitral tribunal to 'conduct the proceedings so as to avoid unnecessary delay and expense and to provide a fair and efficient process for resolving the parties' dispute'. Thus, the arbitral tribunal should put in place arrangements which keep the framework as lean and efficient as possible.

89. Finally, the appropriateness of a measure can, over time, diminish, for example, when 'the threat that led to prohibit such publication dissipated'.[106] It might be appropriate for the tribunal to revisit certain of the arrangements it has made, balancing such a review process with the previously mentioned necessity to prevent an overburdened process.[107]

9.4.4 *Article 7(3)(a): 'Time limits in which a disputing party, non-disputing party to the treaty or third person shall give notice that it seeks protection for such information in documents'*

90. The WG found it important to provide for 'some flexibility in terms of timing, as it was not practicable to require from a party that, at the time it submitted the information to the arbitral tribunal, it also submitted a redacted version'.[108] In some cases such additional time limits might indeed be the most practicable solution. Past tribunals have, however, on various occasions directed the parties to raise issues of protection at the time of their submissions already, for example by: (i) designating all of their documents (including exhibits and witness statements) containing confidential information;[109] and/or (ii) identifying the confidential information in the documents by, for example, placing it in

[105] UNCITRAL (n. 43) UN Doc. A/CN.9/760 [92].

[106] UNCITRAL (n. 60) UN Doc. A/CN.9/736 [130]. [107] *Ibid.* [108] *Ibid.* [129].

[109] *Fireman's Fund Insurance Company* v. *Mexico,* ICSID Case No. ARB(AF)/02/01Award (17 July 2006) (redacted version) [222]–[223] www.italaw.com/sites/default/files/case-documents/ita0331.pdf.

square brackets.[110] In view of the duty to provide for efficient arrangements, it might therefore be a time-saving solution to require from the parties making a submission to the arbitration to already designate any information they seek protection for at the time of submission.

91. The wording 'disputing party, non-disputing party to the treaty or third person' clarifies that not only the disputing parties, but all parties in the arbitration have the right to seek protection of confidential or protected information. In *Glamis Gold Ltd.* v. *United States of America*, for example, the protection of certain information as to their tribal lands seems to have been requested by the Quechan Indian Nation (QIN) acting as third party to the arbitration,[111] and not by any of the disputing parties.

92. Finally, the provision also provides that any party can seek protection of information notwithstanding in which party's submission this information is enclosed. The party having an interest in the non-publication of any information does not necessarily have to be the same as the one that introduced it into the arbitration. This might happen, for example, in situations in which the information had been provided to the other party before or during the arbitration on a confidential basis or at least on a basis excluding dissemination to the public. This situation, created by the wording of this provision, causes problems in the application of Article 7(4) of the Rules.[112]

93. To summarise, Article 7(3)(a) of the Rules calls for two different steps: first, the designation by each party of protected information in its own submission, and, second, the notification of possible protected information in the submissions of another party. While the parties might be best asked to do the first directly in their submission, the arbitral tribunal will in any event need to set an appropriate time limit to do the latter.

9.4.5 Article 7(3)(b): 'Procedures for the prompt designation and redaction of the particular confidential or protected information in such documents'

94. Once the information for which protection is requested has been designated, the arbitral tribunal needs to make a decision on such a

[110] *Philip Morris Asia Limited* (n. 64) [53.B.2].

[111] See, e.g., *Glamis Gold Ltd.* v. *United States of America* (NAFTA, UNCITRAL Arbitration Rules 1976), Award (8 June 2009) fn 10 www.italaw.com/sites/default/files/case-documents/ita0378.pdf.

[112] See below, section 9.5.

request and, if it decides that the information is indeed worthy of protection under Article 7(2), to ensure that such information is redacted from all documents.

95. The structure of Article 7(3) of the Rules does not strictly follow the logical sequencing of such a procedure: while Article 7(3)(a) of the Rules refers to 'giving notice', Article 7(3)(b) of the Rules jumps directly to the 'designation and redaction', skipping the part of the process in which the arbitral tribunal reaches its decision on the notifications/ designations of potentially confidential or otherwise protected information. This step is only referred to later, at the very end of Article 7(3) of the Rules. Of course the procedure also has to include a step in which the disputing parties are consulted on the notifications made and in which the arbitral tribunal takes its decision.

96. Article 7(3)(b) of the Rules clarifies that any procedure to designate and redact information in the documents has to be of such a nature as to make the redacted documents available within a short period of time. The WG felt that 'the linkage between Article 3 and Article (then) 8 should be . . . clearly set out . . . and that the question of the promptness of making documents available be addressed'.[113] Hence, the element 'prompt' in this provision is to be read together with Article 3(4) of the Rules, which provides that the arbitral tribunal has to communicate the redacted documents to the repository 'as soon as possible, subject to any relevant arrangements or time limits for the protection of confidential or protected information'.

97. The arbitral tribunal shall oversee the process of redaction, 'regardless of whether there is an objection by a party to such designation'.[114] The WG, therefore, intended the arbitral tribunal to take an active role in such process. This means that the arbitral tribunal has to at least control the redactions made. Such a redaction process applies 'to all documents, including reports by tribunal appointed experts, submissions by third parties, and not only documents submitted by the disputing parties'.[115]

98. There are examples for both time limits and the procedure to designate, comment and decide on (disputed) designations: in *Apotex Holdings Inc.*, for example, the time limit to designate information for which protection was requested in a document submitted by another party was thirty days.[116] For disputes about the designation as 'eyes of

[113] UNCITRAL (n. 43) UN Doc. A/CN.9/760 [110].
[114] UNCITRAL (n. 60) UN Doc. A/CN.9/736 [129]. [115] *Ibid.*
[116] *Apotex Holdings Inc.* (n. 7) [3].

tribunal and counsel only', the challenge had to occur within five days, the response within four days and the reply within three days, while the arbitral tribunal undertook to decide within a week.[117] In *Philip Morris Asia Limited*, a party had twenty-one days to produce a redacted version of its document, for which it had in its submission indicated the confidential information.[118] The other party had sixty days from the submission of the information to object to the designation, following which the dispute could be brought by either party before the arbitral tribunal in writing within twenty-one days after the objection, triggering a time limit of fourteen days for the other party to respond in writing to the application to the arbitral tribunal.[119] In *William Ralph Clayton et al.*, the party was to provide a redacted copy of its submission within twenty days after the submission of the unredacted version.[120] For any dispute on the designation, five-day time limits were set for submissions to the arbitral tribunal.[121]

9.4.6 *Article 7(3)(c): 'Procedures for holding hearings in private to the extent required by article 6, paragraph 2.'*

99. The arrangements to protect confidential or protected information during the hearing will largely depend on the arrangements that have been made for the public hearing as such and the possibilities of the hearing location and the service provider in this respect.[122]

100. An early assessment of available hearing venues and the different technical solutions provided might therefore be necessary. It might be appropriate to not set in place the respective procedures contemplated by Article 7(3)(c) of the Rules together with the arrangements for the designation, decision on and redaction of protected information in documents at the start of the arbitration. Rather, this should be contemplated once the arbitral tribunal has an indicative idea on the extent,

[117] *Ibid.* [Addendum 6bis]. [118] *Philip Morris Asia Limited* (n. 64) [53.B.3].

[119] *Ibid.* [53.B.5].

[120] *William Ralph Clayton, William Richard Clayton, Douglas Clayton, Daniel Clayton and Bilcon of Delaware Inc.* v. *Canada*, Procedural Order No. 2 (Confidentiality Order) (4 May 2009), [4]–[5] www.pca-cpa.org/showfile.asp?fil_id=1374.

[121] *Ibid.* [6]; and Procedural Order No. 1 (9 April 2009) [30]–[31] www.pca-cpa.org/showfile.asp?fil_id=1373.

[122] Service providers experienced in administering investment arbitration hearings, such as the PCA and ICSID, are probably best placed to not only accommodate or provide for various means of public hearings, including broadcasting and web-streaming services, but also to provide or suggest solutions for the protection of sensitive information based on their experience with this kind of arbitration.

nature and distribution of the information that needs to be protected during the hearing. Only at that time will it be possible to assess the need for arrangements to make sure this information is not made public. These arrangements are issues that need to be discussed with the parties during the hearing preparation.

101. The procedures to protect information during hearings depend on how the arbitral tribunal plans to provide for public access to the hearing. If there is to be live attendance and it is conceivable that the discussion will touch on protected information, the booking of a separate room with closed-circuit broadcast is an appropriate option. This has several advantages: first, it minimises possible disruptions of the hearing. Second, it also gives the arbitral tribunal the possibility of interrupting the broadcast when protected information is discussed. This will be less disruptive than having to ask the audience to leave the room every time the discussion comes to protected information. Depending on the circumstances, the predictability of the witnesses' behaviour and the degree of delimitation between protected and non-protected information, it could be advisable to provide for a slight deferral in the broadcast and a 'red flag' system with the parties. This would ensure that if protected information is addressed in an impromptu manner, the broadcast could immediately be interrupted, so to prevent the 'slip of tongue' from being broadcast to the public.

102. Depending on the division of work contemplated by the arbitral tribunal between its members and the secretary to the tribunal during the actual hearing, it might be necessary to appoint an additional person under the arbitral tribunal's supervision to be responsible for the broadcast and its possible interruption. It is in any event highly recommended to test the whole system before the hearing.

103. Finally, it might be necessary to provide for different levels of 'publicity' of the hearing. In *Glamis Gold Ltd.* v. *United States of America*, part of the confidential information discussed in the hearing concerned the sacred grounds of the QIN for which the same had requested (and obtained) that they not be made available to the public. The hearing was reported via closed-circuit television to a separate room, where the public could view it. In addition, a second broadcast line was installed for members of the QIN, which was not interrupted when the discussion turned to confidential cultural resource information.[123] So, various types of third parties with different 'clearance levels' when it comes to

[123] *Glamis Gold Ltd.* (n. 111), [290] and fn 614; also Procedural Order No. 11 (9 July 2004) [15], [22], [25] www.state.gov/documents/organization/88173.pdf.

protected information can exist, i.e., one group is allowed to witness certain confidential information while the wider public is not.[124] In such cases, arrangements for different broadcast lines[125] or different versions of the transcript have to be made.

104. If a third party has requested the protection of certain information and the arbitral tribunal has granted such protection, it might also be necessary to involve this third party in the control of the broadcast or the redaction of the transcript as to the information protected on its request.[126]

105. If, as contemplated by Article 6(3) of the Rules, a hearing is neither held in private nor broadcasted due to logistical restrictions, the publicity of the hearing may be ensured by publication of the hearing transcripts or posting of audio or video recordings on the internet. In such instances, the procedure to ensure the protection of confidential information will broadly follow the same principles as the one for the designation and redaction of confidential information in documents.

106. Article 6 of the Rules does not make any difference between third parties and non-disputing parties to the treaty. Therefore, where the arbitral tribunal decides that information is confidential or protected, the non-disputing party to the treaty is similarly prohibited from receiving it and/or from being present when the information is discussed at the hearing.[127]

9.4.7 Article 7(3): 'Any determination as to whether information is confidential or protected shall be made by the arbitral tribunal after consultation with the disputing parties'

107. In the past, arbitral tribunals have regularly restricted themselves to the function of deciding issues on which the parties disagreed when it came to the publication or non-publication of information.[128]

[124] See Klint Alexander, 'Article 6', [27]–[28].

[125] *Glamis Gold Ltd.* (n. 123) Procedural Order No. 11 [15].

[126] *Glamis Gold Ltd.* (n. 111) fn 10 and [290].

[127] See in this respect *Detroit International Bridge Company* v. *Canada*, PCA Case No. 2012–25, Procedural Order No. 7 (25 March 2014) www.italaw.com/sites/default/files/case-documents/italaw3162.pdf; and Procedural Order No. 8 (12 May 2014) www.italaw.com/sites/default/files/case-documents/italaw3169.pdf. In this case, the USA was denied access to the hearings of a NAFTA Chapter 11 arbitration.

[128] *Standard Chartered Bank* v. *Tanzania*, ICSID Case No. ARB/10/12, Procedural Order No. 3 (4 May 2011), [3] www.italaw.com/sites/default/files/case-documents/italaw1378.pdf.

108. In practice, arbitral tribunals would at times let the parties decide on the wording of a confidential order without participating in such discussion,[129] and, consecutively, adopt the text provided jointly by the parties without questioning the solution presented to them.[130]

109. The WG did consider this solution, i.e., that the arbitral tribunal would content itself to rule on exceptions on which the parties disagreed,[131] but decided against it. In fact, the *travaux préparatoires* show a salient distrust of the WG towards the arbitrating parties when it comes to the issue of ensuring transparency:[132] This distrust also seems to have been the reason why the WG did not retain an additional subparagraph under Article 7(2), providing for an exception to transparency for 'information that both disputing parties agree not be made available to the public unless it constitutes a breach of the public interest', but struck out this proposal without further ado.[133]

110. Article 7(3) explicitly elevates the arbitral tribunal to the sole decision maker when it comes to the exceptions mentioned in Article 7 (2) of the Rules. Even if the parties agree that certain information shall not be made available to the public, the arbitral tribunal is supposed to overrule the disputing parties' consent and order the publication of any information if it concludes that the information is not protected by any of the exceptions under Article 7(2) of the Rules. Thus, the arbitral tribunal is supposed to dispel a party agreement in favour of an interest stemming from outside of the dispute before it. Such a situation is highly unusual for an arbitration, where the arbitrators derive their powers from the parties' agreement to arbitrate and not from the power of the State. A provision like Article 7 is unproblematic in a State or standing international court. Investment arbitration, as every arbitration, on the contrary, is based on party consent and serves the resolution of a particular dispute between the investor and the State. It might well be

[129] *Standard Chartered Bank* (n. 128), Procedural Order No. 1 (25 March 2011) [4] www.italaw.com/sites/default/files/case-documents/italaw1376.pdf; and Procedural Order No. 2 (29 April 2011) www.italaw.com/sites/default/files/case-documents/italaw1377.pdf.

[130] *Standard Chartered Bank* (n. 128); *Talbot & Pope Inc.* v. *Canada*, Cover letter by the Arbitral Tribunal to the Amended Procedural Order on Confidentiality No. 5 (17 September 2002) www.international.gc.ca/trade-agreements-accords-commerciaux/assets/pdfs/disp-diff/pope-19.pdf.

[131] UNCITRAL (n. 60) UN Doc. A/CN.9/736 [134].

[132] UNCITRAL (n. 60) UN Doc. A/CN.9/736 [112], [129]; UNCITRAL (n. 43) UN Doc. A/CN.9/760 [115] *in fine*.

[133] UNCITRAL (n. 55) UN Doc. A/CN.9/765 [63]–[64].

that many arbitral tribunals will feel uncomfortable in taking a decision over the head of the parties. In a situation where there is no disagreement between the parties about how to deal with certain information, some arbitral tribunals might perceive it as counterproductive to the efficient resolution of the parties' dispute to overrule such a joint agreement by the parties. There might be cases in which such a decision will be perceived by the arbitral tribunal to run against the endeavour to maintain a civilised and constructive atmosphere. Practice will have to show how arbitral tribunals and parties deal with this new situation.

111. The corollary to the arbitral tribunal's power to solely decide on the confidential or protected nature of information is the duty of all participating parties (notwithstanding if disputing party, participating third party or participating non-disputing party to the treaty) to subordinate themselves to the arbitral tribunal in this respect. This means that the parties cannot unilaterally disseminate information before the arbitral tribunal has decided on it, as this would circumvent the sole authority of the arbitral tribunal in this respect.

112. Once the arbitral tribunal has decided that a particular information is not confidential or protected, the party that disagrees with such finding has only one possibility to prevent the publication of such information: the withdrawal of the information from the arbitration under Article 7(4) Rules.

9.5 Article 7(4): Withdrawal of information

113. Article 7(4) of the Rules is the safety break for a party that feels that the arbitral tribunal does not sufficiently protect its sensitive information. Article 7(4) of the Rules allows a party to withdraw from the arbitration any information, or the document in which the information is contained, for which the arbitral tribunal has found that it does not fall under any of the exceptions under Article 7(2).

114. At the same time, however, the party can no longer rely on the information in the scope of the presentation of its case. Due to that dual impact, the withdrawal of information requires careful consideration and balancing the consequences of a publication versus the consequences the non-reliance on this evidence might have for the party's case.

115. In its fifty-fifth session, the WG gave the Secretariat the mission to draft the procedural provisions of Article 7 in a way, *inter alia*, to include the possibility for 'the party that submitted the information [to] withdraw all or part of it, and not rely on it, when that party felt that

confidential and sensitive information would not be sufficiently protected' because the arbitral tribunal rejected granting protection to such information.[134] This solution is, basically, the one retained in Article 10.21 CAFTA-DR and Article 29 of the US Model BIT 2012. In its fifty-seventh session, however, the WG felt that this situation 'overlooked the circumstance whereby a party compelled to produce a document by the arbitral tribunal could subsequently withdraw that document on grounds of confidentiality. It was agreed that [the relevant paragraph] was only intended to apply in circumstances where a party had voluntarily submitted a document'.[135] The wording of Article 7(4) of the Rules was amended accordingly and adopted in its amended form.

116. The starting point for the possibility of withdrawing a document is a negative decision of the arbitral tribunal that a particular information is not confidential or protected by any of the exceptions under Article 7(2).

117. The party that has introduced the document can withdraw it either completely or partially. A partial withdrawal might be particularly suitable where the document also contains separate, valuable information on which the same party relies.

118. Article 7(4) restricts the possibility of withdrawing documents to situations in which the document was voluntarily filed into the record.

119. The term 'record' requires clarification. For instance, it is unclear whether a document is to be considered 'in the record' when one party provides it to the other in the scope of a (voluntary) document production, or if, on the contrary, a document is only 'in the record' once it is filed as evidence or presented otherwise to the arbitral tribunal. The distinction is important insofar as in the second case the party introducing any information or document is not necessarily the same as the party that has an interest to have that information protected.[136] In other words, is it the party that has produced the document to the other party voluntarily that can withdraw it from the arbitration, or only the other party that included said document in its exhibits?

120. Both interpretations have their pros and cons. The first makes sure that the party which considers that the arbitral tribunal does not

[134] UNCITRAL (n. 60) UN Doc. A/CN.9/736 [129].

[135] UNCITRAL (n. 43) UN Doc. A/CN.9/760 [113].

[136] We have seen earlier that Article 7(3)(a) of the Rules does not limit the designation of sensitive information to documents a party has submitted itself, but that it can also designate information in submissions of other parties as requiring protection, see above section 9.4.4.

protect its information sufficiently can withdraw the information. This solution, however, would mean that the other party, i.e., the one that has filed the document as evidence, would have to bear the negative consequences of such withdrawal, as it could no longer rely on it as evidence. The second interpretation (thus that 'record' refers to what is presented as evidence) would guarantee the identity of the person who can withdraw it and the person that has to suffer the consequences of such withdrawal. It does, however, make it impossible for the party from which the document originated to withdraw it.

121. The second distinction is favourable as it minimises possible interferences into the way a party presents its case by another party. This interpretation is corroborated by the *travaux préparatoires*, according to which this provision shall prevent 'a party compelled to produce a document by the arbitral tribunal' to subsequently withdraw that document, not the party that voluntarily disclosed it. This solution might, however, diminish any desire of the parties to voluntarily disclose documents to the other party.

122. One possible way out of this dilemma might be that the arbitral tribunal deviates from Article 7(4) of the Rules applying its power to do so under Article 1(3)(b) of the Rules to prevent the situation discussed above.

123. In sum, Article 7(4) of the Rules amounts – for public interest considerations – to a limitation of a party's right to present its case in the way it chooses: While the party has a 'last resort' to prevent the publication of information it deems protection-worthy (but the arbitral tribunal does not), this will also prevent it from relying on that information in the arbitration proceedings. This means that the party's right to be heard is limited for a reason that has nothing to do with the dispute itself, but stems from the public interest in transparency.

124. The withdrawal of information by a party also has the consequence that the other parties cannot make reference to the information in question in their submissions. In this sense, the arbitral tribunal in *Philip Morris Asia Limited* v. *Australia* included in its confidentiality order a provision explicitly stating that '[i]f the information is withdrawn, it cannot be relied upon by the opposing Party or the Tribunal'.[137] Article 10.21(4)(d) of the CAFTA-DR states the same and even directs the opposing party to resubmit newly redacted versions of its

[137] *Philip Morris Asia Limited* (n. 64) [53.B.5.f].

submissions (deleting any reference to the withdrawn information[138]). The same principle has to be applied under the Rules. Otherwise the same information could be reintroduced by another party into the proceedings and Article 7(4) of the Rules would be emptied of any practical meaning.[139]

9.6 Article 7(5): The essential security interest exception

9.6.1 Introduction

125. Article 7(5) creates a distinctive category of information for which the rules set forth in Article 7(1) to (4) do not apply: information relating to essential security interests of the respondent State. Article 7(5) breaks with the principles put forward in the rest of Article 7: unlike the other exceptions in Article 7, the wording of Article 7(5) does not subject the (non-) disclosure of such information to the decision of the arbitral tribunal. It is left to the State to define the 'information the disclosure it considers to be contrary to its essential security interests' and for which 'nothing in these Rules require a respondent State to make [it] available to the public'.

126. The 'essential security interests' exception was not included in the first drafts of the Rules but put before the WG during its fifty-seventh session by some members of the WG in the scope of a proposal for an additional (and beforehand undiscussed) new paragraph also containing exceptions for public interest and law enforcement considerations.[140] Some delegations supported the view that these exceptions shall be determined by the State itself (and not the arbitral tribunal),[141] noting that the same wording is broadly applied in BITs and trade agreements, and arguing that the importance of these interests justified a self-judging exception.[142] In particular, some developing countries seemed to be concerned about the sufficient protection of their national security interests.[143] Other delegations opposed the introduction of these exceptions, stating that because they were overly broad, a State could give them practically any meaning in order to create a justification to withhold information and that such exceptions would thus contradict the very goal of the Rules.[144] It was argued that this would give any State the possibility

[138] See above, section 9.1.2. [139] Cf. *Biwater Gauff (Tanzania) Limited* (n. 57) [158].
[140] UNCITRAL (n. 43) UN Doc. A/CN.9/760 [105]. [141] *Ibid.* [106].
[142] UNCITRAL (n. 55) UN Doc. A/CN.9/765 [65]–[66], [65]ff.
[143] UNCITRAL (n. 43) UN Doc. A/CN.9/760 [103].
[144] UNCITRAL (n. 43) UN Doc. A/CN.9/760 [106].

of circumventing the Rules unilaterally.[145] As no consent could be found, the paragraph was part of the compromise proposal, counter-proposal and a revised compromise proposal. The latter contained Article 7(5) as it was retained.[146] Thus, while the public policy exception was dropped and the law enforcement exception made subject to a decision by the Arbitral Tribunal by incorporating it under Article 7(2), essential security interests remain a self-judging exception withdrawn to the free consideration by the arbitral tribunal.

127. A discussion as to the content of the term 'essential security interests' or the extent of the self-judging character did not take place.

9.6.2 The notion of essential security interests

128. The WG did not define the term of essential security interests.

129. As had been stated by the WG, the notion of essential security interests is regularly found in BITs[147] or trade agreements.[148]

130. The definitions found therein regularly enclose the trafficking in arms, military materials or other goods, materials, services or technologies in relation to military or security establishments, issues related to war or other emergencies in international relation and issues relating to nuclear weapons.[149]

131. Where there is no definition of the term itself, the notion of essential security interests has to be interpreted according to customary international law.[150] In investment arbitrations the term has regularly been interpreted more broadly than in other cases, for example before the

[145] UNCITRAL (n. 55) UN Doc. A/CN.9/765 [66]. [146] *Ibid.* [69]–[78].

[147] For examples, see Katia Yannaca-Small, 'Essential Security Interests under International Investment Law' in OECD, *International Investment Perspectives 2007: Freedom of Investment in a Changing World* (OECD, 2007), 112ff. (annex 5.A2); OECD, *Security-related Terms in International Investment Law and in National Security Strategies* (OECD, 2009), 32ff. (annex 2).

[148] Cf. Article XXI(1) GATT 1994, Article 74(a) TRIPS, Article 2102(1)(b) NAFTA; Article XIV GATS.

[149] Cf. Article 38(7) of the Canadian Model BIT 2004, Article 26 of the Norway Model BIT 2007, Article 2102(1)(b) NAFTA, Article XXI GATT 1994, or Article 24(3)(a) Energy Charter Treaty.

[150] *Enron Corporation and Ponderosa Assets, L.P.* v. *Argentina*, ICSID Case No. ARB/01/3, Award (22 May 2007) [333] www.italaw.com/sites/default/files/case-documents/ita0293.pdf [annulled]; *Sempra Energy International* v. *Argentina*, Award (28 September 2007) [375]–[378] www.italaw.com/sites/default/files/case-documents/ita0770.pdf [annulled].

ICJ.[151] It is in particular controversial if an undefined security interest clause also encloses economic considerations.[152]

132. Thus, the extent a responding State can rely on the exception in Article 7(5) of the Rules depends on the extent the underlying treaty or customary international law defines the scope of essential security interests. In other words, while it is the respondent State which unilaterally decides if making available any information to the public is contrary to its essential security interests, it cannot unilaterally define the scope of these essential security interests beyond what these interests cover according to the treaty the arbitration is based on.

9.6.3 The arbitral tribunal's power to review an exception under Article 7(5): the 'good faith' test

133. The self-judging character of Article 7(5) of the Rules does not mean that the arbitral tribunal is completely excluded from reviewing an essential security interest exception raised by the responding State: the arbitral tribunal has to conduct a good faith review of such exception.[153]

134. Not allowing such minimal review would indeed open the door to possible abuse of Article 7(5) of the Rules, undermining the very purpose of the same.[154]

135. Conducting such a review, on the other hand, takes into consideration the concerns that the self-judging exception could be used by a State to circumvent the Rules by interpreting the notion of

[151] William J. Moon, 'Essential Security Interests in International Investment Agreements' (2012) *Journal of International Economic Law 15* (2) 481, 499–501.

[152] Pro: *LG&E Energy Corp., LG&E Capital Corp., and LG&E International, Inc.* v. *Argentina*, ICSID Case No. ARB/02/1, Decision on Liability (3 October 2006) www.italaw.com/sites/default/files/case-documents/ita0460.pdf; Contra: *CMS Gas Transmission Company* v. *Argentina*, ICSID Case No. ARB/01/8, Award (12 May 2005) www.italaw.com/sites/default/files/case-documents/ita0184.pdf; *Sempra Energy International* (n. 150); *Enron Corporation* (n. 150).

[153] *LG&E Energy Corp., ibid.* [214], *CMS Gas Transmission Company, ibid.* [366]–[374]; *Sempra Energy International* (n. 150) [388]; *Enron Corporation* (n. 150) [339]; *Continental Casualty* v. *Argentina*, ICSID Case No. ARB/03/9, Award (5 September 2008) [182] www.italaw.com/sites/default/files/case-documents/ita0228.pdf; in relation to Article XXI GATT, which also contains a self-judging essential security interest exception: Peter Van Den Bossche, *The Law and Policy of the World Trading Organization* (2nd edn., Cambridge University Press, 2008) 666ff.

[154] Cf. Andrew Newcombe and Lluís Paradell, *Law and Practice of Investment Treaties: Standards of Treatment* (Kluwer Law International, 2009) 493.

essential security interests so broadly as to justify the non-publication of any information. It does make sense all the more as the exception of Article 7(5) applies to information that has already been disclosed in the arbitration procedure and that is thus known to the arbitral tribunal.

136. In summary, Article 7(5) of the Rules does not give a respondent State a free pass to take recourse to its essential security interests to prevent the publication of information:

- first, the respondent State is bound by the definition of essential security interests in the treaty, of which the Rules cannot derive; and
- second, any objection to publication based on essential security interests have to be made in good faith.

These two issues have to be reviewed by the arbitral tribunal facing an objection to transparency based on Article 7(5) of the Rules.

9.7 Articles 7(6) and 7(7): Integrity of the arbitral process

9.7.1 Introduction

137. Articles 7(6) and 7(7) provide for another category of exceptions to the principle of transparency. They are not concerned with the information as such and its protection, but with the possibly deteriorating effect their publication could have on the arbitral process itself.

138. The regulation of the integrity exception in Articles 7(6) and 7(7) falls somewhat short of the detailed framework provided for the exceptions made for confidential or protected information.

139. Article 7(6) contains the principle that the publication of information can be restricted due to integrity reasons, while Article 7(7) encloses both material and organisational guidance for the arbitral tribunal on when and how to do so.

140. Several past arbitral tribunals have restricted the dissemination of information by the parties due to considerations in connection with the integrity of the arbitral process.[155] This case law, however, dates

[155] See e.g. *AMCO Asia Corporation and others* v. *Indonesia*, ICSID Case No. ARB/81/1, Decision on the Request for Interim Measures (9 December 1983) in 24 *International Legal Materials* (1985) 365–9; *Metalclad Corporation* v. *Mexico*, ICSID Case No. ARB (AF)/97/1, Decision on a request by the Respondent for an order prohibiting the Claimant from revealing information regarding ICSID Case No. ARB/(AF)/97/1 (27 October 1997) www.italaw.com/sites/default/files/case-documents/ita0505_0.pdf; *World*

from before the Rules and does not, therefore, take into appropriate consideration the transparency principle of the Rules and the particular guidance given to the arbitral tribunal in Articles 7(6) and 7(7) of the Rules.

9.7.2 Analysis in view of the WG deliberations

141. Early on, the WG found that 'specific exceptions should be contemplated to deal with the question of protection of the integrity of the arbitral process'.[156] The wide discretion of the arbitral tribunal under Article 17(1) of the Arbitration Rules (2010) to conduct the arbitration in such manner as it considers appropriate was to form the basis of such exceptions.[157] To prevent this exception from becoming an overly broad and vague category inappropriately limiting the principle of transparency, the WG felt that it needed to define what the integrity of the arbitral process meant.[158] Different types of situations that could fall under this term were discussed, such as intimidation or physical threats to participants in the arbitration process, disruptions of hearings by the audience, general politicisation of the dispute or manipulation by the mass media.[159] After some discussion, the WG decided that a high threshold should be applied, rejecting wording used in the past by arbitral tribunals to define the term, such as 'risk of aggravation of the dispute' or 'rendering the resolution of the dispute difficult or impossible', as being too broad.[160] Similarly, 'issues of due process or disturbance of the hearings should not be understood as falling under the category of the protection of the integrity of the arbitral process'.[161] The WG decided that a short list of examples should be included to provide 'adequate guidance to the arbitral tribunal by clarifying that restrictions to

Duty Free Company Limited v. *Kenya*, ICSID Case No. ARB/00/7. Award (4 October 2006) [16] http://italaw.com/documents/WDFv.KenyaAward.pdf; *ADC and ADC & ADMC Management Limited* v. *Hungary*, ICSID Case No. ARB/03/16, Award (2 October 2006) [57]–[68] www.italaw.com/sites/default/files/case-documents/ita0006.pdf; *Biwater Gauff (Tanzania) Limited* v. *Tanzania*, ICSID Case No. ARB/05/22, Procedural Order No. 3 (29 September 2006) www.italaw.com/sites/default/files/case-documents/ita0089.pdf; *EDF (Services) Limited* v. *Romania*, ICSID Case No. ARB/05/13, Procedural Order No. 2 (30 May 2008) www.italaw.com/sites/default/files/case-documents/ita0263.pdf.

156 UNCITRAL (n. 34) A/CN.9/712 [72].

157 *Ibid.*; UNCITRAL (n. 56) A/CN.9/717 [142].

158 UNCITRAL (n. 56) A/CN.9/717 [137], [139]. 159 *Ibid.* [138]. 160 *Ibid.* [139].

161 *Ibid.* [140].

publication could only occur in circumstances that met the threshold of exceptional circumstances'.[162]

9.8 Article 7(6): The principle

9.8.1 'Information shall not be made available to the public pursuant to articles 2 to 6...'

142. This part of the provision clarifies that Articles 7(6) and 7(7) are only to guide the arbitral tribunal as far as transparency in the context of Articles 2 to 7 of the Rules is concerned. If the arbitral tribunal contemplates a measure to uphold the integrity of the arbitral process that does not impact on the publication of information under the Rules, it is not bound by Articles 7(6) and 7(7).

9.8.2 'where the information, if available to the public, would jeopardize the integrity of the arbitral process'

143. Although the WG discussed examples of when the integrity of the arbitral process would be jeopardised, it did not discuss what the integrity of the arbitral process encloses and protects.

144. In *EDF (Services) Limited* v. *Romania*, procedural integrity was regarded as an objective in itself 'meant to preserve the parties' rights to be heard on an equal footing and to be able to collect and provide the necessary evidence in support of their claims and defences'.[163] In *Quiborax S.A., Non Metallic Minerals S.A. and Allan Fosk Kaplún* v. *Bolivia*, the arbitral tribunal considered the procedural integrity of the arbitral proceedings as a right of the parties distinctive from the one to the non-aggravation of the dispute. The tribunal in particular considered it in connection with the parties' right to present their case by having access to documentary evidence, witnesses and evidence through potential witnesses.[164] The arbitral tribunal in *Biwater Gauff (Tanzania) Limited* v. *Tanzania* listed the following issues as falling into the scope of the integrity of the arbitral process:[165]

[162] UNCITRAL (n. 60) UN Doc. A/CN.9/736 [114].

[163] *EDF (Services) Limited* (n. 155) [46], [48]ff.

[164] *Quiborax S.A., Non Metallic Minerals S.A. and Allan Fosk Kaplún* v. *Bolivia*, ICSID Case No. ARB/06/2, Decision on Provisional Measures (26 February 2010) [142], [148] www.italaw.com/sites/default/files/case-documents/ita0698.pdf.

[165] *Biwater Gauff* (n. 155) [135].

- to preserve the Tribunal's mission and mandate to determine finally the issues between the parties;
- to preserve the proper functioning of the dispute settlement procedure;
- to preserve and promote a relationship of trust and confidence between the parties;
- to ensure the orderly unfolding of the arbitration process;
- to ensure a level playing field;
- to minimise the scope for any external pressure on any party, witness, expert or other participant in the process; and
- to avoid 'trial by media'.

145. Arbitral tribunals might take inspiration from these interpretations when contemplating an exception to transparency for procedural integrity reasons.

146. The wording 'would jeopardize' clarifies that the arbitral tribunal will regularly have to initiate a measure to protect the integrity of the arbitral process before it has been endangered or even breached. The arbitral tribunal, thus, does not have to restrict itself to a reactive role, but is encouraged by the Rules to actively prevent any breaches of the procedural integrity.

147. Finally, the reference to 'information' clarifies again that the tribunal shall make exceptions to transparency based on an assessment of the information that might cause a problem (as opposed to making an exception for types of documents, as the *Biwater Gauff* tribunal had made).[166]

9.8.3 'as determined pursuant to paragraph 7'

148. This wording shows that the WG did not want the arbitral tribunal to have total discretion when it comes to an exception to transparency for reasons of procedural integrity. The reference to Article 7(7) serves to clarify that only under the conditions set forth in Article 7(7) shall the arbitral tribunal consider such an exception.

[166] See above, section 9.2.1.

9.9 Article 7(7): Directions as to the integrity of the arbitral process exception

9.9.1 Introduction

149. Article 7(7) contains both a substantive and an organisational part: on one hand it provides guidance as to what kind of circumstances shall give rise to an exception for procedural integrity reasons; on the other hand it indicates how the decision-making and implementation process shall work for such an exception.

9.9.2 'The arbitral tribunal may, on its own initiative or upon the application of a disputing party, after consultation with the disputing parties where applicable'

150. An exception due to the confidential or protected nature of information under Article 7(2) of the Rules will only be contemplated by the arbitral tribunal on the initiative of a party alleging that a certain information falls under any of the exceptions in Article 7(2)(a)–(d). Without a notification by a party to the procedure that it wishes certain information to be treated as confidential, the information will be published.[167] For exceptions to protect the integrity of the arbitral process under Articles 7(6) and 7(7) of the Rules, this is different: the arbitral tribunal can both initiate and take measures to implement such an exception on its own. As a matter of principle, the arbitral tribunal should consult the disputing parties (but not the other parties to the procedure, if any) before taking any measures to protect the integrity of the procedure. The arbitral tribunal shall do so 'where applicable'. Thus, where time is of the essence, it does not have to consult the parties beforehand. The WG found that 'in urgent situations, the arbitral tribunal would not necessarily have the ability to consult the parties' and that in such a situation 'the arbitral tribunal should, at a later stage, consult the parties on its proposed way forward'.[168]

9.9.3 'take appropriate measures to restrain or delay the publication of information'

151. In referring to 'appropriate measures', the Rules confer to the arbitral tribunal a large degree of discretion when deciding on how to

[167] See above, section 9.4.4. [168] UNCITRAL (n. 60) UN Doc. A/CN.9/736 [113].

prevent the violation of the procedural integrity. In line with the general principle of transparency in the Rules, this part of the provision ('restrain or delay') also directs the arbitral tribunal to choose the measure that will infringe least on this principle. As the arbitral tribunal in *Biwater Gauff* observed, restrictions for the sake of procedural integrity often become obsolete after a certain time.[169] This means that the arbitral tribunal will have to keep its measure under continued review and re-assess its appropriateness from time to time.

152. As discussed,[170] a measure would be emptied of any use if the parties were to be allowed to disseminate information. It might be cautious for the arbitral tribunal to remind the parties of their obligation in this respect.

9.9.4 Direction to the arbitral tribunal as to the kind of intensity of the danger for the integrity of the arbitral process

153. As discussed by the WG, possible attempts to endanger the integrity of the arbitral procedure have to feature a certain intensity to justify an exception.[171] The examples in Article 7(7) may serve as a model in connection with the degree of intensity required to trigger an exception under Articles 7(6) and 7(7).

9.9.4.1 'hamper the collection or production of evidence'

154. The parties' right to present their case and to present evidence is a basic necessity of due process. Where this is jeopardised, the proper course of an arbitral procedure is no longer guaranteed.

155. The use of the word 'hamper' indicates that it is not necessary that the collection of evidence is made downright impossible by the publication of a particular piece of information in order to justify its retention, but that it is enough if its publication would make the gathering of evidence more difficult.

156. Depending on the sequencing of the arbitral procedure, the collection and/or production of evidence takes place at a certain time, and not throughout the procedure. It might therefore be possible to limit in time a measure of information retention.

157. In view of the restricted publicity of expert reports and witness statements pursuant to Article 3(2) of the Rules, the situation might arise

[169] *Biwater Gauff* (n. 155) [140], [142], [162].

[170] See above, section 9.2.4.

[171] See above, section 9.7.2.

that an expert or witness requests that his or her written or oral testimony is not made public without his or her explicit consent. Where the expert or witness in question refuses such consent, the arbitral tribunal might want to consider granting an exception under Articles 7(6) and 7 (7) of the Rules to ensure that the expert or witness evidence can be collected.

9.9.4.2 'an exception under intimidation of witnesses, lawyers acting for disputing parties or members of the arbitral tribunal'

158. Intimidation, harassment and/or repercussions taken against actors of an arbitral proceeding is not a new issue in investment arbitration.[172] Intimidation can be overt or subtle.[173] Not always does it become as apparent to the arbitral tribunal as when a witness threatens another witness during the hearing of 'obtaining satisfaction' and, to do so, requests a copy of the other witness's statement.[174] A more 'subtle' example can be found in *Libananco Holdings* v. *Turkey*, where one of the expert witnesses of the claimant withdrew from the arbitration for fear of Government reprisal and harassment after it transpired that the respondent held the claimant's witnesses and legal representatives under surveillance.[175] The examples are, sadly, abundant.[176] The parties involved in an investment arbitration are in particular exposed to the risk of intimidation when they are located in the respondent State and such respondent State is an authoritarian State.[177] Certain States have assembled a track record in using such means to influence investment arbitrations in their

[172] Abba Kalo, 'Witness Intimidation, Tampering and Other Related Abuses of Process in Investment Arbitration: Possible Remedies Available to the Arbitral Tribunal' (2010) 26 *Arbitration International* 45ff.

[173] *Ibid.*, 49. [174] See *ADC Affiliate Limited* (n. 155) [68].

[175] *Libananco Holdings Co. Limited* v. *Turkey*, ICSID Case No. ARB/06/8, Decision on Preliminary Issues (23 June 2008), [72] www.encharter.org/fileadmin/user_upload/Investor-State_Disputes/Libananco-Turkey_decision_preliminary_issues.pdf.

[176] See e.g. the examples given by *Kalo* (n. 172) 49ff, Thomas W. Wälde, '"Equality of arms" in investment arbitration: procedural challenges' in Katia Yannaca-Small (ed.), *Arbitration Under International Investment Agreements: A Guide to Key Issues* (Oxford University Press, 2010) 168ff; or Günther J. Horvath, Stephan Wilske, Harry Nettlau and Niamh Leinwather, 'Categories of Guerrilla Tactics', Günther J. Horvath and Stephan Wilske (eds.), *Guerilla Tactics in International Arbitration* (Kluwer Law International, 2013) 6–8.

[177] Wälde (n. 176) 167ff.

favour.[178] This being said, it is evident that a powerful corporation can often apply the same pressure as a State.[179]

159. In any event, facing a risk of intimidation, the delay or restraint on releasing certain information seems to be one of the least drastic measures an arbitral tribunal can take. This might go from the delay of certain publications to the redaction of the names of witnesses in all documents.

9.9.4.3 'or in comparably exceptional circumstances'

160. This part of the provision shows that the two examples given in Article 7(7) are not to be understood as the only events in which the arbitral tribunal is allowed to limit the public access to certain information. Thus, it is up to the discretion of the arbitral tribunal to decide if a situation jeopardises the integrity of the arbitral process or not.

161. The wording 'comparably' does, however, indicate that any such situation needs to have a certain intensity, for which the intensity of the two examples given in Article 7(7) of the Rules shall serve as model. In other words, the application of Articles 7(6) and 7(7) by the arbitral tribunal shall serve to prevent a situation that has the same potential to jeopardise the integrity of the arbitral process as impediments to the collection and production of evidence or the intimidation of persons in the arbitration. There needs to be a real risk to the efficient and fair resolution of the parties' dispute.

9.10 The parties' unilateral dissemination of information

162. As we have seen, it was the clear intention of the WG to establish the arbitral tribunal as the decision maker and 'channel' when it comes to regulating access by the public to the arbitral procedure, the documents and the information in it.[180] A repository as provided in Article 8 of the Rules would not serve much use if this was not the case.[181] Transparency cannot be without limits. This is the very purpose of Article 7 of the Rules. Such purpose would be circumvented if the parties were free to

[178] Noah Rubins, 'Particularities when dealing with State entities' in Günther J. Horvath and Stephan Wilske (eds.), *Guerilla Tactics in International Arbitration* (Kluwer Law International, 2013) 86–90.

[179] Horvath, Wilske, Nettlau and Leinwather (n. 176) 6–7.

[180] See above, sections 9.2.3, 9.4 (in particular 9.4.7), 9.6.3.

[181] See Giuseppe Bianco, 'Article 2', [18]–[20]; Kathleen Claussen, 'Article 8', [6]–[13]; and also the Guidelines of the UNCITRAL Secretariat (Transparency Registry) on how to submit documents to the Registry www.uncitral.org/transparency-registry/en/guidelines.html.

disseminate information as they wish before the arbitral tribunal has ruled on the issue of protection as provided for in Article 7 of the Rules. Where a party disseminates information that is in the arbitration before the arbitral tribunal has ruled on its protection or if one party diffuses such protected information although the arbitral tribunal has decided that it shall be confidential, this violates the integrity of the arbitral procedure. Hence, the parties have to respect the decisions of the arbitral tribunal when it comes to confidentiality or protection of information and abstain from any behaviour that would render this power of the arbitral tribunal obsolete. This is a direct result of the Rules taking the power to decide on the confidentiality of given information from the parties and putting it into the hands of the arbitral tribunal.

163. This principle applies to both parties alike. If one of the parties is allowed to disseminate information while the other one is not, such a preferential treatment would undermine the fair and equal treatment of the arbitrating parties and, therefore, go against the fundamental principles of every arbitration proceeding.

164. We have seen that Article 7(2)(c) of the Rules directs national laws to define what confidential or protected information is.[182] For information of the respondent State, the arbitral tribunal is directed to apply the law of the respondent State. This option was retained to prevent the situation that the respondent State has to make information accessible to the public by virtue of the Rules that it is not allowed to publish under its national laws. This rule does not, however, give the respondent State the right to circumvent an order by the arbitral tribunal based on the ground that its national laws (such as any kind of freedom of information act) do not convey the same protection to an information the arbitral tribunal has protected.[183]

165. Some treaties do reserve the respondent State's right to do so. For example, Article 10.21(5) CAFTA-DR states:

> Nothing in this Section requires a respondent to withhold from the public information required to be disclosed by its laws.

166. More explicitly, the Canadian Model BIT 2004 provides in its Article 38(8):

> To the extent that a Tribunal's confidentiality order designates information as confidential and a Party's law on access to information requires public access

[182] See above, section 9.3.3.1. [183] See above, section 9.3.3.1.

> to that information, the Party's law on access to information shall prevail. However, a Party should endeavour to apply its law on access to information so as to protect information designated confidential by the Tribunal.

167. In many treaties, however, the issue is not dealt with. During the deliberations of the WG the concern was raised that the State 'could be obliged under legislation to disclose information, and an arbitral tribunal could not be granted the power to prevent such disclosure'.[184] This is wrong. While arbitral tribunals have acknowledged the statutory duty of respondent States to disclose information under their national legislation for the public access to governmental information,[185] Articles 26 and 27 of the VCLT are very clear in this respect: a State cannot hide behind its national laws to neglect its international duties. As Article 7 of the Rules encloses a duty to not disclose information that has been declared as confidential by the arbitral tribunal, disclosing this information would not only violate any arbitral tribunal's order, but also the Rules and the Treaty they are included in.[186] This does not, however, necessarily have to become such a pressing issue in the scope of an application of Article 7 of the Rules.

168. First, many freedom of information acts leave a certain degree of discretion to the State when it comes to the granting of access to information based on requests in this respect.[187]

169. Second, it is not uncommon that national laws regulating access to information provide for explicit exceptions, e.g.: (i) information coming from an arbitration in which the State is a party; (ii) information upon which confidentiality has been ordered by a court or tribunal; or (iii) information that has been given to the State by a third party under an undertaking to keep it confidential.[188]

[184] UNCITRAL (n. 60) UN Doc. A/CN.9/736 [127].

[185] See e.g. *Mondev International Limited* v. *United States of America*, ICSID Case No. ARB (AF)/99/2, Award (11 October 2002) [29] www.state.gov/documents/organization/14442.pdf.

[186] *Pope & Talbot Inc.* v. *Canada*, Decision and Order by the Arbitral Tribunal (11 March 2002) [18] http://italaw.com/sites/default/files/case-documents/ita0683.pdf.

[187] See e.g. Australia's refusal to make accessible its Statement of Defence in an Investment Arbitration under UNCITRAL Rules upon a request made under the Australian Freedom of Information Law for what seem to be purely discretionary reasons; cf. Jarrod Hepburn, 'Australia denies access to its "plain packaging" arbitration defence under freedom of information law' (12 May 2014) *Investment Arbitration Reporter* www.iareporter.com/articles/20140512_1.

[188] See e.g. ss. 27, 32, or 41 of the UK Freedom of Information Act 2000; ss. 8(1)(b) and 8(2) of the Indian Right to Information Act 2005; or Article 3(1) of the Swiss Law on the Principle of Publicity in Public Administration.

170. Where the State can exercise any discretion to keep information which has been protected by the arbitral tribunal under Article 7 of the Rules confidential, the State shall act in a way so as to ensure the confidentiality of such information. In other words, where the statutory obligation to disclose certain information leaves any kind of discretion to the respondent State which it could use not to do so, the respondent State shall not release protected information.[189] Everything else would be contrary to the obligations undertaken by the respondent State in implementing the Rules and would seriously impede the arbitral procedure: a party has to make sure that the information it provided in good faith, and for which the arbitral tribunal has granted protection, remains protected. Otherwise, one party's interest in keeping any information confidential, certified by the arbitral tribunal as being protected under the Rules, is overridden by the other party's interest in full disclosure, which is not protected by the Rules. Such a selective adherence to the rule of law and international obligations endangers the integrity of the arbitral procedure and, in the end, results in a loss of trust in arbitration as a valid instrument to settle investment disputes.[190]

171. It has to be kept in mind that, according to the Rules, the parties are consulted before the arbitral tribunal decides on the status of information.[191] In doing so, the arbitral tribunal has to take into consideration the public interest in transparency in the given case and the disputing parties' interest in a fair and efficient resolution of their dispute.[192] This means that by virtue of the Rules, the arbitral tribunal will balance the public interest in transparency against the interest of the party requesting an exception. If now the respondent State was to make a second appreciation of these issues when facing an access to information request under its national laws, it renders the arbitral tribunal's decision obsolete, empties Article 7 of the Rules of any meaning and substitutes an arbitral tribunal established under an international treaty with a national court.

172. It is noteworthy that Article 1(8) of the Rules, an almost verbatim adoption of Article 1(3) of the Arbitration Rules (2010), does not apply to this case. Said rule only governs the law applicable to the arbitration from which a party cannot derogate, in particular the arbitration law at the seat

[189] *Metalclad Corporation* v. *Mexico* (n. 150) [10].

[190] J. Cameron Murphy, 'UNCITRAL's Efforts to Ensure Transparency: Right back where we started from' (2013) 16 *International Arbitration Law Review* 185–7.

[191] Article 7(3) UNCITRAL Transparency Rules; see above, section 9.4.1.

[192] Article 1(4) of the UNCITRAL Transparency Rules.

of the arbitration.[193] The freedom of information law of the respondent State is no such law. Nothing in the *travaux préparatoires* of the WG would allow such interpretation.

173. In any event it might be diligent to address the issue of the respondent State's law providing for access to information at an early stage of the arbitration, and also address the respondent State's discretion in dealing with such requests. This might be combined with an undertaking by the parties to keep any information for which the arbitral tribunal has determined that it shall be protected, confidential and/or that the respondent State will exercise any given discretion in a way as to keep such information confidential.[194] This might be best achieved in an (countersigned or agreed on) order providing for the arbitration proceeding's framework for public access and its limits.[195]

174. Where the respondent State cannot or will not give such undertakings, even footing and equal treatment can be achieved by another means: some information would not be shared with the respondent State, but only with its counsel. Both the arbitral tribunals in *Apotex Holdings Inc. and Apotex Inc.* v. *United States of America* and in *William Ralph Clayton, William Richard Clayton, Douglas Clayton, Daniel Clayton and Bilcon of Delaware Inc.* v. *Canada* have chosen such an approach.[196] In this situation the information concerned would not come into the sphere of the government of the respondent State, so that it cannot produce this information under a freedom of information request, simply because it does not have it.

9.11 Case management and manageability of the procedure

175. In its first deliberation of the Rules, the WG intended for Article 7 of the Rules to enclose an additional exception: information not to be

[193] See David D. Caron and Lee M. Caplan, *The UNCITRAL Arbitration Rules – A Commentary* (2nd edn., Oxford University Press, 2013) 22; Thomas H. Webster, *Handbook of UNCITRAL Arbitration* (Sweet & Maxwell, 2010) 1-111–1-114; Peter Binder, *Analytical Commentary to the UNCITRAL Arbitration Rules* (Sweet & Maxwell, 2013) 1-049–1-051.

[194] In this respect, see *Appleton & Associates and Barry Appleton* v. *Canada (Privy Council Office)* 2007 FC 640 [12]ff, according to which the wording of the order/undertaking can have a decisive effect.

[195] See below, section 9.13.

[196] *Apotex Holdings Inc.* (n. 7) Addendum; *Clayton* (n. 120) Procedural Order No. 2 (Confidentiality Order) [11]ff.

disclosed for the purpose of case management and the manageability of the arbitration procedure. The WG discussed to what extent efficiency reasons shall give rise to an exception in its own rights under Article 7. It was found that questions of case management are of enough importance 'to be further considered in respect of each substantive matter'.[197] The Rules should 'not create delays, increase costs or unduly burden the arbitral proceedings'.[198] Exceptions to transparency – and rules on transparency in general – 'should also aim at preserving the right of effective access to court'.[199] It was feared that the additional costs created in providing for a transparent proceeding under the Rules 'could jeopardize a party's human right to effective access to justice'.[200] The WG, thus, considered that a right balance had to be found between the public interest in having transparent procedures and the manageability of the procedure from a cost and efficiency point of view.[201] On the other hand, the WG raised concerns that including an explicit exception for case management reasons into Article 7 would 'contribute to a significant erosion of transparency'.[202] In the end, the WG did not attempt to reconcile these different views when redacting Article 7, but found that 'the right balance might well need to be found in relation to each provision in the rules on transparency, rather than as part of the limitations to transparency',[203] i.e., within Article 1(4)(b) of the Rules. This provision makes explicit reference to the disputing parties' interest in a fair and efficient resolution of their dispute'. Also, Article 1(3)(b) of the Rules gives the arbitral tribunal the power to adapt, where necessary, any provisions of the Rules to the particular circumstances of the case. Finally, Article 17(1) of the Arbitration Rules (2010) directs the arbitral tribunal to exercise its discretion so as to 'conduct the proceedings so as to avoid unnecessary delay and expense and to provide a fair and efficient process for resolving the parties' dispute'.

176. As a result, the arbitral tribunal has all the tools necessary to reduce costs, time and effort of the parties if the strict adherence to Articles 2 to 6 of the Rules would unduly burden the procedure and/or limit a party's right to access effective justice in the particular case. It might, for example, be too burdensome for an individual investor or a least developed country to undergo a fully fledged transparency procedure,

[197] UNCITRAL (n. 34) A/CN.9/712 [72]. [198] UNCITRAL (n. 56) A/CN.9/717 [144].
[199] *Ibid.* [145]. [200] *Ibid.* [145]. [201] *Ibid.* [144]. [202] *Ibid.* [146].
[203] *Ibid.* [147].

while a large corporation or a developed country would handle the same procedure without much effort.

9.12 Sanctions

177. At some point the WG discussed the issue of how to ensure the enforcement of the exceptions in Article 7 of the Rules and 'whether a sanction should be provided in case a party would breach confidentiality obligations'.[204] Possible sanctions contemplated were related to costs, as is, for example, provided for in Article 9(7) of the IBA Rules on the Taking of Evidence in International Arbitration (2010).[205] In another context, the WG contemplated that the non-compliance of a party with its duties could be sanctioned by drawing adverse inferences.[206] In general, however, the WG did not seem to be inclined to pursue the issue of sanctions or to provide for them in the framework of the Rules.

178. Article 7 of the Rules does not, therefore, contain a specific provision on the enforcement of the exceptions or the sanctions available to the arbitral tribunal should one of the parties not adhere to Article 7 or an order of the arbitral tribunal based on Article 7.

179. As the Transparency Rules do not contain any provisions dealing with the arbitral tribunal's powers to impose sanctions the next step is to turn to the applicable arbitration rules.

180. Neither the UNCITRAL nor the ICSID Arbitration Rules contain a specific provision dealing with the matter of enforcement or sanctions by the arbitral tribunal.

181. In general, the arbitral tribunal will not have the *imperium* to compel a party to comply with its orders.[207] The question of whether an arbitral tribunal can threaten the parties with a certain sanction, such as a fine, in the case of non-compliance with its orders is controversial.[208] It

[204] UNCITRAL (n. 34) A/CN.9/712 [71]. [205] *Ibid.*

[206] UNCITRAL (n. 43) UN Doc. A/CN.9/760 [115].

[207] Jean-François Poudret and Sébastien Besson, *Comparative Law of International Arbitration* (2nd edn., Sweet & Maxwell, 2007) [538]; Nigel Blackaby, Constantine Partasides, Alan Redfern and Martin Hunter, *Redfern and Hunter on International Arbitration* (5th edn., Oxford University Press, 2009) [5.17].

[208] Jean-François Poudret and Sébastien Besson, *ibid.* [540]; Jeffrey Waincymer (n. 5) 117–18; Gary Born, *International Commercial Arbitration* (2nd edn., Kluwer Law International, 2014) 2315–18; Lucy Reed, 'Sanctions available for Arbitrators to Curtail Guerilla Tactics' in Günther J. Horvath and Stephan Wilske (eds.), *Guerilla Tactics in International Arbitration* (Kluwer Law International, 2013) 101.

does, however, have the possibility of taking the behaviour of a party into consideration when deciding on how to conduct the arbitration, for example, appropriately changing an existing order on transparency. Where, for example, a party is disseminating information although such information has been decided by the arbitral tribunal to fall under an exception of Article 7 of the Rules, the arbitral tribunal could restrict the party's access to certain information by declaring it 'tribunal and counsel's eyes only'.[209]

182. A possibility of sanctioning the non-compliance with the tribunal's directions as to confidentiality is to take the party's behaviour into consideration in the cost decision.[210] Article 42(1) of the Arbitration Rules (2010) provides that the arbitral tribunal is free to apportion particular costs to a party 'if it determines that apportionment is reasonable, taking into account the circumstances of the case'. One of these circumstances is party conduct.[211] Article 42(2) of the Arbitration Rules (2010) gives the arbitral tribunal the possibility of issuing costs decisions in the course of the arbitration, so that it could use such costs decisions as sanctions.

183. In ICSID arbitration, arbitral tribunals can also take into consideration the misconduct of parties in the apportionment of costs and in practice do so.[212]

184. The arbitral tribunal in *Pope & Talbot Inc.* v. *Canada* found the claimant in breach of the confidentiality order issued earlier in the arbitration, because its counsel had disseminated to the press a letter he had received in error by counsel to the respondent. The arbitral tribunal directed the claimant to pay USD 10,000 to the respondent under the cover of a cost decision. The *Pope & Talbot* tribunal did little to conceal that this decision on costs was in fact a sanction of the claimant's (or rather its counsel's) behaviour.[213] In the same arbitration, Canada had revealed documents in the scope of an access to information request, although the arbitral tribunal had explicitly designated these documents as being confidential and prohibited Canada from making them

[209] See e.g. the solution retained by *Apotex Holdings Inc.* (n. 7) Addendum; *Clayton* (n. 120) Procedural Order No. 2 (Confidentiality Order) [11]–[14].

[210] Reed (n. 208) 100. [211] Caron and Caplan (n. 193) 871–3.

[212] See Christoph H. Schreuer, *The ICSID Convention: A Commentary* (Cambridge University Press, 2001) 1227–32; Lucy Reed, Jan Paulsson and Nigel Blackaby, *Guide to ICSID Arbitration* (Kluwer Law International, 2011) 156.

[213] *Pope & Talbot Inc.* v. *Canada*, Decision by the Arbitral Tribunal (27 September 2000) [11]–[13] www.italaw.com/sites/default/files/case-documents/ita0677.pdf.

available. As Canada had not adhered to this order, the arbitral tribunal took this behaviour into consideration in its award on costs.[214]

185. In summary, the Rules give no direction on how the exceptions in Article 7 shall be enforced and a non-compliance sanctioned. The arbitral tribunal will have to do so taking recourse to the means at its disposal under the applicable arbitration rules.

9.13 The need for a procedural order on transparency

186. As we have seen above, Article 7 of the Rules directs the arbitral tribunal to make the necessary arrangements in connection with exceptions to transparency. While at some points Article 7 of the Rules directs the arbitral tribunal to take a certain approach, it nonetheless leaves much to the arbitral tribunal to decide when it comes to the administrative and logistical details of such arrangements. In many cases it will therefore be necessary to provide a comprehensive framework for this issue in the arbitration.

187. The scope of such a transparency order will largely depend on three factors:

- first, the wording of the underlying treaty, superseding the Rules;
- second, the nature of the case; and
- third, the behaviour of the parties.

188. For example, the Peru–United States Trade Promotion Agreement does contain a very detailed provision not only regarding transparency, but also regarding the procedure the arbitral tribunal and the parties are to follow to detect, redact and protect confidential or protected information.[215] In view of those detailed treaty provisions, the arbitral tribunal in *The Renco Group, Inc.* v. *The Republic of Peru* did not see it necessary to address the issue of public access and the limits thereto further than by simply referring to the treaty provisions.[216]

[214] *Ibid.*, Award in Respect of Costs (26 November 2002) [11] http://italaw.com/sites/default/files/case-documents/ita0688.pdf.

[215] Articles 10.21, 22.2 and 22.4 of the Peru–United States Trade Promotion Agreement (12 April 2006) www.ustr.gov/trade-agreements/free-trade-agreements/peru-tpa/final-text.

[216] *The Renco Group, Inc.* v. *Peru*, ICSID Case No. UNCT/13/1, Procedural Order No. 1 (22 August 2013) http://italaw.com/sites/default/files/case-documents/italaw5006.pdf; see also the discussion regarding transparency during the first session of the arbitral tribunal held on 18 July 2013, Transcript of the First Session of the Arbitral Tribunal, 114:4–119:4 http://italaw.com/sites/default/files/case-documents/italaw3266.pdf.

Most treaties will not, however, provide such a comprehensive regulation of the matter.

189. On the other hand, the nature of the case will have an impact on the extent of a possible transparency order. Where the case involves delving into sensible areas where many different issues of confidential or protected information have to be considered, it might be valuable to set a more comprehensive set of rules from the start to avoid later delay during the procedure.

190. Finally, the approach of the parties will be of significant importance. Some parties tend to include the media and the public in their dispute resolution strategy.[217] Where mediatisation of the dispute is an issue, the arbitral tribunal might want to establish a clear level playing field for the parties from the start.

191. As we have seen, the framework provided for the protection of confidential or protected information in the Rules can in some instances become obsolete if the national laws of a respondent State do not provide for the same protection as Article 7 of the Rules.[218] In such instances it might be adequate to set the record straight from the start and to provide, if possible, for ways to ensure the respect of any confidentiality duty under Article 7 of the Rules.[219] At least this would ensure that the parties are aware of the *de facto* protection they can (or cannot) expect from their counterpart. Otherwise the parties might rely on the protection provided for in Article 7 of the Rules, when in fact such protection is not given.

192. A 'catch all' template of a transparency order is difficult to provide, as such an order will have to be carefully crafted around the specifics of the particular case. An arbitral tribunal might, however, want to draw inspiration from the work of past tribunals when contemplating an order regulating public access for the sake of the exceptions in Article 7 of the Rules.[220]

[217] Meg Kinnear and Aïssatou Diop, 'Use of the Media by Counsel in Investor-State Arbitration' in Albert Jan van den Berg (ed.), *Arbitration Advocacy in Changing Times*, ICCA Congress Series, 2010 Rio Volume 15 (Kluwer Law International, 2011) 40.

[218] See above, section 9.10. [219] See above, section 9.10.

[220] Such as, e.g., *Clayton* (n. 120) Procedural Order No. 2 (Confidentiality Order); *Philip Morris Asia Limited* (n. 64); *Apotex Holdings* (n. 7); *Windstream Energy LLC* v. *Canada*, Confidentiality Order (16 December 2013) www.italaw.com/sites/default/files/case-documents/italaw1587.pdf; *Detroit International Bridge Company* (n. 127) Confidentiality Order (27 March 2013) www.international.gc.ca/trade-agreements-accords-commerciaux/assets/pdfs/disp-diff/detroit-po-07.pdf.

10

Article 8. Repository of published information

KATHLEEN CLAUSSEN*

The repository of published information under the Rules on Transparency shall be the Secretary-General of the United Nations, or an institution named by UNCITRAL.

10.1 Introduction

1. The efforts in the area of transparency by the United Nations Commission on International Trade Law (UNCITRAL) Working Group II (Arbitration and Conciliation) (WG) fill a void that has plagued the international arbitration community for several years. Although many cases will remain confidential despite these advancements, the Rules take important steps to make more arbitral proceedings public.

2. While the Rules generally create and encourage transparency in the public interest, the most valuable tool to achieve this overall goal will be the repository – a searchable electronic database – set out in Article 8. In just twenty-four words, Article 8 breathes life into the other Articles by creating a space for access to the information that the Rules make public. In effect, the Rules will only be as successful as the repository's functionality.

3. Under Article 8, the UNCITRAL Secretariat will host a repository containing valuable information about cases to which the Rules apply. Intended to be the first instrument of its kind, the repository breaks new ground by putting an end to the otherwise haphazard collection of arbitral materials available through blogs and subscription services today, which is both unreliable and necessarily incomplete. The repository may

* Kathleen Claussen is a Visiting Assistant Professor at Indiana University Maurer School of Law and Legal Counsel at the Permanent Court of Arbitration in The Hague. She previously served as a Visiting Scholar at the Lauterpacht Centre for International Law, and holds degrees from Yale Law School, Queen's University Belfast, and Indiana University.

serve as a highly significant resource not just by bringing more cases within the reach of the average citizen, but also by filling this void.

4. This brief chapter examines Article 8, its origins, and the intentions behind it, as well as its possible significance.[1] It argues that the repository serves two functions. First, and true to the term 'repository', it serves the basic role of acting as a container for all the information to be made known through the other Rules.[2] Second, the chapter argues that the establishment of an effective repository may have the consequence of re-shaping the practice or the jurisprudence of the 'system' of international arbitration by making a wider range of case decisions more accessible than ever before. The repository will not only allow the general public to easily locate information on cases of interest, but it will also serve as a valuable legal tool for lawyers, allowing them to develop an argument based on past decisions. This trend may, in turn, either contribute to, or challenge, the increasing consistency in decision-making that has become a systemic value and has been heralded as enhancing the system's legitimacy both within the profession and towards the public at large.

5. Put differently, without the repository, the Rules do not amount to much. Article 8 is, in some ways, the *pièce de résistance* of the entire regime the Rules set out to create. Because earlier Articles rely on the repository as the holder of the information, without it, there is no central location for information. At the same time, however, the text of Article 8 is hardly profound or even reflective of any of the values underlying the Rules. It simply names and assigns the task of holding the information mandated by earlier Articles to an entity upon which the Rules regime is intended to rest.

10.2 Background and purpose

6. As reported by the United Nations Conference on Trade and Development (UNCTAD), in 2013 alone fifty-seven new investment arbitration cases were filed.[3] The Permanent Court of Arbitration (PCA) and the

[1] It will do so while also asking: for whom? and why? These questions are reminiscent of those raised by Julie Maupin in her chapter 'Transparency in International Investment Law: The Good, the Bad and the Murky' in Andrea Bianchi and Anne Peters (eds.), *Transparency in International Law* (Cambridge University Press, 2013).

[2] The origin of the word is 'repositorium' – that in which anything is placed; an abundant supply or source; storehouse.

[3] UNCTAD, 'Recent Developments in Investor-State Dispute Settlement (ISDS)' (1 April 2014) IIA Note No. 1 http://unctad.org/en/PublicationsLibrary/webdiaepcb2014d3_en.pdf.

International Centre for Settlement of Investment Disputes (ICSID) each recorded about forty new such cases.[4] Regardless of the exact figure, it is clear that the number of investor-State cases past and present is high and the stakes are even higher.

7. In the early days of the WG's study of the transparency 'problem', it identified different approaches taken by investment agreements to the availability of documents in an arbitration. In the Secretariat's original note on the subject to the WG, it stated that 'dispute resolution clauses . . . usually provide that documents submitted to, or issued by, the arbitral tribunal shall be publicly available, unless the disputing parties agree otherwise, subject to the deletion of confidential information'.[5] In fact, more often than not, investment instruments are silent on publicity or confidentiality when it comes to dispute resolution.[6] This silence has led to controversy in the early stages of cases in which the parties to the dispute may take different views as to confidentiality, and where the tribunal may not feel empowered by the applicable rules to direct more publicity when the parties have agreed to none. This problem does not arise in the same way in ICSID cases where at least basic information on cases is publicly available on the ICSID website.[7] Among UNCITRAL cases, however, the practice on publicity and transparency varies widely.

8. In most instances, UNCITRAL cases are not made known in any formal way, which is especially problematic in the absence of a repository cataloguing them. An award may be made public after its issuance by one side, or the parties may have agreed in advance to make the award public.[8]

[4] Permanent Court of Arbitration, 'Annual Report 2013' www.pca-cpa.org; ICSID, 'ICSID Caseload Statistics', 2014-1 https://icsid.worldbank.org/ICSID/FrontServlet?requestType=ICSIDDocRH&actionVal=CaseLoadStatistics.

[5] UNCITRAL, 'Settlement of commercial disputes: Preparation of rules of uniform law on transparency in treaty-based investor-State dispute settlement' (2010) UN Doc. A/CN.9/WG.II/WP.160 [8].

[6] The lack of such provisions may be seen by carrying out a general review of BITs concluded over the last ten years. While some include provisions on transparency for investors and vis-à-vis investment laws, they say very little about publicity of any dispute settlement proceedings.

[7] See ICSID Cases https://icsid.worldbank.org/ICSID/FrontServlet?requestType=CasesRH&actionVal=ShowHome&pageName=Cases_Home.

[8] See e.g. *Bilcon* v. *Canada*, NAFTA dispute administered by the Permanent Court of Arbitration, Procedural Order No. 2, dated 4 May 2009 http://pca-cpa.org/showpage.asp?pag_id=1341.

In other cases, documents such as an award, other decisions or submissions may be leaked by one side.

9. Public availability or release is only one piece of a larger initiative related to ease of access, however. The instruments that do make reference to publicising an award or the existence of a dispute, such as the North American Free Trade Agreement (NAFTA), only make that particular document information available and do not go so far as to make all cases arising under that instrument available in a single location.[9] These complicated circumstances have led to the creation of ad hoc 'repositories' – personal or professional services that endeavour to collect awards or other documents from cases and make them publicly available.[10]

10. As discussed elsewhere in this volume,[11] the NAFTA provides for publication of awards where Canada or the US acts as a respondent; a resolution passed by the treaty parties in 2001 resolved to make available even more information from each case so that today the public has access to a wide range of documents from NAFTA dispute resolution.[12] While Canada and the US host websites with documents from their several cases under these and some similar instruments (and refer to their sites as 'repositories'), one must dig through several hard-to-follow links on each State's website to download documents of interest; even then, those documents are merely posted and no mechanism exists on the pages to search inside those documents. It should be no surprise that Canada and the US were, therefore, strong advocates for the Rules.[13] Likewise, the Dominican Republic–Central America–United States Free

[9] As discussed in more detail below, the Canadian government provides links to pending and past cases on its website, although these are often scattered on other pages, sometimes outside the government website. See Department of Foreign Affairs, Trade and Development Canada, 'Cases filed against the Government of Canada' (2014) www.international.gc.ca/trade-agreements-accords-commerciaux/topics-domaines/disp-diff/gov.aspx?lang=eng.

[10] See e.g. ITA Law: www.italaw.com/about.

[11] See Maxi Scherer, Markus Gehring and Dimitrij Euler, 'Introduction'.

[12] NAFTA Free Trade Commission, 'Notes of Interpretation of Certain NAFTA Chapter 11 Provisions' (31 July, 2001) part A www.naftaclaims.com. See a longer discussion in Julie Maupin, 'Transparency in International Investment Law: The Good, the Bad and the Murky' in Andrea Bianchi and Anne Peters (eds.), *Transparency in International Law* (Cambridge University Press, 2013).

[13] They also advocated expanding the reach of the Rules. See Lise Johnson, 'Inching Toward Consensus: An Update on the UNCITRAL Transparency Negotiations' (30 October 2012) *Investment Treaty News* www.iisd.org/itn/2012/10/30/inching-towards-consensus-an-update-on-the-uncitral-transparency-negotiations/.

Trade Agreement (CAFTA-DR) provides for public hearings, among other measures, as does the latest US Model BIT (2012).[14]

11. In the absence of institutional case repositories, some commercial providers have sought to create case search tools, seeing a need and being aware of lawyers hungry for easy access to information. The popular legal search engines were slow to pick up this trend, though today both LexisNexis and Westlaw have something akin to a database of investment treaty decisions. New services have emerged, such as the Investor State Law Guide; even other UN bodies such as UNCTAD created case databases – some of these free, some by subscription only.[15] What has resulted has been an unsystematic collection of tools. Most of these service providers, at least those that charge subscription fees, cater to the legal community with less interest in serving a broader transparency goal.

12. Why have more institutions not stepped up to fill the void in the public interest? It is often advantageous to an institution to make its administration of a case known to enhance its own reputation. However, the institution would not be able to do so without permission from the parties and the tribunal. With little leverage to act on, the institution may not be in a position to convince those involved to make that choice. A further limitation is the capacity and budget to realise such a goal. Even ICSID, with its greater public exposure, lacks a searchable repository of its cases with the same degree of flexibility as that of search engines used in other areas of the legal profession.

13. Without a prompt in an underlying instrument towards transparency, we have seen very little movement in this area. The tide may be changing, though; a paradigm shift may be underlying the movement towards the realisation of the Rules. For example, while States may have previously opted for confidentiality on the basis that an unfavourable decision could be used against them, transparency may also be a way to highlight abusive claims by some corporations. Transparency could help the system to function better, bringing it to the attention of broader constituencies. Even if such a movement is underway, as stated by the UNCITRAL Secretariat, '[i]n general, [international investment]

[14] Dominican Republic–Central America–United States Free Trade Agreement (adopted 2004, entered into force 2006) (CAFTA-DR), Article 10.21; US Model BIT, Article 29.

[15] See e.g. www.investorstatelawguide.com/; http://unctad.org/en/pages/DIAE/International%20Investment%20Agreements%20%28IIA%29/IIA-Tools.aspx; www.italaw.com/.

agreements do not provide details on the manner in which the information is to be conveyed to the public'.[16] Herein lies the prompt for Article 8.

10.3 Origins of the registry concept

14. From the WG's first meeting in October 2010, the repository was on the list as an item or task for inclusion.[17] When options were first considered as to who or what would host such a thing and how it would collect case information, two suggestions were made by delegates. The first suggestion was for any State involved in an arbitration to publish information on the website of its relevant ministries; the second idea was for the creation of a central registry.

15. Regarding the first suggestion, a divergence was noted in the experience of States, some of which had the 'right channels in place' to publicise such information, whereas for less experienced States, 'that option would be practically difficult to implement'.[18] Concerning the option of establishing a central registry, the UNCITRAL Secretariat and the PCA were mentioned as possible hosts.[19] It was further noted that the Office of Legal Affairs of the United Nations, to which the UNCITRAL Secretariat belongs, had 'experience in handling comparable types of services, including the publication of instruments of deposits of ratifications, access or acceptance of international conventions'.[20] Through its Secretary-General, the PCA also confirmed its readiness to provide such services, citing its long-standing practice of administering UNCITRAL cases and its work already underway to create an electronic database of an appropriate nature, independent of the Rules initiative.[21]

16. The WG generally felt that there was a need to better delineate the role that such a database would play before deciding whether parties or other entities should be entrusted with that task. Several questions circulated with respect to the possibilities for such a repository. For example, it was questioned whether the registry or repository would also have to make a *prima facie* examination of the information received to determine whether the case fell under the scope of application of the

[16] UNCITRAL (n. 5) UN Doc. A/CN.9/WG.II/WP.160 [10].

[17] UNCITRAL, 'Report of Working Group II (Arbitration and Conciliation) on the work of its fifty-third session' (2010) UN Doc. A/CN.9/712 [36].

[18] *Ibid.* [37], [73]. [19] *Ibid.* [37], [73]. [20] *Ibid.* [75]. [21] *Ibid.*

legal standard on transparency.[22] Likewise, delegates asked whether the registry would be in a position to make judgments that could be viewed as substantive in nature, such as whether there was a valid arbitration agreement in each case.[23] Other questions included whether the scope of the repository would extend to cases arising under contracts between States and investors, under national investment laws or under other instruments.[24] In that regard, it was further questioned whether the registry would be in a position to refuse publication of such cases.[25]

17. By February 2011, the Secretariat prepared a draft Article based on the hypothesis that the respondent State would be responsible for making the information public, unless the WG subsequently decided to establish a repository of published information.[26] At the WG's next meeting, a concern was expressed as to whether establishing a 'neutral registry' fell within the mandate of the WG or of UNCITRAL itself.[27] It was, however, generally agreed that discussion of a neutral registry 'should be considered as an integral part of the mandate received from the Commission to prepare a workable legal standard on transparency in treaty-based investor-State arbitration'.[28] As recorded by the Secretariat 'the existence of a central registry would be crucial to provide the necessary level of neutrality in the administration of a legal standard on transparency'.[29]

18. In October 2011, three very different proposals for the 'registry' were considered, differing principally as to 'who' would host the database.[30] The first proposal was to establish a single independent or free-standing registry. The second proposal set up a list of arbitral institutions that could fulfil the function of a registry:

> 1. In case the arbitral procedure is administered by one of the following institutions, that institution shall be in charge of making information available to the public pursuant to the Rules on Transparency.

[22] UNCITRAL, 'Report of Working Group II (Arbitration and Conciliation) on the work of its fifty-fourth session' (2011) UN Doc. A/CN.9/717.
[23] UNCITRAL (n. 25) UN Doc. A/CN.9/717; UNCITRAL (n. 20) UN Doc. A/CN.9/712.
[24] UNCITRAL (n. 25) UN Doc. A/CN.9/717; UNCITRAL (n. 20) UN Doc. A/CN.9/712.
[25] UNCITRAL (n. 20) UN Doc. A/CN.9/712 [74].
[26] UNCITRAL (n. 25) UN Doc. A/CN.9/717. [27] *Ibid.* [148]. [28] *Ibid.* [148].
[29] *Ibid.* [150].
[30] See UNCITRAL, 'Report of Working Group II (Arbitration and Conciliation) on the work of its fifty-fifth session' (2011) UN Doc. A/CN.9/736.

> 2. In case the arbitral procedure is administered by one of the following institutions, that institution shall be in charge of making information available to the public pursuant to the Rules on Transparency.[31]

19. A third proposal followed the procedure for the designation of an appointing authority as contained in the Arbitration Rules (2010), 'i.e. disputing parties would agree on the choice of a registry and in case they could not agree, an institution would designate the registry'.[32]

20. Consensus was reached that the UN Secretariat would host the registry if possible;[33] if not, it was recalled once again that certain arbitral institutions had expressed an interest and a readiness to create such a system.[34]

21. At that point also, the WG asked the Secretariat to provide information on the cost of a database in cooperation with the arbitral institutions that had expressed an interest in the matter. Thus, in late 2011, the Secretariat approached several arbitral institutions to seek their responses to the following four questions:

> (1) How much do you estimate it would initially cost your organization to put in place an online public registry system (either through tailoring existing electronic systems or developing a new system)?
> (2) How much do you estimate the registry would cost your organization on an annual basis? Please, consider the costs of staff, electronic publication of case documents, data security, preservation of paper documents, server and system maintenance and any other recurrent expenses.
> (3) How would your organization expect to cover the costs of the registry system (e.g., by charging a fee to parties to the dispute)?
> (4) If your organization would expect to charge a fee to parties, how much do you estimate that fee would be?

22. Comments from the organisations reflected a wide spectrum of responses with cost estimates for the creation of the database ranging from 0 to €150,000.[35] If the UN Secretariat were to act as a unique registry provider, the estimated one-time cost of establishing the online

[31] *Ibid.* [131]. [32] *Ibid.* [132].

[33] UNCITRAL, 'Settlement of commercial disputes: preparation of a legal standard on transparency in treaty-based investor-State arbitration' (2011) UN Doc. A/CN.9/WG.II/WP.166/Add.1.

[34] UNCITRAL (n. 25) UN Doc. A/CN.9/717 [148].

[35] See UNCITRAL, 'Settlement of commercial disputes: preparation of a legal standard on transparency in treaty-based investor-State arbitration' (2011) UN Doc. A/CN.9/WG.II/WP.170 and (2011) UN Doc. A/CN.9/WG.II/WP.170/Add.1.

system was said to be €27,000. The estimated cost of system maintenance, technical support and data hosting would be €7,000 per year.[36]

23. These responses led to the following proposal from the Secretariat in early 2012, which seemed to retreat from the earlier consensus on the UN Secretariat as the host institution:

Article 9. Repository of published information

1. Draft article 9 — Repository of published information

Option 1

... shall be in charge of making available to the public information pursuant to the Rules on Transparency. [Other services to be determined, such as storage of documents].

Option 2

1. If the arbitral proceedings are administered by an arbitral institution, that institution shall be in charge of making information available to the public pursuant to the Rules on Transparency. [Other services to be determined, such as storage of documents].
2. If the arbitral proceedings are not administered by an arbitral institution, the respondent shall designate an arbitral institution among the list of institutions in annex, which shall fulfil the functions referred to in paragraph 1.[37]

24. If Option 2 were to have been selected, the WG would have considered whether and how the annex could be updated on a regular basis by UNCITRAL. Again, the WG considered a role for UNCITRAL in coordinating or standardising registry qualities across these several institutions.[38] The Secretariat also proposed that under Option 2, the choice of the institution be made by the respondent.

25. The February 2013 meeting worked through many of the outstanding details related to the registry. The WG took a final decision at that time that its preference would be to use a single institution rather than to create a system whereby various institutions would maintain their own databases under the management of UNCITRAL,[39] agreeing that

[36] UNCITRAL (n. 17) UN Doc. A/CN.9/WG.II/WP.169/Add.1. [37] *Ibid.*

[38] UNCITRAL, 'Report of Working Group II (Arbitration and Conciliation) on the work of its fifty-seventh session' (2012) UN Doc. A/CN.9/760.

[39] UNCITRAL (n. 18) UN Doc. A/CN.9/765.

UNCITRAL would be best positioned but taking note of ICSID and PCA's willingness if UNCITRAL could not take on the task. The WG also considered once more the possible costs, including the retention of a staff member to manage the site, and the possibility of implementing a cost recovery mechanism.

26. The WG also made clear its intention that the repository would have immunity from legal process, which would have been automatic if it were administered by certain, but not all, of the proposed institutions. It considered, without deciding, whether a waiver of liability clause would be needed.

27. In late 2013, with the finalisation of the Rules, the UNCITRAL Secretariat was given the option of locating the necessary funding by 1 April 2014, when the Rules came into effect, for creating and sustaining the repository. If it were unable to do so, one of the arbitral institutions would probably have been charged with that role. UNCITRAL was able to locate the funding and launched the repository in late spring 2014.[40]

10.4 Textual analysis

28. To play off a familiar expression, the text of Article 8 as adopted (the shortest of any of the Articles) leaves much to be defined. In a sense, it feels less like a rule and more like a notice. With so few words, one is left wondering what the repository will entail, and perhaps even, what a repository is at all. Likewise, the Article discusses 'published information' without clear reference to what 'information' is intended. At least on the latter question, 'information' appears to capture all the documentation intended to be published under the earlier Articles of the Rules, such as the information submitted under Article 2, documents published under Article 3 and awards under Article 4. The Rules do not foresee the publication of recordings of public hearings, but they also do not prohibit it; it is not clear from the text of Article 8 whether the repository would include such recordings.[41] The *travaux* confirm that the WG intended that the guidelines on the functioning of the repository (which they occasionally also refer to as the 'registry') would be drafted by the entity

[40] The repository is available at www.uncitral.org/transparency-registry/registry/index.jspx. As of the date of publication of this volume, it still had not been populated.

[41] UNCITRAL, 'Settlement of commercial disputes: preparation of a legal standard on transparency in treaty-based investor-State arbitration' (2012) UN Doc. A/CN.9/WG.II/WP.169/Add.1.

responsible for the registry's sponsorship and upkeep.[42] The UNCITRAL Secretariat recently issued some preliminary guidelines with guidance to disputing parties as to how to submit information.[43]

29. Questions left unanswered in the WG discussions concerned some of the most critical matters, such as those of governance, language and a mechanism to verify the legitimacy of the documents submitted. One discussion not reflected in the text, but which participants noted in the final days, was that all submitted decisions would be included the repository, making it a non-derogable condition within the application of the Rules. This choice was made despite concerns from arbitral institutions that this lack of discretion could be unwise in terms of what may be necessary to ensure quality and legitimacy, among other factors.[44] Basic questions with an impact on the reach and the capacity of the repository, such as what constitutes a treaty-based investor-State arbitration, remain to be clarified. Considering the limitation on the reach of the Rules, which apply only in respect of treaties concluded after 1 April 2014, in the absence of any agreement to include others, if the administrators of the repository secure only case documents from that point forward, the content will be very limited indeed.[45]

30. The last, and perhaps most striking, feature of the Article from its plain text is the lack of any enabling language for the registry or repository to carry out its implicit task and robustly apply the Rules. There is no sanction for non-compliance. The repository will have to define not only its scope and content but also its capacity to implement the other Articles. Should the participants in any given case elect to ignore the repository, the repository administration seems powerless to put any pressure on them to comply.

10.5 Publication to what end?

31. At an early stage, the WG recorded that the purpose of the repository follows the object of the Rules more generally: 'to ensure that information on treaty-based investor-State arbitration cases are made known to the

[42] UNCITRAL, 'Report of Working Group II (Arbitration and Conciliation) on the work of its fifty-eighth session' (2012) UN Doc. A/CN.9/765 [87].

[43] See Guidelines, www.uncitral.org/transparency-registry/en/guidelines.html.

[44] Discussion notes on file with the author.

[45] Krista Nadakavukaren Schefer, 'Article 1', [54]–[59].

interested public'.[46] The task of the WG was to develop a service for widespread access to documents and awards against States. What is more difficult to decipher is where the principal impetus for the transparency 'movement' came from. Was it the non-governmental organisations (NGOs)? Was it States, as predicted above, in a move to protect themselves against abusive claims by powerful corporations? Or did it perhaps come from the legal community, which had seen some cases but wanted to see more to strengthen the system and its practice? The information given by the Secretariat does not answer that question, but suggests that it may have been some combination of forces.[47]

32. Impetus aside, it remains to be seen whether the 'interested public' will take advantage of the opportunity to learn more about published cases. Likewise, it is too early to predict whether the repository's greatest contribution will be that which it makes towards the development of a common law system of precedent for international investment law, or a *jurisprudence constante*, by making more decisions readily accessible for citation, study and argumentation. The increase in the availability of submissions, including while cases are still in progress, is likely to prompt additional references to those decisions as a basis for future arguments. This opportunity therefore raises the question as to whether such references are appropriate, or helpful, in a system that was arguably designed to operate as a series of independent cases without precedential effect.

33. Tribunals have confronted this issue in their decision-making. In *SGS* v. *Philippines*, the tribunal commented:

> In the Tribunal's view, although different tribunals . . . should in general seek to act consistently with each other, in the end it must be for each tribunal to exercise its competence in accordance with the applicable law, which will by definition be different for each BIT and each Respondent State.[48]

[46] UNCITRAL, 'Settlement of commercial disputes: preparation of a legal standard on transparency in treaty-based investor-State arbitration' (2011) UN Doc. A/CN.9/WG.II/WP.162/Add.1.

[47] One may question why the 1976 and 2010 UNCITRAL Arbitration Rules did not include some reference to transparency. Whether due to a lack of consensus at the time, a need for further study or a later realisation of the need for added transparency, some participants in the Working Group have expressed their views that the Arbitration Rules revision in 2010 was a missed opportunity to fully implement a transparency regime.

[48] *SGS Société Générale de Surveillance S.A.* v. *Philippines*, ICSID Case No. ARB/02/6, Decision of the Tribunal on Objections to Jurisdiction, 29 January 2004, para 97.

34. Three years later, the *Saipem* v. *Bangladesh* tribunal approached the issue differently, stating that 'due consideration' should be paid to earlier decisions of arbitral tribunals:

> [The Tribunal] believes that, subject to compelling contrary grounds, it has a duty to adopt solutions established in a series of consistent cases. It also believes that, subject to the specifics of a given treaty and of the circumstances of the actual case, it has a duty to seek to contribute to the harmonious development of investment law and thereby to meet the legitimate expectations of the community of States and investors towards certainty of the rule of law.[49]

35. The idea that tribunals refer to other tribunals for guidance is not unique to investment arbitration. Even at the time of the founding of the PCA, the world's oldest international dispute resolution body, at the beginning of the twentieth century, one commentator bemoaned the individualised, fragmented nature of the system of international dispute resolution:

> The present [institution] (PCA) has not gone far in the direction of establishing and developing international law. Each case is isolated, lacking both continuity and connection with the other. A permanent tribunal, deciding cases in relation with each other, would evidently be a means of unifying the law, and therefore claims on this account the attention of the world.[50]

36. Is unification of the law a goal? Or should it be? While not made explicit in the context of the Rules, one wonders if it will be an inevitable consequence, imbuing or strengthening the value of consistency in this area of law. If the system was made to be purposely pluralistic – is that a value in itself that should be preserved? Or is consistency more important and, if so, why and for whom? The creation of a repository may further demonstrate that the 'system' is no longer as *ad hoc* as once thought. Article 8 moves closer to the centralisation and systemisation of international investment arbitration practice, and raises a qualitative question as to which direction is 'better' for the system, its credibility and its legitimacy.

[49] *Saipem S.p.A.* v. *Bangladesh*, ICSID Case No. ARB/05/07, Award, 30 June 2009, para 90.

[50] Statement by Mr. Joseph Choate, Proceedings of the Hague Peace Conferences, Conference of 1907, Vol. II, First Commission, First Subcommission, Committee of Examination B, first meeting, p. 595.

10.6 Conclusion

37. Article 8 simultaneously completes the transparency function and serves dispute resolution professionals. This repository is more than a container or archive; it may come to serve as a valuable tool for the entrenchment of a system by finally bringing to one central location a means by which to access the galaxy of case law. This would explain the interest among institutions to serve as its host. The repository has the potential to contribute to the constitutionalisation of the investor-State regime, if it is successfully maintained. It is not alone in that effort. Other possible contributions to this effect might be the creation of an appeals court for arbitration – an idea that has been much mooted but has seen no concrete progress.[51] Likewise, the repository will not be the only instrument of its kind. The PCA, for one, has undertaken to create such a database that contains some of the same information as the UNCITRAL repository.[52]

38. While the repository is the critical piece of the Rules that makes effective so many others, an unintended consequence may be its effect on the practice of international investment arbitration, toward a *jurisprudence constante.* The success of the repository, however defined, will depend on the strength of its implementation and its functionality. Article 8 has already begun to come to fruition, but to what extent and with what ease of access remains to be seen.

[51] See e.g. Deepu Jojo Sushama, 'Appellate Structure and Need for Legal Certainty in Investment Arbitration', Kluwer Arbitration Blog (1 May 2014) kluwerarbitrationblog.com/blog/2014/05/01/appellate-structure-and-need-for-legal-certainty-in-investment-arbitration/; Jaemin Lee, 'Introduction of an Appellate Review Mechanism for International Investment Disputes – Expected Benefits and Remaining Tasks' in Anna Joubin-Bret and Jean E. Kalicki (eds.), *Reform of Investor-State Dispute Settlement: In Search of A Roadmap* (Transnational Dispute Management, 2014) www.transnational-dispute-management.com/article.asp?key=2076.

[52] The database was launched in July 2014 and can be accessed at http://pcacases.com/web/.

11

The application of transparency

JOHANNES KOEPP* AND CAMERON SIM**

11.1 Introduction

1. As the preceding chapters illustrate, the UNCITRAL Rules on Transparency in Treaty-based Investor-State Arbitration (the Rules) were adopted following much consultation, deliberation and negotiation. In heralding their arrival onto the field of investor-State arbitration, UNCITRAL expressed with confidence that the Rules 'constitute a robust, innovative set of procedural rules that will make arbitrations involving a State, initiated under an investment treaty, accessible to the public'.[1] Yet when the Rules came into effect on 1 April 2014, they did not become immediately and universally applicable to all treaty-based investor-State arbitrations. Most notably, they did not dispose of the transparency mechanisms provided for in existing treaties and arbitration rules. Rather, for the time being at least, the Rules will coexist alongside arbitration rules utilised in, and other provisions governing, investor-State arbitrations.

2. In this chapter, we voyage through the paradoxically 'murky territory'[2] of transparency to cast light on the likely application of the Rules in the context of investor-State arbitration. This includes consideration of when the Rules apply, when they might be invoked, when any such application or invocation might give rise to conflicts with existing

* Johannes Koepp, Dr iur, LLM, is a Partner at Baker Botts (UK) LLP, London.
** Cameron Sim, LLB, BCL, is an Associate at Baker Botts (UK) LLP, London.
The authors would like to thank Manuel Gomez Carrion and Hayk Kupelyants for their helpful research assistance in the preparation of this chapter.

[1] UNCITRAL Press Release, 'UNCITRAL adopts Transparency Rules for treaty-based investor-State arbitration and amends the UNCITRAL Arbitration Rules', 12 July 2013 www.unis.unvienna.org/unis/pressrels/2013/unisl186.html.

[2] Julie A. Maupin, 'Transparency in International Investment Arbitration: The Good, the Bad and the Murky' in Andrea Bianchi and Anne Peters (eds.), *Transparency in International Law* (Cambridge University Press, 2004) 171.

arbitration rules and other provisions governing the arbitral proceedings, and how any such conflicts are to be resolved.

3. This chapter is comprised of three sections. In the first section, we outline the scope of the application of the Rules, noting the classes of investor-State arbitrations to which the Rules will apply, and might apply. In the second section, we summarise the duties imposed by the Rules on parties and arbitral tribunals alike. These first two sections are intended to bring together and provide an overview of the issues analysed in greater detail in the preceding chapters of this book. In the third section, we move on to consider when conflicts might arise between the Rules and other provisions governing the arbitration, namely the applicable arbitration rules, the treaty pursuant to which the arbitration was initiated, and the laws applicable to the arbitration; and analyse how any such conflicts might be resolved. This includes consideration of the Arbitration Rules, the ICSID Convention and ICSID Rules, the ICSID Additional Facility Rules, the ICC Rules, the LCIA Rules, the PCA Rules and the SCC Rules. We conclude that conflicts concerning the Rules should not be difficult to resolve, because the Rules can easily be accommodated within the existing framework of arbitration rules. As such, the application of the Rules within the framework of existing arbitration rules is unlikely to give rise to interminable conflicts. The true battles will concern disputes over the content of the Rules, as explored in the other chapters of this book.

11.2 Applicability of the Rules

4. The Rules were adopted in a form consistent with viewing them as both mandatory and aspirational. They are mandatory in the sense that their application is compulsory in specified classes of investor-State arbitrations. However, in all other instances, the Rules remain aspirational, as they have been drafted as a stand-alone instrument available for optional use in all other investor-State arbitrations. Whilst Article 1 (9) of the Rules promotes their use in non-UNCITRAL arbitrations by making clear that they may be used in ad hoc proceedings or in investor-State arbitrations initiated under rules other than the UNCITRAL Arbitration Rules, at this stage, it is difficult to predict when the Rules will apply in this aspirational sense. In this section, we offer a checklist approach to the applicability of the Rules.[3]

[3] For detailed analysis of the applicability of the Rules, see Krista Nadakavukaren Schefer, 'Article 1'.

11.2.1 Mandatory application of the Rules

5. As of 1 April 2014, the Rules apply by default to arbitrations that satisfy the following five conditions:[4]

(i) The arbitration is classified as investor-State.
(ii) The UNCITRAL Arbitration Rules govern the arbitration.
(iii) The arbitration was initiated pursuant to a treaty providing for the protection of investments or investors.
(iv) That treaty was concluded, or renewed, on or after 1 April 2014.
(v) The parties to that treaty have not expressly or impliedly excluded the application of the Rules.

11.2.2 Aspirational application of the Rules

6. The Rules only apply by default if the five conditions set out above are satisfied. However, there is likely to be a significant number of other situations in which the Rules also apply where the following five conditions are satisfied:[5]

(i) The arbitration is classified as investor-State.
(ii) The UNCITRAL Arbitration Rules govern the arbitration.
(iii) The arbitration was initiated pursuant to a treaty providing for the protection of investments or investors.
(iv) That treaty was concluded, or renewed, before 1 April 2014.
(v) Either:
    (a) that treaty grants the parties to the arbitration the freedom to select or vary the arbitration rules prescribed, and the parties agree after 1 April 2014 to the application of the Rules; or
    (b) the arbitration rules prescribed by that treaty confer the parties with the right to modify their operation, and the parties agree after 1 April 2014 to the application of the Rules; or
    (c) the parties to that treaty have agreed after 1 April 2014 to the application of the Rules; or
    (d) that treaty is multilateral and the State of the claimant and the respondent State have agreed after 1 April 2014 to the application of the Rules.

7. It will be important for the status of three likely developments to be monitored, which concern a number of additional steps States have

[4] Article 1(1) of the Rules. [5] Article 1(2) of the Rules.

taken, or will take, in order to increase the prevalence of the Rules in investor–State arbitrations.

8. First, and most significantly, on 10 December 2014, the United Nations General Assembly formally adopted the United Nations Convention on Transparency in Treaty-based Investor-State Arbitration (the Convention) to seek to widen the application of the Rules to investor-State arbitrations initiated pursuant to treaties existing prior to 1 April 2014, irrespective of the applicable arbitration rules. In the event that in an investor-State arbitration, both the investor's State and the respondent State have ratified the Convention, then the investor from the non-signatory State has the option to have the Rules apply to the arbitration. This development will significantly increase the numbers of investor-State arbitrations in which the Rules are applied.

9. Second, the issuing of joint or unilateral interpretive statements by States in order to manifest their consent for the Rules to apply in arbitrations arising under investment treaties concluded before 1 April 2014.

10. Finally, the broadcasting by States of unilateral offers of advance consent for the application of the Rules under an investment treaty concluded before 1 April 2014.

11. Furthermore, the Rules may well come to be used in investor-State arbitration initiated under rules other than the Arbitration Rules, or in ad hoc proceedings, which use is promoted by Article 1(9) of the Rules.

11.3 Duties imposed by the Rules

12. In the event that the Rules are applicable to the investor-State arbitration in question, it is helpful to understand how the Rules impact on the proceedings. In this section, we summarise the various duties the Rules impose on the parties, the arbitral tribunal and the repository at all stages of the proceedings, as analysed in detail in the preceding chapters of this book.

11.3.1 Duty imposed on the parties

13. The sole duty imposed by the Rules on the parties themselves concerns disclosure of the commencement of the arbitration.[6] Once the

[6] See further, Giuseppe Bianco, 'Article 2'.

respondent has received the notice of arbitration, each of the disputing parties is to provide a copy of that notice to the repository of published information under the Rules, which is the Transparency Registry at the United Nations in Vienna.[7] The onus then falls on the repository, and not on the parties, to make available basic facts about the arbitration promptly and publicly.[8] At this stage of proceedings, neither the parties nor the repository are required by the Rules to make the actual notice of arbitration publicly available.

11.3.2 Duties imposed on the arbitral tribunal

14. The duties imposed by the Rules on the arbitral tribunal can be grouped into four categories. These are: (i) the disclosure of documents; (ii) the role of third persons; (iii) the role of non-disputing parties; and (iv) the conduct of the hearing.

11.3.2.1 Disclosure of documents

15. The first category of duties imposed by the Rules on the arbitral tribunal concerns the automatic, mandatory and discretionary disclosures of documents created for the purposes of, or relied upon in, the arbitration.[9]

16. The first form of disclosure provides for automatic provision by the arbitral tribunal to the repository of several important documents created in the course of the arbitration by the disputing parties, other parties and the arbitral tribunal.[10] These documents include the notice of arbitration,[11] the response to the notice of arbitration, the statement of claim, the statement of defence, any other written statements or written submissions made by any disputing party, transcripts of hearings, and, if they have been created, a table listing exhibits to the aforementioned documents and expert reports and witness statements (but not the exhibits themselves). In addition, the tribunal must provide the repository with any written submissions made by non-disputing parties to the

[7] Article 2 of the Rules. [8] *Ibid.* [9] See further, Christopher Kee, 'Article 3'.

[10] Article 3(1) of the Rules.

[11] Whilst some of the information contained in the notice of arbitration is to be provided by the parties to the repository prior to the formation of the arbitral tribunal, the actual notice of arbitration will not be provided to the repository until the arbitral tribunal has been constituted and so provides. Therefore, there may be a significant time lag between the arbitration being commenced, and the notice of arbitration being publicly available.

treaty or by third persons. Finally, the arbitral tribunal must provide to the repository any orders, decisions and awards it makes.

17. The second form of disclosure pertains to the mandatory provision of certain documents by the arbitral tribunal to the repository only where a person requests them from the arbitral tribunal.[12] These documents are limited to expert reports and witness statements (but not any exhibits to these documents).

18. The third and final form of disclosure stems from the discretion conferred on the arbitral tribunal to order the publication of various other documents.[13] Upon a person's request, or even upon its own volition, the arbitral tribunal may consult with the disputing parties and then decide whether to place in the public domain exhibits and any other documents which themselves are not subject to the automatic or mandatory disclosure provisions. The tribunal may either make any such documents available at a specified site,[14] or provide them to the repository.[15] Any party requesting such documents from the arbitral tribunal might be inclined to request that they are provided to the repository, as they will then not be liable for the costs of the arbitral tribunal making those documents available to the public. If they are made available to the person through other means, that person is to bear the incurred administrative costs (e.g. photocopying or shipping costs), but not the costs of making those documents available to the public through the repository.[16]

19. All of the automatic, mandatory and discretionary mechanisms for disclosure are subject to the exceptions to transparency contained in Article 7 of the Rules,[17] which seek to prevent disclosure to the public of confidential or protected information[18] and to protect the security interests of States,[19] as well as the integrity of the arbitral process.[20] In the event that the arbitral tribunal determines that information is to be classified as confidential or protected, then, following consultation with the disputing parties, the tribunal must make arrangements to ensure that the information in question is prevented from being made publicly available.[21]

12 Article 3(2) of the Rules.
13 Article 3(3) of the Rules.
14 Article 3(3) of the Rules.
15 Article 3(4) of the Rules.
16 Article 3(5) of the Rules.
17 See further, Thierry Augsburger, 'Article 7'.
18 Articles 7(2) and 7(3) of the Rules.
19 Article 7(5) of the Rules.
20 Articles 7(6) and 7(7) of the Rules.
21 Article 7(3) of the Rules.

11.3.2.2 Third persons

20. The second category of duties imposed by the Rules on the arbitral tribunal is in respect of submissions made by third persons.[22] The arbitral tribunal is empowered in specific circumstances to accept written submissions from a third person who is 'not a non-disputing Party to the treaty', i.e. from a person who is not a signatory party to the treaty pursuant to which the arbitration was initiated, such as an *amicus curiae*.[23] The tribunal must take several factors into consideration in determining whether to grant the third person permission to make written submissions,[24] including any significant interest the third person has in the arbitral proceedings;[25] the assistance that would be afforded by the submission in the tribunal's task of determining a relevant factual or legal issue, but only to the extent that it would bring a perspective, particular knowledge or insight that is different from those of the disputing parties;[26] and any other factors the tribunal determines to be relevant.[27] These other factors must necessarily include those that the tribunal must take into account when exercising its discretion, namely the public interest in transparency in both treaty-based investor-State arbitration generally and, more specifically, in the particular arbitral proceedings themselves; as well as the interests of the disputing parties in a fair and efficient resolution of their dispute.[28]

21. If the arbitral tribunal grants permission to the third party to make a written submission, then the submission must address only matters that fall 'within the scope of the dispute'.[29] Further, the arbitral tribunal must ensure that the third party's submission is not disruptive or unduly burdensome to the conduct of the arbitration, nor unfairly prejudicial to any disputing party.[30] The arbitral tribunal must also provide the disputing parties with a reasonable opportunity to respond to the third party's submission.[31]

11.3.2.3 Non-disputing Parties

22. The third category of duties imposed by the Rules on the arbitral tribunal is in respect of submissions made by parties that are non-disputing parties to the treaty pursuant to which the arbitration has been

[22] See further, Mariel Dimsey, 'Article 4'.
[23] Article 4(1) of the Rules.
[24] Article 4(3) of the Rules.
[25] Article 4(3)(a) of the Rules.
[26] Article 4(3)(b) of the Rules.
[27] Article 4(3) of the Rules.
[28] Article 1(4) of the Rules.
[29] Article 4(5)(d) of the Rules.
[30] Article 4(5) of the Rules.
[31] Article 4(6) of the Rules.

initiated.[32] The arbitral tribunal must accept, or may invite, written or oral submissions in relation to issues of treaty interpretation sought to be made by non-disputing parties to the treaty,[33] but only after consultation with the disputing parties, and only to the extent that any such submissions are not disruptive to or unduly burdensome on the proceedings, nor unfairly prejudicial to any disputing party.[34] Further, the arbitral tribunal may accept written or oral submissions by non-disputing parties on other matters falling within the scope of the arbitration.[35]

23. In deciding whether to accept such submissions, the arbitral tribunal must take several factors into consideration. These factors include the same factors to be taken into account in respect of prospective submissions by third parties.[36] In addition, the tribunal must pay due regard to the need to avoid accepting submissions offered in support of the investor's claim, where doing so would be tantamount to affording diplomatic protection to the investor.[37] If any submissions by a non-disputing party are accepted, then of course the arbitral tribunal must ensure that the disputing parties to the arbitration are given a reasonable opportunity to respond to those submissions.[38]

11.3.2.4 Conduct of the hearing

24. The fourth and final category of duties imposed by the Rules on the arbitral tribunal concerns the conduct of the hearing. The default position is that the arbitral tribunal will hold hearings in public.[39] However, there are three circumstances in which the tribunal must hold part of or all of a hearing in private: where there is a need to protect confidential information;[40] where there is a need to protect the integrity of the arbitral process;[41] and where it is necessary to do so for logistical reasons (such as when the original arrangements for public access are rendered infeasible by a change in circumstances) and the arbitral tribunal has consulted with the disputing parties. In all instances, it is for the arbitral tribunal to determine whether any of these circumstances arise. Significantly, any agreement between the disputing parties that the circumstances are

[32] See further, Martins Paparinskis and Jessica Howley, 'Article 5'.
[33] Article 5(1) of the Rules. [34] Article 5(4) of the Rules. [35] Article 5(2) of the Rules.
[36] Article 5(2) of the Rules. The factors are those specified in Article 4(3) of the Rules.
[37] Article 5(2) of the Rules. [38] Article 5(5) of the Rules.
[39] Article 6 of the Rules. See further, Klint Alexander, 'Article 6'.
[40] Articles 6(2) and 7 of the Rules. [41] Articles 6(2) and 7 of the Rules.

such that a private, or partly private, hearing is warranted is irrelevant to the arbitral tribunal's determination on the matter.

11.3.3 Duties imposed on the repository

25. The repository (which, as mentioned above, is currently the Transparency Register at the United Nations in Vienna) is also subject to duties by virtue of the Rules to provide to the public access to the information it receives.[42] The repository must ensure that the public, on request, is provided with the name of the disputing parties, the economic sector involved and the title of the treaty under which the claim is made.[43] In addition, any of the documents that are provided to the repository (as outlined above) must be made available to the public 'in a timely manner' and in the form and language in which the documents are received.[44]

11.4 Conflicts between the Rules and other provisions governing the arbitration

26. In the event that the Rules are applicable in an investor-State arbitration, the duties summarised in the previous section will not fall to be performed by the parties and the arbitral tribunal unopposed. That is because the Rules will operate alongside other provisions governing the arbitration, including the applicable arbitration rules, the treaty pursuant to which the arbitration was initiated, and the law applicable to the arbitration. As is almost always the case where different rules and laws are operating in parallel to one another, this gives rise to the potential for conflicts to arise between the Rules on the one hand and these other provisions governing the arbitration on the other. In this section, we contemplate when any such conflicts might arise, and how any such conflicts should be resolved. This includes consideration of the Arbitration Rules (as revised in 1976 and 2010), the International Centre for Settlement of Investment Disputes (ICSID) Convention and ICSID Rules, the ICSID Additional Facility Arbitration Rules, the Rules of Arbitration of the International Chamber of Commerce 2012 (ICC Rules), the Arbitration Rules of the London Court of International Arbitration 2014 (LCIA Rules), the Permanent Court of Arbitration

[42] See further, Kathleen Claussen, 'Article 8'.

[43] Article 2 of the Rules.

[44] Article 3 of the Rules.

Rules 2012 (PCA Rules), and the Arbitration Rules of the Arbitration Institute of the Stockholm Chamber of Commerce 2010 (SCC Rules).

27. As a starting point, Articles 1(7) and 1(8) of the Rules pre-empt three situations where a conflict might arise between the Rules and other provisions relevant to the arbitration. These other provisions include: (a) the applicable arbitration rules; (b) the treaty pursuant to which the arbitration was initiated; and (c) non-derogable laws applicable to the arbitration. Broadly speaking, in the event of a conflict, or inconsistency, arising in respect of these three categories, the Rules prevail over the applicable arbitration rules, but are trumped by the relevant treaty provisions or non-derogable laws applicable to the arbitration. In this section, we consider in detail how such conflicts might arise in each of these three situations, and how they should be resolved.

11.4.1 Conflict with the applicable arbitration rules

28. Several sets of arbitration rules are utilised in investor-State arbitration. As noted above, Article 1(9) promotes the use of the Rules in investor-State arbitrations initiated under rules other than the Arbitration Rules, as well as in ad hoc proceedings. In the event that there is a conflict between any set of arbitration rules and the Rules where the latter are applicable, then the Rules trump. Article 1(7) of the Rules provides that the rules are intended to 'supplement any applicable arbitration rules'. However, to the extent that there is a 'conflict' between the Rules and the applicable arbitration rules, it is the Rules that 'shall prevail'.

29. How is it that the Rules can themselves determine that they prevail over the applicable arbitration rules in the event of a conflict? In terms of the legal hierarchy, the Rules sit at the same level as the applicable arbitration rules and, as with the applicable arbitration rules, also work as a procedural mechanism governing the conduct of the arbitration. Regardless of the gateway leading to the application of the Rules, whether by way of mandatory or aspirational application, ultimately the Rules apply only because the treaty or the Convention so stipulate, or the parties to the arbitration so agree. It would be erroneous to accept that the treaty or the parties' agreement permitting the concurrent application of two sets of rules should be seen to give rise to a mutually inconsistent regime governing the arbitral proceedings. Rather, the sensible conclusion is that this is simply an issue of contractual interpretation of the

agreement providing for resolution of disputes by way of investor-State arbitration. The Rules prevail, because they expressly deal with the resolution of conflicts arising with the applicable arbitration rules, which are silent on the issue.

30. We now turn to consider the conflicts that are likely to arise between the Rules and the most prevalent rules used in investor-State arbitration.

11.4.1.1 UNCITRAL Arbitration Rules

31. The Rules have been incorporated into the Arbitration Rules (2010). The new Article 1(4) of the Arbitration Rules, as adopted in 2013 into the 2010 version of the rules, makes clear the link between the Rules and the Arbitration Rules. The new Article 1(4) of the Arbitration Rules (2010) came into force on 1 April 2014 (i.e. the same date on which the Rules came into force). Thus, the Rules are part and parcel of the Arbitration Rules (2010). The scope and manner of application of the Rules is subject to their Article 1, as to which see the above summary in section 11.2 of this chapter. In addition, many arbitrations will continue to be conducted under the Arbitration Rules (1976), which, unlike the Arbitration Rules (2010), do not incorporate the Rules.

32. Article 1(1) of both the 1976 and 2010 Arbitration Rules permits the parties to the arbitration to agree to modify the operation of the Arbitration Rules to their dispute. However, if the Rules are applicable to the arbitration, any such agreement between the parties does not extend to modification of the provisions of the Rules. Article 1(3)(a) of the Rules provides that 'the disputing parties may not derogate from [the Rules], by agreement or otherwise, unless permitted to do so by the treaty'. If the position were otherwise, then the disputing parties would be able to defeat the objectives of the Rules.

33. Two key modifications to the Arbitration Rules result from the application of the Rules.

34. The first modification concerns the publication of arbitral awards. Article 3(1) of the Rules provides that all arbitral awards are to be published, subject to the exceptions to disclosure contained in Article 7. Article 3(1) has the effect of modifying Article 32(5) of the Arbitration Rules (1976) and Article 34(5) of the Arbitration Rules (2010), which provide that awards may only be made public with the consent of the parties. Where the Rules apply, such consent is not required, and publication of the award becomes compulsory.

35. The second modification is in respect of the conduct of hearings. Article 6 of the Rules mandates public hearings, subject to the Article 6 (2) and (3) exceptions, which permit parts of hearings to take place *in camera*. This modifies Article 25(4) of the Arbitration Rules (1976) and Article 28(3) of the Arbitration Rules (2010), which provide for hearings to be held *in camera*, unless the parties reach an agreement to the contrary.

36. In addition to these two modifications, the Rules supplement the Arbitration Rules in two ways.

37. First, Article 1(3) of the Rules confers the arbitral tribunal with the power 'to adapt the requirements of any specific provision of [the Rules] to the particular circumstances of the case', providing standards for the arbitral tribunal's exercise of discretion by permitting any such adaptation only if three conditions are satisfied. First, the arbitral tribunal must have consulted the disputing parties to the arbitration. Second, the change must be necessary to conduct the arbitration in a practical manner. Third, the nature of the change must be consistent with the objective of the Rules. There is nothing which renders Article 1(3) of the Rules inconsistent with the discretion afforded to the arbitral tribunal to conduct the arbitration in 'such manner as it considers appropriate' provided for by Article 15(1) of the Arbitration Rules (1976) and Article 17(1) of the Arbitration Rules (2010). Rather, Article 1(3) of the Rules is *lex specialis*, giving the arbitral tribunal guidelines as to how to exercise the general discretion it otherwise enjoys under Article 15(1) of the Arbitration Rules (1976) and Article 17(1) of the Arbitration Rules (2010).

38. Second, Article 1(5) provides that the Rules do not affect the authority of the arbitral tribunal under the Arbitration Rules to conduct the arbitration in a manner that promotes transparency, for example by accepting submissions from third persons. Article 4 of the Rules empowers the arbitral tribunal in specific circumstances to accept written submissions from third persons, and Article 5 provides the same power in respect of written and oral submissions from non-disputing parties to the treaty pursuant to which the arbitration is initiated. These two articles should be interpreted as a codification of how an arbitral tribunal should proceed in respect of potential submissions by third persons and non-disputing parties to the treaty. Pursuant to Article 1(5) of the Rules, however, these two articles cannot be interpreted as limiting an arbitral tribunal's authority to allow submissions by third parties even if they do not comply with the requirements of Articles 4 and 5. Thus, while an

arbitral tribunal under Article 5 of the Rules does not have the authority to invite a non-disputing party to make a submission, it does seem to have such authority under Article 15(1) of the Arbitration Rules (1976) and Article 17(1) of the Arbitration Rules (2010).

39. This is so despite the fact that the Arbitration Rules do not contain provisions on submissions from third persons. In two cases, however, arbitral tribunals operating under those rules relied on the discretion afforded by (the now) Article 17(1) of the Arbitration Rules (2010)[45] to 'conduct the arbitration in such manner as it considers appropriate' (discussed above) in order to justify accepting submissions from third persons. In *Methanex* v. *United States of America*, the tribunal justified the filing of *amicus curiae* briefs by reference to the public interest in the subject matter of the dispute, as well as the wider considerations of transparency in investment arbitration,[46] but in so doing considered the burden and cost on the disputing parties.[47] Similarly, in *UPS* v. *Canada*, the tribunal, in reaching its determinations on the filing of amicus briefs, stated that it was necessary to bear in mind the wider public interest in the dispute and issues arising from it, as well as considerations of openness.[48] In addition, the tribunal had regard to the need for the just, efficient and expeditious resolution of the case, in a manner not unduly burdensome on the parties, or unnecessarily complicating the arbitral process.[49]

40. It should be emphasised that the factors referred to by the tribunals in the *Methanex* and *UPS* decisions bear similarity to those contained in Article 1(4) of the Rules, which list factors the tribunal must take into account when exercising its discretion. Those factors are the public interest in transparency in both treaty-based and investor-State arbitration generally and, more specifically, in the particular arbitral proceedings themselves; as well as the interests of the disputing parties in a fair and efficient resolution of their dispute.

[45] Article 15(1) of the 1976 Arbitration Rules.

[46] *Methanex Corp.* v. *United States of America*, Decision of the tribunal on petitions from third persons to intervene as 'amici curiae', dated 15 January 2001, at [49].

[47] *Ibid.*, [50].

[48] *United Parcel Service of America Inc* v. *Canada*, Award, 24 May 2007, at para 3. See also the tribunal's decision of 17 October 2011, Decision of the Tribunal on Petitions for Intervention and Participation as Amici Curiae, at [65].

[49] *United Parcel Service of America Inc* v. *Canada*, Award, 24 May 2007, at [69].

11.4.1.2 International Centre for Settlement of Investment Disputes

41. There are two sets of procedural rules used in arbitrations conducted under the auspices of the ICSID. Unlike most arbitration rules, which are designed for commercial arbitrations between private parties, the two sets of ICSID rules were specifically developed for disputes between host States and investors, and provide for a certain degree of transparency.

42. The first set of procedural rules consists of the ICSID Convention,[50] Regulations,[51] Institution Rules,[52] and Rules of Procedure for Arbitration Proceedings (2006) ICSID Rules. This set of rules is used for disputes where the home State of the investor and the host State in question are both parties to the ICSID Convention.

43. The second set of procedural rules consists solely of the ICSID Additional Facility Rules (2006 ICSID AFR).[53] This set is available for use in disputes where either the home State of the investor or the host State in question is a party to the 2006 ICSID AFR. We refer to both sets of rules together as 'the ICSID Rules'.[54]

44. The obligation of the parties to provide to the repository copies of the notice of arbitration pursuant to Article 2 of the Rules supplements existing obligations imposed on ICSID, which is under an obligation to publish basic information about each dispute it administers.[55] The Secretary-General of ICSID is required to maintain a register for each dispute containing basic procedural information.[56] This information includes 'all significant data concerning the institution, conduct, and disposition of each proceeding', which extends to the method of constitution and the membership of each arbitral tribunal.[57] It also

[50] Convention on the Settlement of Investment Disputes between States and Nationals of Other States, 17 UST 1270, TIAS 6090, 575 UNTS 159.

[51] ICSID Administrative and Financial Regulations (2006).

[52] ICSID Rules of Procedure for the Institution of Conciliation and Arbitration Proceedings.

[53] ICSID Rules Governing the Additional Facility for the Administration of Proceedings by the Secretariat of the International Centre for Settlement of Investment Disputes.

[54] It is worth noting that ICSID also administers arbitration proceedings governed by other rules on an ad hoc basis, and so an arbitration administered by ICSID may not necessarily be governed by one of these sets of procedural rules.

[55] Article 5 of the 2006 ICSID AFR provides that Regulations 14–16, 22–30 and 34(1) of the ICSID Administrative and Financial Regulations (2006) shall apply, *mutatis mutandis*, in respect of fact-finding, conciliation and arbitration proceedings under the 2006 ICSID AFR.

[56] ICSID Administrative and Financial Regulations (2006) regulation 23(1).

[57] ICSID Administrative and Financial Regulations (2006) regulation 23(1).

extends to information about requests made in respect of post-award remedies, namely to any requests for the supplementation, rectification, interpretation, revision or annulment of the arbitral award, and to any stay of enforcement.[58] The register containing this information must remain open for inspection by any person.[59] Currently, the Secretary-General allows access to this register through ICSID's website.[60]

45. In addition, ICSID operates under confidentiality obligations in respect of arbitral awards rendered in disputes conducted under its auspices. Article 48(5) of the ICSID Convention provides that ICSID must not publish the arbitral award rendered by the tribunal without the consent of the disputing parties. Article 48(4) of the 2006 ICSID Rules and Article 53(3) of the 2006 ICSID AFR also prohibit ICSID from publishing the award without the consent of the parties (although permit the publication of excerpts of the tribunal's legal reasoning in ICSID publications). These provisions do not conflict with Article 3(1) of the Rules, which requires the arbitral tribunal (as opposed to the arbitral institute) to provide the repository with any orders, decisions and awards it makes. In any event, in practice, ICSID awards are often publicly available, because either the parties tend to consent to publication, or publish the award on their own volition.

46. In arbitral proceedings conducted pursuant to ICSID's first set of procedural rules (i.e. pursuant to the ICSID Convention and the related procedural rules), the parties cannot agree to alter the provisions of the ICSID Convention under which the tribunal operates. Article 44 of the ICSID Convention provides that an arbitration shall be conducted in accordance with Section 3 of the Convention's provisions 'and, except as the parties otherwise agree, in accordance with the Arbitration Rules in effect on the date on which the parties consented to arbitration'. As the arbitration agreement will have included an agreement to incorporate the Rules, any conflict between the Rules, on the one hand, and the ICSID Rules, on the other, must be resolved in favour of the Rules. In contrast, the Rules are trumped by the provisions of the Convention itself.

47. Article 32(2) of the 2006 ICSID Rules and Article 39(2) of the 2006 ICSID AFR empower the arbitral tribunal in identical terms to hold either part or all of the hearing in public, subject to consultation with the Secretary-General of ICSID, and the putting in place of 'appropriate logistical arrangements', alongside 'procedures for the protection of

[58] *Ibid.* [59] See (n. 58) regulation 23(2). [60] See http://icsid.worldbank.org.

proprietary or privileged information'. However, pursuant to these articles, if either party objects to part or all of the hearing being held in public, then the hearing must proceed *in camera*. A direct conflict therefore arises with Article 6 of the Rules, which provides that hearings are to be held in public, and which, according to Article 1(9), 'prevails' over Article 32(2) of the 2006 ICSID Rules and Article 39(2) of the 2006 ICSID AFR. Notably, however, the exceptions to public hearings contained in Article 6(2) and (3) of the Rules are similar to the restrictions imposed on public hearings in Article 32(2) of the 2006 ICSID Rules and Article 39(2) of the 2006 ICSID AFR.

48. Article 37(2) of the 2006 ICSID Rules and Article 41(3) of the 2006 ICSID AFR govern submissions by third parties. The uniform standard governing such submissions is different from the dual standards provided under Articles 4 and 5 of the Rules, which distinguish between participation requests from parties to the treaty underlying the arbitration, and requests from other third parties. The ICSID Rules draw no such distinction. They provide that following consultation with the disputing parties, the arbitral tribunal may allow an 'entity that is not a party to the dispute' (i.e. either a third person or non-disputing party in the sense of Articles 4 and 5 of the Rules) to file a written submission regarding a matter falling 'within the scope of the dispute'.

49. Under the ICSID Rules, in determining whether to accept such a submission, the tribunal must take several considerations into account. First, the extent to which the submission 'would assist the Tribunal in the determination of a factual or legal issue related to the proceeding by bringing a different perspective, particular knowledge or insight that is different from that of the disputing parties'.[61] Second, the extent to which the submission 'would address a matter within the scope of the dispute'.[62] Third, whether the party seeking to make the submission 'has a significant interest in the proceedings'.[63] In addition, under the ICSID Rules, if the arbitral tribunal decides to accept the written submission, then the tribunal is under a duty to maintain the conduct of the proceedings by ensuring that the submission is not disruptive, unduly burdensome or unfairly prejudicial to a disputing party.[64] Further, the

[61] Article 37(2)(a) 2006 ICSID Rules; Article 41(3)(a) 2006 ICSID AFR.
[62] Article 37(2)(b) 2006 ICSID Rules; Article 41(3)(b) 2006 ICSID AFR.
[63] Article 37(2)(c) 2006 ICSID Rules; Article 41(3)(c) 2006 ICSID AFR.
[64] Article 37(2) 2006 ICSID Rules; Article 41(3) 2006 ICSID AFR.

tribunal must afford the disputing parties an opportunity to respond to the submission.[65]

50. These considerations almost mirror those that the arbitral tribunal must take into account under Article 4(3), (5) and (6) of the Rules in deciding whether to accept a written submission from a third person, and in monitoring the impact that submission has on the proceedings. However, other factors the tribunal must take into account under the Rules include those mentioned in Article 1(4) of the Rules, which articulates factors the tribunal must take into account when exercising its discretion. Those factors are the public interest in transparency in treaty-based investor-State arbitration generally and, more specifically, in the particular arbitral proceedings themselves; as well as the interests of the disputing parties in a fair and efficient resolution of their dispute. It is notable that some of these factors were referred to by the arbitral tribunal in *Biwater Gauff (Tanzania) Ltd* v. *United Republic of Tanzania*.[66] In that case, the tribunal was of the view that, in light of the public interest in the dispute,[67] its decision to accept *amicus* submissions was 'an important element in the overall discharge of [its] mandate', and further, 'in securing wider confidence in the arbitral process itself'.[68]

51. However, Article 37(2) of the 2006 ICSID Rules and Article 41(3) of the 2006 ICSID AFR are in conflict with Article 5(1) of the Rules. Article 5(1) compels the arbitral tribunal to accept both written and oral submissions in relation to issues of treaty interpretation, which are offered by parties who are non-disputing parties to the treaty pursuant to which the arbitration was initiated. As regards such submissions, the tribunal has no choice other than to accept the submission, unless it considers the submissions are disruptive to, or unduly burdensome on, the proceedings, or unfairly prejudicial to any disputing party.[69] There is no such compulsion contained in the ICSID Rules, which therefore are trumped by Article 5(1) of the Rules. Pursuant to Article 5(2) of the Rules, the arbitral tribunal may accept written or oral submissions by non-disputing parties on other matters falling within the scope of the arbitration. This also conflicts with the ICSID Rules, as Article 5(2) of the Rules does not limit non-disputing parties to offering written submissions. That said, the factors that the tribunal must take into account in determining whether to accept any such submissions bear similarity

[65] *Ibid.* [66] ICSID Case No. ARB/05/22, Procedural Order No. 5, dated 2 February 2007.
[67] *Ibid.*, at [51]–[52]. [68] *Ibid.*, at [50]. [69] Article 5(4) of the Rules.

to those the tribunal would consider under the ICSID Rules,[70] although they go further and compel the tribunal to consider whether accepting the submission would be tantamount to affording diplomatic protection to the investor.[71] This factor is not mentioned in the ICSID Rules, but must nevertheless be considered by the tribunal, as the Rules take precedence.

11.4.1.3 Permanent Court of Arbitration

52. The PCA Rules are designed for use in arbitrations involving at least one State, State-controlled entity or intergovernmental organisation.[72] They contain two provisions that conflict with the provisions of the Rules in relation to the conduct of the hearing and the disclosure of the award.

53. In terms of the conduct of the hearing, Article 28(3) of the PCA Rules provides that hearings are to be held *in camera* unless the parties agree otherwise. The arbitral tribunal does not have a say in the matter. This provision is rendered inoperable by Article 6 of the Rules, which provides as a general rule that hearings are to be held in public, subject to the exceptions specified in Article 6(2) and (3) of the Rules.

54. As regards disclosure of the award, Article 34(5) of the PCA Rules provides that an award may be made public in four circumstances, the implication being that in all other circumstances it remains confidential. The first circumstance is where all parties consent to public disclosure of the award. The second circumstance is where a party is required to disclose the award in order to comply with a legal duty. The third circumstance is where disclosure is required in order for a party to protect or pursue a legal right. The final circumstance where a party may disclose the award is where it is required to do so in relation to legal proceedings before a court or other competent authority. As these four circumstances are rather limited, Article 34(5) of the PCA Rules conflicts with Article 3(1) of the Rules, which requires automatic provision by the arbitral tribunal to the repository of the award, subject to any necessary arrangements in terms of the protection of confidential or protected information under Article 7 of the Rules. Whether Article 34(5) is disapplied, however, is open to doubt; rather, it may be said that the parties' agreement to apply the Rules constitutes an agreement to publish the award pursuant to Article 34(5) of the PCA Rules.

[70] Article 5(2) of the Rules, cross-referencing the factors listed in Article 4(3).
[71] Article 5(2) of the Rules. [72] Introduction to the PCA Rules.

11.4.1.4 International Chamber of Commerce

55. The Secretary-General of the ICC has stated that the body has made the 'conscious choice' not to include in its arbitration rules an absolute obligation of confidentiality binding on all participants in the arbitral process.[73] Instead, the issue of confidentiality falls to be addressed by the parties and the arbitrators in each case.[74] For these reasons, it is unsurprising that the ICC Rules are mostly silent on confidentiality and prohibitions on disclosure.

56. Article 22(3) of the ICC Rules provides the arbitral tribunal with the power to make confidentiality and protective orders. Subject to the request of any party to the arbitration, this authority extends to the making of orders 'concerning the confidentiality of the arbitration proceedings or of any other matters in connection with the arbitration', and includes 'tak[ing] measures for protecting trade secrets and confidential information'.[75] A confidentiality order may be issued in respect of the confidentiality of the arbitration proceedings, in order to prevent disclosure of information outside the walls of the arbitral process. Similarly, but distinctively, a protective order may be issued before information is disclosed in the arbitral proceedings, in order to preserve the confidentiality of information which a party will subsequently receive from another party in the proceedings.[76]

57. The Article 22(3) power is attenuated, but not emasculated, by the Rules. In circumstances where the Rules are not applicable to the arbitration, Article 22(3) of the ICC Rules empowers the tribunal to make confidentiality and protective orders unless the law applicable to the arbitration prohibits the tribunal from doing so.[77] Where the Rules are applicable, then the power to make confidentiality and protective orders remains, unless either the Rules or the law applicable to the arbitration prohibits the tribunal from doing so. The duties imposed on the arbitral tribunal in respect of the disclosure of documents is one area where conflicts are likely to arise between the broad power under the ICC Rules to make confidentiality and protective orders, and the obligations imposed by Article 3 of the Rules.

[73] Andrea Carlevaris, 'Confidentiality in ICC Arbitration' in Alberto Malatesta and Rinaldo Sali (eds.), *The Rise of Transparency in International Arbitration* (Juris Publishing, 2013) 123, at 125.

[74] *Ibid.*, at 127. [75] Article 22(3) ICC Rules. [76] Carlevaris, n. 73, at 129.

[77] *Ibid.*, at 128.

58. If the arbitral tribunal determines that certain information falls into one or more of the four categories of confidential or protected information, then Article 22(3) of the ICC Rules provides the arbitral tribunal with a useful mechanism in terms of its duty to make arrangements to ensure that the information is prevented from being made publicly available, as required by Article 7(3) of the Rules. Article 7(3) includes three possible arrangements the tribunal might put in place, namely the imposition of time limits within which a party must give notice that it seeks protection of the information;[78] the implementation of procedures for redaction of the information;[79] or the adoption of procedures for holding hearings in private to the extent required to protect the information.[80] The power in Article 22(3) of the ICC Rules for 'tak[ing] measures for protecting trade secrets and confidential information' is broad, and would clearly encompass any of these three possibilities.

59. However, there are certain confidentiality or protective orders that, if issued by the arbitral tribunal, will conflict with the requirements imposed by the Rules. As Article 22(3) of the ICC Rules was drafted in very broad terms, the sole limitation being that the order is issued in respect of a matter 'in connection with the arbitration', there are various matters in respect of which an arbitral tribunal operating under the ICC Rules in conjunction with the Rules will be prohibited from issuing orders. Stated differently, the Rules limit the discretion that an arbitral tribunal operating under the ICC Rules would otherwise enjoy. In particular, the arbitral tribunal will not be permitted to issue a confidentiality order in respect of the confidentiality of the arbitration proceedings themselves.

60. Article 26(3) of the ICC Rules mandates that persons not involved in the proceedings are not to be admitted to the hearings without the approval of both the arbitral tribunal and the parties. In other words, ICC arbitrations are to be held *in camera*, unless the parties agree otherwise, and the tribunal does not object. Where the Rules apply, then the parties have agreed otherwise, and the tribunal cannot object to this, as Article 6 (1) of the Rules provides for public hearings. This is subject to the limitations contained in Article 6(2) and (3) of the Rules, which provide for part of the hearing to be held in private where it is necessary in order to protect confidential information or the integrity of the arbitral process, or for logistical reasons. Therefore, Article 26(3) of the ICC Rules is rendered inapplicable in circumstances where the Rules apply. Unlike in

78 Article 7(3)(a) of the Rules.

79 Article 7(3)(b) of the Rules.

80 Article 7(3)(c) of the Rules.

a normal ICC arbitration, the parties have no control over the privacy of the proceedings. However, the arbitral tribunal maintains control to the extent that it has the power to determine whether any of the exceptions to transparency contained in Article 6(2) and (3) of the Rules apply.

61. One area of conflict which arises from Article 26(3) of the ICC Rules concerns submissions that third persons and non-disputing parties wish to make in respect of the dispute, which are permitted in specified circumstances by Articles 4 and 5 of the Rules. Article 26(3) merely provides that persons not involved in the proceedings are not to be admitted to the hearings. Technically, therefore, no conflict arises with Article 4 of the Rules, which permits the arbitral tribunal to accept written (but not oral) submissions in respect of the dispute. This is because the third party does not need to be admitted to the hearings in order to provide a written submission. However, Article 26(3) clearly conflicts with Article 5 of the Rules, which provides the tribunal with the power to accept both written and oral submissions from a non-disputing party. It would be impossible for a non-disputing party to make oral submissions without being admitted to the hearings. Thus, in this respect, the Rules trump the ICC Rules.

62. In addition, Article 34(2) of the ICC Rules provides that certified copies of an arbitral award are only to be made available to the parties on their request, and not to anybody else. This conflicts with Article 3(1) of the Rules, which provides that arbitral awards are to be made available to the public, subject to limitations in respect of confidential or protected information, or the integrity of the arbitral process, provided for in Article 7 of the Rules.

11.4.1.5 London Court of International Arbitration

63. In stark contrast to the ICC Rules, the LCIA Rules contain several provisions on confidentiality, some of which conflict with the requirements of the Rules.

64. By virtue of Article 30.1 of the LCIA Rules, the parties to the arbitration undertake to keep confidential all awards, materials created for the proceedings (e.g. submissions) and all other documents produced by another party in the proceedings and which are not publicly available. This undertaking does not apply to circumstances where disclosure is required by legal duty, to protect or pursue a legal right or to enforce or challenge an award in legal proceedings before a state court or other legal authority. This undertaking to maintain the confidentiality of the arbitration is disapplied by Article 2 of the Rules, which obliges the

parties to provide the repository with the notice of arbitration. Similarly, the automatic, mandatory and discretionary disclosure requirements imposed on the arbitral tribunal under Article 3 of the Rules relieve an LCIA arbitrator from any duty of confidentiality he or she would otherwise be subject to.

65. As regards the arbitral tribunal, Article 30.2 of the LCIA Rules guarantees the confidentiality of its deliberations. This provision survives the application of the Rules. The Rules do not seek to shed further light on the reasons the arbitral tribunal comes to the decision made. Further, nothing in the Rules impacts on the refusal of an arbitrator to participate in the award, and does not require that arbitrator to disclose his or her reasons for doing so. Therefore, the disclosure of the refusal of an arbitrator to sign an award must still be made by the other members of the arbitral tribunal under Article 26.6 of the LCIA Rules.

66. Article 30.3 of the LCIA Rules provides that the LCIA must only publish an award, or part of an award, with the written consent of all parties to the arbitration and of the arbitral tribunal. Article 3 of the Rules requires the arbitral tribunal to provide any orders, decisions and awards it makes and therefore conflicts with, and prevails over, Article 30.3 of the LCIA Rules.

67. Finally, Article 19.4 of the LCIA Rules provides that hearings are to be held *in camera*, unless the parties have otherwise agreed in writing, i.e. agreed that the hearing shall be held in public. Article 6(1) of the Rules provides for public hearings. Therefore, where the Rules apply, the parties will have agreed that the hearing shall be held in public, and the tribunal must not direct otherwise, subject to the exceptions to public hearings provided for in Article 6(2) and (3) of the Rules.

11.4.1.6 The Stockholm Chamber of Commerce

68. The SCC Rules contain a blanket provision on confidentiality. Article 46 of the SCC Rules provides that, unless the parties agree otherwise, both the SCC and the arbitral tribunal must maintain the confidentiality of the arbitration and the award.[81] However, these confidentiality obligations do not extend to the parties (although the parties may enter into a confidentiality agreement containing congruent or similar obligations).

[81] The obligation on the SCC to maintain the confidentiality of the arbitration and the award is repeated elsewhere in the SCC Rules. See Appendix I: Organisation: Article 9 of the SCC Rules.

69. The consequences of Article 46 of the SCC Rules vis-à-vis the Rules are twofold. Because Article 46 of the SCC Rules does not impose any confidentiality obligations upon the parties, no conflict arises between Article 46 of the SCC Rules and Article 2 of the Rules in respect of the duty on the parties to provide the repository with the notice of arbitration. However, the obligation of confidentiality imposed on the arbitral tribunal under Article 46 of the SCC Rules conflicts with the tribunal's disclosure obligations under Article 3 of the Rules. The arbitral tribunal must still adhere to the automatic, mandatory and discretionary disclosure requirements imposed on it by Article 3. That said, Article 3 of the Rules does not waive entirely the arbitral tribunal's obligation of confidentiality under Article 46 of the SCC Rules, and any disclosure of documents or information made by the arbitral tribunal exceeding the requirements of Article 3 would amount to a breach of the tribunal's Article 46 confidentiality obligations.

70. Finally, Article 27(3) of the SCC Rules provides that hearings are to be held in private unless otherwise agreed by the parties. As is the case with all of the other arbitral rules we have considered in this section, where the Rules apply, the parties will have so otherwise agreed, subject, of course, to the exceptions to public hearings provided for in Article 6(2) and (3) of the Rules.

11.4.2 Conflict with the relevant treaty

71. The application of the Rules in the framework of investment treaties differs from their application in the framework of arbitration rules in two key respects. First, in the event of a conflict between the Rules and a provision of the investment treaty, the former come off second best. As provided for by Article 1(7) of the Rules, the provision of the treaty prevails. Second, whilst there are only a handful of arbitral rules predominantly used in investor-State arbitration (namely, those we have considered above), there are around 3,000 extant investment treaties pursuant to which an investor-State arbitration might be initiated.[82] In considering potential conflicts between the Rules and the provisions

[82] According to UNCTAD, at the end of 2010, there were 2,807 BITs, and 309 other international investment agreements in existence. See UNCTAD, *World Investment Report 2011: Non-equity Modes of International Production and Development* (United Nations Publishing, 2011) at 100.

of the relevant treaty, we do not propose to consider each and every investment treaty in place. Rather, we illustrate the most likely conflicts that will arise, referencing, where appropriate, provisions in existing treaties.

72. By way of general proposition, it is fair to say that provisions in investment treaties, which fall within the realm of transparency-related issues, are included in order to promote, and not defeat, the aspirations of transparency. By and large, investor-State arbitration originated around the practice of international commercial arbitration, for which the provision of confidentiality and the lack of public participation were traditionally, and still remain, central tenets of this alternative form of dispute resolution. The first investor-State arbitration was decided in 1990. During the ensuing decade, following several investor-State arbitrations that took place under Chapter 11 of the NAFTA, these central non-transparency tenets of proceedings generated hostility, and were perceived as inappropriate for resolution of disputes between an investor and a State (as opposed to between two private parties). As a result, the United States and Canada started the trend, since followed by other States, of including provisions promoting transparency within their subsequent investment treaties.

73. Broadly speaking, provisions in investment treaties that govern public access to procedural documents and awards usually provide for the public availability of documents issued by, or submitted to, the arbitral tribunal, subject to the contrary agreement of the disputing parties, and the protection of confidential information. Moreover, modern investment treaties increasingly require transparency in the light of the perceived crisis of legitimacy in international investment arbitration.[83] Conflicts will therefore be less prevalent between the Rules and treaty provisions as compared to conflicts within the framework of applicable arbitration rules.

74. We highlight below the conflicts that might be seen to arise between treaty provisions and the Rules as regards (i) the disclosure of the arbitration; (ii) the disclosure of documents; (iii) the conduct of the hearing; and (iv) submissions from non-disputing parties and third persons.

[83] See e.g. Susan D. Franck, 'The Legitimacy Crisis in Investment Treaty Arbitration: Privatizing Public International Law Through Inconsistent Decisions' (2005) 73 *Fordham Law Review* 1521; Leon Trakman, 'The ICSID Under Siege' (2012) 45 *Cornell International Law Journal* 603.

11.4.2.1 Disclosure of arbitration

75. Several treaties and model BITs impose obligations on disputing parties similar to those contained in Article 2 of the Rules, which requires the disputing parties to provide the repository with a copy of the notice of arbitration. For example, the 2012 US Model BIT provides that after receiving the notice of intent and the notice of arbitration, the respondent shall promptly make both documents available to the public.[84] This provision appears in several US investment treaties.[85] It seems unlikely that the respondent's obligation under the 2012 US Model BIT to make the notice of arbitration available to the public would be satisfied by providing the repository with it. This is because, pursuant to Article 2 of the Rules, the repository is required to make available to the public only the names of the disputing parties, the economic sector within which the dispute arises and the name of the treaty pursuant to which the arbitration has been initiated. Therefore, the 2012 US Model BIT goes further than the requirements imposed by the Rules. However, as no direct conflict arises with them, both disputing parties would still be required to provide the notice of arbitration to the repository.

11.4.2.2 Disclosure of documents

76. Some investment treaties provide for public access to procedural documents and awards in a manner similar to the disclosure requirements imposed by Article 3 of the Rules. Article 29(1) of the 2012 US Model BIT contains relatively strong transparency obligations as regards disclosure, requiring the respondent to make various documents available to the public, including (a) pleadings, memorials and briefs submitted to the tribunal by a disputing party, non-disputing party or third party; (b) minutes or transcripts of hearings; and (c) orders, awards and decisions of the tribunal. The imposition of this obligation on the respondent does not create a conflict with the automatic, mandatory and discretionary disclosure requirements of the Rules. This is because Article 3 of the Rules requires the tribunal, and not the parties, to provide various documents to the repository. These duties imposed on the arbitral tribunal survive any duties imposed on the respondent.

[84] Article 29(1) 2012 US Model BIT.

[85] See e.g. US–Singapore FTA, Article 15.20 (entered into force 1 January 2004); US–Chile FTA, Article 10.20 (entered into force 1 January 2004); US–Morocco FTA, Article 10.20 (entered into force 18 February 2005); US–Uruguay BIT, Article 29(1) (entered into force 1 November 2006).

11.4.2.3 Conduct of the hearing

77. Some investment treaties provide for hearings to be held in public, subject to the protection of confidential information. Such treaties include many of those negotiated on the basis of the 2012 US Model BIT[86] and the 2004 Canadian Model FIPA.[87] The provisions contained in these treaties in relation to open hearings are broadly similar to those contained in Article 6 of the Rules, which provides, as a default position, that hearings will be held in public, unless it is necessary for part of a hearing to be held *in camera* in order to protect confidential information or the integrity of the arbitral process, or where it is necessary to do so for logistical reasons. Where investment treaties provide for open hearings, there is no conflict with Article 6 of the Rules, unless the provision in the treaty provides that there are no exceptions to open hearings (although it seems inherently unlikely such a provision would have been negotiated by any sensible State).

11.4.2.4 Submissions from non-disputing Parties and third persons

78. There are several treaties that provide the arbitral tribunal with the direct authority to accept submissions from non-disputing parties and third persons (e.g. *amici curiae*). These treaties are primarily those entered into recently by the United States and Canada, and are useful to illustrate potential conflicts that might arise with the Rules in relation to the acceptance of such submissions.

79. Article 28(2) of the 2012 US Model BIT provides that non-disputing parties 'may' provide the tribunal with both oral and written submissions regarding the interpretation of the treaty.[88] Similarly, Article 35 of the Canadian 2004 Model FIPA provides that a non-disputing party to the treaty, on written notice to the disputing parties, 'may make

[86] Article 29(2) 2012 US Model BIT. See e.g. US–Singapore FTA, Article 15.20(2) (entered into force 1 January 2004); US–Chile FTA, Article 10.20(2) (entered into force 1 January 2004); US–Morocco FTA, Article 10.20(2) (entered into force 18 February 2005); US–Uruguay BIT, Article 29(2) (entered into force 1 November 2006).

[87] Article 38(1) 2004 Canada Model FIPA. See e.g. Canada–Colombia FTA, Article 830(2) (entered into force 15 August 2011); Canada–Peru FTA, Article 835(1) (entered into force 1 August 2009); Canada–Jordan FIPA, Article 38(1) (entered into force 14 December 2009).

[88] See e.g. US–Singapore FTA, Article 15.19(2) (entered into force 1 January 2004); US–Morocco FTA, Article 10.19(2) (entered into force 18 February 2005); US–Uruguay BIT, Article 28(2) (entered into force 1 November 2006).

submissions' on a question of interpretation of the treaty, which would seem to extend to written and oral submissions.[89] These provisions are not identical to the position under Article 5 of the Rules, pursuant to which the arbitral tribunal must accept, or may invite, written or oral submissions in relation to issues of treaty interpretation.[90] Under the Rules, the tribunal may only accept any such submissions after consulting with the disputing parties, and only to the extent that the submissions are not disruptive or unduly burdensome on the proceedings, nor unfairly prejudicial to any disputing party.[91] The Rules therefore afford the tribunal with the discretion to refuse to accept submissions from non-disputing parties in specified (albeit fairly limited) circumstances. Under the 2012 US Model BIT and the 2004 Canadian FIPA, in contrast, the non-disputing parties have a procedural right to make submissions on questions concerning the interpretation of the subject treaty. Where these or similar provisions apply, the arbitral tribunal thus lacks the discretionary powers it otherwise enjoys and Article 5 of the Rules no longer applies.

80. The 2012 US Model BIT and the 2004 Canadian Model FIPA also include provisions concerning third party submissions, but not in like manner. Article 28(3) of the US Model BIT provides that the arbitral tribunal 'shall have the authority to accept and consider *amicus curiae* submissions from a person or entity that is not a disputing party',[92] but goes no further than that. This leaves the tribunal with a wide discretion to exercise in relation to such submissions. In contrast, Article 4 of the Rules contains various requirements in respect of submissions from third persons, which may only be written and not oral submissions.[93] Further, the arbitral tribunal must take several factors into account in determining whether to accept the submission.[94] Because the treaty provisions prevail, the restriction on the form of submission contained in Article 4 of the Rules is displaced, and third persons may provide written or oral submissions under congruent treaty provisions. As regards the various factors the tribunal is obliged to take into consideration under the Rules,

[89] See e.g. Canada–Peru FIPA, Article 832 (entered into force 1 August 2009); Canada–Jordan FIPA, Article 35 (entered into force 14 December 2009).

[90] Article 5(1) of the Rules. [91] Article 5(4) of the Rules.

[92] See e.g. US–Singapore FTA, Article 15.19(3) (entered into force 1 January 2004); US–Morocco FTA, Article 10.19(3) (entered into force 18 February 2005); US–Uruguay BIT, Article 28(3) (entered into force 1 November 2006).

[93] Article 4(1) of the Rules. [94] Article 4(3) of the Rules.

the better view is not that the tribunal must ignore those factors, but rather that they specify the contours of the tribunal's authority under the investment treaty in deciding whether to accept the third person's submission. In other words, the treaty provision confers the tribunal with the authority to accept written or oral submissions from third persons, and Article 4 of the Rules provides guidance as to how that authority should be exercised. Where the treaty includes factors to be considered by the tribunal in accepting the submission, such as the US–Chile FTA, which mandates that the third party must identify any other party which is providing financial or other assistance in the preparation of the submission,[95] then any factors not specified in the treaty but contained in the Rules ought nonetheless to be considered by the tribunal in the exercise of its discretion.

81. The position under the 2004 Canadian Model FIPA is less generous to third persons. Article 39(1) provides that any non-disputing party that is a national or enterprise of, or 'has a significant presence in the territory of', one of the disputing parties to the treaty, may apply to the arbitral tribunal for leave to file a written submission. Whilst this narrower class of third persons appears in some Canadian treaties,[96] others largely following the model deviate from it and allow for wider participation, extending to 'any person',[97] or any person who has 'a significant interest in the arbitration'.[98] Article 39(4) of the Model FIPA goes on to list various factors the tribunal must consider in deciding whether to accept a submission, including whether (a) it 'would assist the Tribunal in the determination of a factual or legal issue related to the arbitration by bringing a perspective, particular knowledge or insight that is different from that of the disputing parties'; (b) 'would address a matter within the scope of the dispute'; (c) the party seeking to make the submission 'has a significant interest in the arbitration'; and (d) 'there is a public interest in the subject-matter of the arbitration'. Article 39(5) provides that the arbitral tribunal must ensure that any such submission is not disruptive to the proceedings, and that the disputing parties are not unfairly burdened, or unfairly prejudiced, by the submission. These factors to be considered by the tribunal bear remarkable similarity

[95] US–Chile FTA, Article 10.19(2) (entered into force 1 January 2004); US–Chile FTA, Article 10.19(3) (entered into force 1 January 2004).

[96] See e.g. Canada–Jordan FIPA, Article 39 (entered into force 14 December 2009).

[97] See e.g. Canada–Peru FTA, Article 836 (entered into force 1 August 2009).

[98] See e.g. Canada–Colombia FTA, Article 831 (entered into force 15 August 2011).

to those that would be considered under Article 4 of the Rules in the absence of an overriding provision in the applicable investment treaty.

11.4.3 Conflict with a non-derogable provision of the law applicable to the arbitration

82. The final area of conflict envisaged by the Rules concerns non-derogable provisions of the law applicable to the arbitration. Article 1 (8) of the Rules provides that in the event there is a conflict between the Rules and 'a provision of the law applicable to the arbitration from which the disputing parties cannot derogate', the non-derogable provision prevails over the Rules. Whilst Article 1(8) is helpful to remind parties of this position, in a sense, the provision is surplusage, because the Rules could not determine on their own volition that they prevail over non-derogable laws of the *lex arbitri*.

83. The key issue in respect of which conflicts might have been expected to arise between the Rules on the one hand and the non-derogable provisions of the law applicable to the arbitration on the other concerns duties of confidentiality. However, the statutes regulating the conduct of arbitration in France,[99] Hong Kong,[100] the Netherlands,[101] Singapore,[102] Switzerland,[103] Sweden[104] and the United States[105] do not contain provisions on confidentiality.

84. In England, the provisions of the Arbitration Act 1996 are likewise silent when it comes to confidentiality. However, under English law, there is an implied duty of confidentiality in respect of arbitration, subject to limitations determinable on a case-by-case basis.[106] In the United States of America, the courts have rejected such an implied duty of confidentiality to arbitral proceedings.[107] But regardless of whether

[99] Code of Civil Procedure, Book IV (as amended by Decree No. 2011–48 of 13 January 2011).

[100] Hong Kong Arbitration Ordinance.

[101] Code of Civil Procedure, Book IV.

[102] Singapore Arbitration Act 2002.

[103] Federal Statute on Private International Law Act 1987.

[104] Swedish Arbitration Act 1999: 116.

[105] Federal Arbitration Act (1925).

[106] See e.g. *Dolling-Baker* v. *Merrett* [1991] 2 All ER 890; *Hassneh Insurance Co of Israel* v. *Mew* [1993] 2 Lloyd's Rep 243, especially at 247; *Ali Shipping Corporation* v. *'Shipyard Trogir'* [1998] 1 Lloyd's Rep 643, at 651; *John Forster Emmott* v. *Michael Wilson & Partners Limited* [2008] EWCA Civ 184, at [105]–[107].

[107] See e.g. *Industrotech Constructors Inc* v. *Duke University* (1984) 67 NC App 741, 314 S E 2d 272; *Giacobazzi Grandi Vini SpA* v. *Renfield Corp* (1987) US Dist, LEXIS 1783; see also *United States of America* v. *Panhandle Eastern Corp* (D Del 1988) 118 FRD 346.

common law courts should recognise an implied duty of confidentiality,[108] it being an implied duty, it will always be a derogable provision of law, from which the parties to the arbitration may agree to deviate. An implied duty of confidentiality therefore does not give rise to a conflict within the terms of Article 1(8) of the Rules. Along similar lines, the explicit general duty of confidentiality imposed on arbitrators and parties alike under Spanish law does not give rise to a conflict with the Rules, because the duty of confidentiality is not a non-derogable legal provision.[109]

11.5 Conclusion

85. Where applicable in an investor-State arbitration, the Rules are no chameleon, and will not camouflage themselves within the framework of existing arbitration rules, treaty provisions and the applicable law. True conflicts will arise, but fortunately they should be neither painful nor difficult to resolve. The existing framework of arbitration rules generally applying to investor-State arbitrations can readily be used in conjunction with the Rules.

[108] For a particularly sceptical view, see the decision of the High Court of Australia in *Esso Australia Resources Ltd* v. *The Honourable Sidney James Plowman* (1995) 193 CLR 10.

[109] Spanish Law on Arbitration 2004, Article 24.2.

12

Conclusion: The Rules as a swing of the pendulum?

DIMITRIJ EULER* AND MAXI SCHERER**

12.1 'Public interest' and international investment arbitration

1. As mentioned in the introduction to this book, investment arbitration has the potential of affecting 'public interest' issues, i.e. issues that concern a broader public than just the parties to the dispute.[1] Such public interest issues can concern areas as varied as public health, environmental protection, workers' rights, public governance and sustainable development.

2. The important part that 'public interest' issues play in investment arbitration has raised the question as to whether arbitral tribunals are well placed to deal with these types of disputes. According to some, arbitral tribunals are not well placed to deal with investment disputes since arbitrators can only rely on, and are accountable to, the parties.[2] First, arbitration being an adversarial process, arbitral tribunals first and foremost rely on the disputing parties' written and oral submissions to address the issues before them. This limits the tribunal's access to relevant information. In extreme cases, disputing parties may hide unwanted information from the tribunal, which could, however, have an impact for the public at large. Second, the arbitral tribunal is only accountable to the parties. Its mission stems from, and is defined by, the parties' arbitration agreement. It is limited to resolving the parties' dispute before it. As such, arbitral tribunals are different from State courts, which have a broader mission and (at least in theory) are accountable to the public at large. These points arguably show that

* Dimitrij Euler is a PhD student at the University of Basel.
** Dr Maxi Scherer, MA (Sorbonne), LLM (Cologne), PhD (Sorbonne), is Senior Lecturer at Queen Mary, University of London (School of International Arbitration) and Special Counsel at Wilmer Cutler Pickering Hale and Dorr LLP.

1 See Maxi Scherer, Markus Gehring and Dimitrij Euler, 'Introduction', [5].

2 See Fiona Marshal, 'Defining New Institutional Options for Investor-State Dispute Settlement', September 2009 www.iisd.org/pdf/2009/defining_new_institutional_options.pdf 14–16.

arbitral tribunals, as private bodies, are not well placed to address disputes that involve issues of public interest, such as investment cases.

3. Although such a view has some merit, it is, however, important to bear in mind that, so far, no other viable option of resolving investment disputes exists. Whereas being sued before the courts of another State is a no-go for the host State, reverting to the national courts of the host State is unacceptable for the investor in most cases. While the development of an international court dealing with investment disputes could be a possible solution, it is unlikely that such a court will see the light of day any time soon, due to the immense political issues at stake.

4. Moreover, contrary to the view expressed above, treaty-based arbitral tribunals are arguably well placed to address international or transnational public interest. Their foundation in an investment treaty has the potential to establish accountability vis-à-vis its contracting States. When considering issues of public interest, tribunals should consider them in light of the underlying treaty provisions.

5. In any event, investment arbitration is likely to continue to play an important role in the years and decades to come. In this context, the Rules are of crucial importance, since they may contribute to levelling the playing fields between investors and the host States involved.

12.2 Levelling the playing field

6. It is sometimes said that investment arbitration has an inherently investor-friendly bias.[3] While there is no conclusive evidence to this effect, the (real or perceived) investor-friendliness of arbitral tribunals has contributed to a 'legitimacy crisis' of investment arbitration, described in the introduction of this book.[4] The Rules have the potential to ease some of those concerns in that they level the playing field between investors and host States in several ways.

[3] **Pro**: Olivia Chung, 'The Lopsided International Investment Law Regime and Its Effect on the Future of Investor-State Arbitration' (2007) 47 *Virginia Journal of International Law* 953; Ibironke T. Odumosu, 'The Antinomies of the (Continued) Relevance of ICSID to the Third World' (2007) 8 *San Diego International Law Journal* 345. **Contra**: arguing for a neutral forum, see Jan Paulsson, *Denial of Justice in International Law* (Cambridge University Press, 2005) at 265; Charles N. Brower and Stephan W. Schill, 'Is Arbitration a Threat or a Boon to the Legitimacy of International Investment Law' (2009) 9 *Chicago Journal of International Law* 471.

[4] Maxi Scherer, Markus Gehring and Dimitri Euler, 'Introduction', [3]–[6].

7. First, the (real or perceived) investor-friendliness of arbitral tribunals is arguably counter-balanced by powers granted to host States under the Rules to define their policies as to the adequate level of transparency. For instance, in Article 7(5) of the Rules contains an exception to transparency based on the host State's essential security interests. This provision arguably leaves a broad discretion to the host State's legislative powers. As discussed in Chapter 9, the host State's discretion may, however, in some instances, be limited if seen as abusive or against good faith.[5] Similarly, under Article 7(2)(c), the law governing the transparency exception for 'confidential and protected information' is determined differently depending on whether the information is of the host State or of the investor. Information of the host State is governed by the law of that State, whereas information of the investor is governed by rules determined by the arbitral tribunal. As further explained in Chapter 9, host States therefore indirectly have the power to legislate on the scope of this exception to transparency. All these provisions under the Rules show broad powers granted to host States and may, in the context of transparency, alleviate the (real or perceived) concern about the investor-friendliness of arbitral tribunals.

8. Second, and maybe even more importantly, the Rules level the playing field between investors and host States in that *both* will be subject to increased public scrutiny and thus accountability of their actions in relation to foreign investments. For instance, investors will no longer be able to bring disputes 'behind closed doors' without any reputational risk. The investors' conduct will be discussed in the public domain, including where the investor (arguably) contributed, or caused, environmental or even human damage.[6] Such public scrutiny could, for instance, adversely

[5] See Thierry P. Augsburger, 'Article 7', [45]–[80], [125]–[136] and Krista Nadakavukaren Schefer, 'Article 1', [79].

[6] See e.g. *Aguas del Tunari, S.A.* v. *Bolivia*, ICSID Case No. ARB/02/3, Petition by NGOs and people to participate as an intervening party or *amici curiae*, 29 August 2002; IISD, 'Amicus Curiae Fundación Pachamama and The International Institute for Sustainable Development (IISD)—*Chevron* v. *Ecuador*', 2010, www.iisd.org/publications/pub.aspx?id=1718, concerning *Chevron Corporation (USA) and Texaco Petroleum Corporation (USA)* v. *Republic of Ecuador* [II], PCA Case No. 2009-23; Amnesty International, 'Human Rights on the line – The Baku-Tiblisi-Ceyhan (BTC) Pipeline Project', Amnesty International Report May 2003 www.amnesty.org.uk/press-releases/baku-tbilisi-ceyhan-pipeline-project-puts-human-rights-line; UNCTAD, *World Investment Report 2007* (United Nations, 2008) 145; Valerie Sperling, *Altered States: The Globalization of Accountability* (Cambridge University Press, 2009) 83; see also e.g. press statement Michael Keating, 'Nigeria's oil disasters are met by silence', *The Guardian Online*, 9 January 2012, www.theguardian.com/commentisfree/2012/jan/09/nigeria-oil-disaster-silence; Jim Schultz, 'Bechtel vs Bolivia: The People Win!' *Peacework* (February 2006), www.wilpf.

affect the corporations' value, decrease the share price and increase marketing or public relations costs. Similarly, host States will be prevented from keeping a 'veil of secrecy' of their (alleged) unfair or illegal government behaviours.[7] As such, the transparency imposed under the Rules creates a level playing field in which investors and host States alike will have to manage this increased scrutiny and its consequences.

9. In this context, it is worth considering whether 'too much' transparency might result in a possible backlash. Historically, confidentiality in international public law disputes has also been developed to de-politicise such disputes and, eventually, to prevent them from being 'resolved' in an armed conflict.[8] Conversely, imposing transparency in highly politicised investment disputes may sometimes bear the risk of escalating the dispute, perhaps even rendering it impossible to reach a reasonable settlement. It is therefore fundamental, as discussed in Chapter 9, that the transparency obligations under the Rules are subject to a series of appropriate exceptions.[9]

12.3 A look into the future

10. As discussed in detail in Chapter 3, the scope of application of the Rules is basically limited to treaty-based investor-State arbitration if the underlying treaty was concluded after the entry into force of the Rules, i.e. on or after 1 April 2014. For disputes based on treaties before that date the parties have to effectively opt in to the transparency standard of the Rules.[10] As also discussed in Chapter 3, this means that

org/bechtelvsbolivia; Bob Herbert, 'Disaster in the Amazon', *New York Times*, 4 June 2010, www.nytimes.com/2010/06/05/opinion/05herbert.html?_r=0.

[7] See e.g. harassment, intimidation and arrest claims decided in *Veteran Petroleum Limited (Cyprus)* v. *Russia*, PCA Case No. AA 228, Final Award, 18 July 2013 257–76; *Caratube International Oil Company LLP* v. *Kazakhstan*, ICSID Case No. Arb/08/12, Award, 5 June 2012 [170]–[180].

[8] Cf. Jeremy Bentham, 'Essay III. Of War, Considered in Respect of its Causes and Consequences, Entailed in Principles of International Law' in John Bowring (ed.), *The Works of Jeremy Bentham*, Part VIII (William Tait; Simpkin, Marshall & Co.; John Cumming, 1839) 544–5. For instance, in the so-called 'Alabama claims' case in 1872, a tribunal based in Geneva determined the appropriate degree of transparency to reduce the risk of another war between the UK and the US. See Frank Warren Hackett, *Reminiscences of the Geneva Tribunal of Arbitration 1872: The Alabama Claims* (Houghton Mifflin Company, 1911) 160–70.

[9] See Thierry P. Augsburger, 'Article 7' [36]–[174].

[10] See Krista Nadakavukaren Schefer, 'Article 1', [54]–[59]; Johannes Koepp and Cameron Sim, 'The Application of Transparency', [4]–[11].

currently the majority of the investment treaties are excluded from the automatic application of the Rules.[11]

11. This situation, however, changes with the ratification of the UN Convention on Transparency in Treaty-Based Investor-State Arbitration (Transparency Convention). Several States signed the Transparency Convention in Port Louis, Mauritius, on 17 March 2015.[12] In essence, The ratification of this convention undoubtedly increases the interest in, and importance of, the Rules.

12. The application of the Rules (irrespective of a host State's ratification of the Transparency Convention) will significantly influence the way treaty-based investor-State arbitration is conducted and, maybe equally importantly, perceived.

13. First, the Rules have the potential to increase the acceptance of investment arbitration by ensuring both better accountability of the arbitral tribunals, as well as consistency and predictability of the decisions they render.[13] As such, transparency, as framed under the Rules, is in the interests of all the players involved. On the one hand, investors are interested in predictable outcomes so that they can effectively assess their risk when making the investment. On the other hand, host States are interested in being able to evaluate the appropriateness of measures they adopt, the risk of challenges by foreign investors and thus eventually their possible liability.

14. Second, transparency also has the potential effect that arbitral tribunals will be better informed and thus render better awards. Letting third parties (i.e. a third person or a non-disputing party to the underlying treaty) participate in the arbitral process and make submissions, in the circumstances and with the limitations discussed in Chapters 5 and 6,[14] allows arbitral tribunals to broaden their access to relevant information. Compared to a purely confidential setting, arbitral tribunals

[11] See *ibid.*, [21] and [58].

[12] See Resolution adopted by the General Assembly on 10 December 2014, UN Doc. A/RES/69/116. Several States signed the Transparency Convention in Port Louis, Mauritius, on 17 March 2015. Signatories registered on 14 May 2015 were Canada, Finland, France, Germany, Mauritius, Sweden, Switzerland, Syrian Arab Republic, United Kingdom of Great Britain and Northern Ireland, United States of America, see website United Nations Convention on Transparency in Treaty-based Investor-state Arbitration, www.uncitral.org/uncitral/en/uncitral_texts/arbitration/2014Transparency_Convention_status.html.

[13] See Markus Gehring and Dimitrij Euler, 'Public Interest in Investment Arbitration', [5]–[13].

[14] See Mariel Dimsey, 'Article 4' [88]–[208] and Martins Paparinskis and Jessica Howley, 'Article 5'.

might thus receive important information they might not be able to get from the parties alone.

15. In sum, the well-balanced framework of the Rules is likely to positively influence the way treaty-based investor-State arbitration is conducted and perceived. As such, the Rules may help lead to a pendulum swing, away from repeated concerns and a persistent 'legitimacy crisis' of the investment system, and towards a more widely accepted and fairer dispute resolution process. In short, the Rules have the potential to overcome the (real or perceived) lack of legitimacy in international investment law and inspire renewed confidence in a system that was created to avoid unfair or even belligerent means of 'resolving' disputes.

INDEX